The New Communications

SECOND
EDITION

The New Communications

Frederick Williams

University of Texas at Austin

With commentaries by Arthur P. Bochner, Rudy Bretz, Brenda

Dervin, Herbert S. Dordick, Aimee Dorr, Mary Anne Fitzpatrick,

Elihu Katz, John M. Kittross, Mark L. Knapp, Gerald R. Miller,

Mitchell L. Moss, Dan Nimmo, Yash Pal, Linda L. Putnam, Ronald

E. Rice, Everett M. Rogers, Wilbur Schramm, Percy H.

Tannenbaum, and Ellen Wartella

Wadsworth Publishing Company

Belmont, California

A Division of Wadsworth, Inc.

Communications Editor: Kristine M. Clerkin
Editorial Assistant: Melissa Harris
Production Editor: Jerilyn Emori
Designer: Carolyn Deacy
Print Buyer: Randy Hurst
Copy Editor: William Waller
Photo Researcher: Carolyn Deacy, Lindsay Kefauver
Technical Illustrator: Joan Carol, Innographics
Cover: Image House Inc./Stuart Patterson
Cover Photo: Bell Production Inc./Miller Comstock Inc.
Signing Representative: Cynthia Berg

Printed in the United States of America   85

1 2 3 4 5 6 7 8 9 10—93 92 91 90 89

Library of Congress Cataloging-in-Publication Data

Williams, Frederick
    The new communications / Frederick Williams.—2nd ed.
        p. cm.
    Includes bibliographies and index.
    ISBN 0-534-09378-7
    1. Communication.   I. Title.
P90.W49   1989
001.51—dc19   88-11772
                                                                    CIP

Preface

WHY THE "NEW" COMMUNICATIONS?

There is hardly an area of modern life that is changing more than the ways by which we communicate. Although the *whys* of human communication remain unchanged, our *ways* of gathering and exchanging information, instructing ourselves and others, entertaining or being entertained, moving others to belief or action, interacting in groups, making decisions, or managing organizations are changing considerably. As usual, we humans are doing a pretty fair job of adapting to these changes, just as we have for thousands of years. This point was especially reinforced for me during my rare opportunity to work with the Walt Disney staff in developing the communications theme of the Spaceship Earth pavilion at Epcot Center near Disney World in Florida. Communication is certainly a powerful human tool; it has gotten us through (and even into) many crises in our existence on this planet.

With all of the changes in our times, it is not surprising to see the rapid growth in the academic areas devoted to human communication. Rapid change affects not only those schools and departments that call themselves "Communication" but also those that specialize in communication's various facets, such as journalism, speech communication, broadcasting, film, advertising, instructional technology, or business. In all such departments and programs, students are seeking training to adapt themselves to a changing world. *The New Communications* aims to serve this important need.

If educators were to do less, we would not be preparing our students to be consumers in the fast-growing *information society* or to take advantage of the many career opportunities in this society. It is for these forward-looking programs and their students that *The New Communications* is intended.

A FEW NOTES ON FEATURES OF THE BOOK

Orientation

This book draws from a fundamental social scientific view of human communication as well as its quantitative and qualitative research methods. It stresses those communication capabilities that mark the species, how these behaviors evolve in different levels of use, and how they are employed for social purposes. These materials were developed for students who may eventually major in any one of many fields from the liberal arts to the sciences, including specializations in journalism, broadcasting, or speech communication.

Content

Part One, Modern Study of Human Communication, provides an experiential introduction to the study of communication. Student readers are invited to examine examples of communication in human history and to sense the same characteristics in the world about them. Given this introduction, they are urged to develop an analytic view of the communication process.

Part Two, Basic Aspects of Communication, reflects my bias that to understand communication requires that one begin with the study of the communicating nature of the human organism. Topics include verbal and nonverbal behavior, motivation and function in communication, and the psychology of attitudes. The part concludes with a discussion of our ability to extend our sphere of influence by use of the media of communications, including the contributions of new media technologies.

Part Three, Levels of Communication, is traditional, including discussions of interpersonal, group, organizational, and mass communication. (However, I have chosen to adopt the broader term *public communication* in this edition to accommodate an enlarged concept that encompasses alternatives to the traditional mass media, including network information services.) The reader will find substantial cross-references among these chapters, as the new media have begun to blur the distinctions among some traditional levels of communication, for example, in the increasingly personalized uses of public-communications systems.

Part Four, Research in Communication, provides examples of contemporary research in communication, including a sampling of topics and research methods. Chapter topics include relational communication, information and public opinion, political communication, and entertainment. Both qualitative and quantitative research methods are included in the discussions of these topics.

Part Five, Challenges from the Future, emphasizes that the key to students' futures is not so much in the technologies themselves but in how they choose to use them. After all, our students, more so than their instructors, will be setting the life-styles for the twenty-first century.

Commentaries

What does an expert have to say informally on a topic? Scholars representing a variety of research topics have thoughtfully prepared brief commentaries on an issue in their specialty. Inserted in context, these comments often reflect responses to typical student questions such as "What do you think about your theory now?" or "What should I be thinking about now on that topic?"

Topics for Discussion or Brief Papers

Included at the end of each chapter are activities that can be prepared for class discussions or papers. These may be assigned by the instructor as discussion-starters. Assigning a brief paper also offers an incentive for completing the reading assignment.

Exercises for Communication Analysis and Skill Building

The appendix of this volume contains detailed assignments that can be a basis for laboratory or discussion sections of a class or can be exercises for a class itself. The study of communication seems most effective when students directly experience some appointed type of communication behavior. Also, it is important to encourage students to analyze the communications that go on in their everyday lives. The exercises in this section have all been employed in my (or colleagues') classes; we know they work. Note also that they are self-administering by the student.

Glossary

At the heart of any content-oriented course is a fundamental and sometimes technical vocabulary. All key terms that appear in boldface in the text are found in the Glossary. The Glossary also includes other terms that the student may encounter in outside readings or in lectures.

FEATURES OF THE SECOND EDITION

Nothing beats the marketplace as the final evaluator of a textbook, not expert reviewers, editors, or even the insights of an optimistic author. That this second edition was commissioned by the publisher is the best testimonial that *The New Communications* has lived up to the expectations of many faculty adopters and student readers. But this is not to say that there was no room for improvement. The comments from many of these individuals have been invaluable in developing this second edition.

Two major changes were made in this volume. First, many instructors requested an expansion of content, especially to reflect the contributions of new research and theory. There is a trend to introduce such materials earlier in the communication curricula, to add more "meat," as one adopter frankly phrased it. The reader of this edition will find expansions in the chapters of Part Three, on levels of communication, but especially in the addition of two chapters to Part Four, on research.

A second frequent request was to reduce the interruption of the text with "pedagogical features." Consequently, all definitions formerly in the page margins are combined in a new glossary. In-text comments ("probes") directed to students have been omitted or placed at chapter ends as discussion topics. Tables and figures have been improved, and there are fewer photographs.

Among the features often receiving positive comment that are not only preserved but also, I hope, improved in this edition are the following:

Emphasis remains on the importance of seeing relations among the various levels of communication (for example, the interactions of interpersonal and public communication).

In many research examples, I stress that students must understand alternative theory and recognize that the field is still evolving.

The new media technologies are discussed in the contexts of use and not as a separate topic.

I give more attention to the practical links between the study of communication and students' roles as consumers and potential career seekers.

There are new suggestions for discussion and research included at the ends of chapters, as well as exercises for communication analysis and skill building in the Appendix.

The attempt to go the extra mile to achieve an interesting and readable style has again been given special attention.

A BOOK OWES A DEBT TO MANY

In addition to the many faculty members and students who volunteered suggestions that influenced the new edition, many additional individuals have contributed not only to this volume but to the original idea for *The New Communications*. My earliest and foremost debt is to Rebecca Hayden, editor of the first edition, who shared my initial vision that the field was ready for this undertaking and put Wadsworth's talent and financial resources behind it. But ranking a near equal is my new editor, Kristine Clerkin, who, while keeping me on schedule with a new book *(Technology and Communication Behavior)*, did her utmost to keep the present revision on schedule. Kris understands the new world of communication, and it shows in the titles she has developed.

From the field, I owe a special thanks on this new edition to my Texas colleague and longtime friend, Mark Knapp, for his suggestions in the area of relational communication. And to Sandra Ball-Rokeach of the Annenberg School of Communications at the University of Southern California, I owe thanks for sharing materials and thoughts on dependency theory. Also, I acknowledge the able reviews of Jack A. Barwind, Syracuse University; Ken Ksobiech, Marquette University; Norman Markel, University of Florida; Don E. Phillips, Washburn University of Topeka; and Michael D. Scott, California State University at Chico.

In the publishing house, I wish to express special gratitude to Carolyn Deacy, designer; Jerilyn Emori, production editor; and Bill Waller, copy editor.

Finally, I am especially indebted to those scholars who took time from their busy schedules to provide the commentaries found throughout the chapters. No student should study communication without encountering firsthand, albeit in abbreviated form, the words of the experts. That these authorities so willingly contributed to this volume is evidence of the enthusiastic and highly cooperative nature of our colleagues in communication.

Brief Contents

Detailed Contents

PART TWO

Chapter 3

BASIC ASPECTS OF COMMUNICATION   43

Verbal and Nonverbal Communication   45

Chapter 6

Media and Technologies   103

Chapter 9   Organizational Communication   175

Chapter 13   Political Communication   253

Chapter 14   Entertainment   267

PART FIVE — CHALLENGES FROM THE FUTURE   289

Chapter 15 — The Information Society   291

PART
ONE

Modern Study of
Human Communication

The rapid growth of the academic field of communication has

been exceeded only by the changes in communication in our

everyday lives. No matter whether you are studying

communication simply for the knowledge, to be a more

intelligent consumer, or to pursue a career, you'll find the

experience rewarding and exciting. There is hardly a field of

study today that bears more directly upon the sweeping

changes in our lives as our society enters the information age.

In the first two chapters of this volume, we examine the what

and why of communication study and then go on to introduce

steps for analyzing communication as a complex human

process.

Egyptian scribes, relief in chalk (page 2). Egypt, 18th
dynasty ca. 1350 BC. Bettman Archive, Inc.

Preliminaries to the Study of Communication

A half dozen humanlike creatures squat on the clay bank of a prehistoric stream that existed 1000 centuries before the land became desert. They chatter and point in a fashion even then far removed from their more apelike cousins. Silence falls as in the morning mist they position half their group upstream to stir up the lazy carp. Meanwhile their remaining brothers stand downstream poised for the morning catch.

Primordial Humans
c. 100,000 B.C.

Cave paintings,
Lascaux, France
c. 25,000 B.C.

Egyptian "Key of Life" symbol from the Tomb of Tutankhamen
c. 1400 B.C.

Passage from Gutenberg's 42-line printed Bible
1453

Be content to bind America by laws of trade, you have always done it. Let this be your reason for binding their trade. Do not burden them by taxes; you were not used to do so from the beginning. Let this be your reason for not taxing. But if, intemperately, unwisely, fatally, you sophisticate and poison the very source of government, by urging subtle deductions, and consequences odious to those you govern, from the unlimited and illimitable nature of supreme sovereignty, you will teach them by these means to call that sovereignty itself in question. When you drive him hard, the boar will surely turn upon the hunters. If that sovereignty and their freedom cannot be reconciled, which will they take? They will cast your sovereignty in your face. Nobody will be argued into slavery.

Quotation from Edmund Burke's famous oration to the British Commons on "America"
1774

Penny Press
1833

"You'll wonder where
the yellow went when
you brush your teeth
with Pepsodent."
Radio jingle
1940

We all live in a yellow submarine

Beatles
1965

```
100 PRINT "RICHARD BYRNE"

110 GOTO 100
```

BASIC program to list your name on
a personal computer
1978

MTV illustration
1988

"Pass the salt." You today

HUMAN COMMUNICATION IS DISTINCTIVELY *HUMAN*

Nothing is more distinctive about human communication than that its full range of qualities and powers is found in no other species. Yes, we can teach apes to use rudimentary sign language, parrots to mimic sounds, or dogs to respond to voice commands, but there is no other known organism with the communication capabilities of the human. No one or no technology—not even the most powerful computer—matches our human capabilities to communicate, interpret, or act on shared meanings.

Our History as Symbol Users

Although nearly 1000 human generations separate you from the cave painters of Lascaux, their images nevertheless have meanings for you. Your meaning, my meaning, and their meanings may all differ somewhat, but we would all probably concede that the images are of animals. However, whether these animals were sacred images for a religious rite, expressions of the most gifted artist of the tribe, or the aimlessly produced graffiti of a long winter, we will never know.

Much of our human communication does not have to suggest meanings as visually or literally as the cave paintings do. Indeed, there may not be any readily apparent relationship between the physical properties of the "message" and the physical properties of what it is intended to mean. For example, a sketch of an animal has a visible similarity to the real thing, but the word *animal* does not. When we use messages that refer to things or events but do not themselves directly resemble them, we are using **symbols,** the primary and most complex quality of human communication.

Perhaps the illustration of the Egyptian Key of Life meant nothing to you; this is quite possible. But to most readers of this book it will suggest a symbol of religious significance. Perhaps this is because it bears a resemblance to the Christian cross, although it preceded it by around 1400 years. Unless we study more about Egyptian history or become followers of the modern Egyptian Coptic faith, the Key of Life is not likely to be a particularly meaningful symbol for us. We do not have the shared meanings necessary for a full understanding of it.

Humans are remarkably adept at making one thing stand for another, at using sounds, gestures, markings, images, or objects as a basis for complex communication. The words we speak every day are symbols, as is the printed text on this page. A cross scratched in the dust, a hieroglyphic painted on papyrus, the spoken word *mother*, a fleeting wink, a gesture in a Balinese dance, an acid chord of hard rock, the revolting TV image of stuffed nasal passages, the dull green of a computer readout, and the logo *Coca Cola*® are all symbols of one type or another. The examples of communication that began this chapter are also symbols in one way or another. Each was originally created with the idea of affecting other humans, of eliciting a particular reaction that we usually call **meaning.**

Language: Our Primary Symbol System

Our most frequently used human symbols, the sounds of speech, have even less immediate resemblance to what they are intended to mean. There is no more reason why the spoken sound sequence *dog* means a friendly four-footed animal than does *sobaka* (Russian), *perro* (Spanish), *pies* (Polish), or *koira* (Finnish). If you want to know what the word means, then you have to share the meaning with the user of that word. You have to know the **language.**

Although you may not know Latin, its relationship with English is close enough that you can guess the meanings of a few words from the passage shown earlier from the Gutenberg Bible. No doubt you can understand most of the selection from Edmund Burke's famous speech, because English has not changed that much in the last 200 years. If you understand a language, you know meanings for many of its symbols.

If you know something of American revolutionary history, this passage from Burke's speech may be even more meaningful to you. Or consider the example from the penny press. You can read it, but if you knew more about the context of the story, it would mean more to you. The point is that knowing a language is not always enough experience to let one fully realize its meanings.

Grasping a bit of the meaning of the simple computer program illustrated earlier shouldn't have been too difficult if you are a speaker of English. The programming language called BASIC was designed to be a compromise between a concise set of logical commands that can be used to run a computer and words recognizable to anybody who knows English. In this case the designers of the new language were using simple English commands as a basis for setting up a human-and-machine communication system.

Symbols and their meanings, and especially the complex set of associations between sounds and meanings we call language, are the essence of human communication.

The Power of Human Communication

Surely if extraterrestrial beings were ever to study humans, they would find our distinguishing characteristic to be the ability to handle symbols in thought and speech. We are capable not only of knowing but also of preserving and sharing our knowing. A mother raccoon can warn her young of danger, but only if danger is immediately present. She cannot, as we can, talk with her brood about the dangers they might face during that day or their lifetime. We alone are capable of separating our reactions and thoughts from what may be happening to us at any moment. Moreover, we can generalize about our generalizations. We can observe and comment on our own processes of thought and observation.

We are capable of creating an internal, mental world, one for which we or scientists still know no limits. It is a symbolic world, so to speak, which we can manipulate, index, store, retrieve, and, of critical importance to us as a species, share among ourselves. No human capability has been more fundamental to the development of civilization than the ability to collect, share, and use knowledge. Civilization has been possible only through the process of human communication.

The next time that you hear a bird chirp, a dog bark, or a cat meow, consider that they have been making those noises far longer than we have been talking. But bear in mind, too, that their means of communication have not varied in the history of their species. Then think about the noises that you make. Every time you utter a word or hear a sentence, your behavior represents a communication system that has evolved over more than 1000 centuries.

The power of human communication allowed your ancestors to pass down their accumulated knowledge and skills. Meanwhile the birds, dogs, and cats go on tweeting, growling, and hissing just as they did in 100,000 B.C.

That we humans can symbolize, that we can use this capability to share meaning among ourselves, and that we can accumulate our meanings across the span of history are what is uniquely human about human communication.

(And all of this makes your saying "Pass the salt" more profound than you might have thought at first!)

WHAT DO WE MEAN, COMMUNICATE?

Ordinary Definitions

Do not expect to find a single, agreed-upon definition for *communication*. It is too complex and the methods for study too varied for that. There are, of course, uses of the term *communication* that do not directly involve humans or animals, as in electronic circuits and the like. But in most uses and in this book, *communication* refers to human behavior.

In ordinary usage, most people agree, the verb *to communicate* means (1) to exchange thoughts, feelings, information; (2) to make known; (3) to make common; and (4) to have a sympathetic relationship.

Also, you usually find agreement that the noun *communication* refers to (1) the exchange of symbols, common messages, information; (2) the process of exchange between individuals through a common system of symbols; (3) the art of expressing ideas; and (4) the science of transmitting information.

Fundamental Characteristics

Although ordinary definitions are satisfactory in general usage, we will need to be much more specific if we wish to analyze human communication in detail. In one sense this entire book is a definition of human communication. So, again, do not look for a simple definition (especially one to memorize). Instead, we will start by describing selected basic characteristics of our topic. You will find most of these characteristics of human communication compatible with the ordinary definitions just given. The difference is that these characteristics will lead you to a much more precise and deeper meaning of the concept. They are an introduction to the study of human communication.

1. Communication Is the Exchange of Meaningful Symbols. We cannot directly exchange meanings. This is our "communicator's handicap." We can only physically exchange symbols, as in speech or writing or in the more complex exchange of printed, broadcast, filmed, or electronically coded messages. And communication will not take place unless we share meanings for the symbols.

If you want your best friend to go to the movies with you tonight, the simple process of asking is really a rather complicated series of processes. For example:

 a. You convert the intended meaning, "Want to go to the movies tonight?" into a sequence of language symbols.
 b. You generate a sequence of speech sounds representing those symbols.
 c. The spoken symbols travel to your friend.
 d. Your friend translates the spoken symbols into the received meaning, "Want to go to the movies tonight?"

Even if you are doing nothing more than reading a short item in the morning newspaper, there is a symbolic exchange process involved. For example:

 a. You gain a meaning by associating printed marks on the page with the symbol system of your language (that is, you "read").
 b. The symbols were put on the page by a process that included type-setting and printing, and then the page was transported to you.
 c. The symbols were originally selected by a reporter, who recorded them as written notes and then probably typed the story into a computer-editing system, after translating and rearranging the symbols.

2. Communication Is a Process. Communication is an activity, not a "thing." It occurs when humans affect one another. On this page, communication is not occurring through the print, or you, or me (the author). It is occurring through all of these things combined as you interpret meanings the author intended to convey through print. As such, we call communication a **process.**

Figure 1.1 shows one popular way to illustrate the basic process of human communication. This diagram portrays the most fundamental level of the communication process: the basic relationship among **source, message,** and **receiver.** The only new component in this figure is the *message,* which we referred to informally earlier in this chapter. *Message* is simply a word we use to describe the collection of symbols that are transferred between or among

Figure 1.1
The Basic Process of
Communication

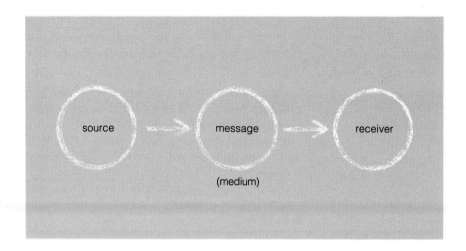

communicators. Messages, like symbols, have a physical basis when being transferred. (This physical basis is often called the communications *medium*, and we will discuss it next.) Messages can be conveyed by the sounds of a spoken conversation; by images in photographs, printed pages, patterns in a television image, data signals; and even by the tone of our voice. But most important, messages—again, like symbols—can be interpreted by humans for their meanings.

We need not restrict "sender" and "receiver" to individual humans. The sender could be a public speaker and the receiver an audience of 500 individuals. Or the sender could be a television producer, the message the program, and the receiver the broadcast audience. (We will see more examples of senders and receivers in Chapter 3.)

3. Communication Requires a Medium. There must be some physical basis for the exchange of messages. This is the communications **medium.** For speech, the medium is provided by sound patterns in the molecular vibration of air. In vision, it is the light waves reflected from a surface or coming directly from a light source. Our human capability for touching one another is a medium. And so, too, is the air when it carries tiny particles that we can smell or taste. All have physical bases for linking sender and receiver and can have a pattern of symbols imposed upon them.

Humans have been clever in extending these "natural media" for communication by using materials from the environment. (In Chapter 6 we explore this in much more detail.) In prehistoric times, humans carved messages on bones, burned them on hides, and scratched them in the dust. Later they painted and sculpted. Eventually the development of writing extended spoken symbols far beyond the scope of the human voice in both distance and time.

When we casually refer to the media of communication, we usually mean print, film, or broadcasting, all of which fit the more technical definition just given. In some circles, disk and tape recordings and even computer circuits are referred to as media.

Again, the medium is the physical basis for conveying a pattern of symbols, whereas the message is what the symbols are intended to convey as meanings. In the 1960s, the media philosopher Marshall McLuhan became well known for his saying "The medium is the message." He meant that some media have particular effects upon meaning in themselves; for example, radio allows us to imagine images, whereas television makes them explicit.

4. Communication Can Be Transactional. In many situations of communication—a two-person conversation, for example—there is no reason to visualize communication only as a one-way, sender–receiver process. Indeed, such a situation is often two-way. That is, it is **interactive** and can be **transactional.** In order to portray this two-way quality, it is important to modify our earlier diagram of the communication process to the form shown in Figure 1.2. This modified diagram much more adequately fits situations where individuals are simultaneously playing the roles of sender and receiver. As we will see in Chapter 7, the most effective personal conversations are highly transactional. That is, both individuals participate equally in the exchange.

The transactional quality of communication also extends to situations that do not necessarily involve two or more individuals. For example, a reader of a newspaper can write a letter to the editor, a viewer can call a TV station to complain about a program, or a listener can participate by telephone in a

Figure 1.2
Communication as a Two-Way Process

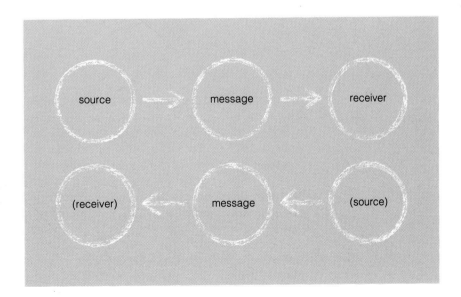

call-in radio show. Sometimes we call such "return" communication **feedback.** It is a reflection of the transactional potential of most (but not all) types of communication.

Feedback differs from interactive or transactional communication. It occurs when the "return" communication is of a different type from the original message (as in the letter to the editor and radio call-in examples). Interactive or transactional communication occurs when the back-and-forth communication is of the same type (as in a conversation).

5. We Communicate to Satisfy Our Human Needs. Most human communication has some purpose to it. You may not always be clear on that purpose, but generally you are not going to spend time talking, writing, gesturing, listening, reading, or viewing (television, for example) unless you can accomplish something. Usually, we say that humans use communication to satisfy different types of needs. For example, you may be reading this book so you can pass an examination and get credit for a college course. Or you might watch television simply to relax.

As we will discuss in greater detail in Chapter 4, our motives for communication are associated with our needs as humans. We use communication to control people, objects, and events around us. We want to make things happen, to get other people to do things for us, to find out what is going on. Communication is also our basis for learning about ourselves and for identifying relations between our "self" and others. We satisfy our desire for human contact through communication situations ranging from face-to-face encounters to watching soap operas. We learn about our culture through communication, and we use communication to transmit our culture to the next generation. Communication is a basis for religious practices—even inspiration. And, not to be overlooked, communication is often a basis for relaxation, for entertainment, or for sheer escape.

WHY STUDY COMMUNICATION?

Communication Is Important to Each of Us Personally

There is hardly a subject that can have more personal relevance to us today than the study of human communication. Our society could not have evolved without it. The development of our personalities depends upon it. Without personal communication skills, we cannot develop the interpersonal relationships so vital to our personal and professional success. We are also communications consumers in an economy that is increasingly dominated by communications products and services. More and more of the "work" in our society involves communication activities. Evident in the expansion of the communication field is the growth of related professions, for example, business communications, banking, and a wide range of entertainment industries. Finally, without an improvement in the methods and practices of international communication, our world may have a short future.

Nothing could be more important to our lives as the twenty-first century approaches than an understanding of human communication—what it is, how it works, where it is going, and, particularly, *where each of us may be going with it.*

We Cannot *Not* Communicate

Here's a story a student told about an embittered man who wanted to cut himself off from the world.

> Once, on the outskirts of a small midwestern town, there was a man who decided to withdraw as much as possible from all human contact. He had an acre of fenced land within which he had surrounded himself with wrecked autos and other miscellaneous junk. The only evidence that a human lived in the midst of this dumping ground was a faded mailbox sign with the name "Bishop" on it. Yet the "Bishop" had to come to town from time to time to get supplies. Whenever he did, he tried as best he could not to talk with anybody. Because of the way he frowned when some newcomer bade him an innocent "hello," the other person always got the "message." And it was probably clearer and more predictable than most of the other messages those folks got during their day.

We cannot separate human existence from communication. This relation is more than the dependence of society upon communication. The relation is direct—being human places us *directly* in the world of communication. Even Mr. Bishop "communicated" in his own antisocial way. In fact, some said that he was probably the best-known person in town!

If we live a generally normal existence, about three-fourths of our waking hours are spent in active communication—in conversations, reading and writing, watching television, listening to the radio or tapes and records, or going to the movies. More of our time is given over to communication than to any other human behavior.

There is no way that we can suddenly withdraw from all of our communication behaviors and still maintain a normal existence. Try it. You'll see how much your life is entwined with daily communication activities. Try not speaking or gesturing in the presence of other people. You'll quickly realize that not responding is a "message" in itself. Again, you cannot *not* communicate.

Communication Is the Basis for Interpersonal Relations

Most of our greatest pleasures in life, including our professional successes, depend on close relations with other people. We humans are markedly social creatures. Our successful existence depends on interpersonal cooperation. Yet interpersonal relations do not automatically spring up in our lives. They require development. Two individuals must know a great deal about each other before trust develops. And becoming acquainted requires the exchange of information, the ability to understand each other's needs, and the willingness to develop mutually satisfying goals. All of these requirements are a part of the communication process underlying the development of interpersonal relations. Effective communication is the basis of interpersonal cooperation whether the relationship grows into a friendship or marriage or becomes simply an effective working relationship between a manager and an employee.

A student whom I'll call Melanie was once a living illustration of the critical role of interpersonal communication in human relationships. Melanie had been reared in a New York apartment by wealthy and somewhat older parents who spent most of their time with their respective careers. The main emphasis in Melanie's upbringing was to be successful in whatever she did. And successful she was—in dance lessons, horseback riding, art classes, and especially in her schoolwork. Melanie had absolutely everything going for her, including an outstanding start on her freshman year in college—except that in the fifth week she had a nervous breakdown. Her attending psychiatrist, in consulting with several of her professors, learned that Melanie, who was living away from her parents for the first time, had never learned how to relate to people. She had concentrated her life on things rather than people. Thus, when other students tried to make friends with Melanie, she had no real experience in how to respond. Fortunately, the therapy was successful and Melanie was back in school by the next semester. It had been necessary for Melanie, now a young adult, to learn how to relate to other human beings.

Melanie's story makes an additional point: Our abilities in interpersonal communication are *learned* behaviors. Like any other behavior, they can fail to develop, develop improperly, or be changed or improved.

New Media Technologies Are Affecting Our Life and Work

As we say many places in this book, the new technologies are changing the way we humans communicate. The modern office is probably the most visible example. Here we see typewriters replaced by word-processing computers, electronic mail augmenting the telephone, and telecommunications networks linking all components of the organization. You will probably work in such an office, if you don't already. A knowledge of "office-automation" technologies will make you a more effective employee, if not executive.

The new technologies of home entertainment are another example. In hardly more than a decade, television has expanded from the three dominant network channels and a few independents into a vast cable-connected system linking almost half of the U.S. population to broadcasters, text services, and even remote shopping systems. Viewing is now shifting away from the networks to the more specialized programming of channels offering news, music, movies, and sports. In the 1980s we have seen the number of people who watch motion pictures at home exceed the number of moviegoers, a result of the burgeoning video cassette business. Even the plain old telephone is changing. Many Americans have multiple phones, phones that can remember numbers to be dialed at the push of one button, and answering machines that can sort or screen calls for us.

Those individuals who understand the opportunities that the new media technologies offer will profit from and enjoy them in the years to come.

We Are All Communications *Consumers*

In the 1980s, no area of the U.S. economy, except for energy and energy-related industries, grew more than the communications industry. The industry includes companies that offer telephone and other telecommunications services, that manufacture computers and related equipment, and that are involved in many areas of home entertainment.

The average number of hours of weekly television viewing was well above the six-hour mark in the first half of the 1980s. And industry analysts see this number increasing with the growth of cable-television services, various pay-television alternatives, and videotape (and perhaps eventually, disk) players.

We can add to this list a host of additional communications services and devices for the home whose use is growing, for example:

Fire, police, and medical alert services via cable television or telephone hookups

Expansion of such telephone services as multiple-party calls, call forwarding, automatic dialing and answering, and perhaps even an electronic Yellow Pages

Greatly improved large-screen television sets with stereophonic sound

The continued installation of small computers for home budgeting, home banking, education, file management, and entertainment

The coming of electronic "text" services that provide everything from airline schedules to "newspapers" at the press of a button

The opportunities for these products and services are dramatic enough, but not as challenging as how we will respond to them. Do we want all these items or services in our homes? Do we want telephones to intrude even more into our lives? Do we want more hours of television—let alone large-screen television—when we have already seen this medium evolve into what some call "programmed mediocrity"? Will we indeed be able to find effective *human* advantages in having computers in our homes? Or could they, like the computerized bills we receive as the bulk of our daily mail, depersonalize us? Should the tradition of the *printed* newspaper give way to television text services? Will the news be reduced to electronic headlines followed by former game-show hosts who offer personal commentaries?

Communication Is Increasingly Critical in Modern Organizations

The importance of communication in modern organizations is growing explosively. This growth can be seen in two areas.

First, communication has become the lifeblood of organizations—of government, education, and other nonprofit organizations, as well as the organizations of business. As such, it is increasingly critical in their operation. From a more theoretical perspective, an organization is itself a communication structure. It receives information in order to guide its actions—as when a manufacturer studies the marketplace. Management communication is the basis for guiding the organization's internal operations. Marketing is largely a communication activity. After sales or services are delivered, the organization again gathers information from the marketplace, and the cycle continues.

Second, businesses and organizations where communication *is* the product or service have grown. There is a strong belief that countries such as the United States are evolving toward a *postindustrial* economy. This term suggests that the growth areas are not so much in the heavy industries (such as automobiles and steel) but in more information- and knowledge-based industries and services, including entertainment. While developing countries of the world move into their own industrial ages, the older industrial countries are moving more into the development of high technology areas. Many of these technology areas involve communications: computers, robotics, home entertainment and services, and satellites, to name a few.

The growth of these two areas has numerous implications for the study of communication. For one, the specialty of *organizational* communication has become a major growth area in the academic fields of communications and business. So, too, has it become critical for communication students to learn more about the theory and development of the communication technologies that are to a postindustrial society what heavy machinery was to the industrial age.

With these implications comes perhaps the greatest challenge of all: As communication efficiency becomes the competitive edge of an organization, how can we keep human communication effective yet pleasurable and essentially *humane?* Ultimately, nothing is more important in human communication than fulfilling basic, personal human needs. Given all of the intervening technologies in the new world of communication, basic interpersonal skills will be at a premium in the years to come.

The Communications Professions Are Changing

At one time studying for a professional career in communications meant essentially studying journalism, broadcasting, film, or speech communication. Now, given the rapid changes in the alternative media of communications in our society, aspiring professionals in any of these areas will not go far if they do not understand the relations of their activities to the broader concept of *communication*. To survive in this era of change, the newspaper professional must understand what it means to be in the *communications*

Wilbur Schramm

An exhibit at the Smithsonian Institution in Washington, D.C., shows two remarkable window panoramas of a Bronze Age village called Bab elh-Dhra, which flourished 5000 years ago in Jordan just east of the Dead Sea. For many centuries Bab elh-Dhra was a stopping place for caravans and travelers in the Jordanian desert, because it was famous for its water. Then, shortly before 3000 B.C., when farmers began to replace nomads, some families moved into Bab elh-Dhra and established a village. That settlement existed for a thousand years, then passed out of human history. But it left its marks on walls and artifacts and tombs; archaeologists dug them up, and the Smithsonian recreated what the village had been.

That exhibit appealed to me as a metaphor for the early history of communication study. For centuries, scholars have stopped to look at communication problems, as travelers stopped to refresh themselves at the oasis of Bab elh-Dhra, and then moved on. Only recently have scholars moved into communication country to stay. But anyone who has studied community has had to pay some attention to communication. Scholars ever since Plato, Aristotle, and Confucius have stopped to look and think about it. In the United States it was a subject of interest to philosophers and political theorists for more than a century before Charles Cooley wrote the first modern analysis of social communication in his 1909 book *Social Organization*. For the most part, scholars like Cooley merely stopped by to visit. Some of them, however, made it a career. Four men, in particular, came from their own disciplines into communication study and made such enormous impacts

that they have every right to be known as fathers of the field in the United States. I mean Harold Lasswell, who came from political science; Kurt Lewin, from social psychology; Paul Lazarsfeld, from sociology; and Carl Hovland, from experimental psychology. We could talk a long time about these four remarkable men, and the younger men (Ithiel de Sola Pool and Elihu Katz, for instance) who followed them into the field. But rather more important than the details is the fact that in the late 1940s and 1950s groups of scholars began to take up permanent residence in communication and established their own settlements there.

By this time, journalism, broadcasting, and speech communication departments had also become increasingly interested in contributing to communications research as well as to skills in the field. In 1947, Illinois, and in 1955, Stanford, set up communications research institutes, specializing in research and doctoral study. Since then, doctoral and research programs have been started in more than fifty universities, sometimes as separate institutes, sometimes as adjuncts to the teaching departments. To a considerable extent these have taken over the obligations formerly carried by the research institutes of the "founding fathers." So now relatively permanent settlements have been established in this scholarly oasis, and they show every sign of continuing to exist until a day, perhaps, when they will be absorbed into a more general social science, which by that time we may be able to call a *science of humanity*.

The late Wilbur Schramm was for years director of the Institute for Communication Research at Stanford University.

Suggested reading: W. Schramm and W. E. Porter, *Men, Women, Messages, and Media* (New York: Harper and Row, 1982).

---

business. (Notice the relation between the profitability of large newspapers and their willingness to diversify into other communications media, such as cable television.) The broadcaster and filmmaker have no choice but to understand the *home entertainment* business. The challenge of keeping personal communication effective yet essentially *humane* fills the future of the speech communication specialist.

Moreover, there are new communications professions. As we move into a society where information and communication are commodities, there is an increasing need for new professionals. Who designs these goods and services, builds them, promotes them, sells them, manages them, services them, or teaches people to use them?

The most successful communications professionals of the next half century will likely be those whose entrepreneurial spirit guides them to best meet the needs of a society entering into a truly communications-saturated future.

For all of recorded history, people have attempted to understand the nature of human communication and put it to its best uses for humanity. As the late Wilbur Schramm, whose research, writings, and engaging manner have influenced many of us who teach and write about communication, says in his commentary, the science of human communication is indeed a part of the larger science of the human condition.

SUMMARY

Symbolic communication is part of human evolution. We humans are distinctively *symbol* users. A symbol elicits a particular reaction, which is its *meaning*. The main symbol system is called *language*, and our powerful use of it is unique to our species.

Fundamentally, communication involves the exchange of meaningful symbols (*messages*) among *sources* and *receivers* via a *medium*. Some communication is two-way, or *interactive*. Most of our communication behavior is *transactional;* that is, it can be seen as a dynamic *process* by which we exchange messages to satisfy our needs. Return communication is called *feedback*. Human communication is (1) an exchange of meaningful symbols, (2) a process rather than a "thing," (3) a medium linking participants, (4) a potential transaction of meanings and intents, and (5) a basic means for satisfying human needs.

The study of communication can be most important to us personally and professionally. Communication is the fundamental basis for human relations, and for this reason, we cannot *not* communicate. We are all communications consumers in a society where communications products and services are becoming a major part of the economy. Communications is increasingly important in the operation of organizations. Even the communications professions are changing.

TOPICS FOR DISCUSSION OR BRIEF PAPERS

1. What are your ideas about the importance of communication to the development of the human species? What might civilization be like if we had never invented writing? Or what if only a very few individuals could write and the rest of us could not?

2. Take three examples of types of communication that are important to you. (For example, these could be conversations with your best friend, the use of TV for entertainment, and the use of textbooks for studying.) Analyze each in terms of a simple source–receiver model. Next, examine

each in terms of the five fundamental characteristics of human communication discussed in this chapter. How do they differ from one another? How are they similar?

3. Think of some examples that support the proposition that "we cannot *not* communicate." How can you explain the communication that does take place? What is different about it as compared with communication that you want to take place?

4. Some say that the new communications technologies (such as video cassettes, video disks, cable TV, pay TV, computers, video games, new types of telephones) are changing the ways by which we communicate. Do you think that this is bad or good? Why? Take a position and defend it.

5. What are your career plans and how do they involve modern communications? Will your career be in communications—for example, in journalism, public relations, teaching, the entertainment business, or communication in business or industry? If so, how might your job change in the next twenty years? If you are not planning a communications career, how will your type of job be affected?

REFERENCES AND READINGS

Agee, W. K., P. H. Ault, and E. Emery. *Introduction to Mass Communications.* 8th ed. New York: Harper and Row, 1985.

Barker, L. L. *Communication.* 2d ed. Englewood Cliffs, N.J.: Prentice-Hall, 1981.

Becker, S. L. *Discovering Mass Communication.* Glenview, Ill.: Scott, Foresman, 1983.

Berlo, D. K. *The Process of Communication.* New York: Holt, Rinehart and Winston, 1960.

Bittner, J. R. *Mass Communication: An Introduction.* 2d ed. Englewood Cliffs, N.J.: Prentice-Hall, 1980.

Book, C. L., et al. *Human Communication: Principles, Contexts, and Skills.* New York: St. Martin's Press, 1980.

DeFleur, M. L., and E. E. Dennis. *Understanding Mass Communication.* Boston: Houghton Mifflin, 1981.

DeVito, J. A. *Communicology: An Introduction to the Study of Communication.* New York: Harper and Row, 1982.

Ruben, B. D. *Communication and Human Behavior.* New York: Macmillan, 1984.

Sandman, P. M., D. M. Rubin, and D. B. Sachsman. *Media: An Introductory Analysis of American Mass Communications.* 3d ed. Englewood Cliffs, N.J.: Prentice-Hall, 1982.

Williams, F. *The Communications Revolution.* New York: New American Library, 1983.

Analyses of
Communication

ANALYSIS AS A BASIS FOR STUDY

How can we discover how communication works? For one thing, we can observe it in its many forms and try to draw some generalizations that fit as many cases as possible. We can try to describe it. But we can also go further. We can attempt to analyze what we are observing. We can "take apart" what we see, study its parts, and then try to explain how it works. This is the process of **social scientific** research in communication: the process of observing, analyzing, and explaining.

But you may ask: "Why analyze communication? Why not just do it?" Although, as with many subjects, we can study communication simply for its own sake, there is a better answer to this practical question. If you have an analytic attitude about communication, you will almost always improve your personal and professional uses of it. More simply, the study of how communication works can help us become more effective persons.

There are many ways in which to analyze the process of communication:

Study the *human being* as a communicating organism. This study is the topic of Part Two of this book, where we ask: "What is language and how do we use it?" "What motivates us to communicate?" "How do we persuade one another?" "How can we extend our communications through using media?"

Study the social *contexts*, or levels, wherein we humans communicate. This study is discussed in Part Three, in terms of individual, group, organizational, and public communication.

Study the *effects* of communication, especially through social scientific research. Part Four contains examples of research into relational, news and opinion, political, and entertainment uses of communication.

Study the *content* of communication, a topic introduced later in this chapter. Such research is a part of many social scientific studies of communications effects.

Study the dynamic *processes* involved in communication behaviors. We now turn to this attempt to identify the processes of communication and divide them into their basic components.

ANALYSIS OF THE COMMUNICATION PROCESS

Diagrams of the Process

One simple analysis of the communication process was already shown as Figure 1.2. It is repeated here as Figure 2.1, with labels added as if we were analyzing *conversation* as a communication process. In some respects, the diagram in Figure 2.1 is also a simple **model** in that it represents the major components of the conversational process. This is not the only model, by any means, nor is it entirely adequate for all facets of communication study. Yet it does capture the essence of what teachers, researchers, writers, and students usually mean by "the communication process."

Figure 2.1
Conversation as a
Communication
Process

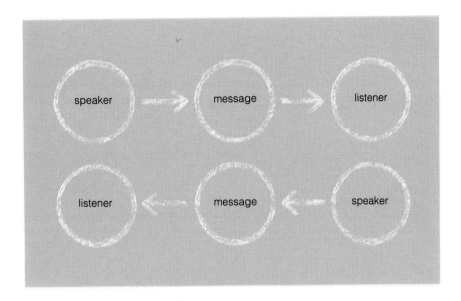

This fundamental model is the framework within which human symbolic transactions take place. It can be a valuable scheme for analyzing any act of communication, especially because it reminds us that the overall communication process is made up of component processes. For example, note in Figure 2.1 how source and receiver have simultaneous roles in this analysis. Conversation is markedly transactional. Consider, too, the different media in this situation: speech, sight, and even touching. And remember to what degree nonverbal communication symbols can enter into this process. Communication in this context can be the most influential of all forms of communication. If the two individuals learn about each other in the process and use their knowledge of their personal needs and wishes to further the relationship, a very *personal* form of communication can develop. This is the process by which interpersonal relationships start and are maintained. We discuss this process in greater detail in Chapter 7.

With a little thought, you'll see how widely applicable this basic source–receiver model is in analyzing different types of communication. For example, let's apply the same model to the operation of a commercial television station, as shown in Figure 2.2. What's different here? For one thing, although the media are still sight and sound, they now also involve broadcasting. Further, as compared with a conversation, the immediate communication is much more one-way. It is not transactional in the sense that conversation is. Feedback here occurs in a different medium from the original communication. Note, too, the differences in communication motives. The broadcaster communicates to gain an audience "share," whereas the viewer tunes in for personal satisfactions. In one sense, the broadcaster is in the business of selling satisfaction to the viewers in return for being able to count them as audience members so as to command a price for commercial messages.

Figure 2.2
Commercial Television
as a Communication
Process

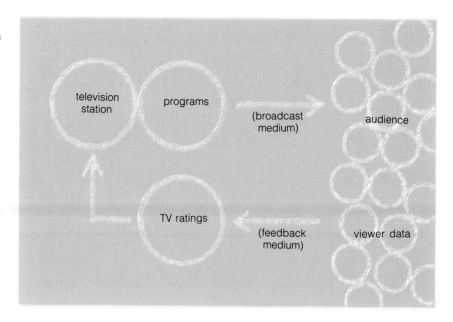

For another example, look at how the model portrays the various formal communications in a business (Figure 2.3). What's different about communication in a company? For one, it is a mix of media forms. Many of the messages are management directives that flow from the top down. Feedback is typically information on compliance with these directives, as well as orders and sales. Can you see how a communication model could help you analyze the communications practices of a specific business? It is not unusual for communications consultants to do such analyses as a basis for evaluating corporate communications.

Other simple models are identified more with specific theorists than with particular modes of communication. Three of these are given next.

The Shannon Model

The model shown in Figure 2.4 depicts message flow in an electronic communications system. This model, developed by a Bell Laboratories scientist, Claude Shannon, stresses the transmitting and receiving aspects of electronic signals in a communications device (a teletype, for example) and emphasizes that "noise" can interfere with the signal. The source and destination are the users of that electronic system. Although Shannon included this model only as an incidental part of a paper on mathematical measures of communication, it is considered the "granddaddy" of most attempts to lay out the communication process in diagram form.

Figure 2.3
Communications in a
Business

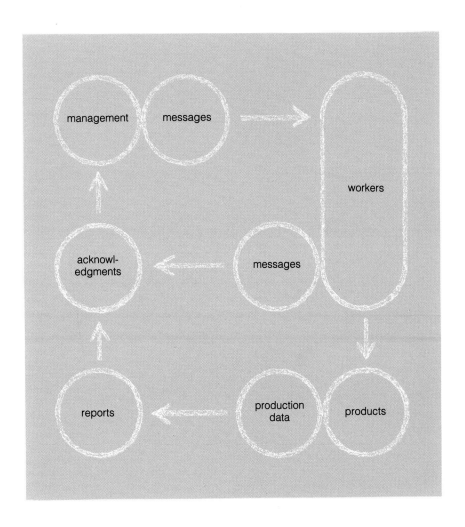

The Berlo Model

Another well-known model, and one developed expressly for students of communication, was included in David Berlo's influential textbook of the 1960s, *The Process of Communication*. As you can see in Figure 2.5, Berlo included many of the factors that could affect how sources and receivers create and react to messages ("communication skills," "attitudes," and so on). He also referred to the topic, organization, and language of messages ("content," "treatment," "code"). His use of the term *channel* instead of *medium* is an example of how these terms are used differently by communications writers. Because Berlo's text was one of the very few around as the communications field grew, this model has influenced many students in the United States and abroad.

Figure 2.4
The Shannon Model of Communication

source
transmitter
signal
receiver
destination
noise
message
message

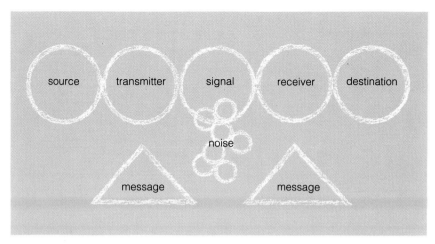

Source: C. Shannon and W. Weaver, *The Mathematical Theory of Communication.* (Urbana, Ill.: University of Illinois Press, 1949), p. 7. Copyright © 1949 by The University of Illinois Press. Used by permission.

Figure 2.5
The Berlo Model

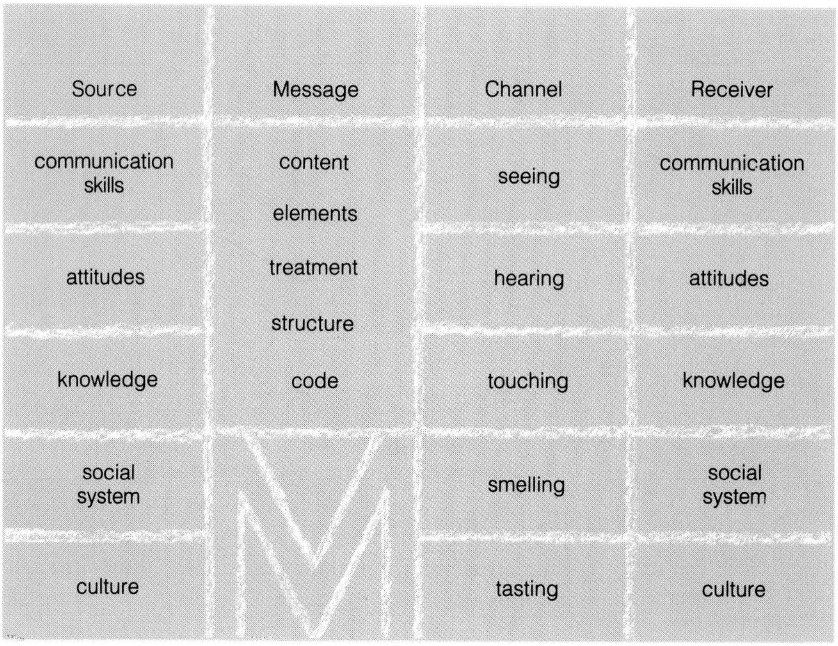

Source
Message
Channel
Receiver
communication skills
content
seeing
communication skills
elements
attitudes
treatment
hearing
attitudes
structure
knowledge
code
touching
knowledge
social system
smelling
social system
culture
tasting
culture

Source: David K. Berlo, *The Process of Communication.* Copyright © 1960 by Holt, Rinehart and Winston, Inc. Reprinted by permission of Holt, Rinehart and Winston, CBS College Publishing.

Lasswell's Verbal Model

Not all models need be as complex as Berlo's, nor do they have to be diagrams. One of the best known and simplest models of communication was contributed by the political scientist and communications scholar Harold Lasswell. It consists only of a few questions:

WHO says WHAT?
in what CHANNEL?
to WHOM?
with what EFFECT?

There is hardly a communication situation that you cannot analyze on the spot if you can remember these four short questions. Notice that Lasswell uses *channel* instead of *medium*, as does Berlo. Sometimes a channel is taken to mean a general type of communication such as sight, print, or the like, whereas a medium refers to the physical basis of communication such as light waves, acoustic vibrations, or broadcast waves.

LEVELS OF COMMUNICATION

We can also analyze communication in terms of levels, or the broad social contexts within which it operates. These levels are often referred to as *intrapersonal, interpersonal, small-* and *large-group, organizational,* and *public* communication. It is easy to remember these levels, because they differ according to how people are involved as senders and receivers. For example:

Intrapersonal: communication within one person

Interpersonal: communication between two persons

Small-group: communication among two or more but usually not more than 25 individuals

Large-group: communication by one or several persons to an audience of, say, 25 or more persons

Organizational: communication among a group of persons related in some type of business or administrative structure

Public, or **mass:** communication from one person or a group of persons through special media to large audiences or markets

One of the best ways to see the differences among these different contexts of communication is to contrast their characteristics; this is done in Table 2.1. Take time to look over this table. Certainly you may be able to think of additions to it. The point is not to present an exhaustive diagram of every possible type of communication but rather to show how the basic source–message–receiver model helps us analyze the different social

Table 2.1 Contexts of Human Communication

Intrapersonal		
	Description	Talking to yourself; monitoring your own speech or writing as feedback.
	Source	Self.
	Message	Anything; but probably most often topics of a personal nature.
	Medium	Speech, writing, film, video or audiotape, computer program.
	Receiver	Yourself.
	Feedback	This type of communication is itself a feedback process.
Interpersonal (Face-to-Face)		
	Description	Everyday conversation, direction giving; social chatter; attempts to develop deep personal relationships.
	Source	Self.
	Message	Usually topics traditionally communicated personally between people whose personal roles are potentially involved. These can become very "deep" psychological transactions, more so than in other contexts.
	Medium	Speech and nonverbal, but could be memos or notes exchanged in close proximity. Offers ideal context for two-way transactions.
	Receiver	One or two other individuals.
	Feedback	Immediate and in the same medium as the initiated communication.
Interpersonal (Point-to-Point)		
	Description	Personal letters, telephone conversations, telegrams, computer conference links, citizen's band (CB) radio.
	Source	Self.
	Message	Topics that require interpersonal exchanges, but with the exception of the telephone, mail, and perhaps CB, usually more formal and less of a highly personal nature.
	Medium	Transported paper, audio and text links via wire or broadcasting.
	Receiver	Another individual.
	Feedback	Potentially immediate and in the same medium for telephone and synchronous computer conference. Delayed for most mail, including telegrams and computer conferences.

Table 2.1 (*continued*)

Small-Group (Face-to-Face)	Description	Small meetings or gatherings, usually with a common purpose in mind. Usually 25 or fewer persons in size, so all individuals may interact.
	Source	Self and potentially all other participants. May have a leader.
	Message	Typical group topics such as agenda setting, decision making, ritual.
	Medium	Usually speech, sometimes augmented with visual aids, note exchange, and so on.
	Receiver	All participants.
	Feedback	Typical face-to-face feedback, perhaps augmented with requests for opinion, voting, "show of hands."
Small-Group (Point-to-Point)	Description	Conferences by telephone or other media that allow participants to confer over large distances.
	Source	Self and potentially all other participants. Usually has a leader.
	Message	Typical group topics, but usually more formal than face-to-face context.
	Medium	Telephone, audio loudspeakers, television, computer links.
	Receiver	All participants.
	Feedback	Usually immediate and in same medium. But participants could share messages via computer files at different times ("asynchronous").
Large-Group	Description	Meetings and gatherings with live interactions, but where most individuals are audience rather than sources: film showings, public performances, TV shows, lectures.
	Source	Usually one or several individuals whose performance or presentation is the object of the gathering.
	Message	Nearly any message is possible, including simply entertainment.
	Medium	Face-to-face speech, often augmented by audio and visual aids; musical, dance, or dramatic performance. If transmitted over radio, film, or broadcast media to larger audiences, it becomes public communication.
	Receiver	The audience in the usual sense.

Table 2.1 *(continued)*

	Feedback	Potentially immediate but not with the same message types as the source: applause, booing, cheering, voting. Sometimes an individual is called upon to respond.
Organizational	Description	Communication that supports the operation of a business, industry, or nonprofit organization; office communication.
	Source	Managers, supervisors, persons who write operations manuals; sometimes employees who must report back information.
	Message	Orders, motivation, information and data, surveillance.
	Medium	The formal network includes speech, memos, documents, telephone, and, increasingly, computer communications. The informal network is mostly speech. Mixture of face-to-face and media.
	Receiver	Employees, workers, lower level managers; in upward communications flow, anyone who receives reports.
	Feedback	Profits, productivity. Immediate feedback is often in same channels and is evidence of compliance.
Public, or Mass	Description	Communication broadly distributed through a media technology: books, periodicals, films, TV and radio, records, tapes, and disks.
	Source	Media institutions such as a newspaper, film studio, TV network, publisher. In many countries the government, through a Ministry of Information, is the controlling source.
	Message	Virtually everything from simple entertainment to attempts at social control. Messages are oriented to segments of the population, if not the entire population.
	Medium	Those media with wide dissemination potential, especially print, radio, TV, films.
	Receiver	Large, identifiable segments of the population, markets, constituencies.
	Feedback	Profits, numbers of readers or viewers, letters, critical reviews. Feedback is delayed and usually in alternate media.

contexts of human communication. Moreover, this table may be useful to you as you study the communications that go on in your life. It should help you to know what to look for.

Intrapersonal Communication

Communication at the intrapersonal level is communication "within one." It could be you reading your class notes, talking to yourself, and, some people would add, simply thinking. There has been relatively little study of intrapersonal communication in the communication field.

However, we may see more analyses on this level as the number of studies increases on how we can use electronic computers to assist us in problem solving. For example, if a civil engineer is going to use a computer to assist in the design tasks of constructing a building, the computer will be of greatest assistance if it solves problems in the same style as its user. In that respect we could say that the more the computer matches the intrapersonal patterns of the engineer, the more readily it can serve as an extension of his or her mental activity. A computer designed to assist a physician would have a quite different approach to problem solving. This is where theory and study of intrapersonal communication should become increasingly important.

Interpersonal Communication

The interpersonal level of communication is the most personal of all contexts of analysis. As we will see in Chapter 7, not all one-to-one communication is necessarily personal. It becomes so only as people begin to address each other as distinct individuals—that is, they address themselves to each other's personal motives and needs. When this level of communication becomes personal, it can be highly transactional. The individuals, being sensitive to each other's needs, will try to work out a relationship that is mutually beneficial.

If you are interested in a career in any type of work that requires close personal relations—such as clinical psychology, social work, personnel work, or even sales—you will find a knowledge of the interpersonal level of communication invaluable. Even if you are not sure of your career area, interpersonal communication is also invaluable for development of the everyday human relationships that make life so interesting and rewarding.

Finally, we have to be careful not to restrict interpersonal communication to face-to-face situations. The most popular media extension of this form of communication is the telephone. Mail, too, can be very personal in nature. These latter types of communication are often called "point-to-point" instead of interpersonal or one-to-one.

Small-Group Communication

In small groups it is possible for everybody to participate actively in a discussion. That is, there are not so many people as to prevent anyone from having a chance to contribute. A committee is a common example of a small group. As discussed in more detail in Chapter 8, people communicate differently when there is more than one other person involved. Groups tend to take on lives of their own, and some communication is necessary simply to coordinate this. Also, people will often be influenced by other members of the group in how they participate; for example, they will be willing to take greater chances with what they say as long as the group is likely to go along with them.

It is difficult to imagine a person in the professional world who does not have many small-group meetings. Management often meets in small groups to collectively plan and review results. As a professional, you will find that "participationship" is often as critical as "leadership."

In modern communications, we have many opportunities for extending small-group behavior beyond the confines of a meeting room. We can connect the participants by telephone, television, and even computer—a procedure called a *teleconference*. One area of research into small groups is seeing what happens to discussions when the individuals are linked by media instead of being in the same room with one another.

Large-Group Communication

The distinguishing characteristic of large-group communication is that there are too many people present for everybody to be a contributor. Large groups often illustrate a one-way communication, where the participants are mainly an audience. The communicator may be an individual speaker or speakers, or perhaps a film or some other type of medium is involved. As distinguished from public communication, the audience is present to give immediate feedback.

It is well known that people react differently to communication if they are in a large group than if they are isolated or in a small group. This contrast is often cited when comparing motion picture and television audiences.

Large groups, like small ones, take on a life of their own, and sometimes it is this "life" that is the most important quality of the group, as with a rally, mob, or demonstration. The group can become the message, so to speak.

Political communications often present interesting challenges for individuals planning large-group communication. The presence of a large audience is itself an endorsement of a candidate. If group response to the candidate is visibly favorable, this is a powerful message that the candidate would like to have conveyed, in turn, via the mass media, especially television. This phenomenon can help create the so-called bandwagon effect in persuasion. The more the home viewer sees people actively supporting the candidate, the more pressure there is on the viewer to make a commitment.

Organizational Communication

Interpersonal, small-group, and large-group communication may take place within an organizational context. By virtue of their membership in the organization, however, people are typically playing out additional organizational

Church congregations are a common example of large-group communication. Here the typical communication flow is from one individual to the group, with the group responding as a whole. Small-group communication, by contrast, provides more opportunity for group members to talk to one another. Church services are also an example of how communication can be highly personalized even if not in a two-person conversation or small-group setting. *Michael Rothstein/ Jeroboam, Inc.*

roles in their communication. One of the motivational factors unique to organizational communication is that the individual is forced to compare his or her personal motives or action or communication with the motives or goals of the organization. (To some extent this takes place in any typical instance of group communication, but it is more pronounced in organizations.)

Almost all professional careers require skill in organizational communication. Organizations operate through communications, and you must know both the formal and informal rules if you are to succeed in this context. You will have a special challenge if you are a member of an organization whose business or purpose is itself to create communications, such as a newspaper, broadcast station, marketing firm, public relations firm, advertising firm, film production company, or one of the many growing areas of the "office" communications business.

Public, or Mass, Communication

Any large-scale communication disseminated mainly by the media of print, broadcasting, film, or the new electronic networks to large audiences is considered to be public, or mass, communication. *Mass communication* is the traditional term applied to communication delivered to large, anonymous audiences (*mass* comes from the nineteenth-century concept of the mass society of largely faceless individuals). Today, many audiences are not so anonymous, since communications and advertising are targeted to specific groups. Also, it is increasingly recognized that large-scale communication is typically a mix of media, individual, and group communications. Hence, it is useful to have a less restricted term, such as *public*, to define this level of communication.

One of the main distinguishing characteristics of public communication is that the communicator is most often an institution. That is, it is a broadcast station, newspaper, publisher, film studio, or something along these lines. Although individuals (newspaper reporters, for instance) create the basic communications, the overall production of messages is a collective effort. The motives of these institutions vary greatly between the free-enterprise and socialist worlds. The purpose of most large communications corporations in America is to make a profit for their shareholders. Although at the same time they may address themselves to social responsibilities, as when a newspaper crusades against crooked politicians, they nevertheless must stay profitable to stay in business.

In the socialist countries, the prime responsibility of most media institutions is to support the political way of life. These media are extensions of the government in power. They are not necessarily concerned with profitability (although many carry advertising to help subsidize themselves). However, they are not without responsibilities. They must demonstrate allegiance to the government and show that they have some influence on the population. As the world's media spill more and more across international boundaries, we must be reminded all the more of the essential differences among institutions of public communication.

Another unique quality of public communication is the vast *multiplication* of its messages, especially in broadcasting. This multiplicity is coupled with a less direct opportunity for audience feedback than is found in most other forms of communication. You may write a letter to an editor, refuse to buy a movie ticket, or call in to a radio station, but your messages are hardly a match for the vast message dissemination power of the mass media. This is why the institutions for public communication are so politically volatile.

THE ANALYSIS OF CONTENT

Whereas analyzing communication by models and levels involves studying the overall process, communication analysis is sometimes concentrated specifically upon the message itself. After all, it is the message that is unique to the communication process. It is the main component in almost any study of communication. Studies of this type are usually called **content analyses.**

Analyses of Public Messages

Most of the best known studies of communication content have examined the print, film, and broadcast media. The general question about content finds many specific forms, for example:

What was in the newspaper to influence voters?
How are workers portrayed on television?
What sex-role stereotypes are contained in books for preschool children?
How much violent content is there in television programming?

Usually the results of content analyses are presented in tabular form. For example, Table 2.2 presents a summary of the number of sexual acts portrayed or referred to per hour in samples taken from television soap operas.

Although these analyses can tell us much about the media environment, they cannot tell us how people respond to this content. In the last decade much has been made of the unbalanced portrayal of men and women in desirable social roles on television. Men, critics say, are too often seen as being smarter than women and more in charge of important events. Women, by contrast, are shown as flighty and worried about trivial things (such as wax buildup on their kitchen floor). But we cannot know without testing television viewers themselves how they perceive these images. Perhaps they pay little attention to them. Or if they do pay attention, they may not relate the images to everyday life. With only a few exceptions, researchers typically have not related the results of content studies to the reactions of users of the mass media.

Table 2.2 Frequency of Sexual Acts or References in Samples Taken from TV Soap Operas

| Act/Reference | Number per Hour | | |
	1976	1979	1980
Rape	4	1	11
Homosexuality	—	—	—
Prostitution	5	—	1
Intercourse (outside of marriage)	6	4	14
Intercourse (within marriage)	1	1	4
Petting	11	34	12
Other intimacies	4	8	9
Total	31	48	51
Rate per hour	2.00	2.28	1.80

Source: B. Greenberg et al., "Sex on the Soap Operas: Afternoon Delight," *Journal of Communication* 31 (1981): 36.

As the author has written elsewhere (Williams, LaRose, and Frost, 1981), the *degree* to which a viewer sees a television character as a role model or as a figure from everyday life may have more of an effect on that viewer's behavior than does the *quantity* of images seen.

Analyses of Other Message Levels

Content analyses of interpersonal communication, although they are found more in studies of language or language behavior, have yielded insights into "rules" that people seem to follow in conversations. An extension of this type of analysis studied the content of what people said to each other in typical telephone conversations (Pool, 1977).

One type of speech content analysis examines the speech to see how it varies according to the social context. There are many studies of the content of the transactions in small-group interactions. Some such research has been the basis for studying the "lives" of groups and how group communication is often carried on simply to maintain the group rather than to talk about the group's ostensible purpose. The Bales guide for Interaction Process Analysis (Chapter 8) is a method for analyzing the contributions made in small-group communication.

Content analyses of large-group communications usually focus on the main message conveyed by a speaker, film, or other medium. There is less emphasis on audience reaction. When a study of such a situation involves an extensive analysis of the meanings of an important instance of communication, it is often referred to as "literary," or "textual," criticism.

Particularly in recent years, researchers have become interested in the content of organizational communication. Many studies of content have also been *network* studies, where the research reveals who communicates with whom, about what, and through which media in an organization. It is often useful for executives to know about discrepancies between how they intend communication to flow in their organization (that is, by the organization chart) compared with how it actually flows (informal communication, grapevine).

Despite the insights that content analyses can provide, we must still bear in mind that what analysts "see" in a message may bear little relation to what effect that message was intended to have or what effect it did have.

Analyses of New Media Technologies

One of the newest areas of analysis is the study of the uses of new media technologies in different communication environments (Williams, Rice, and Rogers, 1988). These studies cover a wide range of topics, which can be examined in terms of level of communication, for example:

Individual: How effective can personal communication be when undertaken on an electronic mail system? Just as we compensate for loss of visual contact when we communicate personal information by telephone, what compensations are likely with electronic text exchanges?

Group: Can teleconferencing be as effective as meeting face to face? Will effectiveness vary according to the purposes of the meetings, differing, for example, between an informational meeting and a negotiation session?

Organizational: What are the consequences for executive decision making as computer-based decision support systems are introduced?

Public: What are the effects of cable television upon viewing of traditional TV programs?

Analyses of the new media are typically (1) feasibility or demonstration studies ("Can the new technologies bring advantages?" "What are the results on a trial basis?"), (2) studies of adoption behavior ("How do people go about learning to use new media?"), or (3) evaluation studies ("What are the effects of the new media?" "Are they meeting the objectives?"). In the next several decades, studies of the new media are a probable growth area in communication studies.

SUMMARY

Social scientists often study human communication by analyzing the process into its component parts and then attempting to explain their operation. *Models* are useful for this purpose, and many have been proposed for the human communication process. Examples of early and influential models include those of Shannon, Berlo, and Lasswell.

Communication is often analyzed in a more concrete sense into different contexts, or levels. These include the *intrapersonal; interpersonal; small-group; large-group; organizational;* and *public*, or *mass*, communication levels. Intrapersonal communication typically involves only one person, whereas interpersonal is person-to-person communication, with messages that are focused on individual interests or needs. Small-group communication typically involves no more persons than can join in conversation with one another, while in large-group communication, one or a few persons address the rest of the group. Communication in organizations is a mixture of different types, but messages typically flow along lines reflecting the operation of the organization. In public communication, messages flow from one to many, and a medium such as print, film, or broadcasting is involved.

We also apply analytic techniques to the content of messages. An example of *content analysis* would be identifying and counting the number of acts of violence in a prime-time television program for a sample week. A deeper analysis of the meanings and attributes of messages is called literary, or textual, criticism. A major growth area of communication analyses is studies of the new media. These may include studies of feasibility in the use of a new communications technology, studies of adoption, or research into evaluation.

1. Take an example of some instance (such as you leading or participating in a group discussion) or system (such as a newspaper) of communication and analyze it into its main components. Then cast these components into a model of some type, either one in this chapter or one of your own design.

2. Take some new (such as video games) or unusual (for example, bird calls) form of communication and analyze it as a process. What generalizations can you draw about its component processes?

3. Make up a chart that includes the six levels, or contexts, of communication (small-group, mass, and so on) described in this chapter. Then for each describe at least two examples of how you engage in that type of communication. Finally, contrast the purposes for which you usually use face-to-face communication as against print, film, or broadcast media.

4. What do you think that the consequences of new communications technologies will be on certain contexts of communication? For example, what is the likely impact of people being able to get television programs from a cable rather than a broadcasting system? Or, if people can communicate with one another in an organization via computers, what will this alternative do to more traditional forms of communication?

5. Do a small example of content analysis. For example, take an evening television program, and analyze the differences in how men and women are portrayed. Whom do you see more? What roles are emphasized? What generalizations do you draw?

REFERENCES AND READINGS

Agee, W. K., P. H. Ault, and E. Emery. *Introduction to Mass Communications.* 8th ed. New York: Harper and Row, 1985.

Bales, R. *Interaction Process Analysis.* Reading, Mass.: Addison-Wesley, 1965.

Berlo, D. K. *The Process of Communication.* New York: Holt, Rinehart and Winston, 1960.

Gerbner, G., and L. Gross. "Living with Television: The Violence Profile." *Journal of Communication* 26 (1976): 173–199.

Littlejohn, S. W. *Theories of Human Communication.* 2d ed. Belmont, Calif.: Wadsworth, 1983.

Pool, I. D., ed. *The Social Impact of the Telephone.* Cambridge, Mass.: MIT Press, 1977.

Schramm, W., and W. E. Porter. "The Process of Communication." In *Men, Women, Messages, and Media,* by W. Schramm and W. E. Porter, pp. 35–53. New York: Harper and Row, 1982.

Shannon, C., and W. Weaver. *The Mathematical Theory of Communication.* Urbana: University of Illinois Press, 1949.

Williams, F., R. LaRose, and F. Frost. *Children, Television and Sex-Role Stereotyping.* New York: Praeger, 1981.

Williams, F., R. Rice, and E. S. Rogers. *Research Methods and New Media.* New York: Free Press, 1988.

PART
TWO

Basic Aspects of Communication

Any study of human communication should begin with a

description of the competencies that underlie our abilities to

exchange messages. We first examine human beings' verbal and

nonverbal communication capabilities and then go on to explore

how these fit into strategies for satisfying needs and wielding

influence. Finally, media and communications technologies are

introduced as bases for the extension of human communication

capabilities beyond our natural endowments. The overall

purpose of the four chapters in Part Two is to orient you to basic

human communication behaviors before examining them in

different social contexts in Part Three.

A portion of the stone circle at Stonehenge, Wiltshire,
England (page 42). *A. F. Kersting.*

Verbal and Nonverbal Communication

OUR SYMBOLIC WORLD

The message you see in Figure 3.1 is a metal plaque that was included in the payload of Pioneer 10, the first space probe to find its way out of our solar system and to travel endlessly into deep space. Notice how the earth is identified from among the other planets of the solar system. Presumably an advanced civilization would be familiar with the relative sizes of these planets and with their distances from our sun. These sizes and distances are a potential bit of "shared" experience. Note also the images along the left of the plaque. These represent certain mathematical relationships that any advanced civilization would presumably have deduced, just as we have. The symbols most prone to misinterpretation in this plaque are probably the figures of the humans. There is no reason for us to assume that beings in some far civilization, who perhaps exist in forms totally different from ours, would have any idea of the meaning of the human sketches on this plaque. (If you were an extraterrestrial being, what bizarre guesses might you make?)

This space-age example of communication reminds us that our symbol system for communicating with others is based on shared experiences. This makes communication a fragile thing. It is no wonder that it often gets us into trouble! Remember from Chapter 1 that a *symbol* represents an idea, object, event, or feeling and that it need have no physical relation to what it

Figure 3.1
The Communications Plaque from Pioneer 10

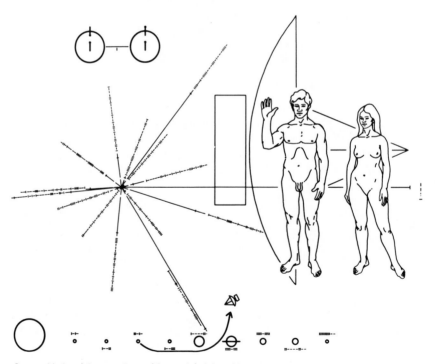

Source: National Aeronautics and Space Administration.

represents. For example, the word *chair* is a symbol; the sounds of that word bear no intrinsic relation to something we sit on. It is arbitrary that we associate that sound pattern with a chair, or that any other language associates its sound pattern with a chair.

Meanings in Search of Words

We live in a symbol-laden world. Much of what we perceive around us—objects, events, and, of course, all forms of direct human communication—suggests meanings beyond the direct characteristics of the stimuli themselves. The room in which you are now sitting has a particular design, a decorating scheme, and furniture, and all of it may suggest a certain mood to you. The clothes you wear have a symbolic value. You probably bought them partly for this value, as a particular fashion or style. Noises in the background may indicate to you whether there is somebody in the next room. Your day is full of spoken symbols, written and printed symbols, text on the television screen, and symbols heard from your radio or tape player. And, of course, you are currently interpreting the text symbols on this page.

In all these examples, you are interpreting meanings as stimulated in your consciousness by objects, markings, images, sounds, actions, or events in your environment. The symbolic values of stimuli are **learned** associations derived from our experiences, and only a few are learned in formal situations of instruction. Learned associations are a result of environmental experiences. As youngsters, for example, we experienced that others called the covers on our feet "shoes." (Or, as was the case with one of my children at the age of 2, golden arches were called "McDonalds.")

Many early theories of language acquisition were oversimplified, in that they tried to account mainly for noun or verb learning, that is, words that could easily be associated with items or experiences in the environment. They also held that rewards were a key part of such learning, as in complimenting or patting a child for learning a word. Current theory holds that we have a strong biological endowment for language and that our early experiences with language are a seeking out of expressions to fit our meanings. Moreover, there are many aspects of language learning, such as the underlying syntactic rules for expressing plurality, the use of modifiers, or sentence structures. We seem to be able to ferret out these aspects from environmental experiences, including deducing the "rules" of usage. Also, direct reward does not seem so important a part of the learning process as was once thought. Either direct reward is not so necessary as it is in other types of behavioral learning, or else learning language itself—the newly experienced ability to use a word—is the reinforcement. Just as we are genetically programmed to walk, we are programmed to develop a symbol system. The specific language we develop, whether it be French, Chinese, or Arabic, is the one we learn from our environment. The language of our environment is also a cultural heritage.

It is important to bear in mind that we embellish our spoken language symbols with a great variety of additional symbols. These include the symbols, or "language," of gestures, facial expressions, and the meaningful movements we make with our entire body. The symbols also include ways in which we use our voice to sound happy or sad, excited or calm, or loving or angry. (Language is placed in quotation marks here because linguists prefer to reserve the term *language* for symbols that make up our basic verbal skills rather than for what some call our nonverbal methods of symbolization.)

As we discuss in a subsequent section of this chapter, there are also nonverbal symbolic qualities in the design of many of our communications media. The layout of a newspaper front page, for example, has communication qualities beyond what is printed on it. So, too, does a scene created for television or film. And believe it or not, the style and format of a computer program can, in subtle ways, also have a quality of nonverbal communication.

Language as a Social System

In addition to the complexity and wonder of human language as a symbol system, language is invaluable for human social relations. *Because humans can share the same symbol and meaning associations—that is, the same "language"—they have a basis for a most powerful communication system.* This suggests a more socially oriented definition of **language** as a system of spoken symbol and meaning relationships shared by a group of people.

When a group of people speaks the same language, it is called a "speech (or language) community." That there are so many different languages in the world is evidence of the arbitrariness of the relations between particular sounds and their associated meanings. If we were to study the history of languages or the relations between them, we would see how much the boundaries of language communities have been set by geographic barriers as well as by the history of transportation.

If you have traveled abroad, you have no doubt experienced the vast contrasts in language and associated communication behaviors that often exist between cultures. Not only are there different ways of saying "thank you" in the various world language and cultural systems, but there are often also critical differences in when people use this phrase. If you decide upon a career that will take you to different cultures for your work, such as the diplomatic corps, the military, or the expanding area of international business, you will have to learn many of these subtle differences among language communities. Practically speaking, you may have to study what we are increasingly calling **intercultural communication.**

Human language is an incredibly complex phenomenon that we should be careful not to slight in our discussion of human symbol systems.

Media Extensions

We humans have become very adept at inventing ways to extend or expand our symbol-based communication beyond our immediate environment. We have developed what the present author likes to call **media extensions,** or our methods for extending our natural media (sight, speech, touch, smell) of communication. Writing, for example, is a media extension. As you are probably well aware, when people in communications refer to newspapers, books, magazines, radio, television, and film, they usually call them simply "media." But remember that speech and sight are based upon media, too (sound waves, light waves).

Through media extensions, we greatly increase our capability for conveying and preserving symbols of communication. The invention of writing (probably around 4000 B.C.) allowed us to communicate in complex ways far beyond the range of our voices. Sculpture, painting, and architecture allow us to embed our symbols in our environment. Printing, as a media extension, made possible the efficient duplication of written messages. The development of the telegraph allowed us to send our symbols at the speed of light. Broadcasting combined message duplication and speed in a media extension. Now the electronic computer is, in part, a media extension that cannot only convey our symbols but also itself act upon them!

LANGUAGE AND BEHAVIOR

Linguistic Theory

As we saw above, our ability to understand and create complex spoken symbols is the result of both our biological and our cultural heritages. This ability is biological because we are born with a brain that gives us the mental basis for learning a language. Our perceptual and mental processes, particularly those that develop before adolescence, give us the capability to draw from our linguistic experiences a set of rules for using the language of our community. Our cultural heritage is the language that has been passed down through generations to our community. The process by which we learn our language—that is, sound patterns, words, grammatical patterns, style—can be summarized by the components in Figure 3.2. This diagram shows that when we learn language, we learn **linguistic rules,** the description of which is **linguistic theory.**

What are linguistic rules? Although nobody knows exactly how they reside in our head, we can write down the rules that seem to explain how our language works. From high school grammar, for example, you may remember that for a statement to be a sentence, it has to have a subject (for example, "John") and a predicate ("hit the ball"). This itself is a linguistic rule of all languages. That is, all languages have subjects and predicates, although they have different ways of expressing them. In any language, therefore, when a listener hears a string of spoken sounds, he or she will be anticipating cues indicating what the subject is and what the predicate is (or if the sounds even make up a sentence).

We still do not know all of the rules of language, but we have made considerable strides over the last twenty years in describing the rules a person would have to "know" in order to speak or understand a given language.

Figure 3.2
A Simple Model of
Language Learning

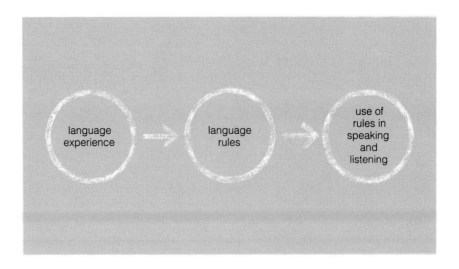

"Know" is in quotation marks here because, although you may reflect the rules of a language in your speech behavior, you usually cannot explain them (not, that is, unless you are a linguist).

As a crude analogy, these linguistic rules can be compared to the rules in a chess game. If we did not know how to play chess, we could analyze the patterns by which people play the game and eventually deduce from those patterns what the basic rules of the game were. And we could do this quite apart from any attempt to describe the detailed mental processes by which these rules are held in memory or executed.

Linguistic rules are our basis for determining meanings. That is, as we interpret a sentence, these rules help us associate basic meanings with the meaningful parts of words and then to combine these meanings in such a way that sentences are patterned grammatically. Say the following sentence aloud, and see how many meanings you can derive:

She is a light housekeeper.

Most people think of three meanings: (1) This is about a person who doesn't have to do the heavy housekeeping. (2) It is somebody who has gone on a diet. (3) It's a pretty lonely job on the coast of Maine. How you hear this sentence spoken—the sound pattern used—will narrow down these meanings for you. So will cues that might be obtained from the context. For example, you may hear it during a discussion on household help. All meanings, then, could be correct under certain conditions.

Psycholinguistic Theory

It is one thing to theorize about the rules that constitute your knowledge of a language, but it is another to explain how you actually behave when using those rules. Psychological theories of behavior involving linguistic rules fall within the realm of **psycholinguistics.**

Psycholinguistic studies are used to inquire how we "perform" with linguistic rules. They are studies of the details of language behavior rather than of the details of the rules themselves (linguistic theory). To help you distinguish linguistic theory from psycholinguistic theory, think of the difference between knowing the rules of chess and putting the rules into action. We can write these rules down, but they say nothing to us about how our brain stores them, how we call them into action, or how we learn them. Nor do they say anything having to do with the details of behavior. Such explanations require a psychological theory addressed to behavior.

Theorists are not sure how we accommodate linguistic rules in our brain. Some think that we may not even store the rules as such but, rather, may learn patterns that allow us to carry out behavior that, at best, reflects abstractly some underlying rules. But the basis of that behavior may be something quite different.

To help yourself understand the mental nature of rules, think about mathematical rules. There are, for example, abstract rules that mathematicians use to describe relationships among simple numbers, such as rules explaining theoretically why $2 + 2 = 4$. These mathematical rules do not describe at all the way in which we learn this easy sum or the way in which we learn any of those simple strategies we used in elementary school to do arithmetic problems. The rules tell us something about the system only in an abstract way. Psycholinguistic theory can so far only speculate on how we must carry out language behavior in ways that reflect what linguistics has been able to tell us about the rules of the language.

There are many other aspects of psycholinguistic theory besides the study of the psychological nature of linguistic rules. For example, psycholinguistic theory examines how we learn language: what aspects of our linguistic abilities are born in us—that is, genetically patterned from the evolution of our brain—and what aspects are learned when we acquire language. Another major area of psycholinguistic research examines the role of language in our thought processes—for example, studying how language helps us with the thought processes involved in problem solving. These studies examine how the ability to frame a problem in our mind using language often helps us find a solution.

Sociolinguistic Theory

When we broaden the study of language behavior to include its social characteristics and contexts, we are in the theoretical domain of **sociolinguistics.** This field studies communication situations (informal speech, a legal contract, a television program); the social roles of those involved in such situations (friends, strangers, the upper class, an ethnic group); and the reasons for the communication. None of us ever talks exactly the same way in all social contexts. From sociolinguistic theory it is possible to describe or to predict some of these socially related differences in communication behavior.

Some studies in sociolinguistics examine ethnic, cultural, educational, or income differences in how people use language in given situations. The theory here is usually that individuals from lower social status groups have less flexibility in using different styles.

Studies of linguistic attitudes are also a part of sociolinguistic theory. Most of us need hear only a brief burst of speech and we are ready to make guesses about the social class, ethnicity, age, or mood of the speaker. Theory in this area consistently shows that certain linguistic characteristics are inevitably tied to social stereotypes.

Some of the most fascinating sociolinguistic studies have tried to describe what we learn when we acquire the "social" rules of language. Most of us are capable of varying our language to suit the situation. But how do we do this? What rules do we learn that govern our use of formal, rather than informal, speech? All of these rules go together to provide us with a theory of what some call **communicative competence.**

Although some communication studies incorporate linguistic or sociolinguistic theories, sociolinguistic studies are most closely related to research into the broader aspects of communication behavior. The greatest area of overlap occurs in what students of communication call studies of interpersonal communication (Chapters 7 and 11). The distinguishing feature of a communication study or theory, as opposed to linguistic or psycholinguistic ones, is usually that the former is concerned not with language details but with the message as it links the sender and receiver. Nonetheless, it is difficult to conceive of any type of theory of human communication that does not include assumptions about a linguistic theory or a sociolinguistic or psycholinguistic one.

Much contemporary research into *conversational analysis* draws from sociolinguistic research. How do people use language to relate to one another, developing or breaking off relationships? Most examples of these processes take place in sociolinguistic contexts.

NONVERBAL COMMUNICATION

Types of Nonverbal Symbols

Not all of our symbols are language (or verbal) ones. Some augment our spoken language, and we call these **nonverbal symbols.** Such symbols are a key part of daily communications. They may reveal to others how we truly feel, as when a smile complements a greeting or when shaky knees disclose our anxiety during an argument. Nonverbal cues may signal when we should take our turn in a conversation or when we are being asked to agree or disagree. Here we will briefly examine seven types of nonverbal symbol: paralinguistics, kinesics, haptics, proxemics, dress and appearance, chronemics, and iconics.

1. Paralinguistics. Paralanguage, as its name implies, is a kind of complementary language. It includes meaningful variations in speech corresponding to patterns of loudness, pitch, rate, and hesitations. On a more complex level, these properties are interpreted by listeners as emotionality, emphasis, nonchalance, certainty, or fear, to name a few. Paralinguistic analyses can also

Often our facial expressions and gestures say more than our words, making our nonverbal messages especially important. In fact, research indicates that nonverbal messages sometimes may be more believable than verbal ones. Some nonverbal symbols, because they reflect the way humans respond emotionally, are similar across cultures, while others are culturally specific. In which category would you place the nonverbal expressions in this picture? *Frank Siteman/Jeroboam, Inc.*

include the social significance of dialect features, such as those that connote educational level, sex role, ethnicity, religion, age, or the fact that a person is handicapped in some way.

2. Kinesics. Our facial expressions, eye movements, gestures, and bodily postures also convey meanings. The study of such expressions and gestures is called **kinesics.**

Kinesics examines most of the normal gestures that humans are known to exhibit in different emotional states unless their culture has taught them to disguise their feelings. These basic emotions include pleasantness, unpleasantness, arousal, fear, surprise, rage, and affection. Hand and bodily gestures do not have as much cross-cultural generality, but the meanings that they signify do, as in explicit gestures denoting the shape of a circle or pointing to an object.

Many gestures, however, are culturally specific. You know their full meaning only if you are a member of the culture that uses it or have learned it from a member of that culture. And, as you have probably learned, there are differences between the sexes and the generations in terms of gestures.

3. Haptics. **Haptics** refers to the use of touch to communicate, as in shaking hands, holding hands, patting someone on the back, putting your arm around a person's shoulder, and the like. Touch may convey emphasis, affection, or greetings, and it varies greatly across cultures. For example, two men walking arm in arm in Western culture may draw attention, whereas in the Arab world this behavior is merely a common sign of friendship. Touch also varies by gender in our culture, as in who can slap whom on the back, when we can touch, and where we can touch.

4. Proxemics. The study of the use of interpersonal space, such as how far one person stands from another, is usually referred to as **proxemics.** In the United States we usually stand farther from one another (as well as touch less) than people in mainly Hispanic cultures. If we stand close, it may be a sign of being overbearing, rude, or socially unaware. In a culture expecting closeness, Americans may convey a message of coldness or distaste.

5. Dress and Appearance. Dress, hairstyles, makeup, jewelry, and any other changeable features we can add to our person constitute a nonverbal code of *dress* or *appearance*. As we know, these features vary greatly by culture, gender, age, and social status. Any bodily feature that is not easily changeable, such as height or weight, is not considered a variable means of nonverbal communication.

6. Chronemics. How time is considered is sometimes a message in itself, a form of nonverbal communication called **chronemics.** In some cultures, punctuality is considered a virtue, whereas in others, one is expected to be late or nonchalant about time. In the Arab world, you may sense a feeling of

Figure 3.3
International Traffic Signs as Iconic Communication

haste in movements and speech when visiting a business office, which seems to be related to a sense of importance. There are differences, too, across cultures in considering the amount of time you may spend in a conversation, transaction, or the like. In some parts of the southern United States, you may be expected to linger momentarily and exchange pleasantries when communicating with a store clerk, whereas in large eastern cities, such behavior would probably be taken as unusual or even silly.

7. Iconics. We can also interpret the symbolism found in objects or designs as a type of communication. We call this nonverbal process **iconics** and the symbols **icons.** Sometimes icons are more literal than symbolic because they illustrate a meaning directly: a photograph, for example, is a literal icon. In this respect, icons are sometimes differentiated by the degree to which they concretely portray their referents, a quality called **iconicity,** or iconic value.

Broadly construed, icons include everything from emblems to works of fine art. The American flag, for example, signifies certain meanings for citizens of the United States. Religious symbols such as the Christian cross, the star of David, or the Islamic crescent are icons. Fashion and design have iconic value as well as being considered symbols of dress and appearance. Similarly, we often purchase everything from pottery to automobiles with an eye toward their design, or, more precisely, the iconic value of their design.

"Full icons" are symbols that attempt to portray their referents. One of the best examples of practical iconic communication is international traffic signs. Look at the signs in Figure 3.3, and see if you can understand their meanings before looking down at the captions.

Intentionality

An important quality of nonverbal communication is the degree to which the communicator intends to convey a particular nonverbal message. For example, imagine a man with a speck of dust in his blinking eye trying to ask a young woman for directions. His blinking is strictly unintentional as it accompanies his communication. Yet, he might be taken as making a pass if the young woman interpreted his eye blinking as a symbolic gesture to her. Or just the opposite could occur: an intentional wink might be misinterpreted as eye trouble. Intentionality reminds us of the tentativeness of some nonverbal symbols and of how some may lead to unintentional communication.

Although we often think of nonverbal symbols as complementing or accompanying verbal ones, they may be main messages in and of themselves, or they may dominate a verbal message. Intentional forms usually fit in these latter categories, as with a shaking fist, a broad smile, a sigh of relief, or a voice filled with rage. We should realize that in our everyday face-to-face discourse with others, the nonverbal symbols we convey may have as many or more consequences than the verbal ones. (Skilled interviewers or negotiators will tell you that a knowledge of nonverbal symbols is invaluable to their work.)

BINARY COMMUNICATION

"Bits" and Binary Digits

We also have symbol systems that have evolved for human-and-machine communication, one example of which is the **binary** communication system. Theoretically, any symbol system could be reduced to only two different digits or symbols so long as you could use many combinations of them. A brief account of a sixteenth-century communication scheme will help introduce this topic.

Around the year 1550, Geronimo Cardano, an Italian mathematician, proposed that messages could be sent visually in a system using five torches on five towers of a castle, lighted in different patterns to represent letters of the alphabet. Each torch could be either lighted ("on") or not ("off"). The five torches, each with a possible message of on or off, could be used to send a total of thirty-two different letters or numbers. Figure 3.4 gives an idea of how this could work, although for purposes of illustration we have updated Cardano's code.

Note that *A* was represented when all five torches were unlighted (off). The letter *B* was signaled when only the easternmost torch was lighted. The letter *C* was signaled when only the torch on tower 4 was lighted, and *D* when both the tower 4 and tower 5 torches were afire. If we kept following this pattern, we would see that thirty-two different patterns were possible with the five-torch system. (How many would be possible with six torches?*)

Figure 3.4
A Renaissance Scheme for Signaling Letters of the Alphabet

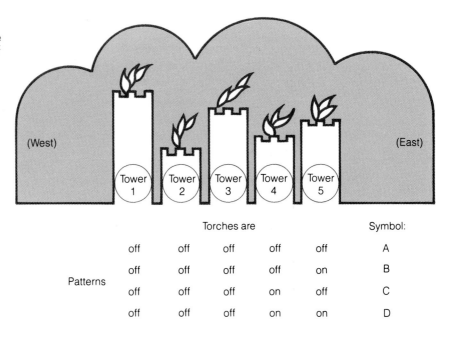

			Torches are			Symbol:
	off	off	off	off	off	A
	off	off	off	off	on	B
Patterns	off	off	off	on	off	C
	off	off	off	on	on	D

*The answer is sixty-four.

Although Cardano did not know it, he was proposing a symbol-encoding system that operated on the same principles as modern electronic devices that store and communicate information, in particular, the computer. Imagine that instead of the five torches you had a set of five tiny switches, each capable of storing one of the on or off signals. This is the principle by which computers store "information" (in quotation marks because it is a special definition of the word). Each on–off switch handles one two-message, or *binary*, unit of information. Each binary unit is called a **bit** (*bi*nary digi*t*) for short.

As you may have deduced, the more switches (or bits) we have in an ensemble, the more different symbols can be represented in the patterns of that set. In fact, to see how many symbols a particular number of switches can represent, we merely need to keep multiplying $2 \times 2 \times 2 \ldots$ a number of times equal to the number of switches. A one-switch system (1×2) handles 2 different symbols; a two-switch system (2×2), 4; an eight-switch, 256. The last system can signal any of 256 letters or numbers at one pattern setting. We can also describe the "information" capacity of the system in terms of its numbers of switches, or *bits*. The last system handles eight bits of information. Cardano's torch system handled "five bits."

Humans and Communicating Machines

Fortunately, it will be easy for us to get along without knowing the details of how computers can store symbols. As we increasingly use electronic devices as aids to human communication and calculation, however, we need to be aware of what it takes to communicate between humans and symbol-handling machines.

For example, we should know that when humans communicate with computers, the computer does most of the "translating" between our language and the binary units (expressed in 0 and 1) of its own language. This translation is made possible by a kind of compromise called a computer programming language. The computer is designed to recognize certain words or symbols in that language (for example, *print* in the language called BASIC), which it turns into binary commands that it needs in order to operate. Programming engineers are busy trying to develop languages that are as much like our own human symbol system as possible. We already have computers that will recognize a selected number of spoken commands.

Probably the greatest advances in human symbol systems over the next century (if not beyond) will be in areas of human-and-machine communication. These advances may influence society no less than did the invention of the printing press, if not the invention of writing.

SUMMARY

Our symbols for communicating with others are based on shared experience. To us, the symbolic values of stimuli are *learned* associations usually derived from our experiences. The primary system for human symbolic communication is *language*, the basic definition of which is the relation between sounds and meanings. The social aspect of language is that groups of people share a knowledge of these relations and therefore can communicate using them. In order to communicate these symbols we often use *media extensions*.

We study the human symbols in terms of the basic *linguistic rules* that seem to relate sounds to meanings (*linguistic theory*); in terms of how we are able to learn and to use these rules (*psycholinguistic theory*); and in terms of how our uses vary with the social aspects of the communicators and the situation (*sociolinguistic theory*). When we learn the rules of communicating appropriately in given situations, we learn *communicative competence*.

Beyond the basic symbol system of language, we have *nonverbal symbols*. The study of these symbols is divided among *paralinguistics, kinesics, haptics, proxemics*, dress and appearance, *chronemics*, and *iconics*. We must also consider the intentionality with which a nonverbal symbol is communicated.

Modern electronic communication systems, particularly those involving computers, represent human language or data in terms of ensembles of binary signal patterns, the basic unit of which is called a *bit*. In the future, human-and-machine communication will have a great influence on society.

TOPICS FOR DISCUSSION OR BRIEF PAPERS

1. Design a space plaque of your own. Give the reasons for the symbols you use.

2. Invent a ten-symbol "language." In order to be able to create new meanings, be sure the symbols can be combined. How many different "messages" will you be able to send?

3. Enlist the help of an acquaintance who is not a close friend. Engage the person in a conversation about something of mutual interest, but as you talk stare at his or her forehead. See if the person notices or mentions this. What did he or she think was happening? What were the consequences of this action for nonverbal communication?

4. Go down to a busy street corner. Select at least a dozen examples of nonverbal communication, and classify them according to the types discussed in this chapter.

5. Think about the old shell and pea game, in which you try to guess which of three shells the pea is under. How much "information" is involved in each guess? How many shells would you need in order to double the amount of information? Triple it? Explain why.

REFERENCES AND READINGS

Burgoon, J. K. "Nonverbal Signals." In *Handbook of Interpersonal Communication*, edited by M. L. Knapp and G. R. Miller. Beverly Hills, Calif.: Sage, 1985.

Hall, E. T. *The Silent Language*. Greenwich, Conn.: Fawcett, 1959.

Harrison, R. P. *Beyond Words: An Introduction to Nonverbal Communication*. Englewood Cliffs, N.J.: Prentice-Hall, 1974.

Knapp, M. L. *Nonverbal Communication in Human Interaction*. 2d ed. New York: Holt, Rinehart and Winston, 1978.

Lenneberg, E. H., ed. *New Directions in the Study of Language*. Cambridge, Mass.: MIT Press, 1964.

Mehrabian, A. *Silent Messages: Implicit Communication of Emotions and Attitudes*. 2d ed. Belmont, Calif.: Wadsworth, 1981.

Shannon, C. E., and W. Weaver. *The Mathematical Theory of Communication*. Urbana, Ill.: University of Illinois Press, 1949.

Williams, F. *Language and Speech*. Englewood Cliffs, N.J.: Prentice-Hall, 1972.

Motivation and Function

THE PURPOSIVE NATURE OF COMMUNICATION

If you are like most people, you can identify some degree of motivation and function in your communication behaviors. For example, one of your motives for reading this book may be to learn material that you will be tested on as part of a university course. Also, you may say that the book has the function of providing you with this information or instruction. In this chapter we make a similar distinction between motivation and function. **Motivation** is how our sense of needs prompts communication as a strategy for satisfying those needs. We use **function** to refer to the purposes that various types of communication serve in fulfilling those needs. These concepts are two sides of the same coin, two parts of the same process of need satisfaction through communication.

Consider your communication experiences this morning. Perhaps you glanced at the newspaper to see what was in the headlines, partly out of a need to find out what was going on in the world today and partly to fulfill a daily ritual. Maybe you had your radio going softly in the background while you were dressing. If so, you probably turned it on out of habit and with the expectation that it would be pleasant listening. Did a casual chat with a friend this morning have a purpose? Perhaps you cannot see this purpose unless you probe deeply enough. The reason may merely have been to fulfill a desire for a brief human contact, which most humans find subtly rewarding.

Most of our daily communications are potentially rewarding to us in direct or indirect ways. Obviously, we do not go around thinking of functions or rewards on a minute-by-minute basis, but **reward** is a key concept in the psychology of motivation. In the long run, we have to feel that we are "getting something" out of a particular kind of communication, or we will not keep doing it. We will avoid devoting time and energy to a type of communication that is not somehow relevant to us. Although we are likely to put up with communications that are negative, as when the boss reprimands us for making a mistake, we actively seek to minimize the frequency of such situations or to avoid them altogether.

We sometimes think of purpose or reward when we find ourselves trapped in irrelevant communications, such as a boring encounter at a party, a dull lecture, or a movie that should never have been released. Also, we often sample likely communications to determine whether they will be pleasing or rewarding to us. Such sampling may involve reading the first chapter of a new book, watching the first few minutes of a TV show, exchanging comments with another person at a party, or skimming over the opening of a magazine article. But for the most part, the communications we initiate or respond to during a day are carried out with some expectation of reward, no matter how subtle.

If our daily personal communications involving other people are generally unrewarding to us, our overall feeling of satisfaction with life may be lessened. Indeed, we may find ourselves without any close relationships with others. We may feel alone, frustrated, and unable to get what we want out of life. Such feelings and the lack of communication satisfactions are common in mental illness. Humans depend on communication for a healthy personal and social existence.

All theories of motivation assume that we humans have a range of needs to be fulfilled and that much of our daily behavior involves this fulfillment process. A distinction is often made between physical and psychological needs. The former are life-supporting, such as the need to eat. The latter refer more to our social existence, such as the need to love. These approaches to motivation are often called **drive-reduction** theories, as if our needs, when in a state of unfulfillment, set up drives (behaviors) toward the promised satisfaction. For example, thirst would be a state of unfulfilled need, setting up a drive to find water. When a need is satisfied, the drive is said to have been "reduced." In this chapter we examine some of the highlights of drive-reduction theory, and we also turn to other, broader theories holding that simple drive-reduction models are insufficient to explain the complexities of motivation. These latter theories are called **humanistic,** because they stress the unique and overall qualities of being human.

Communication has purpose in our lives. Without it, we are in trouble.

DRIVE REDUCTION AS A THEORY OF MOTIVATION

Physical Needs

All motivational theories assume that humans have certain basic **physical,** or bodily, **needs,** including our needs for oxygen, food, water, and certain ranges of temperature and air pressure. These necessities are what we must include in space capsules in order for humans to survive in an environment that lacks them.

Physical needs are sometimes called "biological," because they are part of our genetic inheritance. Often included in this group of needs are other biologically based needs that require not just physical but partly psychological satisfactions. These include an infant's needs for human contact and attention, including love. Another is our biologically based sexual desire. It is set into action by body chemistry, but it requires social behavior for satisfaction.

Physical needs are often associated with so-called drive-reduction theories. These theories emphasize that physical needs are conditions of deprivation; that is, they represent a lack, or absence, of food, water, or air. This "lack" sets up a behavioral drive that is our human attempt to satisfy the need. As the need becomes satisfied, the drive to satisfy is reduced, and we, in turn, reduce or change that given behavior.

We humans, as well as most other species, come equipped with communication capabilities so we can draw attention to our physical needs. If you have been around infants, you know that it is not difficult to tell when they are hungry or in need of a diaper change. Although such behavior is "automatic," in that a baby cries as an innate (or inborn) response to physical discomfort, we adults readily interpret it as a part of our human communication system.

Since it is natural for us to want to stay alive, we often communicate in ways that we hope will sustain our physical needs and ensure their satisfaction. There is probably nothing astounding to you about drive reduction through communication. It is as common as the everyday statement "I'm hungry!" But physical reasons for communication often show up in many different contexts. For example, fear appeals, including threats to our physical well-being, often occur in both interpersonal and public-communication contexts:

Don't drive your car like a madman. You'll kill someone—maybe yourself!

Magazine advertisements for medical checkups often hint that we are risking our lives if we do not have annual physicals. All aspects of contemporary environmental pollution campaigns are direct or disguised death threats. So are antiwar campaigns:

War is not healthy for children and other living things.

In cultures where acquiring the necessities of life is a constant problem, physical bases for motivation are especially powerful. The promises for a better life—for food, clean water, shelter, medicine—dominate human communication channels, particularly the public-communication environment. In contrast, the populations of economically advantaged countries are not so motivated by the promise of physical necessities, but they can be shocked by their unexpected or undeserved absence.

Although we may often be motivated to communicate because of physical needs, many more of our daily communications are associated with needs that go beyond the physical level and involve general feelings about ourselves, our desires and values, and how others feel about us. These are psychological needs, and there are many theoretical formulations of them.

Psychological Needs

When our physical needs are satisfied, we typically seek out situations, things, or people that we believe will make us feel better about ourselves. Usually these needs are classed as **psychological needs** or, when they particularly involve relations with other people, sociological needs.

Motivation theories differ in their perceptions of the origins and nature of psychological needs, but they agree that much of what we do in everyday life is tied to our experiences and expectations regarding these needs. Therefore, many of the gratifications involved in our daily communication behaviors, from friendly conversations to watching the evening TV news, are associated with psychological needs.

Psychological needs are more than a typical mainspring of our communication behaviors. We also use appeals to psychological needs, more often than to physical needs, as a communicative strategy to get people to believe or act in certain ways. Psychological needs are both a reason for communication (the *why*) and a basis for gaining effects through its use (the *how*). That is, we use psychological needs as a basis for **persuasion.**

Psychological needs play a key role in interpersonal communication. With close friends, we typically assume mutual sensitivity to each other's needs. This sensitivity is part of trust and is one basis of an interpersonal relationship.

It is not difficult to identify examples of psychological needs in our personal behaviors. We can think of them in either negative (avoidance) terms or positive (approach) terms. Some negative needs include those for avoidance of:

uncertainty
boredom
fear
appearing foolish

Positive needs include those for:

satisfaction
security
the admiration of others
winning

Most theories of psychological needs are quick to point out that individuals differ on how important these various needs are. Such differences are one dimension of personality differentiations. Some of us are motivated by the promise of security more than by a desire for excitement. To others, love and interpersonal relations may be far more important than business success. And, you've probably heard, some individuals are "people-oriented" whereas others are "thing-oriented."

Curiosity as a Psychological Drive

Theorists differ on the point, but humans (as well as higher life forms) also seem motivated by plain old curiosity, the desire to find out about the world. Curiosity has been proposed as a drive because research suggests that activities like puzzle solving seem to offer rewards in themselves. That is, we will engage in them without the promise of external reward. This type of drive reduction translates easily into a variety of communication activities. For example, we often use personal conversations and the mass media to find out what is going on around us.

One extension of this theory is that "information seeking" may be a fundamental motive for human communication behavior, regardless of whether it leads to some external reward. Perhaps we explore "information" environments to reduce the curiosity drive just as a toddler gets into everything within reach or just as a cat cannot resist exploring every square inch of a room.

A HUMANISTIC THEORY OF MOTIVATION

One trend in the study of psychological drives has been the attempt to derive models of motivation that show human behaviors to be much more than simply responses to needs and drives. These are the growth, or humanistic, theories. Although these theories acknowledge drive reduction as a model for fulfillment of basic physical needs and perhaps of some of the more fundamental psychological ones as well, they propose that we have the capability to seek higher and higher levels of psychological achievement. This is the growth pattern of the theory. We do not react to psychological needs one at a time. Instead, we move from one level of satisfaction to the next, eventually reaching levels that may represent "higher" orders of personal existence.

Maslow's Theory of Motivation

Probably the best-known example of a humanistic theory of motivation, and one especially challenging for communication students, is that of the late Abraham Maslow. Maslow's theory is useful for several reasons. The foremost is that much of what he has proposed as a psychology of motivation has direct implications for motivation in communication. His theory is often cited in books on business communication. Also, we will see later in this chapter how uses and gratifications theory, a specific attempt to formulate a motivational theory of communication use, is compatible with a Maslow-type approach to

According to psychologist Abraham Maslow, healthy individuals often experience feelings of elatedness when everything seems to "come together." One of our aims for psychological growth is to strive for these so-called peak experiences. A question for communications research is how we can use interpersonal and media behaviors for our psychological growth. *Ed Buryn/Jeroboam, Inc.*

motivation. Maslow's work is well known and respected, but as with most psychological theories, it has its critics. Your author has always found it to be a particularly optimistic basis for speculating on the future of human communications (see Williams, 1982).

In his research, Maslow was especially interested in the characteristics of successful, healthy individuals, people who seemed to have reached their full potential. As a result of this research plus his compilation of the clinical experiences of others, he identified a list of psychological traits, or qualities, that are especially characteristic of well-adjusted people.

Moreover, and particularly important for our present discussion, he felt that these traits were akin to psychological needs that we can all knowingly attempt to satisfy. When they are satisfied, we can visibly feel the benefits. Conversely, if they are not fulfilled, we feel unrewarded and unhappy or, at the extreme, become mentally ill. Ten of these needs are summarized in the following list. As you read them, think of how important each is to you personally. (An exercise at the end of this chapter gives you a chance to rate their importance to you and to compare your ratings with those of others.) Think also of how you use communication behaviors to fulfill any of these needs that are important to you. Here are the needs (Maslow, 1968):

1. a clearer, more efficient perception of reality
2. more openness to experiences
3. increased integration, wholeness, and unity of person
4. increased spontaneity, expressiveness, and aliveness
5. a real self; a firm identity and autonomy
6. increased objectivity, detachment, and transcendence of self
7. an ability to maintain creativeness
8. an ability to fuse concreteness and abstractness
9. a democratic character structure
10. an ability to love

Again, these needs, in Maslow's theory, reflect conditions that all humans seek. As with physiological needs, if we are deprived of satisfaction, we will be motivated all the more to achieve them. If we remain deprived of satisfaction, we will fall ill physically, mentally, or in both ways. As mentioned before, "healthy" people often have fulfilled these needs.

Communication and Psychological Well-Being

Unique to Maslow's theory (at least at the time he formulated it) was the idea that, given satisfaction of basic physiological and psychological needs, we go on to seek fulfillment of still higher needs for beauty, knowledge, and order. That is, we are capable of higher and higher levels of psychological striving and growth. The best psychological reward is a feeling of "self-actualization," of total fulfillment, of being fully human. The order of levels of need in this theory is often called the "Maslow hierarchy," a graphic portrayal of which is given in Figure 4.1. Presumably, much of our com-

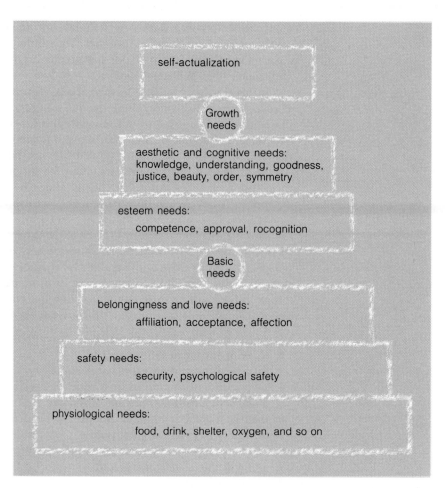

Figure 4.1
The Maslow Hierarchy

self-actualization

Growth
needs

aesthetic and cognitive needs:
knowledge, understanding, goodness,
justice, beauty, order, symmetry

esteem needs:

competence, approval, rocognition

Basic
needs

belongingness and love needs:

affiliation, acceptance, affection

safety needs:

security, psychological safety

physiological needs:
food, drink, shelter, oxygen, and so on

munication relates to fulfillment of these needs. Further, as we are successful in reaching fulfillments, we go on to higher levels, a process of psychological growth.

Another major facet of the theory is that in our striving to fulfill psychological needs, we are sometimes rewarded with brief feelings of self-actualization, which Maslow called "peak experiences." These are momentary feelings of complete psychological satisfaction, an exhilarating or inspiring feeling that everything has "come together" for the moment. Successful and healthy people, according to Maslow, sense more peak experiences in their lives, both because they have higher levels of growth than unsuccessful people and because they are open to such experiences. A powerful form of communication, then, is any that is related to self-actualization.

As inviting as many have found Maslow's theory, it has also been subjected to a variety of criticisms. One objection is that, although Maslow was an accomplished experimental psychologist in his early career, his theory of motivation was not based on detailed scientific study as much as on clinical observation and his own intuitions. Maslow was also criticized as a psychologist with an uncontrolled need to "evangelize." Again, you will have to make your own judgments about a theory of motivation.

NEEDS SATISFIED BY COMMUNICATION

Although much of what Maslow and other psychologists have written about psychological needs has implications for our daily communications, we need to turn to theoreticians in communication for a direct discussion of how communication satisfies our psychological drives.

Take, for example, our fundamental desire to understand the world around us. Certainly, we can think of daily communications that fit this need: talking to friends, reading or watching the news, hearing news flashes on the radio, or reading news magazines. Can this underlying need to understand the world around us be translated into more specific needs? We might be particularly interested in information that immediately affects us—for example, news that it will rain tomorrow. Or the information might have a broader effect, such as knowing that a university education will put us in a better position for a job.

Functional theorists of communication such as Charles Wright, Elihu Katz, and Jay Blumler attempt to identify more precisely the relationship between human needs and the uses of communication. Whereas psychologists such as Maslow are mainly interested in overall theories of motivation, these functional theorists are concerned with how specific types of communication fill certain needs. They use **functional theory** as a basis for explaining the ways in which people use different types of communications, especially as found in public communication.

What needs are most directly or especially satisfied by communication behaviors? Table 4.1 summarizes the needs often found in research literature on this topic. Many come from studies of uses of the mass media, so they have a "receiver" bias, but they can often apply to interpersonal and group communications. Glance at these needs and consider how they apply in your own life.

One important generalization that can be gained from these functional theories is that we do not typically use only one type of communication to satisfy each function. For example, we may gain entertainment from personal conversations, listening to records, or watching television, among other things (see Table 4.1). Although we may use some types of communication more for one need than for another (we will not read the newspaper to fulfill the need for human contact), it is generally possible to fulfill many needs with a single medium of communication. The most universal medium is, of course, face-to-face, oral communication: speech. It served civilization long before other media were of serious consequence, and it is still the principal medium in our media-laden society.

These theories tell us, too, that individuals as well as societies differ in how various types of communication are employed to satisfy needs. For example, in modern industrialized societies, the more highly educated person

Table 4.1 Some Human Needs Satisfied by Communication

Human Contact	Not feeling alone; feeling a sense of relation to other humans. Examples: everyday conversation, turning on the radio so as not to feel lonely.
Surveillance	Watching for things to happen that may be relevant or simply of interest to you. Examples: gossip, reading the paper, or watching the TV news.
Social or Cultural Understanding	Learning what you are culturally or socially a part of; achieving a sense of belonging or identity. Examples: child and parent interactions, news about everyday life as portrayed on television, a novel about a society or culture.
Escape, Release	Getting away from the routines of everyday life; avoiding thoughts about something that is bothering you. Examples: science fiction stories, movie musicals, television prime-time shows, musical recordings, bizarre conversation.
Personal Identity	Learning more about oneself; feeling a sense of self; understanding oneself. Examples: good interpersonal relationships; psychotherapy; seeing oneself in the context of society as gained from a book, film, or television show.
Outright Pleasure	Simply feeling good for the moment: excited, aroused, happy, alive. Examples: stimulating music; a book, film, or television show that is immediately gratifying, such as one with humor or positive human interest materials; a good conversation.
Gaining Knowledge, Know-How	Satisfying a felt need for understanding something or understanding how to do something; having a general feeling of confidence because of new understandings. Examples: self-help books; magazine articles that give personal insights; knowledge-oriented television or radio shows; lectures; group discussions; asking a person about something.
Inspiration	Feeling the stimulation of exciting new ideas; feeling high positive arousal; achieving a "peak" experience or a feeling of transcendence. Examples: a stirring novel, story, film, or television show; a highly successful sermon; a warm and moving conversation.

Elihu Katz

Uses and gratifications research sees the audience as less passive and less powerless than other communications studies. In this view, people cannot be pushed around so easily by the mass media. Proof of this audience power is expressed in selective exposure, selective perception, and selective retention of media and messages. Gratifications studies do not so much emphasize the kind of defensive selectivity that is based on seeking out the media which will agree with one's prejudices and avoiding those which threaten disagreement; rather, they emphasize that selectivity is also based on *interests*—that is, on using mass communications to serve one's psychological and sociological needs. (Defensive selectivity would predict that cigarette smokers will avoid news stories about the correlation between smoking and lung cancer; selectivity based on interest would predict that smokers will read about lung cancer because it is in their interest to do so.)

We have found overall patterns that suggest that individuals specify different media for fulfilling different kinds of needs. By taking human needs, rather than media or messages, as their starting point, gratifications studies are concerned with the need for self-confidence and the need to be diverted as well as with the need to be informed. By studying the various uses to which people put the media, and the gratifications they derive from them, these studies see mass communications not just as a source of information and influence but as an elaborate system of cultural, social, and psychological "services."

Gratifications studies are particularly interested in the role of the media in providing orientation in areas where other people—parents, teachers, friends—fail to do so or fail to satisfy. Consider the new role of radio, for example, as provider of intimate advice on problems of sex, marriage, family, human relations on the job, and so on.

The trouble with gratifications studies, however, is that the concept of *need* is used so unsystematically. That is, we do not have enough agreement on just what we mean by it or on how to measure it. But, on the other hand, this is what makes research so challenging and interesting.

Elihu Katz is Professor of Sociology at the Hebrew University of Jerusalem and Professor of Communications at the Annenberg School of Communications at the University of Southern California.

Suggested reading: J. G. Blumler and E. Katz, eds., *The Uses of Mass Communications* (Beverly Hills, Calif.: Sage, 1974).

---

generally prefers print to broadcasting as a source of information. College-age students prefer movies, records, and the radio over television as a main source of media entertainment, whereas young children and older adults prefer television. Such information is useful to those who "sell" communications, especially advertising. We don't see luxury automobiles advertised in gossipy, sensational newspapers or subcompacts sold in slick, executive-oriented financial magazines.

If you read about the uses of communications in developing countries of the world, you'll see that interpersonal communication is by far the most-used and most-believed medium. Radio, depending on the country, may be more a source of information and orientation than an entertainment medium. Newspapers may be used only by the wealthy and educated, because only they can read.

Needs that can be satisfied by communication are central to **uses and gratifications theory,** which was originally a topic of public-communication research (Blumler and Katz, 1974). It is now proposed as relevant to all levels of communication, including study of the uses of new media technologies (Rosengren, Wenner, and Palmgreen, 1985).

FOUR FUNCTIONS OF COMMUNICATION

In this text, we use the term *function* to refer to types of messages that may serve individually or in combination as information, entertainment, instruction, or persuasion. The concept of function helps us describe how message types may be related to motivation and satisfaction in communication. For example, your need to know the address of a friend is satisfied by information. Or your desire for escape or relaxation could be satisfied by entertainment, and so on. (Although *function* is a fairly common term in communication study, you will see differences among writers in how it is applied.)

It is usually easy to identify common functions of communication in everyday life, including in how people describe communication. For example:

"That movie was sheer entertainment."
"I always find Jane's conversations informative."
"TV could have much greater uses as an instructional medium."
"Frank is so persuasive that he ought to go into politics."

As you are probably ready to interject, functions are often mixed, or overlaid, in typical communications. For example, instructors may mix some entertainment with facts to make a lecture more interesting and appealing. A large corporation may launch an advertising campaign that it wants the public to think is mainly informative but that is really hidden persuasion.

There are also mixtures and differences in effects. A television program designed to be strictly entertainment may be the basis of instruction for a youngster who uses examples of the show's violence to pursue a disagreement with another youngster. Finally, have you ever found another person's persuasive arguments so ridiculous that they were actually entertaining?

It is easy to stir up arguments about whether information, entertainment, instruction, and persuasion are the main functions of communication. Not all authorities in communications agree on such categories or even on the need for them. Nonetheless, it should be helpful, not only in understanding the communication process but also in evaluating our own communication behaviors, to know more about these categories.

Take a few moments to examine Table 4.2, which contrasts the major characteristics of information, entertainment, instruction, and persuasion. Notice how the different functions apply equally well to personal as to public communication. Notice, too, that in many instances sender and receiver may be communicating for different reasons. You may recognize many of these functions in your communication behaviors. Our attitudes about communication functions have a major effect on what we expect to get out of communication situations.

1. Information

All communication, no matter its end purpose, contains information. At a most basic level, **information** can be the recognizable variations in the sound waves of speech or the patterns of lighted dots on your TV screen. Anything in the environment with a pattern whose meaning we can interpret is information. (You may remember that in Chapter 3 there was an even more fundamental definition of information in the mathematical sense: any "bit" of information was an "off" or "on" signal, as in the example of the five torches.)

However, we do not often consider information on such a basic level. Instead, we usually mean by information the fundamental facts about something. This is the information we look for in almanacs, ask for when we need the time of day, or call up from a computer file. The unique quality of strictly informational messages is not so much that they have information—all messages have information—but that they do not also include entertainment, instruction, or persuasion. We want the facts, and that's all. Some of our broader uses of informational communication are as follows:

Traditional journalistic reporting has the ideal of "sticking to the facts." It is supposedly objective rather than subjective. It reports rather than explains or interprets.

The "speech to inform," a common assignment in speech communication, is meant to impart mainly objective information to listeners.

Scientific writing, as in the research and scholarly journals, if properly executed, would show the same objective picture no matter who did the writing. It is supposedly purely objective, unbiased information.

Data communications (financial records, inventories, records of transactions) are mainly informational.

The desired satisfactions from information are awareness, understanding, and perhaps even insight. The informational message leaves its interpretation up to the receiver. Messages that present the facts and a method of interpretation fall more in the class of instruction than information. Relative to the motives for communication, a person's successful use of information should yield a clear perception of reality, in the Maslow sense. Or it should fulfill the need for surveillance of the environment. In public communication, information could be the "news," the stock listings, or the weather report.

As bland as you might think informational communication is, it is nevertheless the subject of several major controversies in modern society. Some media critics argue, for example, that too much of what purports to be information in the mass communications of our society is really not fact at all but, rather, persuasion or entertainment parading as fact. Many examples of this masquerading are found in advertising, as when actors dressed as physicians tell us how to cure our stomach problems. In addition, criticism is often expressed of television news programs that increasingly take on the properties

Table 4.2 Functional Categories of Communication

Information	Basic nature	Specific facts, data, statements, figures, units of a larger knowledge structure.
	Examples	Reports of observations of phenomena; a weather report; computer data file; bank balance; indexes; home addresses; names; labels; phone numbers; radio and TV newscasts; newspaper wire reports.
	Notes on senders	Sender is assumed by the receiver to be an accurate source. Sender may be an information "broker," such as a newspaper, library, bank, telephone "hot line." Reward can be mainly money; sender can be in the "information business."
	Notes on receivers	Receiver is assumed to have a use for the information; getting it will be gratifying, sometimes economically so. Successful receivers will know where to get information. Information can satisfy a surveillance need.
Entertainment	Basic nature	Any communication that is attention-arousing and immediately gratifying, mainly in a pleasurable way.
	Examples	Jokes; an absorbing motion picture where the story line is less important than audience enjoyment; escape reading; prime-time TV shows that are mainly arousal ("junk food TV"); computer games.
	Notes on senders	Senders often are professionals who create entertainment for payment. In interpersonal communication, entertainment may be used to "break the ice" or simply as a means of interpersonal enjoyment. In large-group communication, entertainment may be used to get initial attention.
	Notes on receivers	Receivers often expect immediate gratifications, having paid money for them. If a part of a serious communication, the receiver sometimes appreciates entertainment to lessen tension. Entertainment offers immediate pleasure and sometimes outright escape.
Instruction	Basic nature	Messages that teach basic skills, understandings, and insights. Goes beyond facts to generalizations.

of entertainment. News-show formats are often lightened (for example, with "happy talk") by newscasters who are former actors or game-show hosts. Or news topics may not really be news at all. One Los Angeles TV station had a sports fantasy spot on which, for example, a housewife got to work with pro football cheerleaders for a day! Such formats are slanted more toward stirring up audience attention and interest—and, of course, broadcast ratings—than toward promoting the objectivity of the news, which eventually becomes only a by-product.

If you are interested in objective journalism, you should know that there are even arguments over whether it is humanly possible ever to present any communications that are pure information, since we can never totally eliminate bias. Marxist critics (such as Kaarle Nordenstreng, 1974) raise persuasive arguments that those of us in the supposed land of the free press delude ourselves into believing that the best-trained reporter can be objective. These

Table 4.2 *(continued)*

	Examples	School lectures, textbooks, self-help books and articles; educational computer programs; school in general; parent and child interactions; or simply "learning from experience." "Management" partly involves instruction.
	Notes on senders	Sender is assumed to know the topic, often to be an expert. Gratification motivation is often economic (the sender is a professional). Personal examples are parents, supervisors, managers, usual authority figures.
	Notes on receivers	Receiver is assumed to need the knowledge or know-how. May often purchase it. Sometimes is not gratified until a sense of understanding is gained. The receiver may hold the sender responsible for accuracy. With understanding comes gratification. This can include social or cultural understanding.
Persuasion	Basic nature	Messages aimed at influencing belief or behavior. May include many combinations of other communication functions. The key material of persuasion is an appeal to personal motives. But motives may differ widely between sender and receiver.
	Examples	Most advertising; important interpersonal communication; political speeches; sales pitches; arguments; debates; inspirational editorials or speeches.
	Notes on senders	Sender seeks gratification in the attitudes or behavior of another; must anticipate motivational strategies, be skilled in audience or personal research.
	Notes on receivers	Receiver may not be aware of being persuaded. Has many alternatives for reactions but may not use them. Gratifications will come only from satisfaction of this person's own motives. Receivers may carry out the prescribed behavior and gratify the persuader but not feel gratified themselves.

critics argue that we typically see the world according to our own cultural upbringing and that this perspective inevitably affects not only how we see events but also which techniques we use for describing them.

Another broad criticism of informational communications, particularly as it involves business data, is that the modern technologies are giving us far more information than we can ever possibly use. The information explosion may be really an information glut. Critics argue that what we need is more wisdom, not more information.

Finally, there is considerable controversy over whether vast information files are violating our right to privacy. Every time we make a credit card transaction, file our income tax, have our academic record stored on a transcript, make a credit application, apply for a driver's license—and do many other things—we are contributing information about ourselves. Anyone who can put all those files together will have potential control over our lives.

2. Entertainment

To entertain does not necessarily mean to "roll them in the aisles." Think about the notion more broadly, as when we say "I'm entertaining friends this afternoon" or "She's an entertaining person." Between these two uses is the concept of activities that are interesting, satisfying, and generally have value in and of themselves. This is the broad meaning used in classifying communications as **entertainment.** Although "rolling them in the aisles" is indeed a form of entertainment, so is an absorbing movie, a thrilling mystery novel, an enjoyable conversation, or maybe even a video game. It is not difficult to see how entertainment satisfies such motivating needs as those for escape, release, or outright pleasure. Entertainment may even satisfy the need for inspiration.

As with information, but less so, some characteristics of entertainment are found in many different types of instruction and persuasion. Some teachers are adept at adding a little humor or other interest-arousing devices to classroom lectures. A particularly absorbing and influential film or novel may be a unique combination of entertainment and instruction. The materials give you new insights into life and, at the same time, are highly satisfying. The children's television program "Sesame Street" is a direct attempt to use well-known entertainment techniques to enhance the instructional quality of the program. By clever use of music, motion, shapes, and colors, something as routine as teaching a child the letter E can become interesting, if not downright exciting. And the Disney Corporation, which labels itself an entertainment company, has been a longtime developer and marketer of educational products.

What is typically the most-used or even most-desired entertainment? Many people will immediately begin comparing, even arguing about, the different mass media. For example, are movies always better than prime-time TV shows, or are books better than both? Yet research has consistently shown that when people are asked what kinds of communication they find most immediately satisfying, of great interest, and personally rewarding in and of itself, they typically respond by referring to interpersonal forms. Talking with people seems to be our favorite form of entertainment. Yet we cannot deny that the mass-media forms of entertainment play an important role in our lives; and in a number of countries, such as the United States, they are a major part of the economy.

In the 1970s and 1980s, entertainment-related businesses, along with leisure-time businesses (resorts, sports, vacationing) have become one of the fastest growing components of the U.S. economy. At the same time, studies have shown that television has become the country's most frequently used source of mass-media entertainment, accounting for nearly 40 percent of the average person's leisure time.

How could entertainment, which can be so satisfying, have problems? It does, and mostly in terms of secondary effects. Researchers such as George Gerbner have stressed that television, no matter how entertaining, is at the same time a major source of information for many viewers (Gerbner and

Gross, 1976). A person who spends long hours with television may have a TV version of reality rather than a view based on experiences with the real world. Television presents much "information" that does not fit reality and imparts "instruction" in ways of life that are more fictitious than real. It is known from the work of Gerbner and others that people who are heavy viewers of television often have stereotyped attitudes about sex roles, physicians, and gangsters, for example. They may see the world as populated by stereotyped, sometimes excessively cartoonish, people. In their world, housewives may be more concerned with keeping the "bathroom bowl" clean than anything else. Husbands are the bumblers found in situation comedies. Police officials have minute-by-minute exciting days. People "die" without all the agonies of death. And gangsters are all evil-looking.

A further consequence, and one that was the subject of a $1-million government study in the 1960s (see Comstock et al., 1978), is the effect of explicit violence as portrayed on television. Although violence is meant to contribute to the excitement of dramatic entertainment, it may also be teaching the negative lesson, especially to young children, that it is a primary way of life in our society. Worse yet, it could be teaching that violence is an effective solution to problems. Somewhat similar arguments are consistently raised about the effects of explicit sex in the mass media. Recurrent and excessive portrayals of explicit sex may have the effect of lowering the moral standards of society.

3. Instruction

Instruction, of course, is much broader than a college lecture or textbook. Instruction can include the directions for heating a can of soup, a parent's demonstration to a child of how to use a toothbrush, or a newspaper editorial attempting to provide insights on the status of the economy. Instruction involves generalizations from information. It is also explanation, or the communication of know-how. Instruction can fulfill human needs for such things as social or cultural understanding, an increased sense of personal identity, and detailed knowledge.

The Swiss biologist and psychologist Jean Piaget, who has been very influential in twentieth-century educational thought, often noted that life itself is our "greatest curriculum." Thus, much of what we take advantage of as instruction may not have been intended as such. We can think of such instruction as incidental learning from the environment or as the way individuals seek knowledge by observation or manipulation of the environment.

The environment offers many opportunities to "learn," and as communication receivers we actively seek out that instruction. You may, for example, watch a mechanic change the brake disks on your car so that you can do it yourself the next time and save half the price. Or you may see how somebody dances on a television show and want to try it yourself. In this respect, nearly any situation or any type of information, entertainment, or persuasive communication can have instructional value to a person seeking knowledge or skills.

As you have probably noticed, much instruction includes components of entertainment and persuasion. The less interest a communication receiver has in the instruction being provided, the more persuasion or entertainment will have to be added to the message. As noted, "Sesame Street" increases the attractiveness of its instruction to children by adding dollops of entertainment. If you attend a short course on sales techniques or something similar, you are likely to be persuaded about how important these techniques will be to your success before you get instruction in them (and perhaps have to pay more money).

Conversely, the more highly motivated a person is to gain understanding about something, the less important are the additional components of entertainment or persuasion to the process. If you have been wanting to learn tennis very badly, your instructor can probably spend more time in showing you the game than in trying to get you interested in it. If you know that passing a course in biology will be critical to your later application to medical school, you will be more likely to put up with a dull textbook and instructor than if you couldn't care less about the course.

Another important factor in instructional communication is the effect of a receiver's learning styles on the result of instruction. We all learn better in some modes of communication than in others. Some of us are more visually oriented learners. We acquire knowledge more efficiently if we can see or read about it. Some of us are auditory learners, meaning we are better at understanding things we hear. And some of us are kinesthetic learners, who learn best by carrying out the motions of what we are to learn.

The adaptation to different learning styles is one recognized advantage of using instructional devices in classrooms. For example, lessons in the rules of addition, or at least drills in them, can be incorporated into a television production in ways that stress both auditory and visual learning. A computer program can be varied to employ the different learning styles, including the kinesthetic. These same generalizations can apply in many ways to adult instruction. The challenge is to match the instructional materials to the styles of the learners.

Instruction, particularly public education, is a major institutional undertaking in most countries. In the United States alone, more tax money is spent on instructional communication in public and private schools, universities, academies, vocational schools, and adult education than on any other activity. The new communications technologies (cable television, videotape, computers) offer many opportunities for improving the effectiveness and efficiency of instructional communication, although our schools have traditionally been the slowest of our public institutions to adopt new methods and new techniques.

4. Persuasion

Persuasion is the most complex of the traditional functions of communication. It typically involves the combination of information, entertainment, and instruction. But persuasion is also the most personal of our communication functions. It is the communication by which we attempt to affect the beliefs and behaviors of people. To persuade, we often appeal to the most personal of another individual's motives. In turn, persuasion directed at us individually can become very personal. We are most likely to believe or act the way a persuasive message requests if the materials of that message are especially appealing to our own needs and values.

Persuasive messages, to be successful, must:

1. gain our attention and interest
2. get us to understand the proposition—that is, to understand what we are being asked to believe or do
3. give us personal reasons for responding to the proposition
4. get us to "move"—that is, actually to accept the belief or to take the action

Persuasion occurs in all areas of our lives but, like the other functional categories of communication, is used most often in interpersonal relations. Eventually, our most important interpersonal relationships are based on mutual recognition of each other's unique needs and our willingness to be mutually persuaded through understanding, trust, and commitment. There is a close link between the process of persuasion and the development of deep interpersonal relations, a topic discussed in more detail in Chapters 7 and 11.

Beyond interpersonal communication, probably the most visible form of persuasion in free-enterprise societies is advertising. The more expensive forms of advertising, from display ads in newspapers and magazines to television commercials, are usually in themselves clear examples of persuasive strategies. Almost any ad in this category has readily identifiable attention-getting characteristics, is clear in what it wants us to do, and may appeal directly to our motives for acting or believing. Ads may vary considerably in telling us when we should act. They range from wanting us simply to believe over the long term that "oil companies are good" (as in an institutional ad) to giving us a coupon to clip out and send in NOW! so we will get our free record and Record Club membership immediately.

One of the controversies in public-communication theory is the degree to which mass communications in themselves can have a powerful, persuasive effect on the individual or society. Some theorists hold that because the mass media are impersonal and lack the capability for immediate feedback or negotiation, they are inherently weak as persuaders in themselves. People are more persuaded by interpersonal communication than by mass communication, which may do more to set "agendas" than to change minds (but this generalization is a controversial one). For example, a TV newscast may get people to think about a new political candidate, but their voting decision will more likely be influenced by their conversations with other people about that candidate. Other theorists hold that certain mass media can be very persuasive and that, among other things, this power is inherently dangerous to society. According to this theory, whoever controls the mass media controls the society. One of the most persuasive parts of this argument is the rhetorical question of why advertisers would spend billions each year if the mass media were not influential.

Because persuasion deals so directly with personal motives, it is especially susceptible to rejection or avoidance. If the persuasive message does not appeal to the motives of an individual, it is not likely to receive attention. If you are a male, for example, you probably care little or nothing about the perfume featured in a magazine ad. Even if the picture of an attractive female catches your eye, it is still unlikely that you are going to interpret anything more; the ad simply has no value to you. Or suppose you are a woman at a cocktail party where a man is going on about a hunting trip he has just completed. You may care nothing about hunting, so you selectively withdraw from the conversation, change the topic, or simply "tune out" what is said.

As a negative example, suppose you enjoy smoking cigarettes, yet you inevitably encounter public-service advertisements that warn you of the hazards of lung cancer. In most cases, you skip past such ads, trying to pay the least possible attention to them. And it is unlikely that, if invited, you would attend an evening lecture on the hazards of cigarette smoking. These are examples of the processes called selective exposure and selective attention, and they are part of public-communication theory, which is discussed further in Chapter 10.

In sum, we tend to pay attention to communications that are of interest and value to us and that do not tend to make us feel threatened. Persuasive communications, because they focus on personal motives, are especially susceptible to attention or inattention.

Most simple descriptions of persuasion show it as being "one-way." A political candidate is attempting to get your vote. A newspaper ad screams SALE! at you. Or your best friend relieves you of $5. Indeed, much persuasion, particularly in the mass media, is one-way. There is little you can do to argue back to a television ad, except not to buy the product. Public communications do not typically give us the opportunity to respond to persuasion directly and in the same medium. In that respect, persuasion in the mass media is typically not transactional. It does not allow clarification or bargaining back and forth between the persuader and the one to be persuaded.

Interpersonal communication, because of the opportunity it affords for feedback that is immediate and in the same medium, offers the maximum opportunity for transaction in the persuasion process. Sometimes the distinction is made in interpersonal persuasion between compliance and conflict resolution. In compliance, one person attempts to persuade the other, and the only feedback desired is evidence of acceptance of the proposition. In conflict resolution, the proposition is negotiated; that is, the respondent has the opportunity to clarify the reasons for believing or acting or to offer a modified proposition.

Advertising and interpersonal manipulation are probably two of the most criticized aspects of persuasive communication. Marxists declare that advertising has negative effects in a society because it creates "false markets." It persuades people to buy things that they do not need, including products or services that may be hazardous to them, such as cigarettes or alcohol. (Yet these same products do well even unadvertised in the economies of many socialist countries.)

One vivid example of the "false-market" argument was the aggressive marketing in certain Third World countries during the 1970s of powdered formula for babies' milk. Advertising not only stressed the convenience of bottle feeding over breast feeding but further implied that breast feeding would cause a woman to lose her youthful figure. The negative consequence of this campaign was that infant mortality rose in some areas where women had shifted to bottle feeding because conditions there were so unsanitary. Further, women who ceased breast feeding became fertile again before their health or their family's conditions could ensure another infant's survival.

On the interpersonal level, there is the recurring question of what the repercussions will be for a society in which individuals are out to manipulate one another. Many of the public-speaking textbooks in the United States from the 1940s through the 1960s emphasized the power of personal influence over others more than they did the process of interpersonal communication. Training emphasized how a speaker could secure an intended response from an audience.

Perhaps the epitome of personal manipulation appeared in a popular book in the 1970s called *Winning Through Intimidation* (Ringer, 1974). Although the examples in this book were largely restricted to real estate financial transactions, the strategy was to keep the other person at a disadvantage with intimidation techniques. The social benefits of such techniques are questionable. It is also doubtful whether books and training in business-negotiation techniques are of long-range social benefit when they stress winning out over the other person rather than conflict resolution.

SUMMARY

Most human communication, whether it involves speaking, listening, reading, writing, or simply "viewing," is *purposive*. Communication is among many behaviors we use to satisfy our needs for what we find *rewarding*. It is a consequence of our motivation to satisfy our needs. Human *motivation* is often divided between satisfaction of *physical needs* and *psychological needs*. We use psychological needs as a basis for persuasion. *Drive reduction* means that as a need is satisfied, one's drive for satisfaction is lessened. Curiosity is sometimes considered a distinct human need.

Humanistic theories of motivation stress that humans have a capability for psychological growth. An example of a humanistic theory is Maslow's need hierarchy. Although it has been criticized, Maslow's theory is useful in helping us understand the bases for motivation in communication.

Theories of motivation attempt to specify which needs are satisfied by which types of communication. *Functional theories* explain why humans use different types of communication. *Uses and gratifications research* is one major approach to explaining how people use different communication media to satisfy their needs.

We use *function* to describe the *why* and *what* in communication. Traditional functions of communication are information, entertainment, instruction, and persuasion.

Information is the facts only. We have many uses for and expectations about information in modern societies, and these give rise to "information businesses." *Entertainment* entails more than just pleasure. It is any kind of communication that is gratifying in and of itself. Entertainment constitutes one major growth business of modern society, although many problems are associated with it. *Instruction* is the interpretation of facts. It is knowledge, know-how, or skills. Much instruction takes place in everyday life outside formal schooling. Learning styles make a difference in how instruction is best communicated. *Persuasion* is the most complex form of communication. It often combines all the other forms. In the interpersonal context, persuasion is the basis for developing human relationships and may be transactional. In the public context, it is the basis for the business of advertising. Advertising and interpersonal manipulation are highly criticized aspects of persuasive communication.

TOPICS FOR DISCUSSION OR BRIEF PAPERS

1. Select six advertisements each from a women's magazine and a men's magazine. Analyze them as their appeals relate to the motives discussed in this chapter. What differences do you note between the two magazine groups?

2. Rate the importance to you of each of the ten Maslow-defined needs. Do this by assigning each need a number from 1 through 5, with the numbers indicating (1) very important to me, (2) relatively important, (3) neutral, (4) relatively unimportant, and (5) not important at all to me. Then compare your results with other students' ratings. Be sure to do your own ratings before you look at the results of others. What similarities or differences do you see? Explain.

3. Suppose that you have been hired to develop a television advertising campaign for a dashing new sports car. Prepare some general motivational strategies that appeal to both men and women buyers. Explain your strategies.

4. Take a day's television schedule for a single station from a newspaper listing or *TV Guide,* and classify the different programs into categories based on the functional reasons why people may be watching them (that is, into information, entertainment, instruction, and persuasion, as in Table 4.2). Calculate the relative amounts of time that the programs in each category represent. From the results, generalize about the station's "functional" offerings. Compare your results with another person's analysis. Try to contrast stations in some interesting way—for example, independent versus network-affiliated, cable services or over-the-air, or public versus commercial.

5. Make a list of all the personal information on you that is held in the files of various organizations in your society (such as in academic records,

driver's license files, or health records). Which of those files could you gain access to in order to check the accuracy of the information? Try calling an "information holder" and see what that office says about your rights to see your personal information.

REFERENCES AND READINGS

Blumler, J., and E. Katz, eds. *The Uses of Mass Communication: Current Perspectives on Gratifications Research.* Beverly Hills, Calif.: Sage, 1974.

Comstock, G., S. Chaffee, N. Katzman, M. McCombs, and D. Roberts. *Television and Human Behavior.* New York: Columbia University Press, 1978.

Dance, F. E. X., and C. E. Larson. *The Functions of Human Communication: A Theoretical Approach.* New York: Holt, Rinehart and Winston, 1976.

Gerbner, G., and L. Gross. "Living with Television: The Violence Profile." *Journal of Communication* 26 (1976): 173–196.

Katz, E., M. Gurevitch, and H. Hass. "On the Uses of the Mass Media for Important Things." *American Sociological Review* 38 (1973): 164–181.

Maslow, A. *Toward a Psychology of Being.* New York: Van Nostrand Reinhold, 1968.

Maslow, A. *Motivation and Personality.* New York: Harper and Row, 1970.

Middlebrook, P. N. *Social Psychology and Modern Life.* New York: Knopf, 1974.

Nordenstreng, K. *Informational Mass Communication.* Helsinki: Pammi, 1974.

Piaget, J. *Language and Thought of the Child.* 3d ed. London: Routledge and Kegan Paul, 1959.

Ringer, R. *Winning Through Intimidation.* 2d ed. Los Angeles: Los Angeles Book Publishers, 1974.

Rosengren, K. E., L. A. Wenner, and P. Palmgreen. *Media Gratifications Research.* Beverly Hills, Calif.: Sage, 1985.

Williams, F. *The Communications Revolution.* Beverly Hills, Calif.: Sage, 1982.

The Psychology of Influence

HOW ARE WE INFLUENCED?

Everyday Persuasion

When did you last buy shampoo, perfume, deodorant, after-shave lotion, or a breath freshener? Which brand did you buy? Do you think that advertising influenced your purchase? If you are like most customers, you do not buy items like toiletries for their chemical properties. In fact, you probably have little or no idea of the composition of such products (and it might shock you if you did!). Chances are, instead, that you buy an image, a "feeling," or simply "security." Moreover, in many cases your awareness of what you want to buy comes far more from advertising messages than from the product itself.

We live in a veritable sea of persuasion, from the advertising that surrounds us on television, in newspapers and magazines, on the radio, or on billboards to the messages from the people around us who try to influence our attitudes and behaviors. All of these messages reflect the practical application of the psychology of influence—how messages are used to affect attitudes and behaviors—or persuasion, for short.

Are we bamboozled by advertising?

Marxist critics say yes and it is one of their major criticisms of capitalist mass media. On the other hand, most students feel that they are "wise" to the economic persuasion in their environment. They can take it or leave it, enjoy it or complain about it, and it does not seem to be ruining their lives. In fact, most citizens probably feel that they are bright and experienced enough to sort out what is important to them. Also, any advertiser who seriously misleads you is not likely to stay in business long, although you may be willing to have the truth stretched a bit. You probably make a relatively conscious decision to buy a certain product. You want to be satisfied, and logically, that is what you try to purchase: satisfaction.

So, too, have you probably been influenced by a large variety of sources during most of your life. The greatest source of influence is not advertising but the messages you exchange with the people around you. Interpersonal communication is by far the most influential part of our lives. In the process of trying to get along well with those who are closest to us, we pay particular attention to what they expect from us, and we expect them to do the same. Our messages of influence often promise satisfaction of needs, including our need for human relationships. Indeed, the process of interpersonal influence is the basis for our closest human relationships. These relationships include those with our co-workers, fellow students, close friends, families (when we are getting along with them), and marriage partners.

Are we bamboozled by people?

Not if we can help it! Mostly, we react to others in terms of our personal motives, and with only a few exceptions we respond in ways that we think are entirely logical. It is we who do the responding, so if we are not to be misled, we have the responsibility to evaluate the messages we receive from other people.

Ordinary life is not so dramatic as the lives of the heroes of literature or prime-time television, whose behavior may fly in the face of the "usual" (that's what makes it "dramatic"). If you and another person feel important enough to each other, one of you is usually willing to compromise if differences of opinion arise. So if you and your date want to go to different movies, you'll work out the differences eventually, or else you'll get different dates the next time.

Suppose, in contrast, that you are forced to behave in a way that is contrary to your motives and to what seems reasonable. Perhaps you are put into a position where you may have to drink more than you want to, take drugs, or get too deeply involved in a sexual relationship. Certainly, you could go ahead with the behavior and feel guilty or upset about it. But you will probably take one of three other alternatives: (1) back out of the behavior, (2) make up reasons and motives that justify the behavior, or (3) reduce or lessen the importance to you of the motives or reasons for avoiding the behavior.

Most of our reactions to the psychology of influence reflect the following:

We are constantly being influenced in our daily lives in often undramatic ways by media and, especially, people.

Our reactions are typically conscious ones, reflecting a desire to satisfy motives that have been directly appealed to in the messages we receive. We may also react to satisfy other motives, such as the desire to please another person who is important to us.

We react to influence in a variety of ways, including changing our motives or reasons and, thereby, changing our reactions.

The Role of Attitudes

In most theories of influence, considerable importance is given to the internal mental and emotional states that affect how we react to outside persuasion. These internal states are called **attitudes,** and their place in theories of the persuasion process are illustrated in Figure 5.1. Attitudes are our feelings, beliefs, or ideas that affect how we may eventually behave. For example, I dislike political arguments, so if someone raises one, I am likely to avoid it (or the person). On the other hand, I enjoy talking about tennis, so if somebody brings up the subject, I am likely to be enthusiastic about continuing the conversation.

Many communication theories of persuasion are drawn from theories of how attitudes are formed or changed and how attitudes relate to one another. We next turn to summaries of several of these theories.

SEEKING PSYCHOLOGICAL BALANCE

Most theories of the psychology of persuasion stress people's striving for **balance.** By our nature, we humans seem to desire situations where there is a general harmony, or agreement, among ourselves, our sources of communication, and the messages involved. We try to seek out situations that promise balance and avoid those that do not.

Figure 5.1
The Role of Attitude
in Persuasion

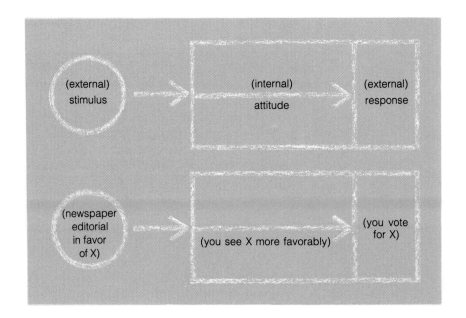

For example, if you hold hostile attitudes toward big business, then you will probably seek out and enjoy the articles in the *Mother Earth News*. By the same token, you will probably avoid the *Wall Street Journal*, unless you want to get fuel for your antibusiness arguments. Similarly, you will tend to seek out friends who agree more than they disagree with you on different concepts or ideas. If you and one of your friends disagree on serious enough concepts, one of you might have to change your opinion about some of the concepts or terminate the friendship.

If there is a general motive in human behavior, it is that we wish to live among our satisfactions rather than our dissatisfactions—among what is agreeable to us rather than disagreeable. Balance seems to be one of our major sources of satisfaction. It is also at the heart of many different theories of persuasion.

Harmony among Concepts and People

For the moment, imagine that you and your best friend are talking about your likes and dislikes in popular music. Picture the relationships among you, this other person, and what you are talking about (propositions), as illustrated in Figure 5.2, a general balance model.

Because you are talking to a friend, the relationship between the two of you in this case will be positive. If you both like the popular music you are discussing, each of you will have a positive attitude toward the proposition. In this case, you and your friend and the proposition are all in a harmonious balance. It is likely that you will continue to talk about such topics and

Figure 5.2
A General
Balance Model

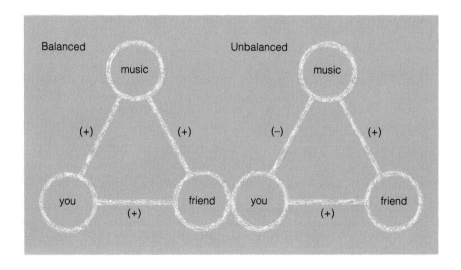

continue to be friends. There is no strain for change. The influences of your messages upon each other are acceptable to the two of you, and you reinforce each other's opinions accordingly.

But, as also shown in Figure 5.2, you may have very negative attitudes about a piece of popular music, whereas your friend may be positive about it. This will put the two of you into an unbalanced state, and the effect of influence here is a motivation for some kind of change in the situation. This change could take several forms. You might, for example, change your opinion about the music to a positive one, bringing you and your friend back into a harmonious relationship. Or your friend might change so that you both have negative attitudes about the music, again a harmonious relationship. The most serious influence in this situation might be one that, because you and your friend disagree so much on the proposition, leads to a change in your relationship from a positive to a negative one.

The fundamental point in this theory, according to Fritz Heider (1946), its originator, is that we humans tend to behave in ways that create harmony for ourselves. Or, as applied to the topic of this chapter, the psychology of influence will typically move in the direction of attempted harmony of our perceptions. Sometimes our striving for balance changes our relations toward other people or sources of communication, rather than the propositions themselves. For example, suppose you were returning a pair of shoes that did not fit. Although you were demanding your money back, the store manager refused to give it to you. You may have had a generally neutral attitude toward the store manager when you entered the situation, but if you cannot reconcile your relations toward the proposition (taking the shoes back) with the manager, the situation will probably create in you a negative attitude toward the manager. Certainly this would agree with your application of common sense to the situation, but note that this kind of negative change in attitude is also predicted as a striving toward balance. If you and the store manager have a negative relationship toward each other, this is in harmony with your differences in relationship to the proposition. That is, balance can be negative all around, too.

Harmony and Media Use. One useful application of all-negative balance to a mass source of communication is as follows. Suppose that your hometown newspaper (the "other person" in this situation) came out with a series of strong editorials in favor of increasing tuition (proposition) for university students. Balance theory would predict (as would common sense) that unless you are also in favor of raising tuition, you will be generating an increasingly negative attitude toward the newspaper. If the situation persists, especially in regard to other propositions, you may not only selectively read the newspaper, avoiding articles with which you disagree, but you may cancel your subscription to the paper. This application of balance theory is often associated with the concept of **selective perception** in theories of communication.

Of course, we do not change friends or newspapers every time we disagree. Balance theory is not meant to be a predictor in each and every instance of relations among yourself, a communication source, and a proposition. Instead, balance theory is meant to apply across a range of cases; if applied to one case, it would be one that is terribly important to you.

Problems of Simple Balance Theories. One of the greatest shortcomings of this type of balance theory is that it does not take into account the *importance* of the relationships among ourselves, the source, and the proposition. For example, perhaps you are ordering dinner on a date, and your friend orders chicken, which you detest. You may express your distaste strongly, saying that you don't like even the smell of chicken when you are eating. At that point, your date, feeling that having chicken is not important, will place another order.

Perhaps the relationship with you is so important that the other person will change his or her perception toward a proposition. Or, by the same token, maybe the proposition isn't of any consequence to the other person, so why make an issue of it? In sum, the prediction of influence according to balance theory is likely to be very changeable, depending on the degree of importance of the relations involved.

Another problem with balance theory is that we are not often influenced by such simple three-component situations. Indeed, you may be the one person in a group of ten who holds an alternative attitude toward a proposition. In this case, the greater the number of people who express a contrary opinion and the more adamantly they express it, the more you may be inclined to change your own attitudes. But even this is not always an adequate predictor of psychological influence, for most people can easily recall individuals who tend to be "holdouts" for their own opinions.

Avoidance of Dissonance

Rather than seeing balance as reflecting a general human desire for harmony, particularly between people and ideas, it is also possible to think of it as mainly the result of avoiding dissonant relationships. In short, behavior is influenced by the desire to avoid a state of psychological discomfort, called **dissonance.**

While Heider's theory would have us consciously striving toward harmony, dissonance theory, developed by Leon Festinger (1957), holds that the key motivator is the dissonant relationship itself. For example, suppose that you smoke cigarettes regularly and that you do not believe they are hazardous to your health. Suppose also that while thumbing through a popular magazine, you see an ad for your favorite cigarette. It promises satisfaction and good taste. Because there is no dissonance being stirred up in this situation—that is, the cognitive elements are harmonious—there are no particular consequences for your behavior. The ad might reinforce your existing positive feeling about smoking, but nothing really changes in your attitudes or behavior.

Contrast this situation with one in which you have just stopped smoking because you feel it is hazardous to your health. Now when you encounter the same ad in a magazine, you sense a dissonant relationship. The point in Festinger's theory is that this is a motivating circumstance. There is pressure toward some type of influence here. You might question your new attitude about smoking and say, "So what? Maybe I'll just smoke anyway." Or, you might look at the ad and say, "How terrible," and try to reject it outright.

Whether you smoke or not, it is difficult to escape dissonance-arousing communications about the dangers of that habit. Advertisements are forever portraying smoking as glamorous and upbeat, even though the law requires them to carry the message that smoking is hazardous to health. Campaigns against smoking often take direct aim at the "glamour"/"hazard" incongruity. *Robert Pacheco/EKM-Nepenthe*

You might even quickly turn the page to "selectively" avoid it. Again, the key issue in Festinger's theory is that harmony or consonance among cognitive elements simply promotes "business as usual," whereas dissonance promotes change.

Dissonance Theory in Application. It is easy to think of examples of how cognitive dissonance is a basis for planning social influence through communication. Take, for instance, rallies opposing nuclear energy. They are filled with negative symbols—mistrust of power companies, pollution, radiation hazards, and very vivid symbols of death itself. The more these rallies are kept in the public eye, particularly on television, the more they are likely to create dissonance and perhaps attitude change in individuals who are neutral or who favor nuclear energy. They force upon such individuals the necessity of either actively rejecting the antinuclear messages or accepting them and changing their minds. If these people do nothing, they will be left with a feeling of dissonance. The premise of dissonance theory in planning social influence is not so much one of directly promising harmony as it is the threat of dissonance that one will wish to avoid.

Dissonance can involve people as well as ideas. For example, you might feel great benefits from studying with another student in class. But, at the same time, that person's political ideas may so incense you that you can hardly stand being in his or her presence. Unless you can tolerate the dissonance, you are either going to have to stop studying with that person or change your feelings about his or her political ideas.

Dissonance theory, of course, has many implications for selective attention. Although we are all willing to tolerate pros and cons of opinion to a reasonable degree in the media we use or in the friends with whom we converse, we are likely to be always biased in a direction of avoiding dissonance. So, as in the earlier example, if you are a reader of the *Wall Street Journal*, you will probably not also be subscribing to the *Mother Earth News*.

Inoculation Theory. One very interesting extension of dissonance theory is an **inoculation** theory of resistance to persuasion. Following the medical analogy, if individuals who are about to encounter massive persuasion on a topic are given small doses of these arguments in a "weakened" form, they will be more resistant when the main arguments are given.

Suppose a salesperson is attempting to sell you a new color television set. Although he knows you will probably shop around before buying, he takes the time not only to extol all the features of his set but also to do one more thing. Because he knows that several competitors will offer you an alternative brand at a slightly lower price, he mentions this in his discussion with you. He might say, "Now you shop around, and you'll see that my set is a good buy. Other dealers may be able to give you some sets for a slightly lower price, but be careful—lower price means lower quality."

Inoculation theory predicts that you will now be less influenced by a competitor's argument about price. Why? Mainly, the effect of his mentioning that you may hear a lower price will set up dissonance, but hopefully a small and manageable amount that you will reduce in one way or another on the spot. Then when you hear the argument in a more powerful form from another dealer, you have already had some practice in reducing dissonance about it. You may choose to stay with what the first salesperson said.

Dissonance about Dissonance Theory. Dissonance theory, like balance theory in general, is not without its critics. For one thing, we can never be sure how carefully people associate different ideas with separate feelings or attitudes that can get into a dissonant relationship. Perhaps people do not think specifically about the "elements" that could be dissonant. Also, it is possible to criticize dissonance research on the basis that it involves reasoning that is "after the fact and therefore because of the fact." There have never been successful independent measures of dissonance so as to demonstrate that it really exists in people's minds and emotions as a main motivator of behavior. Nonetheless, there are many interesting studies of dissonance as a basis for explaining the psychology of influence.

THE ATTITUDE-BEHAVIOR PROBLEM

Many of the foregoing theories of influence, and especially communication research that has been stimulated by them, stress the direct relation between messages and attitudes but only indirectly relate attitudes to behaviors. They assume that if messages affect attitudes, these, in turn, will affect certain behaviors. In some cases, this assumption holds; for example, studies of voter intentions are usually excellent predictors of voting behaviors. In other cases, as discussed in Percy Tannenbaum's commentary, research does not always bear out that attitudes reliably predict behaviors. A number of studies (see Wicker, 1969) have documented the inconsistency between attitude and behavior. What might explain this discrepancy?

One explanation is that researchers poorly designed their measurements of attitudes, that attitudes are more complex than the simple scales or questions frequently used to measure them. This is a continuing controversy. Since most any measure of attitudes involves so many assumptions, it is easily subject to criticism.

Another explanation is that the strength of an attitude, or the degree of importance to its holder, is an important determinant of whether a certain behavior is likely to follow. You might, for example, ask me if I would like to eat some oysters, to which I would respond, "probably not." There is, however, no "cost" or commitment involved in my giving this answer; in fact, the whole issue is of little importance to me. There might be any number of reasons why between the time of expressing that attitude and another time of being asked, or if given the opportunity to eat oysters, I might give another answer. I might be attending an important dinner party and not want to offend the host by refusing his offer to sample the oysters. The point is that weak or superficial attitudes or attitudes of little importance or consequence to an individual may not have the "staying power" to reliably influence behavior.

Percy H. Tannenbaum

The field of study encompassing attitudinal formation, maintenance, and change through communication is alive, but not completely well, and is still looking for a comfortable theoretical home. The following is a bird's-eye view of the past several decades to bring one up to date. The study of attitudinal phenomena, opinions, and belief systems flourished in the 1950s and the early 1960s, mainly under the impetus of the cognitive consistency theories (still probably one of social psychology's major integrated theoretical contributions). It began to wane in the late sixties as the social sciences generally abandoned much of their theoretical and methodological heritage. This was especially true in the case of applying the experimental method to attitudinal phenomena; the process came to be regarded as too artificial a setting, yielding more artifact than true behavioral data. The field all but disappeared during most of the 1970s as social science became less theoretical and more "relevant." Studies did appear in various journals, but they did not add up to a coherent, let alone novel, theoretical formulation. So-called Attribution Theory did assume the vanguard theoretical position in social psychology, but its propositions did not quite address the old dilemmas of attitude change and generally failed to raise innovative notions.

Many of the basic questions involved in attitude theory remain, and deserve repeating:

1. Are attitudes solely pseudotheoretical constructs—figments of the social science imagination, so to speak—or do they have some basis in fact? The jury is still out on this one although it is clear that people do have basic approach–avoidance reactions to objects, events, and others in their environment over long periods. Label them pleasant or unpleasant, favorable or unfavorable, positive or negative, and so on, and you have the equivalent of the way most attitudes are measured.

2. Do attitudes shape cognitions, or vice-versa, or is there no relation between the two? The evidence was mixed on this issue but is of late increasingly coming out in favor of the initial premise—that is, that the more immediate, "primitive" responses represent emotional feeling tones somewhat akin to attitudes, that they are in evidence prior to cognitive formulations and responses, and that they often act to influence the latter.

3. What about the relation between attitudes and behavior? On this, perhaps the most central

Williams, LaRose, and Frost (1981) found strength of attitude to be an explanatory factor in studies of the relation between sex-role stereotypes held by children and their expressed intentions to engage in related behaviors. For example, boys 9 to 12 years of age expressed hesitancy at the thought of forming a football team with girls, as the previous research literature had predicted. (Many similar attitudes had been taken by prior researchers as examples of deep-seated sex-role stereotyping by boys.) When asked why they had reacted negatively, many boys responded that they thought girls did not want to play football because it was too rough. They also thought that other boys would think them to be "sissies" for playing a "boy's sport" with girls. After a brief conversation, in which it was mentioned that "touch" football was seldom any rougher than many sports that girls regularly engage in and in which examples of girls playing football were given, the boys readily

issue in the field, the evidence continues to beguile. There are clearly instances when attitudes do predispose toward a certain type of behavior (as some definitions maintain, seemingly tautologically), but there are also cases where the reverse is true. There seems to be no good reason why both directional influences cannot hold, and no good reason for the many examples where the two appear to be quite independent of each other.

4. What is the role of communication messages in attitude formation and change? While much attitudinal-type behavior is a result of direct firsthand experience, a good deal depends on those indirect, mediated, vicarious social encounters we call *communications*. Obviously, when one is remote in space and time from a particular object of judgment (a particular politician, say) and the only basis for knowing about it is through communication via the media or other individuals, and yet we nevertheless can get to feel and react about the object with partisanship, even passion, the communication messages must be held to play a prime role. On the other hand, it is too easy to overgeneralize such relationships, to ascribe all such influence to communications media, modalities, and contents. Clearly, when mediated messages contradict intimate personal experience, they tend to be discounted.

Clearly, too, the more we learn that such messages are fictional, manufactured, and at best half-true, the more we are inclined to treat all such messages with more than a grain of salt.

5. To what degree are attitudes based on information? This harkens back to the cognition–attitude relation raised before, as well as to the role of communication. Research demonstrates quite strongly that contextual factors other than the informational content of the message influence both the degree and kind of attitude change—for example, the message source and preexisting attitudes toward it, aspects of credibility, the kind of evidential base, other predispositions of the recipient, and so on. In addition, we find evidence that attitudes toward individual objects tend not to be maintained in isolation but in relation to—both positively and negatively associated with— other existing clusters of opinion. It is thus more appropriate to think of "belief systems," relatively stable over time but also dynamic in that change in one or more of their central elements can indirectly lead to change in associated elements.

Percy H. Tannenbaum is Professor of Public Policy in the Graduate School of Public Policy and is Director of the Survey Research Center, University of California at Berkeley.

---

changed their attitudes as well as expressing a willingness to form a boy–girl team. (And in some school settings, they indeed did.) Thus, many of the boys' stereotyped attitudes were superficial, and any number of factors might change them. (The role of television messages in this study is described in Chapter 14.)

Still another explanation is that the situation itself is an important factor in the attitude–behavior link. In expectancy-value theory (discussed in the next section), attitudes are examined as directly relevant to a behavioral situation. In this and similar lines of reasoning, attitudes are only one of several factors that influence behavior.

In all, studies of the process of influence must consider not only how messages affect attitudes but also how attitudes and other factors influence eventual behavior.

Expectancy-Value Theory

One of the problems of balance theory, as well as of other theories in which motives are presumed to affect attitudes, and attitudes, in turn, to affect behaviors, is that the linkage of attitude and behavior is not that predictable. Another theory of influence—one that does not depend on balance theory or stress attitude–behavior relations—comes from the work of Martin Fishbein and his associates. Called **expectancy-value theory,** this approach holds that we are influenced primarily by two types of motives:

Personal rewards: satisfaction of needs for such things as feeling good about ourselves, security, understanding, and physical or monetary rewards.

Social approval: satisfaction based on the fact that those persons ("significant others") who are important to us feel positive about our behavior.

The basic model of expectancy-value theory is presented in Figure 5.3.

Note in this figure how personal and social attitudes are meant to predict a concept called "behavioral intention." Fishbein argues that our motives set up *expectations* of behavior, which we may then further carry out. Of course, outside circumstances that have nothing to do with our personal or social motives may affect whether we actually engage in the behavior.

For example, you may consider washing your car this Saturday. Although it's a bit of a sloppy job, you enjoy getting outside and enjoy the personal satisfaction of having your prized possession looking "like new" again. You also feel that your friends will recognize that you have a nice-looking car and that you are the kind of person who cares about keeping it looking good. All of these motives set up high expectations that you will wash your car Saturday. If nothing occurs to prevent this, you probably will, and behavioral expectation will be a good predictor of behavior. But it may also rain, so quite apart from any of your own original motives, you may fail to wash your car.

Expectancy-Value Theory and Communication

We can use expectancy-value theory to gain insights into communication effects. In fact, expectancy-value theory was used as one of the bases for planning the public television series "Freestyle," in which the objective was to change young boys' and girls' typical attitudes about sex-role stereotyping (see Williams, LaRose, and Frost, 1981).

In one of the programs of the series, a young girl was portrayed as wanting to go out for the junior high school football team. She had strong personal convictions (attitudes) that making the team would be very rewarding to her personally. The show depicted this in dramatic ways. Another part of the plot involved how several of her "significant others" disagreed on her goal of playing football. The coach's wife, for example, was portrayed as thinking this was an utterly horrible desire. On the other hand, the coach, who was particularly close to the young girl, was very supportive. The point of the

Figure 5.3
The Expectancy-Value
Theory of Influence

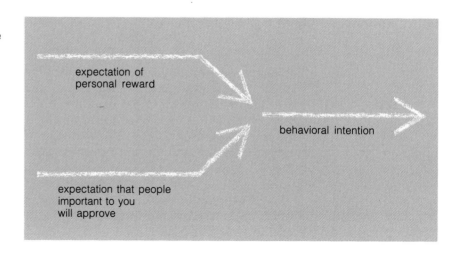

drama was to convey to youthful viewers that if you really stick with your convictions, you may be able to carry them out; moreover, people who are close to you will respect you for it.

One of the key tactics of the producers of the program was to create characters with whom the viewing audience could easily identify. Not only was the young football player attractive and a potential model for identification, but her "significant others" were likely to be similar to those in the viewer's own life—that is, parents, friends, and the coach.

In general terms, expectancy-value theory holds that influence will be greatest when individuals can sense the possibility of personal rewards as well as the approval of those persons closest to them.

ARGUMENT AS INFLUENCE: IS IT "LOGICAL"?

Not all theories of influence involve considerations of balance, dissonance, or attitudes in general: sometimes we talk about **argument.** There are relatively few psychological theories of the use of argument to influence others.

Ways of Arguing

The premises are true, and the logical form of the argument is valid; therefore, the conclusion is true.

This is the implicit overall proposition we follow when we are attempting to use argument as influence. It is the so-called appeal to reason, or rational appeal, and was recognized over 2000 years ago by Aristotle. Nevertheless, arguments in our daily communications seldom follow this tightly formed sequence laid down in formal logic. Instead, the logic is more implicit, even inexact, in everyday communication.

No matter whether we are reading "logical" arguments in a newspaper editorial, hearing "logical" arguments in a TV campaign speech, or arguing with our neighbor about keeping the noise down, we are not necessarily dealing with the type of influence that is strictly rational. The logic may be imperfect—it may be sketchy, and the structure of the argument may even be fallacious. And there is not much use in trying to separate logic from motivational kinds of appeals in persuasion. This is because argument itself—the appeal to truth—can be thought of as a motive in and of itself. Also, as recognized by Aristotle, it is difficult to evaluate logic as a means of influence. Our criteria for judging appeals to reason are about as loose as the communication of reason itself. Often these criteria include the following:

1. *Is the evidence complete and unbiased?* Have all the facts about the proposition been fully revealed? Or have only facts that support the proposition been included? (Research has indicated that two-sided arguments are usually more effective than one-sided ones.) Does the evidence seem to be objective? That is, would any well-meaning person carefully evaluating the proposition come up with similar evidence? Is the evidence readily verifiable by other individuals? Is it directly observable, or is it simply somebody's opinion?

2. *Does the evidence fit the proposition?* Evidence may relate to the proposition but may not directly support it. For example, a political candidate may come from a party that is generally noted for its radical activities. Although evidence of a candidate's relation to that party may suggest that he or she is associated with radical activity, the evidence itself may not necessarily demonstrate that. Sometimes this is referred to more generally as circumstantial evidence. As we sometimes witness in spectacular court cases, a person accused of murder may have been near the scene of the crime, had a motive, and earlier threatened the victim, but none of this evidence directly proves that he or she actually committed the crime.

We do know, however, that as circumstantial evidence mounts, it becomes very persuasive. Arguments on smoking reflect this process. There is abundant correlation evidence that the more people smoke, the greater the probability they will get cancer.

3. *Is the form of the argument logical?* Just as there are certain classic forms of argument, there are classic forms of fallacies. First, consider this example of one classic form of argument:

All Democrats favor social services.

Candidate A is a Democrat.

Therefore, Candidate A favors social services.

On the basis of logical structure, if the first two statements in this argument are true, then the third statement must be true. However, compare that argument with the following fallacy:

All Democrats favor social programs.

Candidate X favors social programs.

Therefore, Candidate X is a Democrat.

This is a famous form of fallacy that, if you studied logical structure, you might recognize right away. If you think about the latter argument, you can see why its conclusion is not necessarily true. (Although all Democrats may favor social programs, other political parties may also favor them, and perhaps Candidate X is a member of one of those.)

As scientifically and philosophically interesting as the evaluation of logic can be, there is abundant evidence that we do not always pay attention to it in our usual communication behaviors. Time and again, studies indicate that in our usual media and interpersonal communication behaviors, we tend to be guided by a complex of personal and social motives, of which the rationality of an argument is but one. It is only when a situation is meant to focus clearly on the quality of an argument—as in a well-reasoned intellectual debate or a point of law in the courtroom—that logic itself seems to have a powerful influence in communication.

Unfortunately, "apparent logic," or people's feeling that something is the truth, may be more influential than the actual quality of evidence in argument.

Toulmin's Model of Argument

One modern model of argument makes it easier to assess the logic of messages. This model comes from the work of Stephen Toulmin, a contemporary philosopher. The key components of Toulmin's (1958) model are as follows:

> The *claim* is the essential proposition of the argument—the conclusion that the listener, reader, or viewer is supposed to accept. We have referred to this in other parts of this book as the proposition.
>
> The *data* are the usual evidence intended to support the claim.
>
> The *warrant* is whatever is supposed to relate the data to the claim—that is, relate the evidence to the proposition.

Now please examine Figure 5.4 and reread the foregoing definitions of the key components of Toulmin's model. Note how the *data* ("My car is a Ford sedan") are related to the *claim* ("My car was made in America") by the *warrant* ("Ford sedans are made in America"). Toulmin's model supposedly applies to any kind of argument, even though the precise logical structure may vary or the criteria differ for the evaluation of evidence.

Examine the next two examples as they relate to the components of argument shown in Figure 5.4. The first is another simple argument:

Claim: The Mark VI gets good gas mileage.

Data: Subcompact cars get good gas mileage.

Warrant: The Mark VI will be a subcompact car.

The Toulmin model also applies to complex arguments such as we often find in advertising or general persuasive communications. Note in this second example how the components of argument are used.

Figure 5.4
Toulmin's Model
of Argument

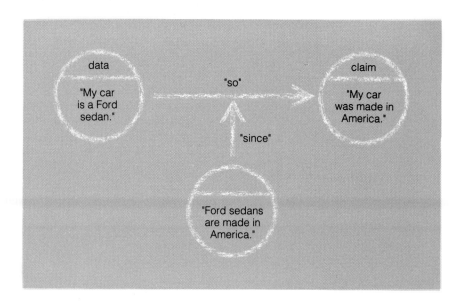

Claim: You should have vitamins in your diet.

Data: 1. Some vitamins build strong bones.
2. Some vitamins aid night vision.
3. Some vitamins promote digestion.
4. Some vitamins aid fertility.
5. Some vitamins promote healthy skin.
6. Some vitamins promote blood clotting.

Warrant: You should judge vitamins by what they do for you.

There are many more details to Toulmin's model than need be presented here to give you a general idea of how everyday arguments can be evaluated. Although there is no psychological evidence that we indeed think about claims, warrants, and data in much detail in everyday communication, the Toulmin model provides a way to analyze their quality in a message.

If logic is to have a rational influence at all, then the quality of these components should be an important part of the process. Moreover, if we are to train people to evaluate the logic of everyday communication, we can use the Toulmin model as a start. Unfortunately, there is little research and even less theory into the exact ways by which we perceive logic when we are influenced by communications, especially public communications.

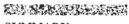

SUMMARY

During our lives we are constantly being influenced, and one of the greatest sources of influence is daily communications. *Attitudes,* or the thoughts or feelings that shape how we respond to stimulation, are a key component in the process of influence.

Many theories of influence have developed around the concept that we wish to keep our attitudes toward ideas and people in a harmonious *balance*. We tend to select our communications accordingly, using *selective perception*. The theory does not always hold, however. *Dissonance* theory holds that we tend to behave so as to avoid conflict (rather than simply seeking balance). Research in *inoculation* theory has indicated that small "inoculations" of an argument can arouse enough dissonance for a person to build up defenses against the major argument when it comes.

Expectancy-value theory holds that our behaviors are shaped mainly by our expectations of *personal reward* and the social approval of people who are important to us. Like balance theories, expectancy-value theory can be used in planning communications.

We also consider *argument* as a process of influence. Although the logic of most everyday arguments is inexact, we humans still feel that reasoned behavior is important to us. The Toulmin model can assist in the evaluation of arguments in communication.

TOPICS FOR DISCUSSION OR BRIEF PAPERS

1. Select an example of modern persuasion—for example, a political campaign, advertising, a sales pitch given to you—and analyze it in terms of the balance theory model given in Figure 5.2. Identify the key components, and describe the negative and positive weightings of the attitudes involved. Explain the different possible outcomes.

2. Using a dissonance theory approach, sketch the outline of persuasive strategies you might employ in public health campaigns, such as in campaigns to get people to stop smoking, to promote exercise, or to prevent drug abuse. How would you combat the problem of selective inattention to your messages if they initially promoted a feeling of dissonance? What evidence might you try to gather to see if your messages did stimulate attitude change through dissonance reduction?

3. Select a popular television advertisement, and analyze its persuasive qualities using any of the models discussed in this chapter. Describe the advertisement both in terms of what it portrays scene by scene and in terms of how this content reflects a persuasive sequence. Speculate on the likely effectiveness of the advertisement. Explain your generalizations.

4. Set up a hypothetical situation in which you are going to persuade a friend to take some type of action such as lend you money, date you, or stay in school. Explain how your persuasive strategy could be based upon expectancy-value theory. Describe your approach in terms of the components in Figure 5.3. What could go wrong?

5. Clip a newspaper or magazine editorial whose content represents a presumably logical argument in favor of something. Analyze that argument in terms of the Toulmin model. Identify the claim, warrant, and data. Evaluate the logical validity of the argument.

REFERENCES AND READINGS

Ajzen, I., and M. Fishbein. *Understanding Attitudes and Predicting Social Behavior.* Englewood Cliffs, N.J.: Prentice-Hall, 1980.

Bettinghaus, E. P. *Persuasive Communication.* 3d ed. New York: Holt, Rinehart and Winston, 1981.

Festinger, L. *A Theory of Cognitive Dissonance.* New York: Harper and Row, 1957.

Fishbein, M., and I. Ajzen. *Belief, Attitude, Intention, and Behavior.* Reading, Mass.: Addison-Wesley, 1975.

Heider, F. "Attitudes and Cognitive Organization." *Journal of Psychology* 21 (1946): 107–112.

Osgood, C. E., G. J. Suci, and P. H. Tannenbaum. *The Measurement of Meaning.* Urbana: University of Illinois Press, 1957.

Reardon, K. K. *Persuasion: Theory and Context.* Beverly Hills, Calif.: Sage, 1981.

Simons, H. W. *Persuasion: Understanding, Practice, and Analysis.* 2d ed. New York: Random House, 1986.

Smith, M. J. *Persuasion and Human Action.* Belmont, Calif.: Wadsworth, 1982.

Toulmin, S. *The Uses of Argument.* Cambridge, England: Cambridge University Press, 1958.

Wicker, A. W. "Attitudes vs. Actions: The Relationship of Verbal and Overt Behavioral Responses to Attitude Objects." *Journal of Social Issues* (1969): 47–66.

Williams, F., R. LaRose, and F. Frost. *Children, Television, and Sex-Role Stereotyping.* New York: Praeger, 1981.

Media and Technologies

EVERYDAY CHOICES

You make many communication choices every waking hour of your life. Suppose, for example, that you feel it is now important to break off a once highly romantic relationship and that you hope to do it gently. You may want to handle this break-up with a face-to-face conversation. But if you can't face the other person at this difficult time, you may simply send a note. For another example, suppose that your mother is ill in a distant city and that you want to convey your love to her. If you are like most other people, you will probably telephone. You want a personal form of communication, but you can't be with her. A letter will take too long. Anyway, you want to hear the sound of her voice so you can get an idea of how ill she really is. Finally, suppose that you hear a rumor that there has been an attempt on the life of the president of the United States. What will you do? If you are like the people studied by Bradley Greenberg (1964) and his colleagues after the assassination of President John F. Kennedy, you will ask another person or turn on your radio.

The point is that we are constantly making choices in modern life about which medium of communication to use in a given situation. As you may recall from earlier chapters, a medium is anything from a face-to-face encounter to any of the most modern forms of communication—a computer, for example. We have many alternatives, far more than did our ancestors, including our parents. Until the invention of writing in about 6000 B.C., most human communication was limited to the range of people's voice or sight or to wherever their travels might take them. Eventually, writing and the development of ancient courier services made long-distance communication easier—if, that is, you were wealthy or influential enough to take advantage of them. By A.D. 100, if you and your lover had been at opposite ends of the Roman Empire, it might have taken months for your written message to get through, if it did at all. Until the installation of transatlantic radio communications, news from the United States to Europe moved at the speed of ships: a few weeks, at least, counting local delivery of a letter. As recently as 1950, if you were to settle back for an evening of television, you'd be lucky to have three stations from which to select.

One of the distinguishing features of our world of modern communications is that we have so many alternatives. We can pick up a telephone to call our next-door neighbor or a friend in Japan. Our society circulates billions of pieces of mail daily, and we get upset if one item is late or lost. Information about our world abounds in newspapers, magazines, and television and radio broadcasts. We use film to record everything from medical records to the fantasies of Hollywood's best writers.

Moreover, the media are multiplying in variety and content by the development of new communications technologies. Television comes into our homes via cable, disk, or tape or directly by satellite. Truly, we are living in a world of exploding communications alternatives. Taking our pick may involve increasingly complex choices. In this chapter we examine media choices, including the so-called new media technologies.

SOME FUNDAMENTAL ASPECTS OF MEDIA

Transmission

A communications medium is, first, whatever allows us to transmit a message between a source and a receiver. In speech, for example, the medium is the acoustic vibrations of air, or simply sound. For communication by gesture, the pattern of light waves that stimulates our visual senses is the transmitting medium. When analyzing a communications medium in more detail, it is helpful to identify the method by which it transforms messages into a form compatible with the transmission and into a form that a receiver can interpret. To use speech as a transmission medium, for example, people must create speech sounds through a neuromuscular process, and others must be able to hear and interpret the sounds. Messages in gesture form have to be made visible to the receiver. As we discuss shortly, the use of any type of communications medium, whether print, wire, film, or broadcasting, requires transformation of a message into a form compatible both with the transmission medium and with the human senses.

"Natural" Media

The **encoding** and **decoding** processes required for media are closely tied to our natural human abilities to create and to perceive message forms. It is not surprising, therefore, that the most fundamental of human media for communication are closely tied to our abilities to see and hear. A **natural medium** is one that we can use without any extra skills, equipment, or the like. Table 6.1 summarizes the natural media.

As you can see in the table, we have added the human senses of touch, smell, taste, and equilibrium to sight and hearing as natural media. Touch is regularly used in face-to-face communication (such as in shaking hands), but we are nevertheless not so capable of creating a variety of messages with touch as with sight or sound. We also make more limited use of our senses

Table 6.1 Natural Media of Communication

Basic Medium	Encoding	Transmission	Decoding
Sound	Human speech articulation	Acoustic vibrations	Human sound perception
Vision	Gestures, visual	Light waves	Human visual perception
Touch	Bodily movements, gestures	Direct contact	Human touch sensation
Smell	Release of molecules	Molecules carried in air	Olfactory sense
Taste	Release of molecules	Transfer of molecules	Sense of taste
Equilibrium	Anything capable of moving the human body or its parts	Direct, physical movement	Sense of equilibrium

of smell, taste, and equilibrium. And when we do use these senses, the messages are simple. For example, perfume has been used throughout the ages as a symbol of attractiveness or pleasantness. We can manipulate the taste of things by selections of ingredients in recipes. But we do not always think of things like these as a direct form of sending messages. As for equilibrium, there are few, if any, examples of how we encode messages to be sensed by a person's perception of changes in equilibrium, except perhaps when we lift someone up out of joy or knock a person down in anger.

The analysis of natural media is useful for a definition of our biologically inherited bases for communication. It also reminds us of how the human senses are extended by the media that we have developed or crafted. Even the most modern communications medium is ultimately limited by the basic human senses. Often, sensory differences are part of our basis for choosing among media.

Primitive "Extensions" of Media

What do cave paintings and the latest satellite communications systems have in common? The answer is that they are both means by which humans have *extended* their basic communication capabilities. Over the millenia of human existence, we have developed the means (1) to communicate across time, (2) to send messages across long distances, and (3) to duplicate messages. Before our ancestors learned how to leave their marks (perhaps scratches in the dust, a pile of rocks, sticks left in a certain position) for another human or themselves to see, virtually all human communication was restricted to the time in which it occurred. Even when humans developed language, speech restricted it to communication of the moment.

For tens of thousands of years the only human communications that could stand the test of time were markings left on the environment. (The cave paintings of Lascaux, depicted at the beginning of Chapter 1, are one example of this technique.) Moreover, until the markings were put on transportable objects (scratches on rocks, marks on pieces of clay, knots on rope, burn marks on hides), our ancestors were not able to communicate beyond the distance of human sight, voice, or hearing. Prehistoric humans had to travel to the cave paintings, just as we do, in order to see them. The ability to put marks on movable objects was the beginning of a long line of capabilities invented by humans for moving messages to people. Later in this chapter, we will see how this process has been especially advanced by the use of new communications technologies.

Most of the messages of antiquity were probably limited to simple iconic representations, such as the animals in the cave paintings. The power to record complex messages was virtually nonexistent until the monumental contribution of the invention of writing around 6000 B.C. In essence, writing allowed human language to extend across the barriers of time and space.

The earliest extensions of the natural media of human communication can be examined in terms of their transmission and encoding components,

Table 6.2 Early Extensions of Human Media

Medium	What It Extended	Recording Basis	Transmission Basis	Symbolization
Writing	Language sounds	Marks on writing surface	Transport of message or receiver	Initially iconic, as "pictowriting," then usually coded, as alphabet
Drawing	Visual images	Marks on drawing surface	Transport of message or receiver	Mainly iconic
Sculpture, architecture	Image and three-dimensional shapes	Physical materials in iconic shapes	Some transport (sculpture), some fixed (design)	Mainly iconic, but can incorporate text

as summarized in Table 6.2. These early extensions include such capabilities as sculpture or design. Certainly, sculpture is a way of capturing a message, if only a highly iconic one. Design (tools, shelters, pottery), although not always a direct message in itself, does communicate some of the subtle intentions or thoughts of its creator. Another characteristic of these fundamental extensions is that they all depend on the basic medium of vision in order for messages on them to be represented and perceived. Also, their transmission requires direct transportation. The speed of communication, except for carrier pigeon or smoke or fire signals, was restricted to the speed of human transportation until the invention of the telegraph in the nineteenth century.

None of these ancient extensions involved a media duplication system, as such. Except for seals impressed on wax, metal, or clay or the rubbing of images from a raised surface to paper or clothlike substances, duplication of messages was to await the invention of printing, first in the Orient around A.D. 500, then in Europe in the tenth century, as impressions "pulled" from inked block carvings. The invention of printing marked the arrival of a communications medium that would have a wide social influence, perhaps as great an influence as the development of writing. Typically we consider printing as among the "traditional" media of modern society.

Contrasts among Media

If you look at the characteristics of modern communications media in some detail, you will soon notice that these media are not all distinguished from one another in similar ways. For example, printing is an advance over handwriting because of the capability it presented of duplicating messages, not because it could transport messages any faster. Printing still depended on the transportation system for transmission. It is a medium with a distinctive basis for recording and duplicating messages, not moving them. In contrast, when the first "wired" communication was developed (the wire telegraph in the last century), its great contribution was the introduction of a new transmission system. The telegraph accelerated messages from the speed of the transportation system to the speed of electrical current. This was a leap from about 10 to 20 miles per hour to 186,000 miles per second!

Table 6.3 summarizes further contrasts among the traditional media of communication. You can see that some media represent changes in the recording or reproduction system, whereas others are distinctive in terms of their transmission system. This table also reminds us that the traditional media are only extensions of our fundamental capabilities for hearing and vision.

Notice also in Table 6.3 that the traditional media vary in the type of symbolization they convey. They may emphasize a linguistically coded message, as with the text of printing or speech on the telephone. Both of these are in contrast with a visually iconic medium such as photography. However, many modern media convey both linguistically coded and iconic materials—for example, television or motion pictures. They are combinations of more fundamental media. The modern motion picture is a combination of photography and our ability to record linguistic sounds either magnetically or optically along with the images. As we see later in this chapter, many of the new technologies of communication are only combinations of the old.

The particular characteristics that distinguish the traditional media from one another represent technological extensions of the process of human communication. Each contribution has expanded the capabilities of human communication. We next examine some of these media in more detail.

Table 6.3 Comparison of Traditional Media

Type	General Medium	Extension of	Recording	Transmission	Symbolization
Books, newspapers, magazines	Print	Vision (writing)	Paper, ink, type	Transportation	Text, still images
Telegraph	Wire Broadcast	Writing Writing	— —	Electric current Electromagnetic	Text Text
Telephone	Wire	Sound	—	Electric current	Speech
Photography	Photography	Vision	Film, chemical	Transportation	Still or moving images
Radio	Broadcasting	Sound	—	Electromagnetic	Speech, music
Television	Broadcasting	Sound, vision	—	Electromagnetic	Speech, images
Phonograph	Recording	Sound	Mechanical acoustic	Transportation	Speech, music

Print

Printing, in essence, is the reproduction of text or other images on a surface, as illustrated in Figure 6.1. Although we often credit Johann Gutenberg with the invention of this technique, he was far from being the first person to develop methods of printing (see box, A Short History of Print). The process itself involves the convergence of several technologies. First, for most traditional types of printing, there is the necessity for paper and ink, both of which were developed and used by the Chinese long before the appearance of printing in Europe. There is also a raised or recessed surface pattern, which when inked transfers the image to the paper. In one respect, the ancient art of taking "rubbings" nearly qualifies as printing, except that the image is achieved by rubbing a darkening material over the paper rather than inking the printing surface.

For the printing of text, the invention of movable type was a major step. Although used in various ways in the Orient, a system to cast movable type probably did make its greatest advance at the hands of Gutenberg. He is also credited with developing a superior press for making the impressions.

Until the beginning of the twentieth century, advances in printing were mostly mechanical improvements in presses, such as the invention of high-speed, machine-driven presses and the invention of typesetting machines. The main advances of the twentieth century have involved bypassing the slow and costly process of casting molten type to form a page image. These advances have been achieved by photo offset printing combined with photo typesetting and, in the last several decades, by computer-assisted systems.

Wired Communication

Wired communication is the process of encoding messages into a pattern of electrical impulses, which then travel via wire to an apparatus that converts them into a message interpretable by another human. As illustrated in Figure 6.2, the simplest and earliest form of wired communication was the telegraph. It was followed about 40 years later by the telephone (see box, A Short History of Wired Communication, on pages 112–114).

The capability for wired communication developed almost simultaneously with the capability for creating and controlling sources of electricity. Given those capabilities, the invention of the telegraph became mainly a matter of how to control patterns of electrical impulses and to work out a code. The first devices used changes in electrical current to cause needles to point to certain messages at the receiver's end of the system. One such system had a separate wire for each letter of the alphabet. These early telegraph systems were used to communicate train schedules that, among other uses, allowed the coordination of trains coming from opposite directions on the same track.

Eventually the telegraph was developed as a simple system of patterns of on–off current flow. These patterns were the basis for a code proposed by Samuel F. B. Morse. In the first demonstration of public use of a commercially available system, its developer, Morse, sent the dramatic message "What hath God wrought?"

Printing proliferated as a business and profession soon after Gutenberg introduced movable type. The new capability for mass dissemination of ideas no doubt played an important role in the coming Reformation and Renaissance. Throughout the Enlightenment, literacy spread rapidly as the number of books in existence multiplied into millions. *Courtesy San Francisco Public Library*

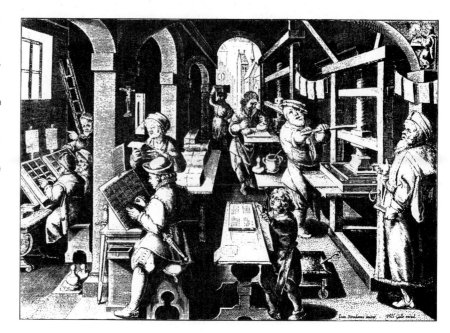

A.D. 100–200	Chinese reproduce designs and texts by inking carved marble surfaces, then laying paper upon them.
500	Printing from wood blocks is developed in China and other parts of the Orient.
700–1300	The art of papermaking travels from the Orient via the Arab world to Europe.
1000–1100	Chinese employ movable type made from clay.
1300–1400	Chinese use individually carved wooden blocks as movable type.
1400?	Koreans create movable type characters from cast bronze.

Figure 6.1
The Printing Process

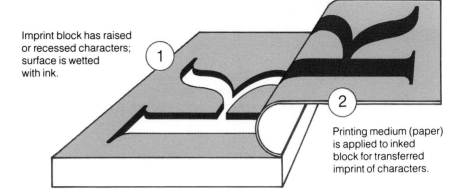

Imprint block has raised or recessed characters; surface is wetted with ink.

① ②

Printing medium (paper) is applied to inked block for transferred imprint of characters.

1400?	Printing using wood blocks and paper appears in Europe.
1400–1450	Single Latin letters are engraved on bronze dies that are used to stamp text on a clay form. The form is hardened; then lead is poured over it to cast a raised text surface suitable for printing.
1450–1454	Johann Gutenberg develops a system for casting individual letters of text.
1830	The steam press is perfected in England, allowing rapid reproduction.
1846	The rotary press is developed, producing up to 20,000 copies per hour.
1884	Ottmar Mergenthaler invents the linotype machine (rapid typesetting).
1900–1920	Offset printing is developed.
1946	Xerography is developed as the basis for photocopy machine.
1950–on	"Programmed" operation of typesetting machines is developed; computer-assisted typesetting is developed.

1700–1800	Experiments are conducted in England and Europe in sending messages via electrical impulses over wires.
1819	Hans Christian Orsted reports how changes in current can move a magnetized needle; suggests this application as a communications device.
1832	Russians install a needle telegraph in the Czar's palace in St. Petersburg.
1830–1850	Various advanced versions of new needle telegraphs are installed along railways in England.
1825–1835	Joseph Henry (United States) experiments with electromagnets, a method ideally suited to telegraphic communication.

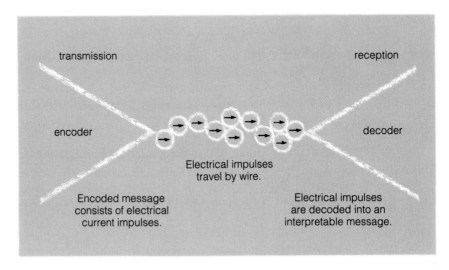

Figure 6.2
A Simplified Diagram
of the Early Telegraph

With the invention of the wire telegraph, the speed of human communication leapt to the speed of light. The critical breakthrough for this invention was the ability to create and control a source of electrical current. The telegraph eventually necessitated time zones, allowed accurate train schedules, and provided the basis for stock market and news wires. *Courtesy San Francisco Public Library*

1832	Samuel F. B. Morse (United States) proposes a form of electromagnetic telegraph.
1832–1845	Morse proposes a dot–dash code for use with telegraph.
1844	Public use of Morse's telegraph is inaugurated between Baltimore and Washington (37 miles).
1856	Western Union Telegraph Co. is established.

Figure 6.3
The Basic Process
of the Telephone

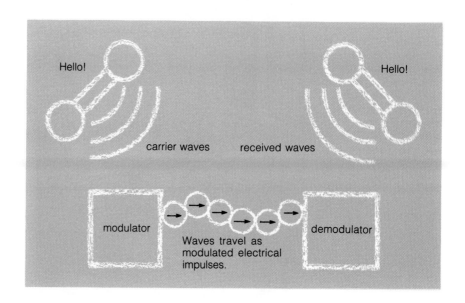

1861	Philipp Reis demonstrates an apparatus in which a vibrating metal strip is used to control the current flowing into a wire; he names it the "telephone."
1872–1875	Alexander Graham Bell and Elisha Gray separately experiment with vibration apparatuses and electromagnets to communicate sounds over wire.
1876	Both Gray and Bell attempt to patent their telephone devices, although neither can yet transmit speech. Bell gets the first patents.
1880	Rapid development of the telephone begins.

Once a simple and reliable telegraph had been developed, it found many immediate applications. It was used to convey information about stock and commodity prices in different markets, a use that eventually developed into the "market wire." It was also used to convey news stories of national and international interest. This use represented the birth of the "wire services," and it changed newspapers. In addition, the telegraph soon put the famous pony express mail service out of business.

As a wired communication apparatus, the telephone differs from the telegraph mainly in that the electrical current carries the much more complex patterns of the human voice over the wire (Figure 6.3). The development of the telephone represented a solution to the technological problem of how to convert the sound patterns of voice into electrical patterns, a problem similar to but more complex than that involved with the development of the telegraph. Alexander Graham Bell's interest in wired communication began as he was studying ways of sending multiple telegraph messages simultaneously over the same wire. In his first approach to the problem, he reasoned that if there were multiple transmitting devices, each at a different frequency, a receiving apparatus at the other end of the line could separate the messages sent on the different frequencies. Although neither Bell nor Elisha Gray (who was also working on the problem) ever developed a multiple-message telegraph, they both realized that if different frequencies could be imposed at the same time on a pattern of electrical impulses and could be separated at the other end of the wire, direct communication by voice was theoretically possible. This is the essence of telephone technology as initially developed. Although we make wide use of the telephone today, not everybody expected such prospects. At one point Bell offered his invention to Western Union, which turned him down because it saw little future in voice communication via wires.

You have probably noticed and perhaps been annoyed by the relative flatness of voices heard over your telephone. Voices are not more realistic because the transmission capability of the telephone has been developed only to the degree that the voice will be clearly intelligible. It is not a high-fidelity transmission system like your home stereo equipment.

The telephone grew rapidly as a commercial venture. By 1880 there were around 30,000 telephone subscribers in the United States; today there are about 90 million, representing 96 percent of all households. In areas like New York City, there are more telephones than there are people. You might be interested to know that in the late nineteenth century, in such capitals as Budapest, London, and Paris, a telephone system was used as a "wired broadcasting" service, offering drama, news, music, and stock market information to subscribers. (Some of the music was even transmitted over two channels for a "stereo" effect!)

Photography

Most of the early development of photography involved methods for "capturing" an image focused on a surface (see box, An Early History of Photography). History does not record who first discovered the "pinhole" effect

Figure 6.4
The Basic Photo-
graphic Process

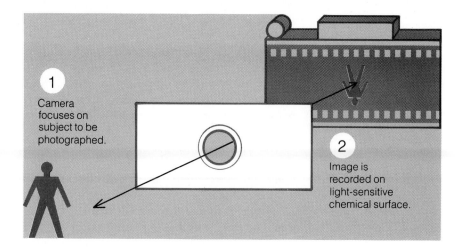

300 B.C.–A.D. 300?	Principle of camera obscura is developed, whereby light coming through a hole in an outside wall of a darkened room projects an image on the opposite wall; similar to a pinhole camera. The principle was mentioned in Aristotle's writings.
1500s?	Crude lenses are used with camera obscuras.
1600s?	Camera obscura becomes regularly used by artists.
1826	Joseph Nicephore Niepce records a crude image by darkening a light-sensitive surface (France).
1829	Joseph Antoine Ferdinand Plateau publishes investigations into "the persistence of vision," and constructs a device giving the illusion of movement ("phenakiscope").
1834	William George Hormer invents the "zootrope," in which pictures mounted inside a moving drum can be seen through slits in the side and look as though they are moving.
1837	Louis Jacques Mandé Daguerre develops and reports on a process that provides positive images (15 to 20 minutes of sunlight exposure are required).
1840	William Henry Fox Talbot in England develops a process for creating a paper negative that, in turn, is the basis for printing positive images.
1851	Frederick Scott Archer develops a sensitized negative material ("wet collodian"), which allows for instantaneous exposures in bright sunlight. This is a "wet-plate" process and requires a portable darkroom along with a camera.

Photography is one communications technology that very early put the ability to create images into the hands of everyday people. (Compare this with the long delay in making home video cameras feasible.) Much development was due to the efforts of George Eastman, whose simplified cameras using celluloid roll film instead of glass plates were mass-produced and heavily advertised early in the century. *Smithsonian Institution*

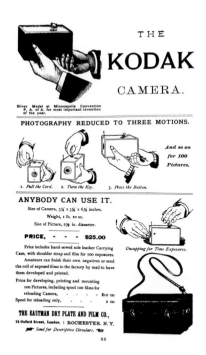

THE

KODAK

CAMERA.

Silver Medal at Minneapolis Convention
P. A. of A. for most important invention
of the year.

PHOTOGRAPHY REDUCED TO THREE MOTIONS.

1. Pull the Cord.   *2. Turn the Key.*   *3. Press the Button.*

And so on
for *100*
Pictures.

ANYBODY CAN USE IT.

Size of Camera, 3¼ x 3¼ x 6½ inches.
Weight, 1 lb. 10 oz.
Size of Picture, 2½ in. diameter.

PRICE,   -   -   -   **$25.00**

Price includes hand-sewed sole leather Carrying Case, with shoulder strap and film for 100 exposures. Amateurs can finish their own negatives or send the roll of exposed films to the factory by mail to have them developed and printed.

Price for developing, printing and mounting
100 Pictures, including spool 100 films for
reloading Camera,   -   -   - $10 00
Spool for reloading only,   -   -   -   2 00

Uncapping for Time Exposures.

THE EASTMAN DRY PLATE AND FILM CO.,
115 Oxford Street, London. | ROCHESTER. N. Y.
☞ *Send for Descriptive Circulars.* ☜

XX

1871	Dry-plate processes become available that allow a photographer to store film; they do not require a portable darkroom.
1880	Eadweard Muybridge captures successive pictures of animals in motion using his "zoopraxiscope."
1887	Thomas Edison develops the kinetoscope, in which movements are shown on 50-foot loops of film.
1889	Celluloid film backing is invented and subsequently manufactured by the Eastman Kodak Company.
1895	Auguste Lumière demonstrates a practical motion picture system.
1927	Sound additions to motion pictures are commercially introduced.
1934	Color motion pictures are introduced.
1947	Edwin Land introduces an instant still photography system (Polaroid films and cameras).

whereby light coming through a small opening will, under certain conditions, focus an image on a surface. But it is known that such a "camera" was used by artists for many centuries as a guide for sketching images. The Frenchman Joseph Nicephore Niepce is credited with what might be called the first photograph. He created the technique by focusing light over a period of time (perhaps up to an hour) on a surface that had been coated with a solution that darkened as it was exposed to light.

The evolution of photographic processes after Niepce was one of creating "film" surfaces that did not require long periods of exposure of a sunlit image, that could retain the image permanently, and that could be used in a subsequent "photographic printing" process to create copies. The essential steps of the photographic process are sketched in Figure 6.4.

Color photography involves initially separating the primary colors from a subject and recording them on a photographic surface. In early color-photography techniques (as in the Technicolor process), the light coming through a lens was actually divided into three images by a prism, and three separate films were exposed. Later, these films plus dyes were used to make a combined full-color transparency, or image. Eventually, the development of color film reached the point at which the surfaces sensitive to each of the primary colors could be sandwiched together on one celluloid base.

Photography, unlike many other media, also developed as an amateur art. The nonprofessional person has been able to create as well as consume the photographic communication product.

Except for the development of motion picture techniques (see box), most of the advances in photography in the twentieth century have involved increasing the quality of images and lessening the need for bright light in the initial exposure.

"Instant" photography, as in the Polaroid camera and film, began in the late 1940s. In instant photography, developing and printing chemicals are embedded in the film as part of the manufacturing process. After exposure, the chemicals are "squeezed" across the exposed image. The most recent innovations in photography are the use of electronic devices for recording still images in much the same way that a video camera records a moving image.

Broadcasting

Broadcasting makes possible long-distance message transmission between sources and receivers without the benefit of transportation or a direct physical (wire) link (see box, An Early History of Broadcasting). Just as the challenge in wired communication was to develop devices for encoding and decoding message patterns imposed upon the flow of electrical current, the challenge in broadcasting was to do the same with energy waves in the **electromagnetic spectrum.** A simplified illustration of the broadcast transmission process is given in Figure 6.5.

When a radio **transmitter** is "on the air," it sets up a chosen **frequency** pattern of electromagnetic wave disturbances called the carrier frequency. When the transmitter conveys a message, an amplitude wave pattern (differing in power or strength) is imposed on this carrier wave. This is the message that travels to a broadcast receiver in **AM** (amplitude **modulation**) radio. In turn, a broadcast receiver tuned to the carrier frequency converts the wave pattern to an electrical one that "drives" a loudspeaker. Not all the disturbances can be extracted from this message wave. Such disturbances were the cause of the bothersome static that affected so much of early radio broadcasting. Modern electronics has allowed us to remove many of these unwanted aberrations.

FM (frequency modulation) radio involves the same links between broadcast transmitter and receiver as AM radio, except that, instead of imposing the message as an amplitude pattern on the carrier wave, it imposes it by varying the frequency.

The broadcast portion of television communication is the same as that of radio except that it requires much more signal space (**bandwidth**) in order to carry the more complex video signal along with the audio one. The audio portion of a television broadcast is simply FM radio at a particular assigned frequency for the television **channel.** Figure 6.6 illustrates the basics for transmitting the video portion of television.

Sending an image over a television circuit involves the following steps. The light on the image is focused through a camera lens onto the face of a light-sensitive tube. This tube is scanned by an electron beam, which registers for each tiny point on the screen the lightness or darkness of that point on the image. What is registered for each of these points is then translated into a broadcast pattern that is received by the television set. In the electronic circuitry of the television set, the lightness–darkness code of each of these points is fed into a picture tube beam, which "paints" an image on a phosphorous screen. Because the scan is so rapid, our eyes perceive the illusion of moving images.

Color television operates under the same general principle, except that the initial image is further divided into the colors red, blue, and green. The codings for these colors are transmitted with the image. As the picture is received and displayed on a color television set, the colors are generated by the scanning beams, which give the illusion of an overall colored image for the viewer.

Sound-Recording Devices as Media

Although we will not go into detail, devices like the phonograph, wire recorder, and tape recorder are also traditional media forms in some regards. Like the telephone and the telegraph, they date back to the nineteenth century. Recording devices allow us to capture a message (including music), and transport it for playback at some other time or place. We can consider them as mass

Early radio was mostly a signaling system, such as in communications between ship and shore stations. But by the 1920s, radio had caught on as a popular medium for entertainment and news. Magazines and newspapers of the period were filled with ads for radios of all shapes and sizes as they became a mass-marketed consumer product. Radio is now by far the world's number one public communications medium. *Historical Pictures Service, Chicago*

The Magnavox Reproducer and the Magnavox Power Amplifier

"These two devices have revolutionized Radio"

MAGNAVOX Radio equipment takes the feeble sound vibrations produced by your receiving set and builds them up into full, round tones in exact accordance with the original broadcasted speech or music.

The development of the Magnavox is one of Radio's spectacular achievements.

Magnavox R3 Reproducer and 2 stage Power Amplifier, as illustrated . . $90.00

R2 Magnavox Reproducer with 18-inch curvex horn; the utmost in amplifying power; requires only .6 of an ampere for field . $60.00

R3 Magnavox Reproducer with 14-inch curvex horn; ideal for homes, etc. $35.00

Model C Magnavox Power Amplifier insures getting the largest possible power input for your Magnavox Reproducer . . 2 stage $55.00
3 stage 75.00

Magnavox Products can be had from good dealers everywhere. Write for new booklet.

THE MAGNAVOX CO.
Oakland, Cal.
New York: 370 Seventh Ave.

MAGNAVOX Radio
The Reproducer Supreme

1864	James Clerk-Maxwell proposes a theory of electromagnetic radiation, eventually the basis for broadcasting.
1887	Heinrich Hertz provides experimental proof of Clerk-Maxwell's theory of electromagnetic energy.
1897	Guglielmo Marconi patents a practical device as a wireless telegraph that uses electromagnetic radiation.
1899	Wireless telegraph messages are sent across the English Channel.
1901	Wireless telegraph messages are sent across the Atlantic.

Figure 6.5
A Simplified Version
of Broadcast
Communication

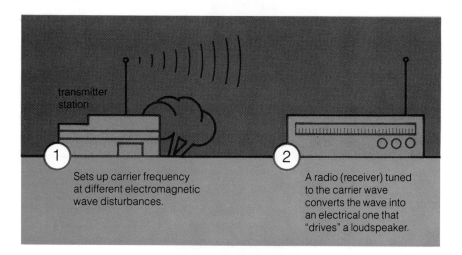

transmitter
station

1 Sets up carrier frequency
at different electromagnetic
wave disturbances.

2 A radio (receiver) tuned
to the carrier wave
converts the wave into
an electrical one that
"drives" a loudspeaker.

1905   Reginald Fessenden patents the heterodyne receiver. The heterodyne circuit is a basis for imposing patterns upon electromagnetic waves.

1906   Lee de Forest patents the Audion (vacuum) tube, a practical basis for encoding music or voice on electromagnetic waves.

1912   Sinking of the Titanic is monitored by wireless telegraphy and rebroadcast in New York by the young David Sarnoff (later founder of NBC).

1914–1918   World War I research accelerates the development of wireless telegraphy equipment.

1920   Radio receivers are sold to the public.

1924   A 22-station "network" carries a coast-to-coast hookup of a speech by President Calvin Coolidge.

1926   Television is demonstrated by John L. Baird in London.

1939   President Roosevelt opens the New York World's Fair on television.

1948   Bell Telephone laboratories develop the transistor, which makes small and inexpensive radio receivers possible.

Figure 6.6
The Basics of Television Broadcasting

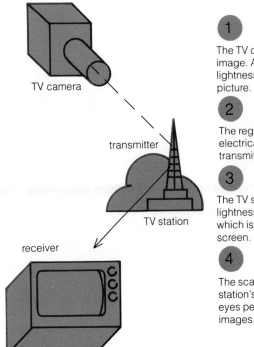

TV camera

transmitter

TV station

receiver

1 The TV camera is used to form an optical image. An electron beam registers lightness or darkness of the image into a picture.

2 The registered picture is converted to electrical signals that are amplified and transmitted by radio waves.

3 The TV set (receiver) reconstitutes the lightness or darkness code of the image, which is "painted" onto a phosphorous screen.

4 The scan of the electronic beam in the station's TV camera is so rapid that our eyes perceive an illusion of moving images.

media if we wish, since many recordings are produced in large quantities, are disseminated over wide areas, and are not usually directed to single individuals but to markets.

The technology of most traditional sound-recording devices is an analog storage of sound wave patterns etched onto a surface (as on a phonograph record) or magnetic patterns of metallic substances coated on plastic (as on tapes). Later in this chapter, we discuss some of the newest recording techniques, which convert sound patterns into binary codes (the 0 and 1 codes discussed in Chapter 3) for storage and replay.

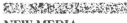

NEW MEDIA TECHNOLOGIES

New Technologies as Media Extensions

Just as we examined traditional media such as print, broadcasting, film, and wired communication as extensions of our basic senses and communication modes, so, too, can we examine the new media technologies as extensions. But there is a difference of degree. Whereas we usually think of the traditional media as communications systems involving components for encoding and decoding, the new media technologies are not usually entire systems in themselves. Instead they extend existing systems.

Take television, for example. If we look broadly at the flow of television from the producing organization to the home receiver, we see a variety of pathways over which the programs may travel. Many people assume that television simply comes over the airwaves from the broadcasting station to their home receiver. However, in many types of television this is not exactly the case. A network television program may travel over special wire or broadcast **microwave** links as it is distributed over the network to the member stations. It may travel by satellite communications. Or it may be distributed to broadcast stations simply by shipping it in videotape form (called "bicycling" in the trade) to the stations.

To get an overall view of the new technologies, we can compare them in somewhat the same way that we compared the traditional media. This comparison is in terms of the basic human communication modes they extend, including the recording and transmission bases involved. Table 6.4 summarizes these comparisons.

This table can be the basis for a few generalizations about the uses of new technologies in communications systems. Notice that these technologies generally provide new alternatives in either the recording or the transmission component of existing communications systems. For example, video cassettes or video disks are simply "stored" forms of television that can be transported and played at a time convenient to the viewer. Satellite communication is nothing more than another form of broadcasting (we will discuss the characteristics of this system in a later section). Digital radio or television is an alternative form for encoding the broadcast message for transmission in the electromagnetic spectrum. Similarly, teletext or videotext are alternative coding systems to simplify the transmission and display of textual information by broadcast or wire transmission, respectively. Cable television is simply a

Table 6.4 Characteristics of Selected Technologies

Type	What It Extends	Recording Basis	Transmission	Message Types
Cable TV	Sound, vision, voice	—	Wire	TV programs, music, text
Satellite	Sound, vision, voice	—	Broadcasting	TV programs, music, voice text
Videotape	Sound, vision, voice	Electromagnetic	Transportation	TV programs, movies
Video disk	Sound, vision, voice	Optical, binary	Transportation	TV programs, movies
Digital	Sound, vision	Electronic, digital	Wire, broadcasting	TV programs, music, voice text, data
Computer	Vision	Electromagnetic	Wire	Text, data, graphics
Videotext	Vision	—	Broadcasting	Text, graphics
Teletext	Vision	—	Wire	Text, graphics

substitute for traditional broadcast transmission. The computer is a storage and retrieval device. We will see, too, that the computer is also a component of many modern communications systems, including those in your own home.

When you think of these new technologies as extensions of old ones, you may begin to sense that they are not so radical as popular writers often make them out to be. Accordingly, when you read or hear some modern critic lamenting the assumed demise of the written word, you should now have a clearer basis for interpreting the arguments. For example, there is more textual material in our environment than ever before in history and the amount promises to increase. The difference is that this material may not always be in traditional paper-and-ink "print" form. It may be on the screen of your television set as a videotext or teletext or on the screen of your home computer as word processing. Or you may soon be "hearing" it, as a scanning device converts printed words into sounds for your convenience.

The effects of the new technologies on traditional media seem to be the same in one respect as the effects that newer media technologies have always had on those preceding (such as the effect of radio on newspapers or of television on radio). One medium never really replaces another. Instead, they tend to be used for different purposes. Telegraphy and the telephone did not do away with letter writing. Television did not do away with motion pictures. And it does not seem that all the new ways of recording and transmitting television programs will do away with broadcast television. But they are changing it.

Cable Distribution

The "cable" of **cable television** is not a new technology at all. It is simply a wire system that is capable of transmitting a variety of different program signals simultaneously (the transmission space, or bandwidth, of one television channel is a thousand times greater than that needed for one telephone circuit.) In essence, a cable system is a wired communication system of high capacity that flows from a central source (**head end**) via a major distribution cable (trunk) to neighborhood lines (**feeders**) and eventually to the line into the house (**drop**). Put more simply, a TV cable is designed to augment or to substitute for over-the-air distribution of television signals. The network of a typical cable system is illustrated in Figure 6.7.

If the TV system is "interactive," there is a single return line for every drop, which allows the household to communicate back to the cable TV service. Whereas the cable distribution from the head to the drops can carry many programs and services, the return line is of small capacity. A cable television system in Columbus, Ohio, QUBE, at one time allowed subscribers to send signals by pressing buttons on a keypad. Included were five buttons so subscribers could answer multiple-choice questions. QUBE's two-way service was unprofitable, however, so it was stopped.

Figure 6.7
A Typical Cable Televi-
sion Distribution
System

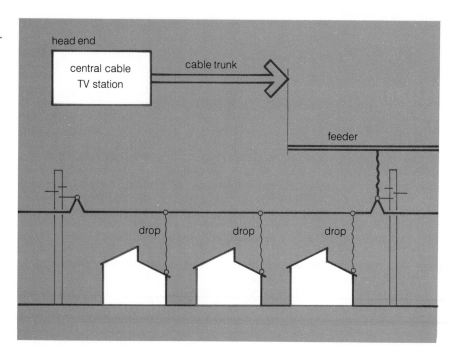

A cable TV system is different from a telephone network. In the latter, local telephones are connected to a central office (switch), where calls can be connected from one party to the other. This is a **public switched telephone network.** In contrast, cable television is not switched. It flows from an original distribution point to the receiving antennas of a cable TV operator, who redistributes it to households. One household cannot be connected to another under the current technology.

Many types of communications signals can be incorporated into a cable television network, including music channels, special information channels, and all types of text service. Further, systems that have an interactive capability can be used for remote shopping, banking, or fire, police, and medical emergency services. As discussed in Mitchell Moss's commentary, cable is changing the nature of the television business.

Satellite Communications

One of the disadvantages of traditional broadcast transmission is that electromagnetic waves travel in straight lines, which limits the distance that signals can be sent. We are able to send and receive some radio signals beyond line of sight because these signals can be "bounced" between the ionosphere and the earth over long distances. This reception varies according to the time

Mitchell L. Moss

Cable television started in small towns during the 1940s where the topography interfered with the reception of over-the-air broadcast signals. Cable grew slowly until the late 1970s, when the relaxation of federal rules governing cable and the advent of communications satellites and low-cost satellite receiving equipment led to the emergence of new cable networks and pay cable services. More than 40 percent of American television households subscribe to cable television, a figure that will soon exceed the 50-percent level.

The remarkable aspect of pay cable is the fact that it is generating a powerful set of alternatives to the major broadcast television networks, simply as a result of private sector initiatives without any deliberate policy-making. Pay cable's success has far overshadowed the development of public and community uses of cable, which were widely heralded in the early 1970s.

Advanced two-way services such as home banking, security alarms, meter reading, and electronic publishing are the next frontier for cable systems. Interactive cable refers to the subscriber's ability to input commands and receive a response from the system or from other subscribers on the system. The Warner-Amex QUBE system was an example of an interactive system in which computers scan all subscribers' terminals every few seconds to determine their status. Other interactive systems, such as Cox Cable's INDAX, use a full-sized alphanumerical keyboard and are capable of transaction services and information retrieval. Over the long run, linking the home computer to cable systems will be an important means of providing interactive services.

Cable systems will face increasing competition from a variety of technologies, such as direct broadcast satellites, subscription television, and multi-channel microwave distribution systems. These technologies do not provide two-way capability or the abundant number of channels that cable has, but they operate with fewer regulations and cost much less to build than technically sophisticated urban cable systems.

In the 1990s, most large American cities will be wired for cable. New urban systems with 100 + channels will pose serious challenges to cities and cable operators. How will this channel space be used? Who will control these channels? What will be the source of cable programming? What audience will programming serve? Will cable systems combine to provide public-access channels and facilities in a deregulatory policy environment? How will the individual's rights of privacy be protected if cable systems are capable of producing detailed records of household behavior?

Cable television is clearly in a state of transformation. It is changing from a medium that once provided improved television reception to rural areas into a telecommunications network capable of delivering a diversity of services to the nation's large metropolitan regions. The role that cable will ultimately occupy will depend on its ability to market new services to cable households, on the changing regulatory climate, and on the ability of cable operators to compete effectively in the marketplace with emerging technologies.

Mitchell L. Moss is Professor of Public Administration at New York University.

Suggested reading: M. L. Moss, ed. *Telecommunications and Productivity* (Reading, Mass.: Addison-Wesley, 1981).

---

of day, however, and it is also susceptible to weather conditions and other natural phenomena. Broadcast emissions in the high-frequency range are strictly line of sight. This is the type of broadcast wave that is the basis for microwave transmission. The satellite **dishes** you occasionally see on buildings or beside homes are microwave receivers (and sometimes also transmitters). A communications **satellite** is like a microwave dish in the sky. It receives signals, repowers them, and then retransmits them to earth. Figure 6.8 illustrates a satellite communications system.

Figure 6.8
A Simplified Version of a Satellite Communications System

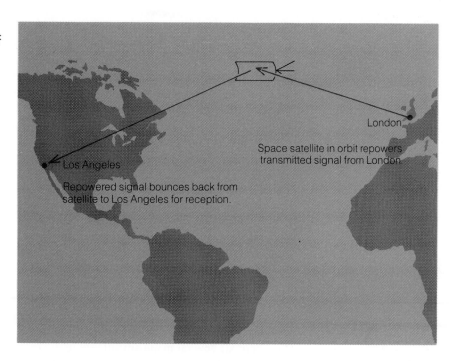

London.

Space satellite in orbit repowers transmitted signal from London.

Los Angeles

Repowered signal bounces back from satellite to Los Angeles for reception.

If a satellite is placed in an orbit 23,500 miles over the equator, it will appear "fixed" in space over that point, because it is orbiting at the same speed as the earth's rotation. The great advantage of such geosynchronous satellites is that earth stations do not have to have complicated mechanisms to track their movement across the sky (as all early satellites required).

The greater the retransmission power of the satellite, the smaller the associated earth stations can be. Over the years, earth stations have been reduced from the size of a large building (and a cost of millions of dollars) to ones you can now buy to put on your housetop. This reduction is possible because newer satellites are increasingly more powerful in their retransmission capabilities. Eventually, satellites could become powerful enough to allow us to have personal send-and-receive dishes no larger than our wristwatches.

Most satellites are capable of receiving and retransmitting more than one signal at a time. The equipment necessary for this process is called a **transponder.** Naturally, the more transponders there are, the more complicated as well as valuable the satellite communications system is.

One of the most desirable characteristics of satellites is that they do not have the extremely high cost that long-distance wired communication systems and even microwave systems have. Thus, satellites are inviting technologies for developing countries that do not have the resources to become fully wired (for example, many African countries). Another advantage of satellite communications systems is that their transmission frequencies can be much higher than surrounding traditional broadcast traffic, and thus more communications signals can be mixed in a given region. Finally—a fascinating factor in the future of electronic communications—once a satellite communications system is in place, the distance costs of transmission are irrelevant. For example, if you were operating a multinational company with satellite communications links between, say, the United States and London, your satellite transmission costs for a message from New York to London would be no different from those for one from New York to Jersey City!

Digital Technologies

Traditionally, the transmission of telephone, radio, and television signals has been in an **analog** form. *Analog* means that variations in the original sound or visual wave forms are transformed into related wave forms in electrical impulses on a wire or in electromagnetic disturbances in the air. This type of transmission requires a fixed amount of signal space even if part of the space is irrelevant to the message. Would it not be more efficient if only those portions of the wave forms transmitted were those critical for the transmission of the message, even in a high-fidelity form? This is one of the main advantages of so-called **digital transmission** (see Figure 6.9).

There are several major advantages to digital transmission. For one, less transmission space is involved in sending a particular message than is involved with the analog form. Also, by using technologies that further change the signal, it is possible to send several messages simultaneously in the same circuit or broadcast frequency. Finally, when messages are in digital form, if all are encoded in a similar way, it is possible to use computers to "read" them, to edit or further change them, or to automatically route them to their designated destinations. In all, there are so many advantages to transmitting messages digitally that we can expect most electronic forms of communication to move toward this type of transmission, a trend that some call "going digital."

The advantage of digital transmission of speech is that many voice transmissions can be compressed simultaneously into the same communications system. The sounds can be transmitted with a high fidelity that conveys more of the paralinguistic qualities than do traditional telephones. Eventually, telephone dialing signals and other administrative codes can be read directly by a computer, which will route the spoken message. Moreover, the digitally coded speech can be stored in the same computer memory with text and data.

Digitally encoded television (along with sound components) can be more distortion-free than analog transmission forms, and it can be much more easily routed over electronic networks that are designed for digital switching.

We can also use digital communications to place an "address" on messages so they can be automatically routed by computers through wire or broadcast networks to their destinations. With packet switching, it is possible

Figure 6.9
General Character-
istics of Digital
Communication

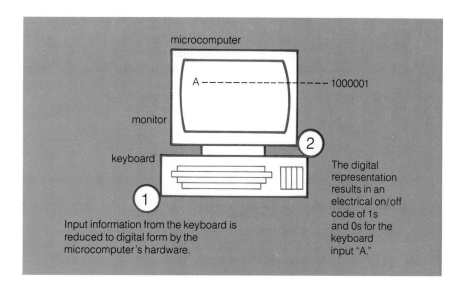

to have radio broadcasts in digital form that would be received and stored by a communications device only if they had a given digital address on them. In this way, it would be possible to fill the airwaves with digital information and to have our receiving devices pick out only the messages we wanted to receive. These messages could be information on the weather, traffic reports, stock market prices, or even our horoscope. Already, there have been feasibility studies about a worldwide personal communications network that would allow us to send and receive alphabetical and numerical messages on pocket-size devices.

Digital technologies have also revolutionized recording techniques. Earlier in this chapter, we examined the technology of magnetic recording. The wave patterns of sound are transferred analogously to magnetic patterns on a film tape. As you have probably already assumed, a videotape is simply an extension of this technique that also allows the storage of TV picture patterns. Recall how a TV image is produced by an electron beam scanning a phosphorous screen. A videotape pattern contains the patterns for this scanning and, therefore, image formulation.

Video disks use different techniques for recording and playback. One type has a device that "reads" electrical patterns in the microscopic grooves of a disk. These patterns are then transformed into sound and image. A more sophisticated type of video-disk recording technique stores the sound and picture information in a binary code on a pattern of ultramicroscopic dots embedded in plastic. A highly focused light (**laser**) is focused on the dots, some of which reflect light and others that do not. This reflection–no reflection binary pattern is then converted into images and sounds. One distinct advantage of this type of disk system is that each still frame of an image is stored in one "circle" (or revolution) of the disk. This makes it possible to store mixtures of still images, text, and moving images (and sounds, too). Perhaps you heard that an experimental version of the Sears Roebuck and Co. catalog has been tried in a disk format. (If you turned to swimming suits, you could see a model not only posing but walking around.)

Videotext and Teletext

The capability to encode text or even graphics of various kinds into a computer's memory and then retrieve them over a communications network is the basis for services now popularly known under such labels as **videotext** or **teletext.** Generally, videotext is an interactive information system that is distributed from a computer via a telephone network. In teletext, a specially equipped television set receives the textual information and stores it in an electronic memory. Then, at your command, "pages" of information can be displayed on your television screen. These terms, however, are undergoing change as new commercial systems are offered. Computer-based textual communications systems are also the basis for **electronic mail.**

Computing and Communications

An electronic **computer** is the prime example of a digital communications device. All the messages we give a computer, whether they be direct commands, programs for later execution, or data of some sort, are eventually converted into a digital communications code stored in the computer's memory. Even the programs that create the exciting sounds and graphics of video games are stored and executed forms of digital communications.

In a large computer system, the operator types information into a data terminal, which converts the keystrokes into digital electronic coded impulses that, in turn, are carried by wire transmission to the main computer. (This is what is happening at an airline counter when you make a flight reservation.) Or perhaps you own or have seen a personal computer in operation. You communicate directly, via the keyboard, with such a computer, whose main circuitry is incorporated right in the machine being operated. These small machines, too, convert your keystrokes into 0 and 1 patterns. If you know how to do it, you can communicate directly with any computer in this code. As you might guess, the code is called "machine language."

When computers communicate with one another over telephone lines, the message is sent in a special code. (The computer terminal at the airline counter is "wired" to a main computer, probably thousands of miles away.) Once the message is in the other computer system, it can be "decoded" into a visual or printed form. Perhaps you participate in services whereby you can connect your personal computer to your telephone and "call in" to a large

Figure 6.10
A Simplified Diagram of a Computer Communications System

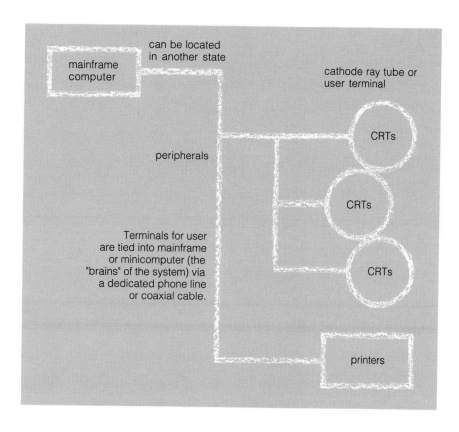

mainframe computer

can be located in another state

cathode ray tube or user terminal

peripherals

CRTs

CRTs

Terminals for user are tied into mainframe or minicomputer (the "brains" of the system) via a dedicated phone line or coaxial cable.

CRTs

printers

computer for information services: stock prices, news headlines, shopping tips, the weather, and travel or theater schedules. All such computer links are communications systems similar to any other communications medium. Figure 6.10 illustrates the major components of a computer communications system similar to those whose services affect you daily.

NEW TECHNOLOGIES IN OLD CONTEXTS

How Media Affect One Another

One of the fundamental generalizations that scholars often make about new media forms is that they seldom fully replace the old ones. Radio did not do away with the newspaper, as we have seen, but it changed some of what newspapers try to do. For example, newspapers cannot compete with radio for spot news. And television did not do away with newspapers, radio, or movies. But it certainly changed them. For example, some media critics claim that the newspaper *USA Today*, because of its color and brevity, is designed for the "TV generation."

Modern media technologies allow us to create our own psychological environments literally at a flick of a switch. With miniaturized tape cassettes you can listen to anything from hard rock to Beethoven while you skate, bike, jog, or wait in a line. Perhaps this equipment will become small enough so that you can shut out a boring class lecture. *S. Oristaglio/ Photo Researchers, Inc.*

Similarly, the new technologies do not seem to be doing away with the old. Our use of the entire range of communications media seems to be undergoing three general changes. First, we are using different media for more specialized purposes. Second, we are using some of the newer forms to give us combined capabilities for voice, image, and text in the same communications systems. Third, we are employing computers and digital encoding to automate many aspects of the transmission and formatting of messages.

Contemporary Applications

Much of the "new" communication is going on at the same old levels of everyday uses. We can analyze some of these uses in terms of the traditional levels of interpersonal, group, organizational, and public communication, as summarized in Table 6.5.

Table 6.5 New Technologies in Traditional Levels of Communication

Level	Traditional Form	Technology Application
Interpersonal	Face-to-face, mail, telephone	Video telephone; personal computer linkage; electronic mail; voicegrams
Group	Face-to-face	Telephone conference; teleconference; computer conference
Organizational	Face-to-face, memo, intercom, telephone, meetings	Telephone conference; electronic mail; computer-aided management; information system; facsimile
Public	Newspapers, magazines, books, television, radio, films	Videotape, video disk; cable TV; direct satellite TV; videotext, teletext; digital information systems

Notice how we can extend some of the qualities of personal communication in the point-to-point contexts of video telephone, electronic mail, and **teleconferences,** and even in personal computer links. For almost every illustration of how new technologies can be "depersonalizing" (and they certainly can be if not used properly), there are illustrations of how individuals can get into personal contact with one another without the need to be in physical contact. Sometimes they need not even be in the same time period. For example, as discussed later in Chapter 9, you can participate in computer conferences at any time of the day or night. You can check the accumulated reports of individual participants, add contributions of your own, suggest new agenda items, or send personal messages to other participants (and then go back to bed!).

For many years, organizations have sought communication channels that could expand the control of managers beyond their immediate office space or wherever they could travel. The telephone, telex, and mail systems have been invaluable in the past. But now the new technologies make it possible to have meetings in which participants join via telephone or video teleconference to complete their deliberations, thus saving travel expense and time. New office communications systems are increasingly integrating voice, text, and data communications into one system that you can operate at the flick of a switch, not only from your desk but also from home or from a hotel room (and for some, even from a phone booth). A business organization need no longer be centralized to have readily available opportunities for communications among its parts. The components of an organization can be as close as its **telecommunications** links. (Note in Rudy Bretz's commentary how new technologies could be extended even to handshakes!)

Rudy Bretz

The sense of touch is an important means of communication mainly in personal, affectionate, and intimate relationships. The exception to this is the handshake. The handshake is so important to social intercourse that the inability of individuals to use it at a distance is often considered a serious and permanent limitation of electronic communications—for example, in teleconferencing. But is a handshake really impossible? It may be that all the necessary technology for the "telehandshake" is now in existence. All that is needed is someone to pay the cost of development. I won't predict who will do this or when it will be done, but neither will I say it will not come to pass. By that time, large-screen, three-dimensional TV will already be in use for teleconferencing. A teleconference group will interact with life-size images of the distant participants as though they were real people across the table.

When people shake hands, they approach to within reach of each other, extend a hand, and look each other in the eye. Their hands meet, and they both "press the flesh," as President Johnson used to say. The hands meet at a point in space that is within a limited vertical and horizontal range. Within this window, in the plane of the teleconference screen, the designers will place a simulated hand. It will be warm and respond according to the exact movements sensed and transmitted by another such hand at the distant conference location. The spot for such introductions or greetings will be to the side of the conference table, where you can

approach to within reach of the screen, or within reach of whatever plane carries the image. The lasers that produce *your* image are hidden behind the screen. The hand will not be seen at either end of the line until both of you extend your hands in the usual fashion. Where your hand touches the image hand, the artificial hand will automatically appear in exact register, and you will seem to be shaking hands with the person in front of you. If he or she produces a weak or limp handshake, that is what you will feel. If the other person habitually squeezes enough to make people want to yelp, you will get this treatment here. And the hand will change size too, according to whether the respondent on the screen has a large hand or a small one.

Science fiction? Possibly, although anyone who has experienced the highly realistic patient simulators now used in medical training will probably agree that this is only a further step in an already amazing technology.

There are other questions, too. Can one person shake hands with many in many locations? Does this have implications for political campaigning? What values will there be to "touching" by telephone, aside from communication between those who lack one or both of the primary senses? And what will be the content of private phone calls, after holding hands by phone has become routine?

Rudy Bretz is well known for his book A Taxonomy of Media *(Englewood Cliffs, N.J.: Educational Technology Publications, 1971). He is currently Executive Vice President of the Bedacom Co., in Santa Clara, California. The major part of this commentary appears in his book* Media for Interactive Communication *(Beverly Hills, Calif.: Sage, 1983).*

Evolving technologies such as cable and satellite television systems are vastly expanding the number of alternative channels you can bring into your home. Added to these choices are alternatives available through the recorded television media of videotape and disk. No longer do you have to adhere to the broadcaster's schedule to watch your favorite program. You can have prime time, anytime. Traditional news services are being augmented with videotext and teletext services, which are especially useful for spot news, classified ads, and directory-type information services. The public-communication distribution system, because of the new technologies, is becoming increasingly personalized. As discussed in Chapter 10, we may be entering an era of "demassification" of our public media.

SUMMARY

Many of the choices that we make in sending or receiving communications involve the choice of a medium. A communications medium is the form of the message transmission. We come equipped with the *natural media* of sight, sound, touch, and smell. Primitive extensions of our natural media include the ways we have been able to "send" messages by such methods as writing, drawing, or sculpting. Most traditional media—print, wired communication, photography, broadcasting, and recording devices—represent differences in storage, transmission, or coding techniques.

Although print media may date back as far as A.D. 500 in China, most printing in the Western world was influenced by the invention of movable type by Johann Gutenberg. Wired communication was made possible mainly by the development of methods to generate and to control—and, hence, to encode—patterns of electrical current. Photography is a process whereby messages are recorded by different light intensities (and color variations) on a light-sensitive chemical surface. Broadcasting represents the capability of transforming sound patterns to patterns of *electromagnetic* radiation that a broadcast receiver converts back into sound patterns. The video portion of television is obtained by "sweeping" an electron beam across an image to encode the light-sensitive variations (and eventually colors). Many modern recording devices are based on an *analog* match between sound or picture patterns and variations in a recording medium. The latest techniques, however, convert these patterns to a numerical code, that is, to digital recording.

The new technologies of communications are extensions of the traditional media. They offer alternative means for the storage or transmission of voice, text, or images. Most of these technologies are a product of the convergence of advances in *telecommunications* and computer systems. Although the technologies are new, most of our uses of them are for traditional purposes of information, instruction, entertainment, and persuasion.

Cable television systems substitute a complex wired communications system for over-the-air broadcasting, making available many additional channels and services. The communications *satellite* is simply a relay station in the sky. It allows us to send broadcast signals inexpensively over long distances. *Digital transmission* is the conversion of voice or images into a numerical code that is much more efficient to transmit and route than traditional analog signals. New recording techniques allow us to combine sound, images, and text in highly compressed forms and on recording media that will not wear out. The *computer* is a digital communications device that we can also program to act on information we give to it. One major communications application is its use in *videotext* or *teletext* systems.

As has been the case with the introduction of most new media, the new technologies are not replacing, but are changing, how we use the traditional media.

TOPICS FOR DISCUSSION OR BRIEF PAPERS

1. Suppose that you were to plan a public-health campaign to provide middle- and upper-middle-class women between the ages of 20 and 50 more information about the dangers of mixing alcohol and tranquilizers. What medium or media would you use, and why?

2. The psychological aspects of the telephone, unlike those of most other communications media, have not been extensively studied. What are the main reasons for its use? How might people differ in their uses? What are your main uses? How would you classify the telephone—as public communication, personal communication, or what? Explain.

3. Do some research on one new technology (for example, cable TV, personal computers, communications satellites, video cassettes, video disks, videotext, teletext, digital broadcasting, or video games). What is available to purchase? What does it cost? What is coming up next? Look in your library for specialized periodicals in the fields of entertainment, information, and communications technology. Also, talk with vendors.

4. Imagine that you are a consultant who has been asked to write a description of how new technologies can be applied to one of the traditional communication contexts in Table 6.5. Do some research on what technologies are available. What will they do? How much will they cost? How do you get people to use them?

5. Take one side or the other in the debate about how technologies can "depersonalize" their users. Is the problem with the technologies or with how we use them? Are manufacturers and vendors "forcing" public acceptance, or is the public actively looking for new types of communication? What are the long-range social consequences?

REFERENCES AND READINGS

Bretz, R. *Media for Interactive Communication*. Beverly Hills, Calif.: Sage, 1983.

Dordick, H. S. *Understanding Modern Telecommunications*. New York: McGraw-Hill, 1986.

Greenberg, B. S. "Person-to-Person Communication in the Diffusion of News Events." *Journalism Quarterly* 41:489–494 (1964).

McLuhan, M. *Understanding Media*. New York: McGraw-Hill, 1964.

Pelton, J. *Global Talk*. Brighton, England: Harvester Press, 1981.

Rice, R. E. *The New Media*. Beverly Hills, Calif.: Sage, 1984.

Singleton, L. A. *Telecommunications in the Information Age*. Cambridge, Mass.: Ballinger, 1983.

Toffler, A. *The Third Wave.* New York: Morrow, 1980.

Wicklein, J. *Electronic Nightmare: The New Communications and Freedom.* New York: Viking Press, 1981.

Williams, F. *The Communications Revolution.* New York: New American Library, 1983. (Also Beverly Hills, Calif.: Sage, 1982.)

Williams, F. *Technology and Communication Behavior.* Belmont, Calif.: Wadsworth, 1987.

Williams, F., R. E. Rice, and E. M. Rogers. *Research and the New Media.* New York: Free Press, 1988.

PART
THREE

Levels of Communication

Strategies and patterns of human communication vary in different social environments. In the next four chapters, we examine communication at the individual, group, organizational, and public levels. Although we contrast behaviors across these environments, we also emphasize that much of human communication is a mix of these levels and that our behavior in any one level is usually influenced by others. The purpose of these chapters is to introduce you to the analysis of human communication relative to the basic social contexts that are often used to divide the field for study.

Henry Moore's *Family Group,* 1948–49 (page 138). Bronze, 59¼″ × 46½″; at base × 29⅞″. Collection, The Museum of Modern Art, New York, A. Conger Goodyear Fund.

Individual Communication

COMMUNICATION ON THE INDIVIDUAL LEVEL

The *individual* communicator is the most fundamental level in the analysis of human communication. Some of our most important communication takes place at this level. It is this level that enters into the more complex levels of group, organizational, and public communication. Among the key characteristics of individual communication are whether it is personal or impersonal, its transactional qualities, and its use for developing personal relationships. When communication on this level is personal and transactional, it is a means for forming a social relationship among individuals. This process is often called **interpersonal, or relational, communication** (the topic of research such as that described in Chapter 11).

Impersonal or Personal?

For most of us, no form of communication exceeds in amount and importance the daily exchanges we have with others. Many of these exchanges are *impersonal* conversations that we use to pursue our simple needs, ranging from saying hello to a passing stranger to ordering an airline ticket. In such communications, we pay little attention to the detailed personality or needs of the other individuals. We interact with them in their roles as sales clerk, waitress, or passer-by giving us directions. This type of communication is impersonal in that we do not get to know the other person. Nor do we need to know him or her.

In contrast, as mentioned above, individual communication can be the highly *personal* form we use to build social relationships. In this process, we exchange information about our personal selves. We begin to learn about each other's personal needs and address our communications accordingly. This is the communication that leads to friendships and, in some cases, to marriages. In interpersonal communication, we address the other person not mainly in his or her role as a student, clerk, boss, or employee but more as a unique individual. For example, if you date a person to whom you are attracted, you are less concerned with that person's social role at the moment (student, for example) than you are with him or her as an individual. This type of person-oriented, one-to-one communication is the topic of this chapter.

Table 7.1 summarizes the major contrasts between impersonal and interpersonal communication. Examine it briefly before reading the next section, on the nature of personal influence. Notice that personal communication does not necessarily have to be face-to-face. The telephone, for example, can be a very personal medium of communication. So can letters. People are sometimes frustrated with new technologies when they seem to be impersonal, as with a computer-generated form letter.

Transactional?

Interpersonal, or relational, communication is much more two-way, or interactive, than impersonal communication. As we exchange communications that are sensitive to each other's personal needs and interests, our interaction

Table 7.1 Contrasts between Personal and Impersonal Communication

Characteristics	Impersonal Communication	Personal Communication
Context	Face-to-face situations, telephone conversations, one-to-one mail correspondence, and possibly computer or video telephone conferences or any other new one-to-one communications links.	
Motives	Usually communication to accomplish some short-term objectives, such as making a purchase, asking questions, commenting simply on something, formal on-the-job orders, cocktail party chatter, or simple requests.	Although communication may at first be directed toward a simple task, the reasons for such communication may either now or later involve deeper, important human motives.
Orientations	The other person may be seen mainly as embodying a social or cultural stereotype or as acting in some practical role (for example, clerk). Communication is to the role rather than to the individual.	Communication is directed to the other person as a distinctive individual. Personal motives are identified and appealed to.
Personal information	Superficial information is involved—only what is needed to maintain the communication. Usually this is not personal information.	Gaining further information is a critical part of the process. It is the basis for creating personal motivation.
Temporal pattern	This is mainly an "at-the-moment" type of communication. Although individuals may communicate again and again at different times, the relationship from one time to the next is not necessarily one of "development." Communication is more an instance of exchange than it is a step in the development of an interpersonal relationship.	Time is necessary for the individuals to learn about one another if the interpersonal relationship is to develop. Each successive situation can be a step in the growth or phase of an interpersonal relationship.

has the form of a *transaction.* We appeal specifically to the motives of the other person and invite him or her to understand ours. There is a give and take to the interaction, an exchanging of personal information and a building of a social relationship. We can try to negotiate until we have a mutual satisfaction of personal motives. By contrast, much of our impersonal communication is one-way or barely transactional. The study of transactionalism in communication has been a major focus in modern communication theory, as you can see from the commentary by Gerald Miller.

The main positive effect of interpersonal communication is the development of close human relationships, ones based on trust, respect, shared motives, and even love. Every friendship is a product of the process of interpersonal communication. Much of our personal and professional success in life is dependent on our ability to understand, cooperate with, and influence the people around us. Interpersonal communication is the key to personal success. It is the most distinctly human of all of the levels, or contexts, of communication.

Gerald R. Miller

People ordinarily talk about communication as a unidirectional activity where one party exerts some effect on the other—for example, Sally convinced Margo to quit smoking. Moreover, when an effect is observed, its occurrence is typically accounted for by offering one of two explanations. The first is environmental pressures: all of Margo's friends had urged her to quit, and Sally's message provided the last little shove. The other explanation is actor intent: after thinking about Sally's arguments, Margo decided it would be best for her to quit smoking.

As used by students of communication, terms such as *transactional* and *transactionalism* describe the communication process differently from the way it is pictured in the preceding paragraph. In one sense, the phrase *a transactional perspective* labels a viewpoint which argues that communication should be treated as a relational phenomenon, rather than as a process of individual action and reaction. Thus, when seeking to understand how Sally and Margo *reciprocally* influence each other in their symbolic exchanges, transactionalism holds that their relationship, not their individual behaviors, is the relevant unit of analysis.

Communication scholars who are guided by this viewpoint treat communication as a serial exchange of messages. Rather than using a single message as a starting point and recording the response to that message, these scholars code sequences of exchanged messages, using these message "strings" to draw inferences about the nature of the relationship in which the parties are socially embedded. For instance, if Sally consistently sends "one-up" messages—that is, messages seeking to establish control over Margo's actions—and Margo consistently transmits "one-down" messages—that is, messages indicating that she accepts and defers to Sally's controlling attempts—the relationship is characterized as complementary, with Sally in the one-up, or dominant, position. By contrast, if the message string contains a large number of matched pairs, such as one-up–one-up or one-down–one-down, then the relationship is described as symmetrical, with both parties manifesting similar amounts of relational power.

A second meaning for transactionalism holds that people's communicative activities can best be understood by taking into account both the influence of the environment on the actor and that of the actor on the environment. Explanations that rely solely on environmental pressures or actor intent are incomplete. Thus, in order to understand why Margo quit smoking after being exposed to Sally's persuasive message, it is necessary to take account jointly of all the relevant factors affecting Margo and Margo's own intentions and motivational states.

Scholars who espouse this viewpoint are likely to design studies that incorporate both relevant environmental and actor variables. Most of the prior work in areas such as persuasion makes use of this mixed conceptual model.

Why all the sound and fury about conceptual topics such as transactionalism? The goals of most communication researchers are explanation, prediction, and control of communicative behaviors. In pursuit of these objectives, a great deal of *metatheoretical* ("theory about theory") debate ensues, that is, debate about the most useful paradigms for studying communication. Proponents of either of these transactional perspectives contend that their approach is more useful than other alternatives. As is usually the case, only time and future scholarship will determine whether they are right. For the moment, it is sufficient to say that transactionalism, in each of its two senses, exerts a strong impact on contemporary communication research.

Gerald Miller is Professor of Communication at Michigan State University.

Suggested reading: G. R. Miller and M. Steinberg, *Between People: A New Analysis of Interpersonal Communication* (Chicago: Science Research Associates, 1975).

Interpersonal Communication via the Media

Although most interpersonal communication takes place in face-to-face contexts, it can develop under other conditions. The next closest contexts are extensions of the one-to-one context, as in the case of telephone calls or the personal exchange of letters or any other type of correspondence. It is quite possible for interpersonal communication to develop in a group context, although the basic transaction still takes place only between individuals.

Obviously, other media can impose restrictions on the process of interpersonal communication. For example, the telephone denies us the exchange of symbols of the nonverbal, visual code. If we cannot see how a person is reacting to our conversation, it is more difficult for the interpersonal communication process to develop. Yet we can also make a telephone conversation very personal. We compensate for the lack of visual emotional cues by using our vocal (paralinguistic) ones. (In training telephone receptionists, it is sometimes said that they should sound as if they are smiling when they answer calls.) Also, we may compensate for the restrictions of the medium by using language that is especially personal. Finally, because a telephone conversation can be thought to be highly private, it aids in developing the interpersonal process.

The psychologist John Short and his colleagues (1976) have made an extensive study of how different telecommunications media affect what they call "social presence." This concept is equated with feelings that a communications experience is "sociable," "sensitive," "warm," or "personal." To the degree that a medium restricts nonverbal cues, is not interactive, or may be public, it will lessen one's feelings of social presence. Yet we can compensate for such restrictions by our language styles and the degree to which we focus our communication upon the individual needs of the other person. Even interaction over a computer message system can have a degree of personal quality (see the commentary by Ronald Rice in Chapter 8).

Influences of the Media

Our uses of face-to-face interpersonal communication can influence our uses of television, radio, newspapers, or other forms of public communication. For example, a conversation with others may create for us an interest in finding out more from the media about a particular topic. We might be interested in reading a newspaper article about a new music group that everybody is talking about.

This relation also works in the opposite direction. We may find that something we have seen or heard in the media, such as a movie, is an interesting topic for conversation.

Also, it has been known for many years that how the media influence our attitudes and behaviors is closely tied to interpersonal communication. For example, we may follow a political candidate in the newspapers and on television, but how we cast our vote will be further influenced by conversations we have about what we read or see. (This is called the "two-step flow theory" and we discuss it in Chapter 12.)

For many years, interpersonal and public communication have been studied separately. But as the media theorist Wilbur Schramm (1982), among others, has maintained, we can never thoroughly understand the effects of the mass media until we know how their uses interact with people's daily conversations about what they read and hear. And we cannot understand the nature of media organizations until we study how people working and communicating interpersonally manage to create such media forms as newspapers, magazines, books, television and radio shows, records, or movies.

COMPONENTS OF THE INTERPERSONAL COMMUNICATION PROCESS

You can look to your own experiences for examples of the process of interpersonal communication. Think of a friend who has been especially close to you. Be sure this is somebody with whom you have shared personal confidences, particularly a person whom you grew to trust. With this person firmly in mind, try to answer the following questions:

1. Where did you first meet this individual?

2. What attracted you to him or her?

3. What motivated you to get to know the person better?

4. Did you consider the other person as a "general type" (for example, student, man, housewife, child) or as an individual?

5. How did you learn what was of most personal interest to the other individual? Was he or she willing to share information?

6. How did you come to trust that individual?

7. How did you manage to maintain the relationship? How did you accommodate any ups and downs?

In answering these questions, you have touched on at least seven components of the developmental process of interpersonal communication. Let us examine these in a bit more detail.

1. Proximity

In order for interpersonal communication to develop, something must have brought you in contact with the other person. Usually, this is some factor of **proximity.** That is, some circumstances brought you into face-to-face contact with each other. You are physically in the same place. But it is possible for contact to develop initially when a communications medium such as the telephone, an exchange of letters, or perhaps even seeing a person's picture in a photo album has been the basis for a type of proximity.

Ironically, and probably among the factors that keep life interesting, many of the individuals with whom we will develop close interpersonal relationships we meet only by chance. We may sit next to them in class, meet them at a party, or work with them on the job. Sometimes we meet them because some third party brings us together for one reason or another. We seldom set out intentionally to find specific individuals with whom we wish to develop interpersonal relationships. We may wish for it, but we seldom do it. Most of our relationships start as chance encounters. (At the 25th anniversary of my high school graduation class, my best friend from high school days reminded me that we met as freshmen when we had mistakenly been assigned to the same locker.)

But simply meeting another individual does not necessarily lead to an interpersonal communication process. Additional steps are involved.

2. Attraction

In the last several decades, we have learned much from research about the psychology of attraction. Why is it that when you first meet people, you often have definite attitudes about whether you want to get to know them better? The answer may be **personal attraction.**

In the most general terms, we know that humans carry around attitudes that may immediately influence their perception of another individual. Although persons usually cannot explain all of their likes and dislikes, their attitudes consistently influence whether they are attracted to others. Most of these attitudes fit into **social stereotypes.** These are our ways of classifying other people.

Among our stereotypes are types of people we would like to know better, would like to have as friends, would like to be seen with, or even would like to have as mates. Some of the stereotypes, with characteristics that individually or in combination may attract us, include:

individuals who appear to be "good looking" ("beautiful," "handsome") according to the standards of our social group

members of the opposite sex whose characteristics (physical attributes, personality, behavior) fit our sexual interest

individuals who seem to merit the attention and praise of others, whose success seems to be recognized

people who we feel are like us or "in the same boat," who may be undergoing what we are undergoing

individuals who resemble people we already know and like

individuals who seem identifiable with family members (such as a father image)

Obviously, there are exceptions and contradictions to these varieties of stereotypes that often influence interpersonal attraction. A person may not fit any of these categories yet greatly arouse your curiosity. Although we do not like to admit it, there are also dimensions of attraction based on attitudes held among ethnic and cultural groups, as well as within them. But despite the many exceptions and the complexity of attraction, nearly any individual who is presented to another (even as a picture), will probably stir up attitudes of attraction or nonattraction.

The psychology of attraction spills over into the selection of individuals who populate our mass media. It is no accident that leading men and women in the movies fit, if not strongly influence, the standards for physical attractiveness of society. Advertising is not populated with the images of "plain" people (unless there is a point to be made about them). Even television newscasters are often selected, and sometimes audience-tested, for their attractiveness. (Beauty may be only skin deep, but it pays off in many parts of the communications business.)

A person's attractiveness, along with other factors, may stimulate the interpersonal communication process. If it does not, there are other factors that may still motivate the process.

3. Contextual Motives

Beyond factors of physical proximity and personal attraction, there can be relatively direct motives for getting to know another person better. Perhaps the two of you have been assigned as roommates. Maybe you have been told that a person would be somebody you "would really like to get to know," so you are motivated to give it a chance.

Similarly, it is a lack of motive, or a negative motive, that prevents many of our everyday encounters with others from developing to the interpersonal level of communication. Take a sales clerk, for example. You could be in physical proximity and the person could be most attractive, but your relative roles of clerk and customer to some degree dictate an impersonal relationship. If, for some reason, your conversation with the clerk did move to the interpersonal level, then the two of you would also be abandoning the clerk and customer roles. Probably for this same reason, managers are sometimes told to get to know their workers but not to get "too personal" with them. If they get to know each other too well, then the authority relationship may be weakened. As a consequence, conversation between a manager and a worker often stays on a relatively formal and impersonal level.

In brief, then, whether communication moves to an interpersonal level depends in part on the presence of motives to do so—or not to do so.

4. Individual versus Stereotypical Orientation

Although the other person may be seen first by you as a stereotype (middle-age male manager, young housewife, graduate student, college athlete), you will have to relate to that person as an individual if interpersonal communication is to develop. And the other person will have to develop a similar individualized orientation toward you.

In the clerk–customer and manager–worker examples given previously, many different individuals could play out their respective roles, and the conversations would probably be somewhat similar. When we converse with a person mainly in terms of the roles involved, we are dealing in stereotypes, and the characteristics of the exchange are often predictable from the motives that usually go along with the roles. For example, a sales clerk will try to "sell." Yet if each of the persons in those roles were to communicate about a topic of personal importance, the conversations would not be all that similar, because a great variety of individual motives would be involved.

As humans, we all have motives. But each of us is unique in terms of what configuration of motives is most important to us at the moment. Part of the process of interpersonal communication is an orientation to individual rather than to role or general stereotype motives. Are you talking to that person as an individual or in terms of the role he or she is fulfilling? Family or marriage counselors often make the point that when a husband and wife concentrate their communication upon their respective roles rather than upon each other as individuals, the relationship is destined for trouble. "Two roles cannot love each other!"

If you try to orient your conversation to the other person as an individual, you are initiating the process of interpersonal communication.

5. Sharing Information

Communication cannot move to the interpersonal level unless the individuals involved gain information about each other. How can communication be directed toward an individual's personal motives unless those motives become known? This necessitates openness and an agreement to share personal information, a critical part of the interpersonal transaction process.

Often, the revelation of personal information or the raising of personal questions communicates much more than the item itself. It communicates that you have a personal interest in the other individual, and it invites a similar response.

However, the degree of how open you should be in revealing information about yourself is a subject of theoretical controversy, as you can read in the commentary by Arthur Bochner.

6. Developing Trust

As communication moves to an interpersonal level and you transact shared information, attitudes, and motives, you are also usually developing confidence that the relationship is mutually beneficial. That is, you expect the other person to respect your motives, and to be predictably "looking out for you" as well as for himself or herself. You do not expect that your developing personal relationship will be used against you. This is the development of trust, and it is the mark of an evolving interpersonal relationship.

Arthur P. Bochner

One of the fundamental problems of social life is determining when to reveal and when to conceal private information. Is it better to be open, spontaneous, and direct? Or is it wiser to hold back, show discretion, and be tactful? Most of us can recall times when we regretted what we said because our words hurt somebody's feelings. Conversely, we can also recall instances when we felt guilty because we lacked the courage to express ourselves candidly.

Studies focusing on interpersonal communication draw a sharp contrast between two ends of the continuum of interaction: openness versus closedness, or frankness versus restraint. In the 1960s many writers championed the cause of open communication. They summoned their many followers to "tell it like it is," "let it all hang out," and "do your own thing." Sidney Jourard, who pioneered research on self-disclosure, regarded expression without reserve as the ideal for all interpersonal relationships.

In principle, the ideal of open communication is difficult to challenge. Children are brought up to believe that honesty is the best policy. But they are also taught to be sensitive to the feelings and thoughts of other people. Most of us can think of instances when telling the truth is insensitive because it hurts the other person. There are other occasions when we withhold information to protect ourselves, because we don't want to lose our job or our friends. The practical situations that confront us in everyday life make it difficult indeed to establish uncomplicated rules about when to reveal and when to conceal.

Thus, social life poses a fundamental dilemma of communication that faces all of us. We must show that we are honest and trustworthy individuals, *and* we must demonstrate that we respect the rights of others. Sometimes these two requirements are contradictory. How can one show ample respect for the other without a certain measure of restraint? On the other hand, how can one maintain a sense of trustworthiness without sharing private thoughts and feelings? Our chances of sustaining a satisfying relationship often rest on whether we know where and when to draw the line between disclosure and secrecy. Research on this subject suggests that it is better to err on the side of self-restraint than on the side of self-disclosure. Still, it is important to remember that the door may swing shut from either direction: If we share too much, we may find ourselves with nothing stimulating left to share, but if we don't share enough, we may ultimately find ourselves too detached to share anything at all.

Arthur P. Bochner is Professor and Chair of the Department of Communications at the University of South Florida.

Suggested readings:
Arthur P. Bochner, "On the Efficacy of Openness in Close Relationships," in *Communication Yearbook 5*, ed. M. Burgoon (New Brunswick, N.J.: Transaction Books, 1982), pp. 109–124.

Sidney M. Jourard, *The Transparent Self* (New York: Van Nostrand, 1964).

Abraham Maslow, the psychologist whose theory of motivation we discussed in Chapter 4, gave **trust** a central role in his conception of psychological growth. People who cannot gain the trust of others are denied the chance to develop close interpersonal relationships, which in turn restricts their ability to fulfill such basic belongingness and love needs as affiliation, acceptance, and affection, or esteem needs such as competence, approval, or recognition.

Similarly, people who cannot trust others are also hampered in psychological growth. According to Maslow, they tend to be guided more by fear

Interpersonal communication is our most fundamental and powerful form of communication. As we increasingly come to share personal information with another individual, we develop trust. People who have strong interpersonal relationships are usually perceived as especially trustworthy. *Laimute Druskis/Jeroboam, Inc.*

of betrayal than by potential rewards of interpersonal relationships. Also, they are denied fulfillment of psychological needs that require the cooperation of others. They tend to become very "closed" and isolated. Trust, in Maslow's reasoning, is essential to psychological health and growth.

Trust seems sufficiently important to interpersonal communication that we often make very significant initial judgments of other people on the basis of first impressions. Often, trust can be influenced by nonverbal cues of voice, gestures, and facial expressions. These cues are often more potent as suggestions of untrustworthiness. Some negative cues in U.S. culture include:

> failure to maintain eye contact
> shifty eyes
> nervous gestures, tics (facial movements), shakiness
> stammering
> a flabby handshake
> a strained or quivering voice
> sweating (including a sweaty palm in a handshake)

Some of the nonverbal qualities identified with trust are similar to the characteristics that influence interpersonal attraction, including physical attractiveness. Also, you can easily see how the apparent characteristics of trust are used in mass media stereotypes. Criminals are often portrayed by actors who are physically unattractive and who can exhibit many of the nonverbal cues of untrustworthiness.

Trust itself is an integral component of the interpersonal communication process. The process cannot develop without it. If trust is seriously violated, whatever level of interpersonal communication has been reached may be lost and possibly irretrievable.

7. Resolving Conflict

Interpersonal communication requires special attention to its maintenance. No relationship is without potential conflict, and it is not the probability of conflict that threatens relationships as much as the inability to resolve it. Perhaps you have heard that "good relationships are sometimes stormy." That is because conflict is brought out into the open. The problem occurs when conflict is suppressed. In practical terms, the process of interpersonal communication requires a capability for conflict resolution.

Conflict can arise from a great variety of specific problems, but these often reflect general categories. For purposes of illustration, here are several of the categories:

Conflict over motives. Because two humans can never have precisely the same set of beliefs and attitudes, it is understandable that what is desirable for one may be less than desirable for the other. (A wife may want to go to a Monday night concert, a husband to watch football on TV.)

Misperceptions. Individuals who frequently communicate and know each other well are apt to take many meanings for granted. One individual may so expect the other one to act in a certain way ("Scott is always on time") that it is difficult to comprehend exceptions to the behavior ("Scott be late? You're kidding. . . . Maybe he doesn't love me anymore").

Desire for false harmony. Two individuals give such priority to getting along well and proving to everybody how well they get along that they will do anything to avoid a conflict—even if it means pretending that a conflict does not exist.

Problems of the balance of authority. In most relationships, individuals work out an informal set of assumptions about the balance of authority. A husband may defer to his wife regarding household decor, whereas the wife may go along with his choice of a family automobile. Problems could arise when the husband wants to decorate his new study or the wife decides she also needs a car.

Maintenance of the interpersonal communication process in such situations is largely a process of conflict resolution. This involves (1) an agreement that both parties value a solution to the conflict more than being "right" themselves or maintaining a false harmony; (2) a willingness to define the conflict as rationally as possible, including differences in motives and problems due to misperceptions; (3) cooperation in identifying a range of possible solutions; and (4) an agreement beforehand to accept the solution that is the most beneficial (or least offensive) to *both* parties.

CHARACTERISTICS OF EFFECTIVE INTERPERSONAL COMMUNICATORS

Some people are better interpersonal communicators than others. Why is this? Certain characteristics seem to be present in the behaviors of successful interpersonal communicators. These include a positive self-concept, positive assertiveness, open-mindedness, the ability to feel empathy, and the ability to employ persuasive strategies. Why not think of your own successes (or failures) in interpersonal communication as we briefly examine these characteristics of effective interpersonal communicators.

Positive Self-Concept

Despite the frequency with which we see the term *self-concept* in popular as well as psychological textbook literature, there are really no fully agreed-upon scientific definitions of the term. Nevertheless, it is clear from the psychology of interpersonal relations that individuals who have positive concepts of who they are (or who they think they would like to be) are in a better position to manage their relations with others.

Self-concept does not necessarily mean a single view of self. And it is not necessarily a consistent view. We may have one concept of who we think we are. We may have another concept of who we think person A feels we are. Still another may be of who we think person B feels we are. Added to all these may be the additional concept of who we would like to be.

Nonetheless, it would be difficult if not impossible to plan or control our communications with others without making some personal assumptions about one or the other of these selves. We use these assumptions as a basis for negotiating our relations with others.

Positive Assertiveness

Whether in its more popular or more conservative clinical definitions, *assertiveness* means that we are willing to make an effort to get another person to believe or do what we want. This is the opposite of an individual who leaves relations with others in the other person's hands, or to chance or fate.

A distinction is often made between positive and negative assertiveness. Positive assertiveness is our willingness to act toward another person in ways that will be maximally beneficial to the two of us. This is the attempt to create "you win, I win" situations. Conversely, negative assertiveness is typically called aggression. This is the attempt to shape the behavior of others to our own ends whether or not the ends will be beneficial to that other person.

The person who is positively assertive will have a strong personal orientation toward other individuals and will attempt to identify their needs and values so as to be able to create maximally beneficial situations.

Open-Mindedness

Openness often refers to the distinction between a person's being closed- as opposed to open-minded. Closed-minded individuals tend to see situations and people in only one way (tunnel vision). They are not open to the suggestion of alternatives and will either shun them or simply fail to understand them. By contrast, an open-minded individual is able to see alternatives in situations, is willing to invite alternative suggestions, and has the ability to assess the alternatives.

Ability to Feel Empathy

Empathy is the ability not only to sense but also to feel the emotions of others. In a sense it is the ability to be in the other person's shoes. Empathy, in part, is an imaginative process. It may involve the ability to role-play, to project, or to react emotionally as another person would in a given situation. There are good reasons to believe that empathy is itself a communication skill. That is, we can learn to recognize certain cues in other individuals that will give us a basis for sensing that individual's deeper feelings. Many of these are the nonverbal cues of vocal and gestural expression.

It is also important to think of empathic communication as a transactional process. That is, we may not sense the full emotions of the other people simply upon perceiving one set of cues. Communication may have to go through a variety of give-and-take exchanges before we can personally sense how the other individual feels.

It is also important in empathic communications to be able to distinguish one's own emotions from those of others. An individual learns to avoid the generalization that everyone reacts emotionally the same way. In part, then, empathy is also based upon information gathering about the motives and values of the other individual, including personality factors. You cannot empathize with another person simply by assuming that they are reacting to a situation in the same way you are.

Ability to Use Persuasive Strategies

Most of the preceding characteristics of effective interpersonal communicators set the stage for personal influence. If you know what you want (self-concept), realize that you must positively opt for it (assertiveness), understand that different alternatives may be involved (open-mindedness), and sense which of the person's deeper feelings may influence actions (empathy), you are then in a position to persuade. This means that you are now able to use strategies of influence that will relate most directly to the needs and values of the other individual.

As discussed in Chapter 5, we can consider strategies of influence in terms of balance theories—that is, creating communications that another person will see as attractive because of the promise of harmony among the factors involved. We can further distinguish the types of motivation, whether generally positive or negative. Or perhaps the persuasive strategies can be interpreted in terms of expectancy-value theory, where the other individuals are promised personal reward and social approval for the belief or action.

The point is that some of us are better than others in employing the strategies of persuasion. Yet, because all of the characteristics of the effective interpersonal communicator are learned ones, it is possible for virtually every person to improve upon their use of this type of communication.

Try it.

SUMMARY

Personal communication focuses on the specific motives and needs of individuals, whereas impersonal communication relates more to the social roles of the individual involved. Highly personal exchanges between individuals, or interpersonal communication, is interactive, or *transactional*, and is the basis for the development of interpersonal relationships.

Personal and impersonal communication are often mixed and can occur in a variety of ways, including via telephone or mail. Often, interpersonal communication can reflect the influence of what has been experienced in the mass media, or the results of a conversation can influence what a person would look for in the media. All communications media, to some extent, can have a personal quality even though there are restrictions upon transaction and nonverbal symbols.

Interpersonal communication is an ongoing process for which we can observe at least seven components: (1) proximity; (2) *personal attraction*, including *social stereotypes;* (3) contextual motives; (4) individual versus stereotypical orientation, (5) sharing information; (6) *trust*, and (7) resolving conflict.

Effective interpersonal communicators have a positive self-concept, use positive assertiveness, are open-minded, and have the abilities to feel *empathy* and to use persuasive strategies.

Make up for
Dyad-Recit.

TOPICS FOR DISCUSSION OR BRIEF PAPERS

1. Prepare a brief history of an interpersonal relationship. Reflect the components of the interpersonal communication process in your description. Compare your history with those of others. What generalizations might you make?

2. What characteristics of people are personally attractive to you? List them, and compare your list with others. What do you think is personally attractive about yourself? Would your best friend agree with you? What characteristics of attraction do you think you could improve?

3. How much social presence do you communicate over the telephone? Get a friend to find an individual who does not know you and have him or her listen to you on the telephone. How would the individual rate you in terms of sociability, sensitivity, warmth, and "personalness"? What might you do to improve your ratings on these dimensions?

4. Think about interpersonal relationships that you or the other person ended. (You could still be friends, but not close ones.) How did it end? What communication, if any, was involved? How could you have kept the relationship going if you had wanted to? Compare your answers with those of others.

5. How would you rate yourself on the characteristics of effective interpersonal communication? Which could you improve upon and how? Have a friend rate you on these also; then compare the results.

REFERENCES AND READINGS

Anderson, N. H. "Likableness Ratings of 555 Personality-Trait Words." *Journal of Personality and Social Psychology* 9 (1968):272–279.

Barnlund, D. C. *Interpersonal Communication: Survey and Studies.* Boston: Houghton Mifflin, 1968.

Knapp, M. I. *Interpersonal Communication and Human Relationships.* Boston: Allyn and Bacon, 1984.

Miller, G. R., ed. *Explorations in Interpersonal Communication.* Beverly Hills, Calif.: Sage, 1976.

Miller, G. R. "The Current Status of Theory and Research in Interpersonal Communication." *Human Communication Research* 14 (1978):164–178.

Miller, G. R., and M. Steinberg. *Between People: A New Analysis of Interpersonal Communication.* Chicago: Science Research Associates, 1975.

Roloff, M. *Interpersonal Communication: The Social Exchange Approach.* Beverly Hills, Calif.: Sage, 1981.

Schramm, W., and W. E. Porter. *Men, Women, Messages, and Media.* 2d ed. New York: Harper and Row, 1982.

Short, J., E. Williams, and B. Christie. *The Social Psychology of Telecommunications.* New York: Wiley, 1976.

Watzlawick, P., J. Beavin, and D. Jackson. *Pragmatics of Human Communication: A Study of Interactional Patterns, Pathologies and Paradoxes.* New York: Norton, 1967.

Group
Communication

COMMUNICATION ON THE GROUP LEVEL

You have doubtless already spent many hours of your life in face-to-face communication that involves more than two persons, a situation that can properly be called **group communication.** However, the number of people involved is not so important as the patterns of communication and how they relate to the structure or maintenance of the group. Again, as in the study of interpersonal communication, we will see an association between communication and the development of social structures among people.

Groups Large and Small

We often make a distinction between small-group communication, which involves approximately three to twenty-five people, and large-group communication, which may involve more than twenty-five people. In small-group communication, there are few enough people so that everybody has a chance to participate in the give-and-take. With larger groups, we are usually dealing with one or a few people communicating to an "audience." A discussion around the dinner table about the day's events is an example of small-group communication. So is a committee meeting of ten people. However, a college lecture delivered to a class of sixty students, some of whom may become involved in discussion with the instructor, is more on the order of large-group communication.

Types of Groups

Groups are fundamental to human existence. We are, for example, born into what sociologists call a **primary group.** As we grow old enough to leave this primary group from time to time, we join other groups, such as children on a playground, a preschool class, other family groups, and eventually regular groups of other children in school. All of these additional groups and ones continuing through adulthood are called **secondary groups.**

In adult life, we also carry out significant amounts of our communication in secondary groups. We socialize with friends and join sports groups, study groups, church groups, school groups, or work groups, to name a few. One mark of adulthood is that we greatly expand the type and complexity of the groups within which we communicate.

Common Types of Groups As you will see in the following list, groups can have quite different sizes and characteristics. But most have some qualities in common. We will spend the bulk of this chapter discussing these qualities.

learning group: a college class or seminar, for example

living group: one or several roommates; a cluster of individuals who live near you; or individuals in a dormitory, sorority, or fraternity

organizational group: a collection of individuals who represent some formal part of a business, institution, or organization, such as the people in the accounting office, the receptionist, the "marketing" group

Much of our daily communication occurs in small-group settings. This communication may have an interpersonal quality but typically will reflect a speaker and listener's awareness of the presence of others. Put another way, when we communicate in small groups we often have a dually focused message—partly for another individual and partly for the group. Some of our communication in small groups is also devoted to maintaining or controlling the group itself. By contrast, in a large-group setting (usually over twenty-five persons), the focus generally is on a single speaker or presentation, and there are too many individuals for them all to exchange messages with one another. *Frank Siteman/Jeroboam, Inc.*

committee: people who come together to accomplish some specific goal, either members of an organization or individuals assembled only because they are needed to solve a particular problem

social group: individuals who are together for purposes of mutual pleasure or enjoyment, such as those invited to a party, a mixer

therapeutic group: individuals who are using the group experience in order to help one another work out personal problems, to stimulate one another, or to engage in any other type of personal growth; "encounter," "assertiveness training," "consciousness raising," or "growth" groups

ritual group: typically a collection of individuals who come together to celebrate certain ideas or feelings or to go through certain prescribed actions that are meaningful to them, for example, a religious service or a traditional, formal meeting of a business group, where the main purpose is to come together and to participate in certain rituals

circumstantial group: a collection of individuals brought together by some course of events, often accidental or circumstantial, as a group of individuals who find themselves waiting in line at the bank or who are traveling together in a section of an airplane

event, ceremony, or public communication group: individuals who come together to attend a presentation or performance of some type, for example, a motion picture audience, the audience for a public speech, people attending a concert

Ronald E. Rice

The bulk of the research to date on how groups *telecommunicate* has originated from social psychologists and sociologists (for example, Short, Williams, and Christie, 1976). Let's consider a few propositions.

The first proposition is that the purposes of group interaction can be divided into those that are task-oriented and those that are primarily socioemotional. The second proposition is that individuals perceive media as having a subjective quality called "social presence." Social presence is the degree to which the medium is able to transmit the full range of visual, auditory, and physical information from one communicant to the other. It is also the degree to which the medium is perceived as "sociable," "personal," or "close." Social presence contributes especially to group communication that involves a socioemotional component or purpose. Print media have the least social presence. Face-to-face communication has the most. Audio channels, telephone, and video have middle-range levels of social presence. Different levels of social presence affect group interaction and, obviously, the choice of media.

The interaction of group purpose and social presence leads to a wealth of implications. Simply put, group goals that are primarily task-oriented do not require much social presence. Therefore, the medium used is not likely to affect the accomplishment of that goal. In this case, the medium may be chosen for reasons of efficiency, appropriateness, accessibility, or cost.

However, highly interpersonal interactions seem to depend on nonverbal and auditory cues, which some media cannot transmit. Print media typically transmit only language information, although even casual users of electronic mail may add clues of a paralinguistic sort (such as indicating a joke). Audio media can transmit both language and paralinguistic information. Video media can also transmit kinesic information (body movements) such as shyness or attention. Finally, face-to-face communication also transmits information about physical distance and territorial space. It's not surprising, then, that because of the importance of perceived social presence of the other members in these interpersonal activities, face-to-face communication seems preferable for getting to know fellow group members or for resolving group disagreements.

The focus of new research in this area considers factors that affect the acceptance and impact of new media on group communication. A new group medium will be used, partly to the extent that it facilitates communication with other people who are

rally, riot, mob, public gathering: usually a large group of people who come together for some cause in which they have some immediate, on-the-spot interests, to which the assemblage gives momentum and strength, as in the case of a protest group

The Media of Group Communication

Typically, we consider group communication to be face-to-face, with speech and nonverbal communication as the main media. But as with interpersonal communication, there are media alternatives for group communication. Technology has expanded these alternatives.

For example, telephone conference calling has been available for many years. The operator simply connects multiple parties at an appointed time. Although group communication by telephone can be quite successful, the loss of visual feedback makes it somewhat frustrating, because you cannot

already known to one another. Because of their growing availability and applicability to group communication, computer conferencing and the more sophisticated electronic mail systems are particularly important for this discussion. Although computer communication has potentially low social presence, designers, managers, and users can call upon the processing capabilities of the computer to structure group communications. For example, a person may select various "circles" of interaction. These may include personal notebooks, interpersonal messages, joint authorship, "closed" group conferences, public read-only bulletin boards, or statewide public conferences. The system can also provide immediate feedback on the group's performance. Such media are called *computer-based communications systems.*

Of course, one's particular job in an organization or specific role in a group may require certain kinds of tasks. Individuals have personality traits that may lead them to prefer more or less social interaction. They may wish to select from the lower social presence forms of computer-based communications systems. Also, the way in which media constrain the structure of group communication affects the appropriateness of a given medium.

The interaction of all these factors leads to a generalized notion of "media style." The more that a media style meets a group's needs and expectations, the less the medium will interfere with desired interaction. The implication here is that new media should not be forced on groups because of the benefits we know are possible from such technology. Rather, we need to match media usage to tasks, group roles and norms, and individuals' personalities.

Ronald E. Rice is Assistant Professor of Communications in the Annenberg School of Communications at the University of Southern California.

Suggested readings:
S. R. Hiltz and M. Turoff, *The Network Nation: Human Communication via Computer* (Reading, Mass.: Addison-Wesley, 1978).

R. Johansen, "Social Evaluations of Teleconferencing," *Telecommunications Policy* 1, no. 5 (1977).

R. Rice and D. Case, "Electronic Messaging in the University Organization," *Journal of Communication* 33, no. 1 (1983).

J. Short, E. Williams, and B. Christie, *The Social Psychology of Telecommunications* (New York: Wiley, 1976).

---

see the immediate reactions of others to what you say. A two-way video teleconference provides at least a partial visual channel for group interaction. But, as you can imagine, it is expensive to set up such groups. At one time, the Bell Telephone operating companies offered a Picturephone Meeting Service. Now it has been replaced with a variety of video communications services, some available through the new regional telephone companies and some from new vendors.

Another medium for group interaction is the computer teleconference. This involves the exchange of keyboarded messages that are sent and received by computer terminals linked by telephone lines to a central computer. The computer stores the messages as a record of the group interaction and also makes them available to individuals who are communicating with the group during "off" times. You can join the group at any hour you wish, no matter whether anybody else is participating at the time. You can look at the proceedings, add your comments, and sign off. This is called an asynchronous computer conference.

The use of new technologies for group communication is growing rapidly. As you can read in the commentary by Ronald Rice, we are learning about the effects of different media on group communication.

A GROUP'S LIFE CYCLE

Although groups vary in how they occur, most follow a cycle of birth, life, and death, or, in group terms, an "establishment–maintenance–termination" cycle of their own. This cycle is most evident in task groups that are formed to solve a particular problem. For example, five individuals in an accounting firm are asked to form an ad hoc committee to select two new accountants from among several dozen applications. The group is formed only to perform that function. It will be maintained while they carry out the review and selection process and will be dissolved upon completion and presentation of its report. The life cycle of a group such as this will be relatively clear if you are a member or an observer of it. In this particular case, the individuals probably know one another well, so it is not difficult for them to come together, do their job, and then get on with their other work.

The life cycles of groups often become a bit more complex when individuals who do not know one another come together to form a group, particularly a task group of some type. Suppose, for example, that you have been selected as one of fifty students, drawn from different colleges and universities around the nation, to come to Chicago for a two-day meeting; the task is to come up with ideas on how to get students to register to vote. If you were participating in this group, you would probably experience phases reflecting both formal and informal aspects of group life cycles. All involve specific types of communication. These phases are:

Birth

1. Invitation: You are invited and agree subsequently to attend. You accept the understanding of your purpose in attending this meeting.

2. Agenda: You arrive and are given a plan for action that you and the group may follow. It may also remind you what you are to achieve.

3. Beginning of activities: You attend an opening session where you begin to carry out the schedule of the group. You are now actively involved in the proceedings.

Maintenance

1. Role assignment: You establish the roles you wish to take as the group "comes to life."

2. Role adjustment: You personally interpret what you wish to make of your role; for example, you are a follower who wants to assert more of a leadership position.

3. Conflict arousal: Not everybody, including you, is likely to be in initial agreement as the group operates. You encounter differences of opinion, personal interpretations, and motives.

4. Conflict resolution: If the group is to be reasonably successful, there will have to be an agreement to resolve differences of opinion sufficiently to get the job done. You will have to be willing to make compromises between your personal goals and those of the group.

5. Problem–solution sequence: This is mixed with all of the other aspects of birth, maintenance, and even conclusion of the group. You will usually participate in the following general sequence:

   a. goal definition

   b. clarification of the goals in terms of importance and implications

   c. identification and evaluation of goals or values or motives against which possible solutions will be evaluated

   d. identification of a range of alternative means for accomplishing the goals or solving the problem

   e. evaluation of alternatives to the values, goals, or motives discussed earlier

   f. selection of the desired alternative, course of action, or solution

   g. consideration of requirements to implement the action or solution

Termination

1. Commitment: You are asked to agree that a decision or a sensible alternative has been reached and to make a commitment to support this solution.

2. Acknowledgment of completion: You participate in the recognition that the group's job has been completed and the crediting of members with the job they have accomplished.

3. Formal dissolution: The group is dissolved but sometimes with an agreement on how it might be reassembled if necessary.

Of course, some groups never seem to come to an end. Some of this is by design, as in the permanent committees of an organization, long-lived family groups, or an institution (such as a university, church, club) that has no intention of concluding activities. However, if you do not already, sooner or later in your life you will find yourself participating in groups that really have no continuing significance, other than their own existence. These are, for example, the committees one runs across in businesses and universities that accomplish nothing more than simply meeting. They may meet because it is useful for the organization to show to its public that it exists. If you participate in many of these groups, you will very soon notice that they have gone beyond a natural or productive life cycle. Nothing could be more efficient than their dissolution.

COMMUNICATION DIFFERENCES IN GROUPS

Group Motivation

Even though you are speaking the same English language in a group as in a one-to-one conversation, how you communicate may differ substantially. For one, maintaining group communication differs from the maintenance of a two-person conversation. Whereas in a two-person conversation you may be concentrating upon accomplishing some simple, immediate goal—such as the relatively impersonal situation of buying a pair of shoes—in group communication it is always necessary to devote some attention to the reason for the group's existence or its goal. The communication that you need in order to keep a group going will focus on the relation between the reason for the group's existence and the motives of the individual members. Conversely, in conversation, maintenance communication is often a much simpler, two-person thing.

Just as two-person communication can grow markedly personal—that is, when individual motives are transacted—group communication can become similarly personal. This takes still another type of group maintenance communication, one where a considerable amount of attention is given to the goals or motives of the individual members participating in the group. Some of the most personal types of groups are those of a therapeutic nature, where individuals are encouraged to share their most private thoughts and deepest emotions on a topic, often themselves. The maintenance communication in a therapeutic group is often of a highly personal nature.

Some maintenance communication in groups is as direct and visible as, for example, an agenda that is circulated at the beginning of a meeting or a group's leader's opening statement of goals and attempts to motivate the group to achieve them. Other group-maintenance communication may be much subtler, as when a group leader discourages a particular member from having a personal goal that is at variance with the group. For example, suppose that all but one member of a committee in a business firm has agreed to work through Saturday in order to get a job done. It will be the leader's task to convince this dissenting member of the priority of the group goals over his or her own.

A variety of maintenance statements guide a group's interactions. These include raising questions or clarifications, summarizing what has been said, intentionally hindering the progress of a group, pleading special or personal interest, requesting more information, criticizing a point, and criticizing information that has been given. (The analysis of patterns of group interaction is taken up later in the chapter.)

Pressure to Conform

Another distinctive characteristic of group communication is the pressure to conform. That is, for most participants, it is often presumed more difficult to disagree with a group in a discussion than with another single individual in a conversation. People are much more likely to make statements and estimates they feel will be in line with a group than they would be to make these statements independently. This is not to say that people will fail to express their own opinion when it is contrary to the ideas of a group but only that, if they do, they will do it in the presence of pressure to conform.

Risky Shift

Conversely, groups seem to offer a type of "haven," or security, that makes people more willing to take risks in what they say or suggest, if this is supported by the group. This is called the *risky shift* phenomenon; it is the reason often given why people may make a riskier or more radical decision if it is with the support of a group. Beyond the "safety in numbers" context of this phenomenon, it also seems clear that as long as a group agrees on a given point, no individual feels totally responsible for that point. In other words, the apparent sharing of responsibility seems to allow people to take greater risks in what they say or agree to.

Brainstorming

Groups can also offer a stimulating context for creativity. An individual can receive immediate and multiple reaction to his or her ideas. Those reactions may immediately suggest new alternatives. Or somebody listening to the exchange may come up with still another set of ideas. Often, when groups are used mainly for purposes of such creativity, this process is called *brainstorming*. The process seems to work best when there is mutual agreement among members of the group that any idea, no matter how outlandish, can be expressed. The emphasis is to get as many ideas out in the open as possible. In order to do this, there is also usually agreement that no one idea will be evaluated, rejected, or even thoroughly discussed until all possible ideas are out on the table. Brainstorming works best where there is a free-wheeling attitude on the part of all involved. In more formal situations, it is often further agreed that as soon as the ideas are out on the table, there will be a systematic attempt to evaluate each and, eventually, to reduce them to a selection or decision affirmed by the group.

Leadership

Finally, communication in groups is highly affected by differences in styles of leadership. As discussed in the next section, a strong central type of leadership will not encourage full and wide discussion by different members in the group unless it is ordered by the leader. This can be contrasted with a very democratic type of group organization where there is mutual agreement among the participants that all should "have their say." Obviously, this leadership difference has a major effect on the type and amounts of maintenance communication in the group, on the spread of participation, and on who contributes in the form of leadership statements or "followership acceptance."

GROUP LEADERSHIP

Who runs the group? If you are like most people, you might say, right off, "the leader." The problem is that upon closer examination, we find that leadership operates in a variety of ways. The stereotype of a conscientious, assertive, and even compassionate leader moving everybody toward the group's objectives seldom really exists exactly in this way. Leadership may vary all the way from an absolute dictatorship to styles of democracy that would impress even our founding fathers. Also, there are many situations where leadership, whether or not the role is defined, really does not exist. A group simply wanders in whatever direction the discussion drifts. Usually we call these three leadership types the *authoritarian*, *group-centered*, and *hands-off* styles of leadership, respectively.

The Authoritarian Leader

Every Monday morning sharply at 6:30, Dr. B meets with the resident physicians on the staff of the local hospital. The meeting lasts exactly 20 minutes. Almost to the second, the first 15 minutes is spent in reviewing the status of the staff for the week, any special financial considerations that may have arisen, and the schedule of events. The last 5 minutes, with almost absolute certainty, are devoted to Dr. B's near "sermon" on the need to uphold standards, image, and profitability of the hospital. Questions are not invited, and, for as long as most people can remember, no member of the group ever made a significant statement at a meeting. It is Dr. B's meeting. When he is unavailable, the group does not meet.

Authoritarian leadership is sometimes called "leader-centered" because what occurs is almost totally under the control of the leader. No participation other than dutiful listening and compliance is invited in the meeting. Communication is mainly one-way from leader to participants. Leader communication in such situations is often impersonal, meaning that the persons attending the meeting are seen more in terms of the roles they are fulfilling than in terms of individuals. Despite the one-way direction of Dr. B's meeting style, the physicians attending it do not necessarily feel that the time is wasted. After all, they do gain a knowledge of what is going on in the hospital, particularly what Dr. B thinks is going on. Also, the meeting gives the resident physicians a chance to mingle sociably for coffee after the meeting, although Dr. B seldom stays long enough to join them.

Group-Centered Leadership

The university's Linguistic Circle meets monthly. It is made up of university faculty in the foreign language, linguistic, and language arts departments and a few of the more advanced graduate students. Although Linguistic Circle is a relatively formal occasion—that is, it isn't a party, and there are certain unwritten rules of behavior—it is a relatively warm and social affair, but primarily an intellectual one. The main program for each meeting is the presentation of a scholarly paper on a topic in linguistics, followed by group discussion of it. Although Professor Z has been the recognized chairman of the Linguistic Circle for as long as anybody can remember, he is mainly a coordinator. Different faculty are invited to sponsor a session, and the group as a whole generally participates equally in deciding any special business of the Circle. Last year, Professor Z was out ill for an entire semester. Although the members of the Circle missed his participation in intellectual discussion, leadership of the group was not perceptibly affected.

Group-centered leadership is sometimes called "democratic" in that all members are invited to participate fully in the decisions and actions of the group. The leader takes on a responsibility more of coordination than of direction. Because the program schedule is chosen by individual members, nearly everybody gets something on the program that is of personal and professional interest. A group-centered style of leadership may create a situation that is not as efficient as the authoritarian-led group, but at the same time it is less dependent on any single individual being present as a leader.

Hands-Off Leadership

The Imagineering organization does research, development, and design for the Walt Disney organization. The most critical of the group structures within this organization are "project" teams that include writers, artists, engineers, and an occasional musician and that develop large-scale exhibits. Although each project has a "leader," who usually has a business background, that person's main task is to see that the projects stay on budget and schedule. Because the individuals in this organization are longtime professionals, once they are assembled as a project team, there really is little need for daily or even weekly monitoring by the project leader. These professionals can get the job done mostly on their own. Recently, one of the project leaders left to take a job with another company, and one of the most important projects in the Imagineering organization continued to progress well, although the leader has not yet been replaced.

This hands-off, or as it is sometimes called, *laissez-faire*, type of leadership does not necessarily mean the absolute absence of a leader. Instead, it means that often there is a leader available for handling problems should they arise or that somebody has been designated as having the overall responsibility. However, there is little direct contact or need for this leader on a day-by-day basis. Whereas authoritarian or group-centered leaders may be in very active contact with members of their groups, the laissez-faire leader is relatively inactive unless called upon for advice or assistance. Of course, this is a positive view of hands-off leadership. We are all aware of situations where hands-off leadership has resulted in a group that gets absolutely nothing accomplished. The success of hands-off leadership depends upon having group members who are self-directing and a task that does not require a high degree of central control.

ANALYSIS OF INTERACTION PATTERNS

The communication patterns of groups can be analyzed by a variety of methods. These analyses are useful for both theoretical and practical purposes. From a theoretical standpoint, interaction analysis can tell us much about the general nature of how people communicate when they are in a group, including how these patterns change depending on the group's past, the relationships among the members, the style of leadership, the relations between the personal motives of the participants, and the reason for the group's existence.

From a more practical standpoint, an understanding of interaction patterns can help you when you are involved in different situations of group communication. For example, if you are leading a discussion, it is important to see if or how the various members are contributing to the group's goals. Or if you are participating in a group, you can find ways to determine your best methods of contribution.

We will look at two widely recognized methods for analysis: Interaction Process Analysis (IPA) and network analysis.

Interaction Process Analysis

The most widely recognized method for analyzing the contribution of individual members to a discussion comes from the research by Robert Bales (1967), as reported in his book *Interaction Process Analysis*. In this analysis method, each person's contribution at any point in a discussion is classified according to twelve basic "types." A contribution might be simply a brief response such as "Yes, I agree," or it might be a fairly involved explanation of a topic. The point is that each contribution has a function in the interaction. The twelve types of contributions fall into four main categories. Two of these categories reflect a participant's attitudes in the situation. They reflect how a person is responding either positively or negatively to what is being said. The Bales categories are summarized in Table 8.1.

Theoretically speaking, Bales's method suggests that most of the relevant contributions to a discussion fall into one of these detailed categories. Moreover, we might expect certain participants in a discussion to emphasize contributions that fall more into some categories than into others. For example, you may remember people who have sat through a discussion and then

Table 8.1 Bales's Categories for Interaction Process Analysis

Positive	seems friendly dramatizes agrees	Attempted Answers	gives suggestions gives opinions gives information
Negative	disagrees shows tension seems unfriendly	Questions	asks for information asks for opinions asks for suggestions

Source: Robert F. Bales, "A Set of Categories for the Analysis of Small Group Interaction," *American Sociological Review* 15 (1950), p. 258.

Figure 8.1
Tabulation Form
for Interaction
Process Analysis

Participants

Categories	Jane	Harry	Phil	Betty	Becky	Tom	Steve
Seems friendly							
Dramatizes							
Agrees							
Disagrees							
Shows tension							
Seems unfriendly							
Gives suggestions							
Gives opinions							
Gives information							
Asks for information							
Asks for opinions							
Asks for suggestions							

Source: Robert F. Bales, "A Set of Categories for the Analysis of Small Group Interaction," *American Sociological Review* 15 (1950), p. 258.

complained about everything that was said, as compared with those who have been genuinely helpful. In order to study this, charts can be constructed, as shown in Figure 8.1, on which the frequency with which each participant makes a contribution in a particular category is tabulated. After the discussion (or samples of it) when the content is analyzed, it is possible to see what types of statements tended to predominate in the discussion. Also individual members can be classified according to their typical types of contributions.

Bales's Interaction Process Analysis has been very useful in studies designed to contrast types of discussion, types of participants, types of topics, and combinations of the three. More recently, the Bales method has been applied to evaluate the effects of holding discussions when participants are linked by audio and video hookups (teleconferencing).

Network Analysis

You could also interpret a Bales analysis chart in terms of the degree to which the participation was spread among the different members of the group. Surely you have been in discussions where one person dominated the exchanges and in others where almost everybody got a word in. A discussion with wide participation would show the check marks on the chart widely distributed among the individuals.

It is also possible not only to gauge the spread of participation in the group discussion but also to chart it in terms of a diagram we usually call a *network analysis*. Suppose, for example, that you constructed a network-analysis chart similar to the one given in Figure 8.2. Anytime an individual made a contribution in response to another individual's contribution, a line would be drawn to connect the two participants. Notice, also, that you could have the option of taking into consideration a person's making a comment that is in response to no one in particular or that is addressed to no one in particular. After the content analysis of a discussion, therefore, it is possible to identify who is mainly addressing whom in the pattern of the discussion, as well as to isolate people who tend not to address or respond to other individuals. You can see, also, how interactions that were not in response to, or addressed to, specific individuals can be plotted relative to "all" in this diagram.

Figure 8.2
Network
Analysis Chart

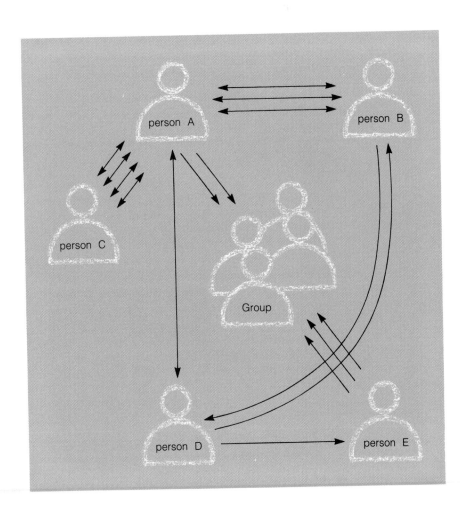

If you conduct a network analysis of this type, you will soon see that groups differ substantially in their patterns of interactions. Notice, for example, the contrast among the three generalized network diagrams in Figure 8.3. You might begin by asking yourself which network diagram illustrates the fullest participation by all members of the group. The answer is that the star diagram (a) represents a situation where all five members of the group have communicated with everyone else. Compare this with the circle configuration (b), where generally, each person has communicated with another, rather than everybody with one another. Although we seldom have a clear example of an "around the circle" communication, the figure does illustrate the general pattern of people interacting with certain partners and they, in turn, with others. When a circle is not complete, as is most often the case, and people are still communicating in partners, it is often called a chain network. This would look like a circle except that one of the links would be missing. Finally, another general pattern of interaction is one in which participants tend to respond to or interact with a central figure in the group process. This is sometimes called the wheel pattern (c).

Two other patterns are often seen in network analysis, and these are illustrated in Figure 8.4. The *isolate* (a) is the individual who tends not to interact with other members of the group. Also there are *cliques* (b). These are small groups of individuals who communicate mainly among themselves and are connected with the larger group only through an individual who serves as a *bridge* (c).

Network analysis goes far beyond applications to small-group situations. The analysis of the flow of communication within a business organization, a village, a city, or any kind of an organization lends itself to network analysis. It is not difficult to plot the interactions—not only face-to-face but also by memo, telephone call, and other forms of communication—and to identify leadership and "followership" patterns and the spread of participation, as well as isolates, cliques, and bridges.

Figure 8.3
Types of Networks

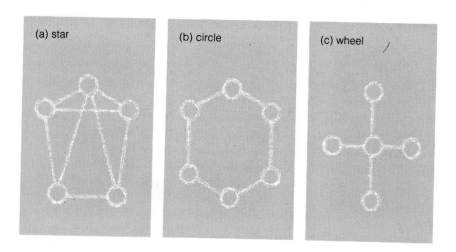

(a) star (b) circle (c) wheel

Figure 8.4
Special Network
Elements

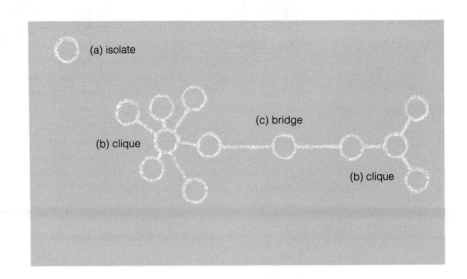

SUMMARY

Much of our daily communication is carried out in groups of many types. Some are small family groups, or *primary groups*. Others are the social groups representing friends, meetings, or organizations in which we participate. These are *secondary groups*. Groups range from three or more persons perhaps meeting as a committee to hundreds or thousands of people who might gather for a public meeting or concert. Although most groups meet face-to-face, there are a growing number of ways for group communication to take place via telecommunications media, as in a video teleconference, for example.

All groups have a life cycle of birth, maintenance, and termination. Group communication deals with the operation of the life of the group in addition to the topic of discussion.

Communication in groups goes on somewhat differently from that in two-person conversations. Some communication is devoted to motivation of the group. There is pressure to conform to group opinions. People tend to take more risks if the group agrees with them. Groups are often an excellent context for developing ideas, as in brainstorming. Finally, group communication is shaped by leadership style.

Types of leadership include authoritarian (one person in total charge), group-centered (leadership is shared among the members), and hands-off (nobody leads).

Participation in group communication can be analyzed by Interaction Process Analysis, in which individuals' contributions are classified into various functional categories. It is also possible to analyze the spread of participation in a group as well as who talks to whom, as in network analysis.

TOPICS FOR DISCUSSION OR BRIEF PAPERS

1. Prepare an agenda for a group discussion. Be sure to specify in detail the *purpose*, the *participants*, and the *agenda*. Also, what type of leadership do you think will work best? Explain why.

2. Describe your plans for arranging a teleconference. Choose a medium from the following and explain your choice: (1) telephone; (2) audio and video one way, audio only the second way; (3) audio and video both ways; and (4) computer-based. Also prepare an agenda that reflects the special needs of telecommunications-based group interaction (for example, being sure the participants have been introduced).

3. What type of group leadership do you prefer to work under? Explain why. What type of leader do you prefer to be? Why?

4. Do a short case study, if only from memory, of a group leader whom you have observed. What were his or her strong points, weak points, or unique characteristics? How did the style of leadership affect the results of group communication?

5. Take any group meeting or discussion in which you participate, and conduct either an Interaction Process Analysis or a network study. What generalizations can you draw from your results? What suggestions would you make for improving that group's communications?

REFERENCES AND READINGS

Bales, R. *Interaction Process Analysis*. Reading, Mass.: Addison-Wesley, 1967.

Fisher, B. A. *Small Group Decision Making: Communications and the Group Process*. 2d ed. New York: McGraw-Hill, 1980.

Rice, R., and D. Case. "Electronic Messaging in the University Organization." *Journal of Communication* 33, no. 1 (1983).

Shaw, M. E. *Group Dynamics: The Psychology of Small Group Behavior*. 3d ed. New York: McGraw-Hill, 1981.

Short, J., E. Williams, and B. Christie. *The Social Psychology of Telecommunications*. New York: Wiley, 1976.

Williams, F., and R. Rice. "Communications Research and the New Media Technologies." In *Communications Yearbook*, edited by R. Bostrom, 200–224. Beverly Hills, Calif.: Sage, 1983.

Organizational Communication

THE ORGANIZA-TIONAL LEVEL OF COMMUNICATION

Organizations are probably the most complex of the social contexts of human communication. They may encompass face-to-face, group, and media-based communication. Some organizational communication is quite impersonal, such as sharing information about cost statistics. But it can also be personal, as in a verbal reward for making a key sale.

Communication in an organization may often entail a substantial amount of group communication, as in staff or committee meetings, presentations, and even brainstorming sessions. Also, communication takes on a great variety of additional forms, as with memos, telephone conversations, posters or notices on bulletin boards, books or pamphlets, rule books, plus a veritable storm of in-and-out written correspondence. Added to these are the new technologies and their applications, such as electronic mail, teleconferencing, management information systems, word processing, and electronic funds transfer.

Communication goes on in special ways in organizations. Everybody plays a mix of individual and organizational roles. Communication in organizations can be very formal, in the sense that certain communication patterns must be established in order for a business or establishment to operate. Yet, communication often evolves in ways very much altered by the individuals involved. Sometimes the true communications networks of an organization are so subtle that you must literally "join" the organization in order to discover them. (The paperback *The Ropes to Skip and the Ropes to Know*, by Richard Ritti and Ray Funkhouser (1977), is delightful reading on this topic.)

Further, the organizational environment is one of the prime targets of the new communications technologies. You can hardly pick up a business magazine today without encountering all types of advertisements for new office technologies and scenarios of the so-called "office of the future." If you are now an undergraduate university student, chances are that your professional success will depend in part upon your ability to employ these new technologies.

How do we look at communication in organizations? One way is to examine how individuals communicate within the internal structure of the organizational context. Another way is to view the organization as a "communicating structure" itself, receiving and disseminating messages and using communication to maintain itself. We will examine the internal level first as a natural extension of our explorations of interpersonal and group communications.

ORGANIZATIONAL COMMUNICATION FROM THE STANDPOINT OF THE INDIVIDUAL

Organizational Roles

The moment that you become a member of an organization, in addition to your existing social roles involving family and friends, you take on another set of role expectations as defined in the context of that organization. Although theoretically speaking, the "organization" can be anything from an athletic team to a business, much of the theory of organizational roles has to do with occupational ones. That is, much of what is said about organizational communication applies to **organizational roles.**

One key characteristic of an organizational role is that, theoretically speaking, it can be accomplished by different individuals. Apart from certain talents that the person performing the role might need, organizational roles are explicitly *impersonal*. Although all of us would like to be in roles that are consistent with our own needs and drives, an organizational role essentially requires only that the actions associated with it are carried out. In the life of an organization, therefore, we may expect the definition of an organizational role to remain much more constant than the personal characteristics of the people who fulfill it.

In most formal organizations, and especially in large ones, the organizational roles are defined as job descriptions. For example:

Field Sales Manager, Eastern Division: Supervises sales staff of 15 representatives; directs regional advertising campaigns; serves as director of the NYC marketing office.

Assistant Editor, Financial Section: Compiles daily market statistics; writes business feature articles; writes Sunday column on personal investment programs.

Given descriptions such as these, as well as descriptions of how the different roles in an organization relate to one another ("organizational chart"), it should be possible to describe how an organization is meant to operate. But as we shall see, there are often many differences between formal and informal rules of communication.

Communication Rules

Any given organizational role requires specific types of communication. Indeed, much of what you need to fulfill an organizational role is communication know-how. You need to learn the **communication rules** that go along with the roles and with the operation of the organization.

Usually we make a distinction between *formal* and *informal* communication rules in organizations. The formal rules are partly a reflection of the formal organizational chart. Suppose, as illustrated in Figure 9.1, sales manager A reports to the organization's vice-president for marketing. This person also supervises three regional sales managers whose territories are the Midwest, South, and Atlantic states, respectively.

For the role shown in Figure 9.1, one of the formal communication rules would be that the sales staffs (shown in the blocks under each of the three regional managers) are to report their expected quarterly quotas to sales manager A. In return, this manager assembles all of the regional information and passes the package on to the vice-president. In turn, the vice-president's office formally recognizes these quotas, then usually announces prizes, bonuses, or other incentives for the sales staff to reach the quotas. In terms of formal communication rules, therefore, each person in this management chain has a particular communication task to accomplish. This is part of the formal definition of all of the individual jobs in this hierarchy.

Figure 9.1
A Portion of a Formal
Organization Chart

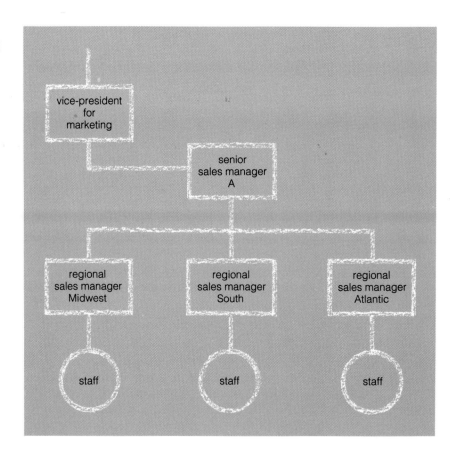

The formal rules do not typically define all the types of communication, however. Suppose that in the same organizational relationship shown in Figure 9.1, it is a custom for the regional sales manager to suggest next year's quotas before the vice-president does. If a new person assumed the sales manager's role and did not know about making this "opening bid" for next year's quotas, an *informal rule* would be violated.

It is usually more difficult to learn informal rules. Whereas you would expect to find the formal rules or routines of sales reporting on official memos, management documents, or other guides for the organization, it is not likely that you will find anywhere official rules for the informal rule just described. Informal rules are based more on the individuals in organizational roles than they are on the roles themselves. They reflect how particular individuals try to do their jobs. Here is another example, this time from a small radio station:

(Roger, the station manager, is speaking.)
"Sally, I know that you'd like to do the early morning news sign-on, so I'll make you a deal. If you'll cover the station one Sunday a month, you can try the morning slot for those four days a month that Jack needs a fill-in. OK?"

In this example, nothing in the regulations or the established formal procedures of the station set the manager and Sally up for that extra bit of persuasion. Instead, it was informally acceptable (they both agreed on this "rule") that if Sally would help out on one problem, she would be *personally* rewarded. Informal rules often also depend on the particular personal relationship between the individuals involved. Practically speaking, your success in many organizations is going to depend as much on your ability to quickly learn the informal rules associated with your role as it is to understand and carry out what is defined for you formally.

Organizational and Individual Conflict

Because organizations are run by people and because the mix of individual motives, organizational roles, and communication rules is not usually perfect, conflict in an organization is often inevitable. There is, after all, often a natural tension between employees and management. Also, there are usually more people who want to be promoted up the ranks than there are positions for them. Conflict in an organization is not unusual. Nor is it unusual that inexperienced employees are surprised to find that organizations are not as ideal an environment as they originally believed.

As a consequence, one of the important areas of organizational communication is negotiation, or conflict resolution. This is a very personal type of interpersonal or group communication. It is a frequent part of the everyday management of an organization, and it is not the kind of communication you would predict from organizational charts. It is the more human side of the organizational picture. The commentary by Linda L. Putnam will provide you with a few more thoughts on the topic.

MANAGEMENT FUNCTIONS

You may recall from Chapter 4 that the general functions of communication are *information*, *instruction*, *persuasion*, and *entertainment*. It is not difficult to see examples of these functions and mixtures of them as used by individuals in their everyday organizational communication. But it is usually more useful to look at organizational communication in terms of its *management functions*. The management functions most often described in the context of organizational communication are (1) planning and organizing, (2) directing and motivating, (3) monitoring and controlling, (4) training, and (5) evaluating and changing.

All of these management functions are carried out by mixtures of the traditional functions just mentioned.

1. Planning and Organizing

Beyond the general obligation to be a productive contributor to society, the general goal of a business is to be profitable or, for a nonprofit organization (such as a university), to deliver its services. Planning and organizing are the means by which managers set their organizations on course toward these

Linda L. Putnam

Communication plays an integral role in the development and management of organizational conflict. A conflict refers to incompatibilities in goals, actions, or values between two or more people. When an incompatibility exists, one person's goals are diametrically opposed to the aims of another. For example, a conflict is likely to develop if the computer department in a corporation needs a standard format for system design and the accounting division wants flexibility in adapting software to fit particular problems. The need for structure in designing computer programs clashes with the user's need for flexibility and frequent change.

But it is through communicative behaviors that incompatibilities are recognized and experienced. Even before these two departments identify their conflict, they exchange verbal and nonverbal messages that signal an impending controversy. Three of these types of messages are:

1. Contradictions between message and action—a computer programmer agrees to design a new system for an accountant, but the system produces deficient and inaccurate data.

2. Verbal digs aimed at the other side but exchanged among members of one department: "Computer folks want everything as predictable as machines." "The accountants are stupid when it comes to system design."

3. Differences of opinion between members of departments: Accountant: "We need a program to perform these functions." Programmer: "It can't be done. We can't write that kind of program—see our guidelines."

As these forms of communication appear frequently in conversations, they begin to define the conflict: its surface and deep issues, its emotional intensity, its parameters, and its meaning to participants. In an organization, conflicts become apparent to both parties during decisions about policies and procedures. Through discussions of preferred courses of action, members realize that their disagreements result from basic differences in values, goals, and priorities. A felt difficulty, then, moves into the realm of conscious recognition of incompatibilities.

The parties involved in a conflict choose communicative strategies for managing it. Even though conflict is not always rational or intentional, organizational disputes are frequently managed through deliberate and strategic choice. At the individual level, people choose to be silent about a disagreement, to gloss over differences, to confront problems, or to argue persistently for a position. At the organizational level, these choices are manifested in such formal procedures as collective bargaining, grievances, majority rule, and third-party intervention. There is no magic formula or "best way" to manage organizational conflicts. Current research indicates that the importance, intensity, and urgency of a conflict as well as the organizational structure affect choices about communicative strategies.

The communicative strategy used to manage a conflict reflects back on and shapes the evolution of the conflict. Many conflicts are never fully resolved. They resurface from time to time and are managed through decisions on select issues. The aftermath of one conflict, then, sets the stage for future disagreements. But since conflict is a viable form of organizational change, both the development and the management of it can be effective means of organizational communication.

Linda L. Putnam is Associate Professor of Communication at Purdue University.

Suggested readings:
L. R. Pondy, "Organizational Conflict: Concepts and Models," *Administrative Science Quarterly* 12 (1967): 296–320.
L. L. Putnam and T. S. Jones, "The Role of Communication in Bargaining," *Human Communication Research* 8 (1982): 262–280.
L. L. Putnam and C. Wilson, "Communicative Strategies in Organizational Conflicts: Reliability and Validity of a Measurement Scale," in *Communication Yearbook 6*, edited by M. Burgoon. Beverly Hills, Calif.: Sage, 1982.

goals. What specific objectives will management try to achieve in order to move toward the larger, more general goal? How can resources best be applied to achieve objectives?

Planning and organizing require a constant supply of information. The supplying of such information, rapidly and accurately, has been one of the contributions of the computer to manufacturing and business. Information files can be established that monitor every step from buying raw materials through manufacturing to final sales. New computer programs—now available even for personal computers—allow a manager to model likely future courses of action. You can ask such questions as "What would happen to profits if we try to double our manufactured output?" or "What are the impacts upon profits if the work force averages a 10 percent wage increase?"

2. Directing and Motivating

"An organization chart cannot run a business" is a favorite phrase of managers. Indeed, that chart must be filled in with real-life people who must be informed of their job objectives and be motivated to meet these objectives in an effective manner. This requires mixtures of all the traditional functions of communication, although possibly with a minimum of entertainment.

As we discussed in Chapter 8, motivating people in groups requires that they see the relationship between their individual motives for action and the motives that are for the good of the organization. The most productive employees will be those whose personal goals are most compatible with the organization's goals. Guiding personnel toward that match is the task of the skilled manager, or, in more general terms, the *leader*.

This functional area also involves the negotiation and conflict resolution tasks described earlier.

3. Monitoring and Controlling

How well are interim objectives being achieved? Are directives being carried out? Are personnel working productively? All such questions require prompt and accurate feedback of information about the operation of the organization. This includes in large part the financial, or "bookkeeping," part of organizational management.

Again, new office technologies provide much-improved means for gathering and presenting information on the operation of an organization. In most businesses, the ability of management to set standards for operations and then to monitor results as a basis for making improvements in their operations marks the difference between profit and loss. Monitoring and controlling can often be the competitive edge for an organization.

4. Training

"Instruction is part of management" is another organizational truism. Organizations are almost always involved in training personnel to handle new responsibilities. Moreover, employees in free-enterprise societies typically expect job advancement as their skills and experiences develop. In many modern organizations, the tasks are too complicated for a person simply to learn on the job as in the "apprentice" system. It is necessary to have formal training, which is either done in the organization or by outside specialized schools or institutes. As our organizations become increasingly technologically sophisticated, we can expect the need for specialized training to increase. (Turn to any business section of a large newspaper or a business newspaper and see the number of specialized seminars and institutes offered to managers.) The largest growth area of higher education is "continuing education" for people beyond the usual college age.

5. Evaluating and Changing

The business writer and professor Peter Drucker is well known, among other things, for his advice that any manager who hopes to be successful will have to ask himself or herself at least every six months: "What business am I in?" Part of the art of management is to sense and take advantage of change. This is change not only in the overall business climate but also in how to operate a specific organization.

Consequently, another key management communication function is to make overall evaluations of an organization's operation and to implement change if necessary. This, of course, requires accurate information, the ability to make intelligent judgments, and the ability to convey change through direction and motivation.

THE MEDIA OF ORGANIZATIONAL COMMUNICATION

Traditional Media

An individual in an organization can expect to use many different types of communications media. These media, like the relationship between general communication functions and management communication functions, vary for different types of organizational communications. This relationship between function and media is summarized in Table 9.1.

One of the most general patterns that you can see in the table is that the more communication involves personal persuasion (as in motivation), the more it is likely to have a characteristic of personal immediacy, as in a face-to-face meeting, a telephone call, or a personally written memorandum. In contrast, communication of a more strictly informational nature may usually take on quite impersonal forms, as in group memorandums, documents, or even a computer data file.

The point of Table 9.1 is not so much for you to try to remember the scheme relating these organizational communication functions with different media but to sense the relatively complex sets of alternatives and mixes we use in modern organizations.

If you participate in organizational communication or study it, you will soon see that you have many alternative ways for carrying out necessary communications. The most effective members of an organization know how

Table 9.1 Communications Media Used for Management Functions

1. Planning and Organizing	Input	records on paper and in computer files; reports, correspondence, personal testimony
	Activity	face-to-face meetings, both individual and group
	Output	small-group meetings with senior managers, memos, directives, organization charts
2. Directing and Motivating	Input	memos, directives, charts, and small-group meetings face-to-face and small-group meetings
	Activity	large-group meetings, directives, memos; some face-to-face interpersonal
	Output	communication for motivation purposes; telephone conversations
3. Monitoring and Controlling	Input	mostly records of production, sales, or services; in modern organizations, computerized files; financial figures; telephone conversations
	Activity	analysis of reports, comparisons of figures with standards, computerized analyses; small-group meetings to discuss evaluations
	Output	production charts, service goals, feedback of evaluations of information obtained earlier; memos, directives; some face-to-face communication for motivational purposes
4. Training	Activity	input instructional objectives; planning; small-group instruction, books, manuals; videotape, disk, or film instructional programs; computer-assisted instruction, lectures, and demonstrations; two-person conversations; output new skills; knowledge for workers and management
5. Evaluating and Changing	Input	paper or computerized records, reports from outside sources on the market or clientele, small-group meetings with analysts, telephone conversations
	Activity	small-group meetings, telephone and face-to-face conversations, computerized analyses or simulations, personal interactions or meetings with consultants, written presentations
	Output	directives, new charts, instructional communication for new product lines or services, public information or advertising, internal directives, small- and large-group meetings

to use these alternatives, and this is often what separates a person who is upward bound on the executive ladder from those who seem destined to be followers rather than leaders. This distinction is likely to become greater as the new communications technologies offer all of us new channels and techniques for organizational communication.

The Office of the Future

The phrase *office of the future* is more a metaphor than an objective description of media technologies. Essentially, it means that the tools of the manager are changing. The needs of management—as described in the five functions—remain the same. It is the techniques for carrying out these functions that are changing. As with all of the technologies discussed in Chapter 6, the changes are in the storage, retrieval, and transmission of information.

Some of the technologies most associated with change in the methods of organizational communication are:

Management information system (MIS): This is not one piece of equipment you "buy" as such, but a configuration of computer terminals and electronic filing systems that allows you to gather, edit, and disseminate information rapidly and efficiently.

Word processing: Single-purpose word processors or computers with word-processor programs are used to replace the typewriter. Essentially, the text is kept in electronic form until all editing is performed, thus saving erasures and retyping. Also, documents that are in electronic form can be filed without having to be saved on paper.

Electronic mail: When point-to-point messages are sent over electronic communications systems such as a computer network or by facsimile machines, the messages are called electronic mail.

Electronic funds transfer: Computers are used to send messages regarding the transfer of funds among different accounts, to obtain balances, or perform other desired banking operations.

Teleconference: As described in Chapter 8, this is a meeting held via a telephone, audiovideo, computer, or combined communications network.

ORGANIZATIONAL COMMUNICATION FROM THE STANDPOINT OF THE ORGANIZATION

Organizations as Communicators

Beyond the detailed behaviors of the individual staff members, committees, departments, or managers, organizations have a communications life of their own. Any organization, for example, has an overall image. Think of the oil company from which you last bought gasoline. It communicates to you in the form of its advertisements, signs on its stations, or perhaps even direct mail to potential customers. Its message to you is "Buy your gasoline and automobile services from me." This organization also has communications with its stockholders, saying, in essence, "Have confidence in how I do business. Depend on me for high dividend rates." That same large petroleum organization may have a communications program designed to nurture its overall institutional image; the program may stress the organization's interest in giving you the latest benefits of scientific exploration, its contributions to the nation's economy, and its attempts to protect the natural environment as much as possible.

On the other hand, there may be environmental and consumer interest groups who are trying to tell you that this petroleum company is "ripping you off," that it is "exploiting the natural environment for its stockholders' profit, and at the expense of a future that belongs to all of us." Thus, companies are also very much in the business of receiving messages from other institutions, groups, and individuals. Perhaps the most vital of this information is the feedback a company gets from marketing its products: sales figures, orders from distributors, investors rushing to buy stock at a given price. Further, it is likely that this same company makes a special attempt to influence what is going on in the minds of legislators, who could easily change regulations that might affect the profitability of the company (this is an example of lobbying).

Just as we thought of individuals and groups of individuals as making up the "communicating units" described in Chapter 2, we can think of the organization as such a unit; this is illustrated in Figure 9.2. And just as with any other type of communications unit, an organization has the capability for overall encoding, decoding, and sensing feedback.

Organizations also have internal structures that are communications systems. Obviously, an organization that can respond to feedback, create new messages, and engage in any type of institutional behavior must have an internal communications system, often a highly complex one. In simple terms, it takes internal communications systems within organizations to operate the external ones. The overall patterns of internal communication within an organization are more often examined under the general concept we call **management.**

Management Structures

We have seen that it takes planning, decisions, direction, motivation, and evaluation to make an organization operate. In the overall sense, these are all part of the management functions of communication. Essentially, the job of management is to control and coordinate the resources (people, raw materials, machinery) so that the organization can accomplish its objectives. These objectives may be the manufacture of automobiles, and the ultimate objective may be that these automobiles can be sold for a profit. Or the "product"

Figure 9.2
The Organization as a "Communicating Unit"

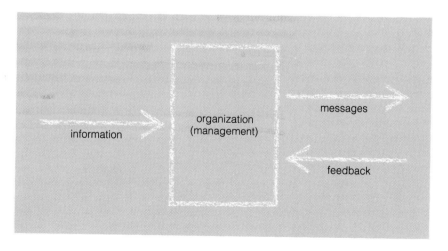

Corporate leaders set the communication image and style of their organization. In many respects, an organization is made up of communication sources and receivers. If you work in an organization, especially in communications work, you may be part of the team that allows an organization to communicate—in addition to carrying out your own personal and professional communications roles. *Ellis Herwig/ Stock, Boston*

might be medical services in a nonprofit institution. In this case, all of the activities of management are focused on the capability of the institution to provide services to its intended market. Being *nonprofit* does not mean that the ultimate financial consequences of management are not also as critical as in the prior example. It simply means that the goal of the organization is mainly to provide its intended services rather than to create an additional financial return to investors.

As a means of control and coordination, most activities in organizations are monitored by communications processes. Thus, it is possible to study organizational communication on this level without necessarily getting down to the details of how communications involve particular individuals within an organization. That is, we can examine the broad patterns of management control and coordination, sometimes called the *communication hierarchy* in an organization.

Management Communication Hierarchy. Upon first examination, a **communication hierarchy,** such as that shown in Figure 9.3, suggests that responsibility is distributed among different managers on the various levels of the hierarchy. For example, the chief executive officer (CEO) has the overall authority, in contrast, for example, to the vice-president for marketing, who has responsibility mainly over the people in marketing. This is the typical downward flow in an organization, and it involves the flows of orders, procedures, regulations, instructions, and all of the other ways by which managers tend to direct the actions of those who report to them.

But there is also some upward flow of communication in all organizations. In a more formal sense, upward communications are typically acknowledgements of management directions, reports of results, questions of clarification, and, of course, letters and memos from people being supervised who may wish to somehow influence the people who manage them. Despite our modern tendency to want to see workers participating democratically in the process of their own management, downward communication remains primarily com-

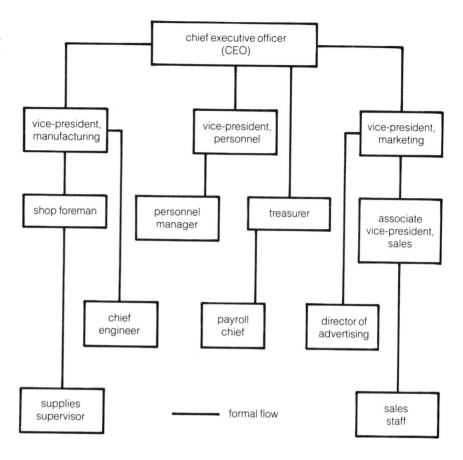

Figure 9.3
A Management Communication Hierarchy

municaton of direction and control, and upward communication remains primarily the communication of feedback. It is often acknowledged that workers' frustrations can greatly increase when they feel that their feedback is going unrecognized. This is one reason for the development of negative rumor, or "grapevine," patterns of communication in an organization. Professional consultants often deal with problems of the upward flow of communication in organizations.

There are also many communication flows that are not distinctively upward or downward but horizontal, as when co-workers communicate with one another for coordination or for clarifying responsibilities.

Networks: Formal and Informal. In our previous discussion, we have emphasized the formal flows of communication; that is, the communication needed in order for the organization to operate. In formal flow patterns, managers survey their markets, evaluate their resources, and give directions to their staffs to apply the organization's resources in ways that will accomplish its objectives. Staffs clarify instructions if necessary, acknowledge them, and eventually report results, all as upward communication. In turn, much horizontal communication may take place as formal communication required for coordination among staffs and departments in the organization.

In general, then, in any organization there will be a complex mixture or overlay of formal and informal flows or patterns of communication. The formal network can be predicted from the organization chart. The informal network, however, will arise from a great variety of factors, including chance social acquaintances among workers, proximity of different staff members who may not be directly related in the management hierarchy, channels explicitly developed by staff members because they cannot get the information they need from formal channels, and all of the broad processes of rumor or grapevine that develop to meet the communication needs of individuals who are not served by the formal network. Figure 9.4 illustrates the overlay of formal and informal networks.

There are many types of organizations for which a hierarchical order of management communication may offer optimum efficiency. For example, it is difficult to imagine how a military unit could be consistently efficient, particularly under fire, if there were not well-established lines of authority. Communication flows or networks in such organizations have a strong hierarchical pattern and are characterized by an authoritarian style of leadership.

Organizations characterized by complex combinations of professional personnel working on projects tend to shy away from strong hierarchical management patterns. One such organization is the modern hospital, where, although there may be a hierarchy of professional administrators, every physician feels generally "in charge" of his or her own professional activities. Administrators in this type of organization—and faculties of major universities would agree with this—are there for the "convenience" of the professional people. These organizations tend to have weak hierarchies because the professional members tend to manage themselves relatively effectively.

This same type of self-management carries over to modern technical organizations—for example, where a group of scientists is working on the development of a new piece of equipment. In such cases, although the overall company or organization has a strong hierarchical management, most of the activities directly concerned with the development of the product are not managed in an authoritarian manner. They are managed by the professionals, who coordinate their own efforts in accomplishing their goals. This is called *project management* and it is found increasingly often in modern service and technological organizations. In this type of organization, the communication flow of project managers is much more a coordination function. Consequently, if you were to find yourself in a position of either participating in such projects or studying the type of organizational communication found within them, you would be examining communication flows that are quite unlike those found in traditional hierarchies. Modern commentators on organizational communication (for example, Peter Drucker, 1974, 1980) observe that the business and service organizations of modern societies tend to be moving in the direction of more project management.

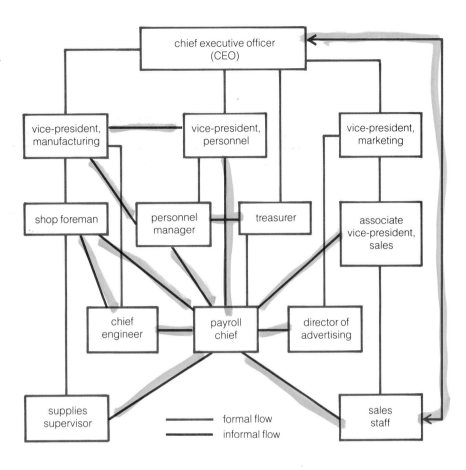

Figure 9.4
Mixtures of Formal and Informal Communication Flows

chief executive officer (CEO)

vice-president, manufacturing

vice-president, personnel

vice-president, marketing

shop foreman

personnel manager

treasurer

associate vice-president, sales

chief engineer

payroll chief

director of advertising

supplies supervisor

formal flow
informal flow

sales staff

COMMUNICATION WITHIN A COMMUNICATIONS ORGANIZATION

A particularly important and somewhat unusual area of organizational communication study involves businesses and service organizations whose product is communications itself. Take, for example, the organizational communication required to operate a daily newspaper. In the broad sense, like any organization, the newspaper has its institutional image, participates in a broad intake and output of messages, and requires a management hierarchy and communication flow in order to operate as an organization. But beyond these general characteristics, since the product itself is communications, there are several additional dimensions for organizational communication analysis.

Despite our idealistic images of newspapers as the "fourth estate," the objective of almost all newspapers in the free-enterprise world is to turn a profit for their shareholders. As will be discussed in several subsequent chapters, the predominant source of income for most newspapers is advertising, and a secondary source is subscriptions and single-copy sales. Here are two distinctly different kinds of communications-for-profit patterns, and in some ways they may be antagonistic to each other.

On the one hand, so that it can call itself a *news*paper, this type of organization will engage in the broad communications processes of news gathering, writing, editing, producing, and distributing a finished product that presumably has enough of interest in it that people will pay for it. At the same time, this newspaper will tell potential advertisers that it will carry their commercial messages for a fee. The more readers a newspaper can provide evidence of, the higher price it can charge for its advertising. Advertising is mostly solicited by a staff of sales personnel who have a specific set of communication behaviors for their activities. Ads are created in communication forms that are also a type of communication. And subsequently they, too, are reproduced and distributed along with the "news" part of the paper.

The natural antagonism between these two components of a newspaper organization raises the possibility that false or misleading advertising might slip past the newspaper manager, compromise the "news" value of the paper, and lessen its profitability as it loses subscribers. Also, the news component of the newspaper, in an attempt to be thorough and objective, may reflect negatively upon a major advertiser, who, in turn, will withdraw business from the newspaper. Not only is the management of both advertising and news functions of a newspaper complex, but the overall management of the organization requires special understanding and tact in order to keep this natural antagonism at a minimum.

It is a credit to newspaper professionals in the free-enterprise world that so many newspapers (but certainly not all) have been able to accomplish this balance. But more important for the present discussion is the fact that organizational communication has further complex extensions when the organization itself is in the business or service of communications.

SUMMARY

Our first encounters with organizations are likely to be confusing, because the way in which they operate is not always clear on the surface. When we communicate in organizations, we often mix our usual communication roles (those involving family, friends) with an organizational role, that is, the way we are supposed to contribute to the operation of the organization.

Much of our *organizational role* involves communication behaviors, most of which are reflected in *communication rules*. Rules are not always formally evident to us, and we must know how to learn the informal, subtle ones.

The traditional functions of communication usually become management functions in organizational communication. These are: (1) planning and organizing, (2) directing and motivating, (3) monitoring and controlling, (4) training, and (5) evaluating and changing.

When carrying out organizational communication, we often use many communications media. We can relate certain media uses to each of the five management functions. The so-called office of the future is more a metaphor than a fact. But there is a steady growth of new technological applications such as management information systems, word processing, electronic mail, electronic funds transfer, and teleconferencing. The successful organizational communicator will know how to make the most effective use of traditional media as well as new technologies.

Organizations themselves are "communicating units" in that they receive and disseminate messages. Traditional organizations have a communication flow—a *communication hierarchy*—representative of a management hierarchy. Flow within such hierarchies is both formal and informal. In some organizations there are variations of the traditional hierarchy, as in project management networks.

Organizations that are communications businesses have a special relation between typical organizational communication and the management of their product or service.

TOPICS FOR DISCUSSION OR BRIEF PAPERS

org make up

1. Create an organizational chart for any organization in which you have been involved or have available for study. What organizational roles are required for that organization to operate? How does communication facilitate that operation? What informal communication also affects the organization?

2. Do a brief case study of communication rules for an organization. How does a person new to the organization learn those rules? What happens if a member breaks them? Would you change the rules if you could?

3. Make a more detailed examination of the communications required for one of the five management functions described in this chapter. What media are involved? What new technologies would be of benefit? How would you train people to carry out that function?

4. Select one of the new technological applications mentioned in this chapter and find out how you purchase the equipment, service, or both. What are the approximate costs? What training is involved? If a purchase were made at this time, how soon would the system be obsolete?

5. Do some additional research on the topic of negotiation, or conflict resolution. What are typical cases? Typical solutions? Is there an "expected" amount of conflict in any organization? How do you know if it is getting out of hand?

REFERENCES AND READINGS

Baskin, O., and C. E. Arnoff. *Interpersonal Communication in Organizations*. Santa Monica, Calif.: Goodyear, 1980.

Bell, D. *The Coming of Post-Industrial Society*. New York: Basic Books, 1976.

Dordick, H. S., and F. Williams. *Innovative Management Using Telecommunications*. New York: Wiley, 1986.

Drucker, P. *Management: Tasks, Responsibilities, Practices*. New York: Harper and Row, 1974.

Drucker, P. *Managing in Turbulent Times*. New York: Harper and Row, 1980.

Farace, R. V., P. R. Monge, and H. M. Russell. *Communicating and Organizing*. Reading, Mass.: Addison-Wesley, 1977.

Putnam, L. L., and T. S. Jones. "The Role of Communication in Bargaining." *Human Communication Research* 8 (1982): 262–280.

Ritti, R. R., and G. R. Funkhouser. *The Ropes to Skip and the Ropes to Know*. Columbus, Ohio: Grid, 1977.

Tompkins, P. K. "Organizational Metamorphosis in Space Research and Development." *Communication Monographs* 45 (1978): 110–118.

Uris, A. *The Executive Deskbook*. 2d ed. New York: Van Nostrand, 1976.

Williams, F., and H. S. Dordick. *The Executive's Guide to Information Technology*. New York: Wiley, 1984.

Public
Communication

THE PUBLIC LEVEL OF COMMUNICATION

One mark of modern societies is an abundance of communication widely disseminated to large groups of people, hence the label *public*. Traditionally, when such communication has involved media disseminated almost indiscriminately to the public, social scientists have called it *mass* communication, reflecting the nineteenth-century concept of anonymous individuals composing the newly emerging, impersonal "mass" society. We have chosen to use the term *public* for this broadest level of communication because, in the present era of selective audiences and markets, the individual is no longer so anonymous, and the growth of this type of communication is as much in the *alternative* sources of messages (radio and TV channels, specialized publications, and the like) as in the growth of any one source. In fact, some public communication can be said to be "demassified" as it is targeted to specific audience groups, a topic developed later in this chapter. Also, it is important to recognize that large-scale public communication may combine word-of-mouth communication among individuals or within groups as a complement to media. In other words, all levels of communication may be involved in the concept of public communication.

Print and broadcast media play an important role in most public communication, for it is through the selection of media from the marketplace or the society at large that we satisfy many of our informational or entertainment needs. For example, think about which of the media—newspapers, magazines, books, movies, television, radio, records, disks, or tapes—you might select to fulfill such needs as:

releasing tension
understanding what is going on in the world
learning about something
developing good taste
sharing a communication experience with a friend
learning more about yourself

If you are like some university students who have expressed their preferences (see Exercise 1 in the Appendix), you have probably selected a wide variety of media options for these uses. Moreover, you may have thought how you might use one medium for two or three different uses, such as television for the news, to release tension, or to enjoy with some friends (watching a soap opera or a football game). Indeed, such choices are the essence of media use in our society. We serve many personal needs with them, particularly those that are not easily served by face-to-face or other forms of communication. For example, it may sometimes be easier to release tension by relaxing with radio music or a few tapes than by trying to talk with friends. Or if you want to find out the news of trouble in the Middle East, chances are that you can get that information only from a print or broadcast medium (that is, unless you know somebody there whom you can call). It is probably no revelation to you that if you want to study up on something, books are a handy reference medium.

How did you answer the question about knowing yourself? Many university students we have polled do not see much use for the media of print, broadcast, or film for this purpose, except for an occasional mention of self-help books. Mostly they feel that highly personal communication is required.

In this chapter we examine some of the general aspects of public, or mass, communications, both as a social process and as a business. Research examples of the effects of public communications are discussed in Chapters 12–14.

FOUR CHARAC-TERISTICS OF PUBLIC, OR MASS, COMMUNICATIONS

Mention "mass communications" or "public media" in an everyday conversation, and most people think that you are about to say something concerning newspapers or television, or even the movies or radio. However, the concept of public, or mass, communications in theoretical or research circles is much more complex. Typically, we are much more concerned with the ways in which media that are distributed broadly in a society are used by and affect their users.

As contrasted with interpersonal, group, or organizational communication, the social context of public communication is the larger society itself. In particular, public media are distributed to selected large groups in a society. Sometimes they are even the basis for defining a large group, as in the audience of a prime-time television series. These media have an effect on what a society learns about itself (for example, as "news"), on forms of leisure, the style of governments, and even on cultural attitudes. Although public communications has many facets, at least four main characteristics set it off from other forms of communication. These are:

1. low cost, rapid duplication, and wide dissemination
2. organizational sources of messages
3. potentially large and varied audiences
4. a role in economic or governance structures

1. Low Cost, Rapid Duplication, and Wide Dissemination

The media of public communications are particularly distinguished by messages that are reproduced in large numbers to be disseminated to an equally large audience. Such messages are often distributed rapidly and are inexpensive to the recipient. This function of the public media is sometimes called "multiplicative."

We can see, too, how the production and dissemination of public media have grown with the technological advances of society. This is one perspective from which to interpret the consequences of the invention of printing, broadcasting, photography, and the development of various recording and transmission devices. Based on this thinking, we date the origin of the system of public communications generally at the time of the invention and spread of printing in fifteenth-century Europe.

Although there were certainly many forms of "one-to-many" communications prior to the invention of printing (for example, public proclamations, inscriptions on temple walls, statues and displays), these messages were not multiplied in large numbers, and they could not be easily distributed to a population. (The people came to the temples, not vice-versa.) Not until the invention of printing could people duplicate messages inexpensively and eventually distribute them widely. We can also see how public communications grew with the development of machinery and the harnessing of energy in the Industrial Revolution. Public, or mass, communications through printing also grew as literacy spread beyond the scholarly class.

For most public media, the main message flow is one-way, from institution to audience. The return flow is often in another medium, as with television ratings, newspaper circulation, or the box-office returns for a motion picture. Often, too, feedback is indirect, as with letters to the editor or critics' reviews of films or television shows.

2. Organizational Sources of Messages

Although individual reporters write the news or an individual author writes a book, all creators of public, or mass, communications depend on an organization for the eventual production and dissemination of their product. If you paused at this moment to take inventory of all the public communications you have used today, every example could be traced to some type of disseminating organization—a radio station, local newspaper, a record company, a motion picture organization, and so on.

Public-communications organizations have several features in common. For one, they either house or coordinate the aforementioned production and dissemination capability. It is a fact of newspaper management that you must somehow take charge of printing your paper, either on your own presses or as contracted with another organization. A broadcasting station is organized in part around its production and engineering departments. The very essence of a broadcast network is its distribution capabilities. Media organizations were reflected in the discussion in Chapter 9 as institutions where communications is the product.

Because the reproduction and dissemination of public messages require a formidable investment of money, equipment, and personnel, there are obvious limits on who or what can be an organizational source of public communications. Whereas with interpersonal, group, or organizational communication it is not usually difficult to initiate a message, it is often difficult for an individual to get a message into the public-communications system of a society. Public relations and advertising professionals spend millions on this task. As we too often witness, some individuals stage riots, demonstrations, or sit-ins in order to gain space in the messages of public media.

Another characteristic of the organizational aspect of public communications is that the persons who make up such institutions are typically professional communicators. They must have certain levels of appeal or quality if they are to compete in the marketplace. Further, in many types of communications institutions, particularly among respected print and broadcast journalists, in publishing, filmmaking, and the public arts, there is a sense of professionalism. This means that there are either expressed or unexpressed standards for performance and conduct. In free-enterprise systems, these professionals must be sufficiently competitive so that their organizations can be profitable. In nonprofit or government institutions, communicators are expected to get results if their organization is to continue support of them and their products.

3. Potentially Large and Varied Audiences

Hand in hand with the multiplicative and wide dissemination capabilities of media institutions is the potential for large and varied audiences of message receivers. The concept *mass* does not necessarily center on the idea of a large audience but on individuals or groups of individuals who may become the audience of the messages. This use of the term *mass* originally reflected its application to mass society, or large groups of people who are not necessarily tied to one another by family, occupation, or other types of social structure. In this older sense of the term, the audiences of mass communications would be anybody (or group) who might choose to buy the newspaper, magazine, or book; listen to the broadcast; or go to the film. However, in the modern public-communications business the characteristics of these audiences are much better known, and messages are directed not so much at an indefinite mass as at particular sociological, cultural, age, or political groups. Success in modern public communications depends increasingly upon knowing and being able to secure an intended and well-defined audience. Although the "mass" quality of mass communications still applies to the audience, the anonymity of the latter does not. If any anonymity still exists, it may be of the individual user of a public medium; it is certainly not anonymity of the groups with which that individual may be associated (social class, politics, age, sex). Indeed, many of the audiences of public communications are referred to as specific "markets" in today's parlance.

One of the major social consequences of the new communications technologies is that they can reach specific and "self-service" audiences. If you decide to watch television tonight, you may have thirty or more broadcast channels to select from, or you may turn to cable TV, videotape, disk, or direct-to-home satellite channels. As a consumer, you may not reflect many of the traditional characteristics of a mass communications user. You may be only one of a few individuals viewing a program, and you will have chosen it from a large variety of selections. You are not one of the huge, anonymous mass of individuals of yesteryear's public communications who had few choices. Your choice may be very personal and self-serving.

This change in the nature of the audience is what some call the **demassification** of the traditional broad public forms of communication. If you are 25 or younger, you may not live out your life in the same mass society and public-communications environment so often ascribed to our culture. We ponder this prospect in the final section of this chapter.

4. A Role in Economic or Governance Structures

In free-enterprise economies, most public-communications organizations are profit-making institutions. Although the communications of that organization will generally serve broad purposes such as information, entertainment, instruction, or advertising, the institution must turn a profit for its owners in doing so. This, more than any other factor, will determine what that institution will produce for its public.

Too often, communication academics have studied public-communications organizations mainly in terms of their avowed social purposes or consequences, at the expense of examining their practical operations as businesses.

One of the most visible examples of the profit motive at work is the inundation of so much prime-time television by superficial and mass-taste entertainment. This is a reflection not so much of the poor taste of TV executives but rather of what type of product they claim they must produce in order to gain a large audience. A large audience means large advertising rates and a maximum profit for their stockholders.

Many public media are also the backbone of the advertising industry in a free-enterprise economy. Newspapers and most magazines devote more space to paid advertising than they do to editorial material. Commercial broadcasting has an abundance of commercial messages. And the amount may even increase as time-limitation regulations are dropped.

Although this book concentrates on communication in U.S. society and the Western world, we must remember that in worldwide terms, more public-communications organizations (by number, not necessarily size) operate as government agencies or under government influence than as free-enterprise businesses. The primary function of public-media organizations in most non-Western or socialist countries (especially communist countries) is to serve the national interest, not to make money for their owners. This is to be expected from the political philosophy of such societies. There is nothing unusual about it. In the ideal sense, the goal of these governmentally controlled communications institutions is to protect and otherwise advance the nation's cultural and political systems. In that respect, their operation is inextricable from the system of governance.

The press in free-enterprise countries also has a special political role as a media institution that can evaluate or influence government actions. It is a "watchdog" for society. The avowed responsibility of a free press is to seek out and expose corruption and mismanagement. (The Watergate scandal was a prime example.) But as we all realize, there are vast differences in the degree to which print and broadcast organizations assume this responsibility.

Even in free-enterprise societies, however, there are laws and regulations that affect how the process of public communications carries on.

In Part Three of the book, we have stressed that we must look at communication as a process if we are to analyze it. We must do the same for public communication. Among the distinguishing features of public communication is, again, that its context is society itself. Within this broad context we can examine it in terms of several processes, the first being an interaction between the *public* and *media* institutions, as illustrated in Figure 10.1.

Figure 10.1
Communication as
a Public Process

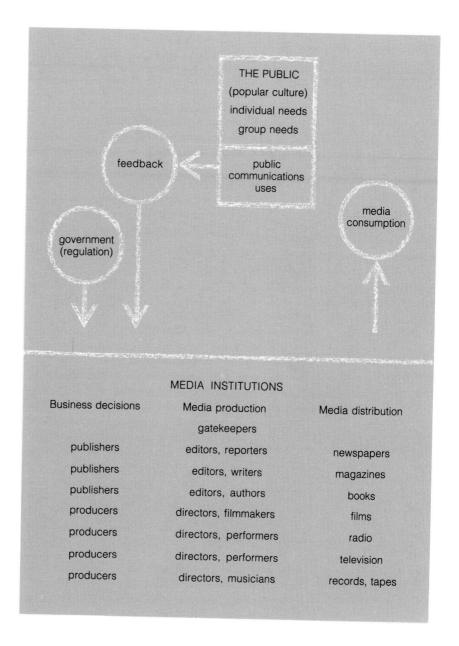

THE PUBLIC
(popular culture)
individual needs
group needs

feedback

public
communications
uses

media
consumption

government
(regulation)

MEDIA INSTITUTIONS

Business decisions	Media production	Media distribution
	gatekeepers	
publishers	editors, reporters	newspapers
publishers	editors, writers	magazines
publishers	editors, authors	books
producers	directors, filmmakers	films
producers	directors, performers	radio
producers	directors, performers	television
producers	directors, musicians	records, tapes

The Public

Notice in Figure 10.1 that the public has been put at the top of the diagram in order to stress its centrality to this communication process. It is the public, its needs and tastes, that creates the market for the media. We are the ultimate consumers who support the media industries.

As discussed in earlier chapters, we tend to use public media for needs that we cannot so easily fulfill in face-to-face or other, more immediate forms of communication. This is what "needs" reminds us of in the diagram—that we typically use public media toward some personal or social end. We turn to records, tapes, or movies to fulfill our entertainment needs. The newspaper, or news on radio or television, helps us to find out what is going on in the world beyond our direct experiences. Theaters and films give us opportunities for public outings with friends and a program for our personal enjoyment. The media reflect the operation of our society, including the current public attitudes, habits, and feelings we often loosely call "popular culture." They convey to us information that we can use to carry out our everyday lives. In all, our needs create the marketplace for media institutions (to do business in).

How well certain media fulfill our needs is eventually reflected in what we purchase, rent, or pay admission to. Our reactions are feedback to media institutions, which then try to adapt to the marketplace.

In the modern world, we have many alternative forms of media, each of which attempts to find its place in the public market. Most media institutions are mixes of business, creative, and production or distribution personnel. They plan, create, and distribute the public-media "product."

Media Institutions

Most media institutions can be divided into business, production, and distribution components. Figure 10.1 includes a few examples of how these divisions are represented in terms of personnel and the ultimate product (what is distributed). As such, a media institution is usually a relatively unique combination of business and creative personnel. And the need for productivity and profit (business) is a goal that is sometimes antagonistic to the freedom necessary for a creative environment. You may witness one side or the other of this if you go to work in either the business or creative side of a media organization—for example, as an advertising salesperson or general-assignment reporter. From either side, though, this is one of the challenging, yet exciting, qualities of working professionally in communications.

Sometimes we say that some creative personnel, especially editors, are "**gatekeepers**" because they control what media content eventually appears in the final product. They are the ones who essentially control what the public sees or hears. Persons who fill such roles have a potentially strong influence on the images society sees of itself.

Yet, there is a longtime controversy in theoretical circles over how much the media simply cater to public tastes rather than shaping them. Although we take up some of this controversy in later chapters (news in Chapter 12, entertainment in Chapter 14), suffice it to say that this process often works both ways. Young children's interests in the fantasy films of George Lucas ("Star Wars") or Steven Spielberg ("E.T.") were no doubt stirred up by monumental advertising campaigns. Yet, at the same time, there were many signs that older children and young adults had an appetite for a new wave of fantasy films.

PUBLIC COM-MUNICATIONS AS A BUSINESS

As we said at the outset of this chapter, too often in the academic study of public communications we overlook the fact that in a free-enterprise society, most of the communications institutions are profit-seeking businesses. We are not so much stressing free enterprise to take a political position here but rather as a reminder that this is what supports the operation of the public media in the United States and other countries with similar economic systems. Remember, again, that in most other countries of the world, the institutions of mass communications are either a direct part of, or an extension of, the government.

If the model in Figure 10.2 seems "commercial," it is meant to be. Unless you keep this commercial quality in mind, it will be difficult for you to understand the public media of the United States, let alone to work in

Figure 10.2
Mass Communications as a Business

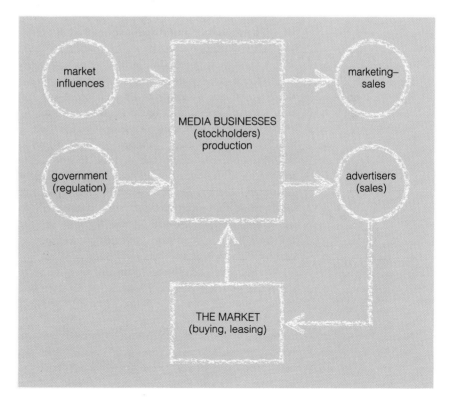

them or even be an intelligent consumer of them. With this in mind, let us examine some of the dynamics that relate the communications business organization with its market.

The Media Business Organization

What influences a commercial media organization to invest in a product for a market? Mainly, in a profit-making enterprise, it is any activity that will generate revenues from the marketplace, increase the value of the investors' holdings, or otherwise be beneficial to the financial status of the organization. For advertising-supported media (newspapers, most magazines, commercial radio and television), will circulation or viewership ("ratings") be large enough to justify the level of advertising rates? If the media product (books, records, tapes, some periodicals) is sold or leased (films to theaters), will the market generate sufficient funds to create a profit on investment?

Sometimes market influences may not suggest an immediate profit but rather a longer range one. For example, many cable-television organizations often are not currently profitable. But their longer range promise for profits as well as the fact that they represent a franchised monopoly for an area make them valuable as investments.

Market influence also reflects government or other types of regulation. For example, broadcast television has been deregulated. This removed the limits to the amount of time that can be given over to commercial messages. All along, cable-television operators have been able to devote entire channels to full-time advertising if they thought enough people would watch it in order to get advertisers to pay for it.

Although anybody who wants to make the investment can start a neighborhood newspaper, you cannot start up your own radio station. You must have a license. Such points may already be well known to you, but we mention them because market influences and investors' reactions to them often operate under the constraint of regulation.

A change in regulation may prompt a change in the dynamics of the marketplace. For example, in this decade debate will continue over the prospects of delivering a television signal directly to the home from a communications satellite. If or when regulations make it easy to go into this business, the marketplace for such services will soar in value (and traditional broadcast stations may lose value). No wonder so many special-interest groups try to influence how the government regulates certain aspects of public communications.

As we have seen, antagonisms can arise in an advertising-supported medium over whether to publish or broadcast content that is possibly damaging to a major advertiser. In most major news organizations, there is a large measure of independence for those who select stories. Editors in such organizations have a professional commitment to do their best, within the context and style of their medium, to deliver objective reports of the news. On the other hand, relations between story selection and advertiser revenue are not uncommon

Compact disks are one example of the wide distribution of media products by "rack sales" methods. Distributors sell large blocks of titles to retailers, who then sell individual items, with options for returning unsold ones. This puts more of the initial selection in the hands of the manufacturer and distributor, rather than the individual retailer or customer. *PhotoEdit / Tony Freeman*

in smaller, especially local, media organizations. For example, it is not unusual for smaller newspapers to carry promotional "stories" for their bigger advertisers. This is called "puff" in the business, and it represents questionable behavior to a highly professional journalist.

But for entertainment television, the selection of program content can be influenced by advertiser interest. A program will not be run long without a sponsor! Selection of programming for network prime-time television is almost exclusively tied to the advertising marketplace. The larger the audience, the higher the rates for commercial insertions. That prime-time television is marked by so many programs of mass-public taste is a commitment to deliver the largest possible audience to the commercial period. But the fact that prime-time programs can sometimes be of exceedingly high quality and also attract a large audience is evidence that our broadcast industry could serve us better. As *Roots* producer David Wolper has maintained: "If somebody has an idea that if the audience is large, the material is less intellectual, that's not true. The audience can be large and the material can be intellectual."

One of the major trends in the magazine business is that it has slowly been shifting from an advertiser-supported to a sales-price-supported medium. The old mass-market magazines such as the weekly version of *Life* sold for far less than it cost to produce each copy of the magazine. Profits were gained from advertising revenue. Now, in the late 1980s, about half of all magazines make money from their cover price in addition to advertisements.

Books are an example of media products that are not linked to advertising revenue. Acquisition editors are given a budget to develop a given number of books. In the world of trade books (those for the general public), manuscript ideas often flow from authors through literary agents to editors. Or editors may ask agents to be on the lookout for certain types of projects. If an editor favors a proposal, the project may be reviewed by the publisher's marketing department to estimate its potential sales. Also, all proposals need a final clearance by a committee. The marketability of a book is a mixture of the author's reputation and an estimate of the market interest in the topic, coupled with the amount of promotional money the publisher is willing to invest.

Content selection in the motion picture business is even more of an entrepreneurial operation. Except where a major studio will invest its own funds in a potential production, selection is closely tied to a producer's ability to raise funds from investors. Because the film business is such a high-risk investment (most films are not profitable, but a few are spectacularly so), decisions are often influenced mainly by the reputation of the producer or simply his or her ability to attract investors.

Market research is also a major practice in the modern business of mass communications. That is, what do audiences want to read? What types of shows might they watch? How will they like this film that will have a trial showing (sneak preview) in five cities? How much will they be willing to spend on new pay-TV programs? Since such questions are partially answerable by assembling trial audiences and testing media materials, sometimes only a few people (focus group) who are thought representative of a general type (such as housewives) will be assembled for a trial viewing or discussion of a product.

The Market

How the audience reacts to media products or services is the most important component of market influence (to complete the process "cycle"). What is a newspaper's circulation and, in turn, its advertising revenues? What is a film's box office, especially in the first week or so? What orders are initially placed for a forthcoming book? (The fact that bookstore chains make huge orders is the reason why some popular authors have best sellers before you can buy the book on the market.)

But the most publicly visible reactions in the media industries are television rating services. For example, the Nielsen Company selects a nationwide sample of 1500 households that are taken as representative of the U.S. viewing audience. They regularly fill in diaries of what programs they watch. The results are then converted into population viewing estimates—a "30 share" (30 percent of total households viewing at that time), for example, or "30 million viewers," a projection of households multiplied by the average number of persons in each. Some households in special samples have small meters connected to their television sets, so that they can be read literally "overnight" and become the basis for ratings referred to by that name. Ratings, as you have no doubt experienced, will usually make or break a new program before it is even well into a television season. Is this good show business? Probably not. But, after all, it is more fundamentally the *advertising* business we are witnessing.

SOME NOTES
ON REGULATION

Laws and Codes

Regulation is a factor to consider in examining mass communications either as a public or a business process. Mostly this refers to government rules or laws, but it could also include the influence of codes, or industry-supported agreements to operate in certain ways. An example of the former is that you cannot just go out and start your own radio station. You must have a license, which is required, among other reasons, so stations won't drown one another out. Another example is that the U.S. Constitution forbids the government from censoring news stories. (If you looked at several Pakistani newspapers during the early 1980s, you could regularly see blank spots where government censors required removal of stories unfriendly to the current government.)

An example of the effect a code has is the agreement among broadcasters not to advertise hard liquor on television or radio.

Although we are mainly concerned with public communications in this chapter, we should remember that there are also regulations affecting other forms of communication. For example, telephone companies would very much like to develop advertising services that you could use via your phone and television set. Current regulations bar these companies from so-called electronic publishing, because under the law they are mainly to sell transmission services. Such regulations are no doubt influenced by newspaper publishers who do not wish such competition for the advertising dollar. However, recent telephone deregulation will eventually permit telephone companies to sell information.

We cannot really account for public-communications processes in a society without understanding the regulatory forces at work. The problem is that these forces differ substantially from country to country and within a country in terms of the different media of mass communications. It may surprise you to learn that the language of regulations is often similar among different countries (the constitution of the U.S.S.R. also guarantees freedom of speech and of the press). The main distinction is in how the regulations are interpreted.

Regulatory Principles in the United States

In the United States, two broad principles have influenced the regulatory context of public communications. The first is the literal interpretation we make of the First Amendment to the U.S. Constitution: "That Congress shall make no law . . . abridging the freedom of speech, or of the press. . . ." Although our founding fathers were thinking mainly of freedom of political expression, the First Amendment has been used as a premise in legal arguments to guarantee freedom of expression in a great variety of applications, from the advertising of patent medicines to the right to march on city streets.

The second principle has been the need to create an environment that maximizes the orderly development and public benefits of certain communications media. This is especially reflected in the phrase "public interest, convenience, and necessity" as found in the U.S. Communications Act of 1934. This is the type of regulation that allocates the broadcast spectrum among different types of services as well as coordinates the licensing of com-

John M. Kittross

In recent years, the volume of the Code of Federal Regulations that deals with broadcasting and cable television has expanded considerably. This growth alone would tend to justify the current campaign for deregulation of the broadcasting industry. Although many of these regulations can be eliminated, most were originally installed for valid reasons; that is, their intent was to benefit the public, not to give bureaucrats an excuse to employ more bureaucrats. It is a shame that the buzzword *deregulation* has eclipsed the undefinable but comforting goal of the "public-interest" standard as the touchstone of public policy.

The goal of deregulation, according to FCC Chairman Mark Fowler in 1981, was "to create to the maximum extent possible, an unregulated, competitive marketplace environment for the development of telecommunications." This goal assumes a great deal—with limited evidence and logic—about both the marketplace and competition.

The basic argument of deregulation is that the day of "scarcity" of channels in the electromagnetic spectrum is over, and with deregulation, true competition among businesses will benefit the public in the long run by providing a greater selection of channel services. But this dogmatic assertion assumes that additional channels of television programming provided by the different technologies present today, such as cable, direct-broadcast satellites, or videotape and disk, are all part of the same market.

This assumption remains to be tested. As late as 1969, the Supreme Court, in the *Red Lion* case, held unanimously that "scarcity is not entirely a thing of the past." This remains true today, with respect to over-the-air television and radio, since new stations squeezed onto the same number of channels generally cause interference, not more service. Indeed, hundreds of new stations have squeezed onto the same number of channels. Is a home video computer game in direct competition with ABC, CBS, or NBC? Is it a factor in the same market? I believe not, except insofar as *all* activities are in competition for our attention, from our families and pets to all sorts of other natural and human-made stimuli.

For most Americans, there *is* scarcity—not just scarcity of the kinds of programs that an individual wants to see or hear. The 35 to 104 channels of cable television offered in some communities must be weighed against the fact that only a little over one-half of American homes now have cable service. The typical cable system only offers twelve channels, and there is a single cable operator selecting channels for the consumer. Many Americans have access to only two or three channels of television, and a small proportion live where none are available. Furthermore, the existence of multiple channels does not guarantee even distribution of the economic resources to purchase or subscribe to them or a wide diversity of programs. It certainly doesn't guarantee outlets for local expression or programs of high quality!

Two traditional principles of American broad-

mercial radio and television broadcasters. It is also the type of regulation under which the telephone business grew as a legalized monopoly in the United States and which now is being modified in our era of deregulation. (In most countries, the telephone system is operated by the postal, telegraph, and telephone branch of the government, or "PTT," as they say.)

As you might assume, wired and broadcast types of communication have required the most coordination. The regulatory agency most identified with these activities is the **Federal Communications Commission** (FCC). The operations of this agency have not been without controversy during its roughly half-century of history. Much of the criticism has centered upon its lack of aggressiveness in regulation, its sometimes apparent subservience to industry, and its predictable slowness in responding to change. Also highly controversial have been situations where the *content* of communication has been

casting policy have prevented monopoly and the enhancement of localism. But the FCC is allowing direct broadcast satellite (DBS) television service without requiring service to local audiences, and FCC rules preventing one entity from owning an unlimited number of stations do not apply to cable or low-power television. In a way, broadcast deregulation is analogous to granting leases for private gain to the forests or other public resources in perpetuity. Although many "have-nots" have been deluded into thinking that deregulation will give them a chance to obtain a channel, the acquisition will require either lots of money—enough, say, to outbid a member of the Fortune 500—or a challenge to an existing licensee. But license terms have just been substantially lengthened, and the burden of proof on challengers has grown almost impossibly heavy. Deregulation, in spite of its superficial attractiveness, doesn't always lead to healthy competition. History tells us that the end product of uncontrolled competition often is the absence of competition, or monopoly.

Who will benefit most from deregulation? As "Deep Throat" said to Bob Woodward, "Follow the money." Without the legal and enforceable requirement to operate in the public interest, many entrepreneurs would have no commitment to anything other than a profitable bottom line. Such investors care little about the social values of what they communicate.

Will the public benefit? Well . . . not very much. It is unlikely that there is much undiscovered talent of high quality just waiting for new media to employ them or that the general public will find much more variety in entertainment or news con-

tent, as is already the case with the repetition of movies on different pay-cable services. The "marketplace of ideas" may be adversely affected by competition in the marketplace of business if the latter doesn't lead to a greater diversity of voices and outlets. More competition isn't the cure for a shortage of talent to produce good programming.

While the FCC may not have an immediate need for annual financial data or for station logs, without them it may be impossible to determine whether this great ideological experiment is serving the public interest. One shouldn't have to throw out the concept of accountability with the red tape.

So, since the push toward deregulation is aimed only at government, we may find ourselves at the tender mercies of (monopoly) business. Since the loved and the rich don't really need much protection, only government can enable the minority and the mass publics to mobilize against economic power. While government doesn't always recognize or act for the "common good," who else is equipped or willing to even try on this role? Deregulation will be beneficial to some—but probably not to thee and me.

John M. Kittross is a Professor with Emerson College, Boston.

Suggested reading: Christopher H. Sterling and John M. Kittross, *Stay Tuned: A Concise History of American Broadcasting* (Belmont, Calif.: Wadsworth, 1978).

---

an issue. Prominent controversies of this type have included the equal-time provision for political candidates who appear on television or the public outcry over the amounts of violence on television, especially in programs available to children. But any type of regulation of the content of communication can run head on into the regulatory principle of freedom of speech in our society.

Deregulation

The reluctance to regulate cannot be explained as bureaucratic ineptness. For one thing, the sometimes conflicting regulatory principles, as just mentioned, make decisions virtually impossible under existing law. But more important is that the United States is not by tradition or philosophy a society that takes easily to regulation. If there are not compelling reasons for regulations of certain types, it becomes exceedingly difficult to enforce them (note, for example, the controversy over the legality of home taping of television programs). For these reasons, regulations affecting communications in the United States have undergone more change in the decade of the 1980s than at anytime since the early regulation of radio and the Communications Act of 1934. We are in a period of active **deregulation.** And it is changing the structure of many communications businesses, from broadcasting to telephone. The pros and cons for broadcasting are summarized well in the commentary by John M. Kittross, a broadcast historian and critic. Deregulation is one of the forces speeding the apparent demassification of broadcast media in the United States.

THE CONCEPT OF DEMASSIFI- CATION

In contrast to processes of interpersonal, group, and organizational communication, the receiver of a public communication is selecting medium and content from what is often a vast variety of alternatives. In a free-enterprise, public-communications system, the audience member is often a consumer who must make an outright purchase of the media product—newspaper, magazine, book, record, tape, and so on. In other cases, this consumer is subsidizing the medium through the purchase of a product promoted by an advertiser, as with television and radio, in particular. One mark of modern communications is that the variety of these alternatives has been constantly increasing. As the alternatives increase, there is less opportunity for large, anonymous—that is, *mass*—audiences to be attracted by any one medium. There is less attraction for the mass advertiser. One very visible trend since the 1950s has been increased competition among the different public media for this broad (and profitable!) audience.

From the 1920s through most of the 1950s, certain magazines had large audiences. *Life, Look, Post,* and *Colliers,* for example, commanded huge circulations and could charge high prices for advertising space. But in the 1950s and early 60s, television drew away the audience from magazines and, subsequently, their advertising dollars. The once mass-audience magazine was superseded by many specialized ones—by publications devoted to hobbies or to particular types of content. Most such magazines were designed to appeal to specialized rather than general audiences. Audiences were, so to speak, "demassified." They became much more specifically identified. Content was targeted for them, just as the content of, for example, *Playboy* magazine is designed to appeal to a certain type of reader. Additionally, advertisers were persuaded that they could now buy space in publications that were particularly targeted to certain audiences.

Radio underwent a similar change in audience. From the 1930s into the 50s, people huddled around their living room radio sets as we now do in front of our television sets. But when television attracted these audiences, radio had to become specialized in order to hold some type of audience. This led to the growth of station "formats," which you can experience especially in urban areas where many stations are competing for an audience. These are the all-music or all-news formats, "talk radio," as well as stations specializing in certain types of music ranging from country-and-western to rock. Radio went from broadcasting to "**narrowcasting,**" as they say in the trade. It also, in many cases, became more of a "background" medium, one to which the audience might not always pay direct attention. No longer could a Jack Benny attract a national audience for a weekly show. Radio, too, became demassified.

Films have undergone a somewhat similar transition. In the 1930s and 1940s many families went to the movies regularly on Friday or Saturday night. Just as many television viewers turn on their sets just to "watch TV" and not always a specific program, moviegoers simply "went to the show." Now, the audiences of films also has become demassified. There is no longer a truly mass audience. In the movie business, producers think of markets as "preteens," "young adults," or the "drive-in crowd." Even the audiences of highly profitable films do not represent much of a cross-section of the public.

One common question is whether we are now entering a period when network, prime-time television will be losing its large mass audience. As viewers turn more and more to specialized programs offered by cable TV, videotape, video disk, videotext, pay-TV systems, and, soon, satellite ones and have their individual needs fulfilled, will we see the demise of television as a mostly *mass* medium? As with magazines, will advertisers who seek more specialized audiences pull their dollars out of advertising budgets and, thus, the support of "mass programming" strategies of the networks? Will we see the demassification of the last truly mass medium?

SUMMARY

As communications consumers, we become involved in the processes of public, or mass, communications as we make choices among media for purposes of fulfilling our needs. The media of public communications tend to fulfill those needs that cannot otherwise be accommodated through face-to-face and other more immediate forms of communication. *Mass* traditionally refers to large, anonymous audiences.

The four characteristics that distinguish public communications are (1) the messages are inexpensive, rapidly duplicated, and widely disseminated; (2) the messages are produced and disseminated by institutions, often commercial ones; (3) the audiences are potentially large and varied; and (4) most mass media fit into the economic or governance structures of a society.

The content of the process of public communications is society itself. As a public process, mass communications is an interaction between a public with individual and social needs existing in a contemporary culture and institutions that may both supply and influence those needs by the creation and distribution of information, entertainment, and various services. This process is further affected by the regulatory environment.

As a business, public communications in a free-enterprise society is an interaction between institutions that attempt to return a profit on the investments of their stockholders and a "market" that will purchase, lease, or pay admissions. A further, key component is the selling of message time or space for profit—that is, the "advertising" component of the mass communications business. These processes are also affected by the regulatory environment.

Regulation of media in U.S. society through laws and codes mainly reflects an interpretation of the First Amendment (free speech) and attempts to create an orderly growth and operation of certain media for "public interest, convenience, and necessity." In the decade of the 1980s there is a strong trend in the United States toward *deregulation* of wired and broadcast media.

The burgeoning growth of new communications services and the expansion of old ones, coupled with deregulation, may be causing the *demassification* of public media, particularly network television. The large, often anonymous, mass audience may be replaced by a public-communication process of many alternative types of communication and content to meet the specialized interests of individuals and groups.

TOPICS FOR DISCUSSION OR BRIEF PAPERS

1. Examine several of the books listed in the references to this chapter for their definitions of the public-communication process. What do the different definitions have in common? How do they differ? What definition do you prefer? (Can you create one of your own?)

2. Do some research on the First Amendment to the U.S. Constitution. How did it come about? What are some of the landmark ways it has been interpreted by the courts? Do you think it should now be revised or modified?

3. Look up the annual earnings of some of the major mass-communications corporations in America. Which are the largest? How do they compare with other businesses in size and return on investment? (*Business Week* carries annual earnings statements; and look up its publisher, McGraw-Hill, while you are at it.)

4. Write out an analysis of your personal uses of public media. Distinguish what you use for information, instructional, or entertainment purposes. What sources of media persuasion do you experience? Which medium could you least do without? Do you see your uses of any medium growing in the future?

5. Reexamine the John Kittross commentary on deregulation. What are your own ideas and attitudes? Take a position on the topic, and be prepared to defend it.

REFERENCES AND READINGS

Agee, W. K., P. H. Ault, and E. Emery. *Introduction to Mass Communications*. 8th ed. New York: Harper and Row, 1985.

Atwan, R., B. Orton, and W. Vesterman. *American Mass Media*. New York: Random House, 1982.

Becker, S. L. *Discovering Mass Communication*. Glenview, Ill.: Scott, Foresman, 1983.

Bittner, J. R. *Mass Communication: An Introduction*. 2d ed. Englewood Cliffs, N.J.: Prentice-Hall, 1980.

Davison, W. P., J. Boyla, and F. T. C. Yu. *Mass Media: System and Effects*. New York: Holt, Rinehart and Winston, 1976.

DeFleur, M. L., and E. E. Dennis. *Understanding Mass Communication*. Boston: Houghton Mifflin, 1981.

Dennis, E. E. *The Media Society: Evidence about Mass Communication in America*. Dubuque, Iowa: William C. Brown, 1978.

Head, S. W., and C. H. Sterling. *Broadcasting in America: A Survey of Television, Radio, and New Technologies*. 4th ed. Boston: Houghton Mifflin, 1982.

Pemper, D. R. *Mass Media in America*. 3d ed. Chicago: Science Research Associates, 1981.

Sterling, C. H., and J. M. Kittross. *Stay Tuned: A Concise History of American Broadcasting*. Belmont, Calif.: Wadsworth, 1978.

Whetmore, E. J. *Mediamerica*. Belmont, Calif.: Wadsworth, 1982.

Wolper, D. "Docudrama Conference." *Emmy*, Summer 1979.

PART
FOUR

Research in Communication

Communication is still a relatively young field, with new ideas

being contributed continually through scholarly reports in

books and journals. The four chapters in this part review four

topical areas of research: relational, or interpersonal,

communication; information and public opinion; political

communication; and entertainment. Most of the research

reviewed in these chapters represents variations of the social

scientific approach. Systematic observations are made, and

generalizations are drawn from them. The variations reflect

quantitative and qualitative methods, formal and selective

sampling, and innovative attempts at studying interaction

processes across time. Thus, these chapters sample not only

research topics but also methods.

Relational Communication

Certainly among the most important uses of human communication are the interpersonal exchanges that allow us to develop and maintain social relationships. Research into relational communication between the sexes is especially interesting because it can examine the process by which two complete strangers develop not only a friendship but the intimate relationship of marriage. By the same token, research can also look into how communication is used when a relationship is deteriorating. *Photo Edit/Alan Oddie*

Guy R. Lefrancois, author of the textbook *Psychology*, relates this anecdote about the beautiful Celine:*

Sam has been too occupied to read all of this manuscript, but he has taken the time to read the chapter introductions.

"You have no choice," he said. "No choice whatsoever."
"About what?"
"About the introduction for Chapter 19," he answered. "You have to tell them about the time you fell in love with Celine."

I can't. I choose not to. I do not want to tell you about Celine. It would be meaningless for you and embarrassing for me to describe how I lay awake at night dreaming of that girl, planning our incredibly happy future, and

*From Guy R. Lefrancois, *Psychology* (Belmont, Calif.: Wadsworth, 1980), p. 577. Reproduced by permission of the publisher.

listening to my grandmother snoring. I could not show you our poetry—my poetry. "My soul is sick with sores of misery," I wrote in imperfect iambic pentameter, beginning a heart-rending sonnet expressing my fear that she might not love me, for I had not yet spoken with her. Elsewhere I penned, "Oh sweet, oh love! Oh you, my dove" in a burst of romantic agony. And there were other lines, other poems, too private for me to share. Even with Celine.

I could not bring myself to tell you of the countless clever coincidences I arranged to bring us close enough to each other that I might see her, even if only for a brief instant. It would shame me to admit that I almost failed my French class because she sat in the row two over to the right and three desks forward from where I sat, and I could see her out of the corner of my eye whenever Luke left his seat.

Ah, Celine. She was with me night and day. I could not rid my mind of her. I didn't want to. I was in love. At the age of fifteen and for three whole weeks!

I should have spoken to her.

Lefrancois's charming anecdote reminds us that relational communication may well begin as a process of interpersonal perception. These perceptions set up expectations that we may pursue or test through interpersonal communication. Sometimes the exchanges lead to lifelong friendships or marriage, or they may lead nowhere. But they are sure to lead nowhere (except perhaps to pleasant memories) if we remain silent!

In this chapter, we examine several examples of social scientific research into relational communication. As you will see, much of the theoretical emphasis is on correlations between types of communication and stages in the development or deterioration of interpersonal relationships.

THE RESEARCH PERSPECTIVE

Prior to examining several examples of research, let us review a few points about relational communication. A fundamental premise is that the more that message exchanges involve personal information about the communicators involved and the more that this information affects the persons' expectations about each other, the more the interaction can be said to be *interpersonal*, or *relational*. As described in Chapter 7, this is the process of getting to know the other person as an individual rather than as a stereotype.

The main point is that communication is a part of the development, maintenance, deterioration, or termination of a relationship. Also as discussed in the earlier chapter, there may be important distinctions about the degree to which a role relationship is influenced by initial stereotyping, by sexual attraction, or expectations associated with the communication context (for example, at a party, at work, or in an impersonal situation). Although relationships are often discussed in terms of dyads (two-person units), they can also involve small groups of, say, three to five persons or even more in family networks.

Relationships can be said to evolve through a series of steps. Although researchers differ somewhat on the details of the steps, they all include a range from a general step of initiation to one of formalization, with the option of continued maintenance or termination of the relationship. Most of these relationships evolve within a social context of some type (school, work, group, club). Research has tended to focus on marriage relationships, in the study of interpersonal communication; leader–participant relationships, in group communication; and manager–employee relationships, in organizational communication. Again, the basic characterization of the process of relational communication is that it is *not* a one-dimensional exchange like the following:

$$\text{PERSON} \longrightarrow \text{PERSON}$$

Instead, communication affects the individuals so that they grow in their knowledge of each other. Therefore, the relationship at time 2 may be different from that at time 1, for example:

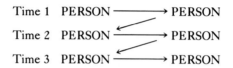

The diagram above could reflect your getting to know your professor as you communicate during a semester, for example.

The research methods used in relational studies have several distinguishing characteristics. First, they are often a mix of qualitative and quantitative methods. A qualitative study might interpret message segments as they represent different intents or functions—for example, attempts to disclose or gain personal information, attempts to dominate the behavior of another, or attempts to persuade. A quantitative study might count the number of exchanges in a given conversational period or use rating scales to describe attitudes. Another important characteristic is that research often focuses on the *interaction* process rather than on a single point in time. That is, rather than sampling messages as independent units, researchers attempt to understand their interrelation as a communication sequence develops. Indeed, interaction is a fundamental aspect of the communication process, and relational studies lead in contributions to knowledge in this area.

Much of the research interest in relational communication is an attempt to develop a theory about the types of communication that contribute to developing (or dissolving) interpersonal relationships. If we are to examine this theory, it is important to identify the characteristics of personal communication that seem to reflect different relationships.

TYPES OF COMMUNICATION IN RELATIONSHIPS

What kinds of communication characterize the relationship process? This is a topic of much research. One of the clearest summaries of the broad range of these characteristics is given by Mark Knapp (1984). He discusses eight dimensions along which individuals' interpersonal communication varies according to the stage of their relationship:

Narrow–broad: Broad conversations encompass a wide range of topics, rather than concentrating on one or only several topics. As a relationship develops, one expects a broader range of topics to be accommodated in conversation. By the same token, as a relationship comes apart, fewer topics may be exchanged.

Stylized–unique: Unique communication is adapted to another person as a specific individual, whereas stylized communication is suitable for a wider range of people. Uniqueness could involve special ways of saying hello, particular tones of voice, or even gestures that seem to be effective in a particular relationship.

Difficult–efficient: As a relationship becomes established, it should take less planning or overall effort to communicate, thus making message exchange more efficient. Thus, there is less tendency to misunderstand each other. Individuals who come to know each other well and share considerable personal experience can refer to mutual experiences without the need for a large amount of description.

Rigid–flexible: In new, less-developed, or deteriorating relationships, communication may become more inflexible and routinized, as, for example, mumbling "uh-huh" to most everything the other person says. As relationships develop, communication may involve an increasing variety of ways of expressing topics or emotions. There may even be an intent to explore that flexibility.

Awkward–smooth: As we get to know other persons well, it is usually easier for us to communicate with them, because we know what they understand and what will motivate or interest them. With people about whom we know less, we are likely to make occasional mistakes in explaining or appealing to them, and communication may not always be clear.

Public–personal: As we come to know another person, we often learn more of the personal, intimate details of his or her life, and our communication may take these into account. This knowledge is in contrast to the more general, or public, image that a person reveals. The more the communication is personally oriented, the greater is the "social penetration" in the interaction.

Hesitant–spontaneous: Conversations among people in a close relationship may be marked by considerable spontaneity, in that there is less fear of saying the wrong thing or taking time to calculate how something should

Mark L. Knapp

What scholars choose to study is often influenced by societal trends. During the 1960s and 1970s, more and more Americans were divorcing, freely experimenting with relationship styles from dual careers to communal living, questioning messages based solely on authority or status, exploring the values of a philosophy rooted in self-fulfillment above all else, and moving more than at any other time in U.S. history. These factors, among others, were influential in launching what is now a rapidly growing area of communication research, which seeks answers to two interrelated questions: (1) How does the definition of a relationship (between friends, boss and employee, lovers) affect communication behavior? (2) How do various patterns of communication affect the way an interacting pair choose to define their relationship?

The study of communication behavior in the context of developing relationships has raised some issues that are in sharp contrast with those in the days when the prevailing paradigm for studying interpersonal communication was the analysis of initial interactions between strangers.

For example, interaction patterns manifested during initial interaction are heavily laden with stereotypical behavior—that is, behavior adapted to people in general. But as the relationship develops, idiosyncratic patterns also develop, patterns that reveal the communicator's knowledge of the specific characteristics of his or her partner. Stereotypical patterns can be seen in long-term relationships, but only in special circumstances, for example, when clarity is of paramount concern.

Studying relational communication has also raised important questions about the fundamental unit of communication study. For many years we tried to understand the nature of face-to-face communication by administering questionnaires and rating scales to individuals. Later, it became clear that we had to examine how each person mutually influenced the outcome of the interaction. But as we learned more about the nature of relational communication, we realized that a full understanding of what happens between two persons also has to account for each person's larger interaction network of family, friends, and community.

Our perspective on time also changed. It is true that one use of the term *relationship* concerns a spe-

be said. When a relationship has developed, there may be more mutual tolerance for interpretation of what is being said.

No overt judgment–presence of overt judgment: Overt judgment refers to openly giving responses to another person, as contrasted with not expressing a judgment because you do not know the person well. Although in dealing with strangers (as in making a purchase from a clerk), we may often express judgments, we are not likely to be as free with them when they relate to us personally as we will be when the individual is a long-standing friend or companion.

If we were to analyze relational communication at different sampling points in time, we would expect to find patterns reflecting some of the major distinctions described above. As you can see from the above descriptions, we would expect communication associated with a developing relationship to be open, revealing, and fluent. Communication associated with the lack of a relationship or with a disintegrating relationship should reflect the opposites of these characteristics. Researchers often study openness, or *self-disclo-*

cific time: "I just had a talk with my new boss, and I feel we have a good relationship." But the other use of the term, as a summary for *many interactions over time*, involves studying people for a longer period. We have had to move from a single encounter to entire communication episodes, from interaction snapshots to films.

Studying people with a relationship history has also made us appreciate the difficulty an observer has in understanding a couple's behavior. For instance, some of what the interactants are reacting to are things *not shown*, things that have meaning only to the participants in the relationship. And even observable behaviors may have very different meanings for the participants than for the observers. This difficulty has prompted researchers to seek participant accounts of their own behavior to supplement other analyses. Our methods of measurement have also changed as we learned more about relational communication. In the past, how often a behavior occurred (quantity) was considered an important relationship indicator. And for the period when relationships are being established and reestablished (following some threat), quantity *is* an important measure for understanding relationships. But the quality of behavior (timing, sincerity, and magnitude) is critical to measuring how relationships

are maintained after they are established. In a romantic relationship, for example, how often self-disclosure and affection signals (kisses, hand holding, saying "I love you") take place may be critical in getting the relationship established or reestablished when faced with threat, but *how well* such behaviors are performed is likely to be the key for sustaining the relationship.

The challenges to effectively studying the complex world of communication in ongoing relationships are formidable. We can no longer be comforted with the simplicity of tightly controlled laboratory experiments with interacting strangers if we wish to generalize to those relationships we value most. Nevertheless, it is an exciting challenge to edge, no matter how slowly, closer to understanding the very essence of our daily lives.

Mark L. Knapp is Professor of Speech–Communication in the College of Communication at the University of Texas at Austin.

Suggested reading: M. L. Knapp, *Interpersonal Communication in Human Relationships*. Boston: Allyn and Bacon, 1984.

---

sure, as an indicator of whether relationships are developing or disintegrating. This dimension was a key variable in the next study to be described, in which the communication patterns of married couples in different types of relationships were compared.

RESEARCH INTO COMMUNICATION DIFFERENCES IN MARRIAGE

Couples as a Research Paradigm

Judging from the sheer amount of research, one of the most interesting social relationships for researchers is that between marriage partners. After all, these are intimates who at one time were strangers and who by marriage have created a new and socially sanctioned social unit. It has long been known, not only from research but also from therapeutic intervention into distressed marriages, that the communication interactions between a husband and wife are often the key ingredient for success or failure in a marriage. This may be particularly so in modern societies, in which there is less conformance to the traditional expectations of marriage.

Partners in a modern marriage in the United States are expected as never before in history to be open and understanding of each other, even to the extent of serving as mutual therapists. All these factors make communication and the modern marriage an important as well as an intriguing topic for communication research.

Communication Differences

One would expect that as individuals in a marriage hold different attitudes toward one another, this difference would show in their communication. For example, J. M. Gottman (1982) distinguishes between the characteristics of distressed and nondistressed married couples:

> Satisfied couples typically report that they spend time discussing mutual interests of a personal nature. They are able to understand each other's idiosyncrasies in communication, including being sensitive to the subtleties of feeling conveyed by a spouse's nonverbal communication.

> Nonverbal communication tends to be visibly negative among distressed couples. There is more intermittent breaking off of communication. Satisfied couples, in contrast, show more positive emotional cues in their communication and offer frequent positive enforcement as agreement or approval.

> On a level of conflict resolution, there are easily distinguished contrasts between distressed and nondistressed couples in terms of their willingness to use strategies for positive problem solving. Distressed couples may include more coercive strategies in their communication, with examples of attempting to dominate the marriage partner or to use strategies for gaining control.

> Nondistressed couples seem more natural in their positive behavior by sitting close together, touching each other, and using easily seen and friendly gestures.

> Distressed couples may tend to send inconsistent messages in terms of tone of voice, words used, or nonverbal cues, as if they lack control of these channels or else are purposely sending a mixed message.

> Distressed couples tend to feel that each other's interpretations of messages are more negative than an objective assessment might yield and have expectations that future communication will tend to be negative, even to the point of seeing it as negative whether it is or not.

Differences such as these should promise much opportunity for finding correlations between couples' attitudes toward each other and their communication patterns. Following is one example of this type of assessment as undertaken by Mary Anne Fitzpatrick.

An Analysis of Competitive Exchanges

In a long line of research based upon responses to a questionnaire, Fitzpatrick (1983, in press) distinguished among three types of individuals by their communication expectations:

> *Traditionals* see interdependence as important for a couple and feel that they are open and understanding toward each other. We would expect them to be highly expressive in interactions and to reciprocate in self-disclosures. They would favor interdependence even if it involved minor disagreements.

> *Independents'* attitudes are not so conventional as those of traditionals. They recognize a need for interdependence but also favor autonomy, and they feel that they are open with each other. Although we would expect them to be expressive, they are protective of their own attitudes and probably not so sensitive to each other as are traditional couples. Minor disagreements are likely to be voiced.

> *Separates* have varied conventional and nonconventional attitudes and do not feel a close sense of companionship or openness with their mates. If there is disagreement, they probably do not voice it; they may seem to agree on the surface.

The above types also represent couples in which both members exhibit the aforementioned characteristics. Obviously, there are *mixed* couples with, for example, a traditional individual and an independent. One objective of Fitzpatrick's research was to study differences in "competitive symmetrical exchanges" within couples of the foregoing types. These are exchanges in which the partners attempt to assert control over each other; neither wishes to give in to the other. They are contrasted with exchanges in which one individual asserts control and the other is submissive. Presumably, couples of the types just discussed should vary in terms of their use of competitive exchanges.

Figure 11.1 shows the results of a study of forty-three couples who discussed issues upon which they were known to disagree. A distinction is also made between the disagreements they thought most important to them (the left side of the figure) as against those less important (right side). Notice that regardless of the importance of the disagreement, couples comprising "independent" individuals engaged in proportionately more competitive exchanges than couples of any other type. By contrast, "separates" made the least use of these exchanges. "Traditionals" used the exchanges, but less so as the disagreement was rated as less important to them. "Mixed" couples did the opposite of traditionals: they used slightly more competitive exchanges as the topic was less important.

Although the details of this type of study are valuable for understanding communication in marriage, they illustrate the larger generalization that how two persons communicate is highly tied to the status of their perceptions and

Figure 11.1
Competitive Symmetrical Interactions of Different Couple Types

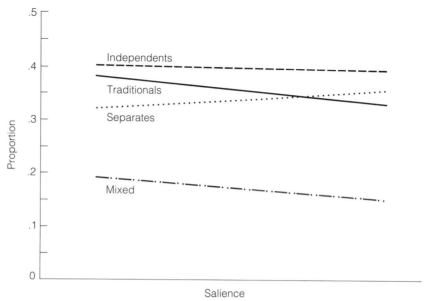

Source: "Predicting Couples' Communication from Couples' Self Reports," by Mary Anne Fitzpatrick in *Communication Yearbook–7.* Reprinted by permission of Sage Publications, Inc., and the author.

attitudes toward each other. In fact, the communication pattern itself may be the process by which that relationship is maintained or changed. (See the accompanying commentary.)

SEX DIFFERENCES IN SELF-DISCLOSURE

The Importance of Self-Disclosure

To what degree does gender difference affect communication in interpersonal relationships? Do men and women communicate differently to each other as a factor in the relationship process? A study by Rebecca Cline (1983) revealed evidence of such differences. She began the research on the assumption that correlations between interpersonal communication and relationships be studied in terms of the communicative qualities of *control, intimacy,* and *trust:*

Control is how people use interpersonal communication to affect the behavior of another person and how that person responds.

Intimacy relates to people's disclosure of personal thoughts, ideas, and situations.

Trust is the degree to which people feel that another person's behavior and attitudes are predictable and in their best interests.

It is not difficult to see the relation between these categories and those described by Knapp (1984) as characteristic of relational differences in com-

Mary Anne Fitzpatrick

Nearly all Americans marry at least once, and those who divorce usually remarry within five years. Personal experiences, fiction, and folklore provide colorful examples and anecdotes about marriage, but they often contradict one another. Do birds of a feather flock together, or do opposites attract? Although Ann Landers may believe that opposites attract, research demonstrates that liking and attraction are produced by similarity. Systematic, scientific observations provide reliable generalizations and improve our understanding of marriage and other personal and social relationships in modern society.

Throughout this century, scholars have been searching for the social or demographic factors—such as income, education, age at marriage, and age differences between spouses—that can predict whether marriages will survive or fail. Such factors are far less important than the communication that occurs between partners. A lack of money in itself does not cause marital problems. What causes marital problems is the couple's inability to discuss and make decisions about financial troubles.

Communication is the major predictor of material success in the twentieth century. There are two major scientific approaches to the study of communication in marriage. The first approach categorizes couples as "happily" or "unhappily" married and then examines the communication between couples for different styles and patterns. Many intriguing, yet counterintuitive, style differences emerge in this research. For example, the sheer number of negative messages exchanged does not always reliably discriminate the happily from the unhappily married. What differentiates these couples is how negative messages are received. Unhappily married people are significantly more likely to reciprocate the negative messages of their spouses, whereas the happily married do not respond to a negative message with a negative message.

Ten years ago, my colleagues and I developed the second approach to studying communication in marriage, the typological approach. We developed this approach because we believed that examining people's values, attitudes, and beliefs about marriage, as well as their communication behavior, would tell us why certain communication patterns lead to satisfaction or dissatisfaction. Happiness in any aspect of life is always a function of the expectations that people have set for themselves minus the expectations being met in a given circumstance. For some couples, open conflict is a sign of severe marital distress, because they believe that good communication involves very little conflict and a great deal of emotion control with each other. For other couples, "a good fight" is fun and energizing. Conflict and negotiation between these spouses clears the air and brings them closer together. People have remarkably different philosophies about marriage and family life, different views on the nature of companionship possible or even desirable in marriage, different attitudes about male and female roles in marriage and in society in general, and very different views on how to approach conflict and disagreements. Some people believe that stability and predictability are exceedingly important in a marital partner, whereas others look to the spouse for excitement and the satisfaction of personal needs.

Uncovering the various philosophies and attitudes that couples have about marriage and the role of communication in satisfying human relationships has enormous practical consequences. Different types of interventions and therapies are needed for couples with traditional sex roles and fears of expressing themselves to a spouse than for couples with modern views of male and female roles and a high tolerance for conflict and the expression of negative feelings.

Mary Anne Fitzpatrick is Professor and Director of the Center for Communication Research at the University of Wisconsin—Madison.

Suggested readings:
M. A. Fitzpatrick, "A Typological Approach to Marital Interaction: Recent Theory and Research," in *Advances in Experimental Social Psychology*, edited by L. Berkowitz, vol. 18, pp. 1–47 (New York: Academic Press, 1984).

M. A. Fitzpatrick, *Between Husbands and Wives: Communication in Marriage* (Newbury Park, Calif.: Sage, in press).

munication. Similarly, these types of transactions, as well as others, enter into the process by which communicat   partners define their relationship and how that relationship may build.

Within the context of relational communication, Cline saw self-disclosure as an important function for controlling the privacy and intimacy of a relationship or, on a wider scale, the degree of closeness or distance between communication partners. Relational communication patterns were assumed to be the overall process by which individuals interact on the aforementioned dimensions and others and thus come to know and relate to each other. This process of self-disclosure involves a seri   f bids and responses in which one partner makes a disclosure and the othe   her reciprocates or does not make a disclosure.

Differences in Acquaintance Communication

Given the above assumptions, Cline paired students, who were initially strangers, in male, female, and mixed dyads. These students then engaged in a conversation in which individuals were given a topic to disclose to the other as an "acquaintance" exercise. Topics included family, attitudes about religion, sex, physical appearance, emotions and feelings, relationships with others, and attitudes about money, school, and property. Participants rated the intimacy of these topics as well as ir perception of how the acquaintance process was proceeding.

Among Cline's general findings were that:

There was more disclosure by males in the mixed dyads than in the all-male ones.

In the process of disclosing intimate information, females were more likely to reciprocate to their male partners than vice-versa.

Females often showed more responsiveness and acceptance of female definitions of the relationship than did males.

Table 11.1 summarizes a few of th   details in the analysis of how much intimate information males and females revealed. Note that females revealed the most information to each other in a same-sex dyad, followed by male–female dyads. Males talking to each other were the most restrained.

RESEARCH INTO THE DISENGAGEMENT PROCESS

Types of Disengagement

Given that much popular attentio   to the process of developing relationships, it is equally importa   rstand how relationships can deteriorate and how two individuals   ge from a highly interpersonal relationship. The process involved w   relationship is coming apart has also been a focus for theory and research. Davis (1973) makes a distinction

Table 11.1 Revelations of Intimacy in Conversations between Male–Male, Female–Female, and Male–Female Dyads

	Male	Female
Male	111.67*	120.33
Female		124.50

*The higher the value, the more intimacy was revealed.

Reprinted by permission of Sage Publications, Inc.

between relationships that terminate rapidly ("sudden death") and those that fade or deteriorate over a period of time ("passing away").

As denoted by its name, a sudden-death termination, on the surface at least, may not be marked by a period of communication exhibiting a deteriorating relationship. One obvious cause of sudden breaches is that the individuals are separated by physical circumstances. One person moves to another city, for example, or two university students go their separate ways for the summer break. There are also cases in which a relationship has been deteriorating under the surface, so to speak, but the participants have been motivated enough to keep the image of the relationship alive. A common example involves parents who postpone divorce until the children are old enough to go off to college. A sudden termination may also occur when only one of the individuals has wanted to leave the relationship but there has been compensating behavior on the part of the other to keep the relationship going ("I'll change"). But at some point the relationship cannot be held together, and at that moment it appears to have ended abruptly.

Longer-term disengagements are marked by contrasts with the communication patterns described earlier for healthy, growing relationships. That is, there is decreasing openness and intimacy. At the heart of a disengagement is usually a lack of mutual motivation to maintain the relationship. Numerous studies have cited boredom, growing differences in interests, or a new desire to be independent as reasons for divorce. In such cases the causes of the breakup grow over time, thus contributing to the longer-range process of disengagement. Because of the rapid social changes in the United States in the 1950s and 1960s, many young couples found themselves growing in different directions. This estrangement, combined with increasing social tolerance for divorce, is reflected in the soaring divorce rates. The social milieu may thus be a contributing factor in disengagement. In terms of communication, interaction during the process of disengagement is likely to be marked by movement toward the negative end of the eight dimensions mentioned earlier: communication may become more narrow, stylized, difficult, rigid, awkward, public, or hesitant, with overt judgments not being expressed.

Perception of Dissolution

We should expect certain patterns (for example, lack of openness) to be marked in the dissolution of a relationship. Some of them were discussed earlier in this chapter in terms of general communication characteristics. However, one further area for research is the ways in which individuals perceive relational dissolution. An example of a contemporary study of this type is one by William Cupach and Sandra Metts (1986), who studied the accounts of breaking up given by fifty divorced individuals and fifty individuals who had broken off a dating relationship. The researchers were interested in finding similarities in how people accounted for relational dissolution and also in distinctions between the terminated marital and nonmarital relationships. The researchers analyzed the accounts in terms of four main features:

1. Problems and relational stresses that motivate one or both members to dissolve the relationship: What are the factors that the subjects thought contributed to the breakup?

2. Attributions of responsibility for these problems: Whose fault was it?

3. The attempts to repair or manage the dissolving relationship: How do people try to avert a breakup and renew the relationship?

4. The factors that impede termination of the relationship: What events, attitudes, or situations would delay a breakup?

In essence, the research looked into the communications describing the breakups and attempted to code narratives in terms of the problems involved. Who was responsible? What attempts were there to turn the tide? What reasons were given for trying to slow the breakup?

Research Design

Cupach and Metts obtained answers to questionnaires from twenty-five males and twenty-five females who had been divorced at least once (some had remarried). The nonmarital samples were taken from lower-division students, also twenty-five males and twenty-five females. Questionnaires given to individuals involved the usual variety of background information (age, income, and the like) as well as specific questions about the relationship, such as length of marriage or physical separation before the breakup. The key question for which descriptive responses were analyzed in detail was:

> Give an account of the sequence of events leading up to and culminating in divorce (or break-up). Begin your story at the point in your marriage (relationship) where you considered (or were told) that divorce (break-up) may be a possible option. What was the situation at this time and how did it lead to dissolving the marriage (or relationship)? (1986, p. 316)

Six broad subcategories of problems were eventually defined for the analysis of data relative to this question:

1. references to the individuals involved in the relationship, including their attitudes, actions, or the like ("I began to feel lonely." "We just couldn't cope anymore.")

2. references to the performance of relational roles, such as sex roles, parental roles, or marriage roles ("We were not ready for the responsibility of marriage.")

3. references to relational cohesion and intimacy, or "we-ness," reflecting the expected closeness in a relationship ("Our personalities didn't mix." "I knew I would never marry this girl.")

4. references to regulation of interaction, relating not just to regulation via communication ("All we ever talked about was his job and his problems.") but also including physical episodes ("He raped me the night I left.")

5. references to third-party involvement that influences the partner or the relationship, including comments on affairs, unfaithfulness, or adultery

6. references to external factors that are ostensibly beyond the direct control of partners, such as losing a job, changing colleges, or getting deeply into debt

Findings

Table 11.2 summarizes the frequency of problem statements. The researchers extracted 402 problem statements from the marital sample and 296 from the nonmarital one, reflecting the fact that the formerly married people probably had much more to talk about. Several of the main findings related to problem statements can be paraphrased as follows: Although the married and

Table 11.2 Types of Problem Statements Made by Men and Women after Dissolution of Their Relationship

Category	Formerly Married		Formerly Dating	
	Female	Male	Female	Male
1. Individual references	40%*	30%	41%	33%
2. Role references	10	13	11	10
3. Relationship references	19	19	23	20
4. Regulation references	13	18	12	13
5. Third-party involvement	16	09	08	14
6. External forces	04	11	05	10

*Because of rounding, columns may not add up to 100%.

Adapted from W. R. Cupach and S. Metts, "Accounts of Relational Dissolution: A Comparison of Marital and Non-Marital Relationships," *Communication Monographs*, by permission of The Speech Communication Association.

nonmarried groups were different in total amount of problem statements cited, the proportion of those statements was relatively similar across the two groups. In both cases, most problem statements were those reflected directly to individuals (Type 1). The greater frequency of items under the individual category may also reflect a movement away from the "we" character of a positive relationship, now seeing one another more as individuals, and the problems oriented to those individuals may be part of the process of communication of disengagement.

Women tended to produce more problem statements than did men, particularly in the category of statements relating to individuals. Several further contrasts were evident, for example, on questions about problems in category 5. There was more reference to third party involvement by females than males among the formerly married, but just the opposite among the males from the formerly dating group. For attributing problems to factors external to the relationship, there was a somewhat greater frequency of problems cited by males among the divorced as well as those in the formerly dating group.

As for the question of responsibility, in most cases the majority of individuals tended to place more responsibility for the breakup on the other individual than on themselves. However, there were some differences in the subgroups. In the formerly dating sample, for example, 45 percent of the individuals attributed the breakup to the partner and only 30 percent to themselves. In the formerly married sample, the difference was greater, with 23 percent attributing the breakup to themselves and 54 percent to their partner.

On the question about repairing the relationship, females typically initiated more repair attempts, in both the marital and the dating samples. What most stood out in the results was the effort made by females to change themselves in an effort to mend the relationship. As might be expected, there were more attempts to repair relationships among the formerly married couples than among the formerly dating ones.

The researchers found fewer statements about factors that impede dissolution than they did about the other three categories in their analysis. About 78 percent of these statements were made by the formerly married individuals, as against 22 percent by the formerly dating individuals. Again, there was a greater proportion of attempts to impede the dissolution among the formerly married couples, surely reflecting that a married couple has a much higher degree of engagement not only in experience but also in material and social expectations.

A NOTE: NEW MEDIA AND "PERSONALNESS"

You may recall that in Chapter 7 we mentioned the research by John Short into the "personalness" of selected media, including comparisons of face-to-face communication with business correspondence and telephone conversations (see Short, Williams, and Christie, 1976; Williams, Rice, and Dordick, 1985). There were perceived differences in how warm, sociable, sensitive,

or p   communications are. The major question in research of this
typ   rent media technologies may place restrictions on styles of
com   , including relational communication.

I.   , especially personal letters, or in using the telephone, we may
compens   for the lack of nonverbal cues or voice quality by specific uses
of language to communicate openness, good feelings, or personal interest in
the other person. Mass-media technologies sometimes achieve that effect by
the use of camera angles, lighting, setting, or an individual communicator
who is ac pt at "personalized" use of the medium. The same techniques
can be use to facilitate more informal and personal communication in a
teleconfer ce. Some teleconferences, including ones where only computer
text is exchanged, can become highly personal.

Being able to avoid the restrictions of a medium—or, better, to capitalize
on a medium—is the mark of the well-trained and talented modern com-
municato o matter whether one is talking on the telephone, giving a speech
on television, or interacting with electronic mail.

SUMMARY

Relational communication refers to communication processes involved in the
development, maintenance, or dissolution of interpersonal relationships.
Research into this process typically focuses on the interactive quality of human
exchanges and on how different patterns of exchange can be associated
with different types and stages of relationships. Different types, or dimensions, of interpersonal communication patterns include narrow–broad,
stylized–unique, difficult–efficient, rigid–flexible, awkward–smooth,
public–personal, hesitant–spontaneous, and no overt judgment–presence of
overt judgment.

Fitzpatrick has studied communication differences among individuals
classified as "independents," "traditionals," or "separates" in their attitudes
toward their marriage partners. This research illustrates how personal communication is highly tied to interpersonal perceptions. Cline has investigated
gender differences in self-disclosure in relational communication. She found
females to use more disclosure than males in same-sex dyads, but males
increased disclosure when paired with females. Finally, Cupach and Metts
have sho . how communication patterns can also reflect the social disengagement process.

The uses of new technologies in relational communication raise challenges for future research.

TOPICS FOR DISCUSSION OR BRIEF PAPERS

1. Was Professor Lefrancois's experience with Celine a situation of relational communication? Was it even communication? Take a side on these
   questions, and defend your position.
2. Describe the communication characteristics of one of your personal expe-
   rienc   that might be comparable to characteristics and situations in a
   stud   scussed in this chapter.

3. Which characteristics of nonverbal communication would you consider as indicators of a developing or disintegrating relationship? What would you theorize about the role of nonverbal communication in these processes?

4. Refer to the original report of the Fitzpatrick (1983) or Cline (1983) study described in this chapter. Prepare a brief critique of the study. How would you improve the design?

5. Prepare a brief proposal for a study of relational communication. What questions would you try to answer, or what hypotheses would you test? How would you design the study so that the results would allow you to clearly reach the desired conclusions?

REFERENCES AND READINGS

Cline, R. J. "The Acquaintance Process as Relational Communication." In *Communication Yearbook 7*, edited by Robert N. Bostrom. Beverly Hills, Calif.: Sage, 1983.

Cupach, W. R., and S. Metts. "Accounts of Relational Dissolution: A Comparison of Marital and Nonmarital Relationships." *Communication Monographs* 53 (1986): 311–334.

Davis, M. S. *Intimate Relationships*. New York: Free Press, 1973.

Duck, S. *Human Relationships: An Introduction to Social Psychology*. Newbury Park, Calif.: Sage, 1986.

Fitzpatrick, M. A. "Predicting Couples' Communication from Couples' Self Reports." In *Communication Yearbook 7*, edited by Robert N. Bostrom. Beverly Hills, Calif.: Sage, 1983.

Fitzpatrick, M. A. *Between Husbands and Wives: Communication in Marriage*. Newbury Park, Calif.: Sage, in press.

Gottman, J. M. "Emotional Responsiveness in Marital Conversations." *Journal of Communication* 32 (1982): 108–120.

Knapp, M. L. *Interpersonal Communication in Human Relationships*. Boston: Allyn and Bacon, 1984.

Littlejohn, S. W. *Theories of Human Communication*. 2d ed. Belmont, Calif.: Wadsworth, 1983.

Millar, F. E., and E. Rogers-Millar. "A Relational Approach to Interpersonal Communication." In *Explorations in Interpersonal Communication*, edited by G. R. Miller. Beverly Hills, Calif.: Sage, 1976.

Reardon, K. K. *Where Minds Meet*. Belmont, Calif.: Wadsworth, 1987.

Short, J., E. Williams, and B. Christie. *The Social Psychology of Telecommunications*. New York: Wiley, 1976.

Williams, F., R. E. Rice, and H. S. Dordick. "Behavioral Impacts in the Information Age." In *Information and Behavior*, edited by B. D. Ruben. New Brunswick, N.J.: Transaction Books, 1985.

Information and Public Opinion

FROM REVOLUTIONS TO TOOTHPASTE

How do you start a revolution? How do you stop one? Or in calmer times, how do you get people to buy the new brand of toothpaste for which your advertising agency has a $10-million account? In all such cases you would no doubt try to use powerful forces of communication to get at people's minds, to influence their actions. Lenin expounded on this point in his underground newsletter, *Iskra,* before the Russian Revolution. It wasn't surprising, then, that one of the first acts of the new Bolshevik leaders in 1918 was to set up radio loudspeakers on city corners broadcasting the new party line. Or if you mistakenly think that revolutions are un-American, you need only remember 1776. You may recall, too, that the First Amendment to the U.S. Constitution is meant to guarantee freedom of the press.

In this chapter, we review several theories that, together, should give you a greater understanding of how news, other information, and persuasion tend to influence large groups of people. (You may even be able to put some of this understanding to practical use if you enter a career in politics, advertising, or public relations.) Further, you will see that the relationship is really an interactive and multiple one. Communication, public opinion, and society all mutually affect one another. Toward the end of this chapter, we introduce a model of that interrelation.

This chapter is not the only one to examine the relations between communication and society. In Chapter 13, we will see some of these same uses of communication as applied to politics. Further, in Chapter 14, you will recognize that mass entertainment also contributes to social influence.

As for toothpaste, any good account executive can tell you what it will cost in radio, television, magazine, and newspaper ads to put your brand name on people's lips, and how much more to get your product on their teeth!

THE RESEARCH PERSPECTIVE

Research in news and public opinion has traditionally involved **survey research,** including content analysis of the mass media. What content has been printed or broadcast? Who has read or viewed what materials? What are their attitudes on certain current topics? And can any relation be drawn between exposure to communication and the opinions held by the public?

Currently, however, there is more interest in the *process* nature of this interrelationship. News, public opinion, and change are all seen as parts of the same process. They act and react with one another. Although their relationship appears simple on the surface, it is actually a complicated one. Evidence has shown repeatedly that most public opinion seems affected by a great range of communication experiences, especially interpersonal ones. We must also consider the consequences of the expansion in types of information available to us. The news is coming to us in many alternative forms, including personalized data-base information sources into which we can "dial" our computers. Traditionally, if we wanted information, we were largely restricted to sources that were mass oriented rather than individually oriented. Now, with so many more alternatives, we have more personal choices open to us. As you will see in this chapter, modern research in this topical area is much more concerned with the nature of the public-opinion process than with raising questions of who has read or seen what. Although we do not treat the subject in this chapter, there is also a strong tradition of historical research into the nature of the press, especially as it has reflected the First Amendment of the U.S. Constitution.

In this chapter we examine theories that have been developed to explain the social and public effects of communication. Although many of them come from the reports of public-communication researchers, all are relevant to interpersonal and group communication as well.

THE FLOW OF IDEAS FROM THE MASS MEDIA

The idea that a story in a newspaper, a television program, or any type of public-communication message has a direct, one-to-one effect on its readers or viewers has often been called "magic-bullet" thinking. In the bullet analogy, communication effects are considered to be the direct consequence of particular acts or events of public communication. That is, for every public message, we can expect a corresponding, and predictable, public response. As any public relations or advertising executive can tell you, it is extremely difficult (and expensive) simply to attract the attention of large groups of people, let alone get them to think or act in certain ways. So, too, has it been difficult for social scientists to find convincing examples of large-scale magic-bullet effects of communication on society. One-to-one influences on the public seem to be an exception rather than a rule.

Questions about Direct Effects

In the 1930s there was concern among some political observers that the presumably all-powerful newspaper, newly coupled with radio broadcasting, was having more influence upon political campaigns than was desirable. The assumption was that the press had a direct effect upon how people voted. The history of media in society no doubt contributed to this point of view, since there have been numerous examples of books, treatises, and public announcements that have literally turned the tide of history.

But a landmark study by Paul Lazarsfeld and his colleagues (1948) brought an abrupt change in this type of thinking. The study was of the influences of radio and newspaper coverage on the 1940 U.S. presidential election, and it drew its samples from Erie County, Ohio. The unexpected finding was that neither radio nor print had the self-reported greatest influence on voters. When individuals reported influence from communication, it was mainly from situations of interpersonal or group communication. In other words, if we are to believe the people's reports, interpersonal communication had much more to do with voting decision than did any use of the media.

Two-Step Flow

As a consequence of the finding of his study, Lazarsfeld advanced what became known as the **two-step flow theory** of mass-media influence. The theory held that the flow of communication generally incorporates two steps: (1) The media influence certain individual opinion leaders, and then (2) those individuals personally influence others. Although for many reasons the two-step flow theory is inexact and misleading, it subsequently altered much of the thinking about the effects of public communication. No longer was it assumed that audiences were simply anonymous individuals who responded directly to the effects of a mass medium. Instead, they were considered active reflectors of information who might receive influential information from a variety of sources, interpersonal sources being perhaps the most influential in decision making.

What are the consequences of the new media for flow theories? For one, the increasing availability of personalized information sources (as in computer data banks) cuts out the middleman in the flow of communication from a centralized source to the receiver. That is, the message flow is direct rather than via opinion leaders and the like. Although media such as videotext are like mass media, they, too, add to our choices as media consumers. If everybody has access to media that give him or her personal choices, will we have any capability left to influence public opinion on a mass scale? An optimistic view is that citizens could become such efficient information seekers with such varied sources of information that it would be difficult for them to become swept away by an individual politician. On the other hand, a pessimistic view is that people could become so bewildered by the glut of information sources competing for their attention that they would simply turn off or, worse yet, turn to leaders who offer them simplistic alternatives. It is one thing to have information available but quite another to interpret and use it.

Like so much other communication research, studies on the question of direct media influence versus two-step influence have yielded complex and equivocal answers over the years. This is probably due both to more detailed examinations of the process and to the fact that the public communication environment has itself vastly increased in complexity, even since the 1940s (when there was little television, for example).

In general, we cannot deny that the media do have direct effects on society, but these effects are often the exception rather than the rule. Instead of directly persuading people to hold opinions or to act in certain ways, more often the media are part of a larger process. Among other things, there is substantial research suggesting that the media most often call attention to certain ideas or issues, a phenomenon called "agenda setting" (see the next section).

Critics of two-step flow theory have often pointed to situations in which no opinion leaders could be identified in the flow of information of a particular topic. In contrast, there are many examples of direct effects, as in some well-coordinated advertising campaigns. Mostly, however, theorists now recognize that the flow of ideas from media takes many forms: direct, two-step, and many-step. With the many communications options available to us through the new communications technologies, the flow is likely to become even more varied but also direct in some cases.

Lazarsfeld's concept of two-step flow, then, was not accurate for all types of communication, but it did alert us to the fact that mass media do not typically have the direct effects that were earlier assumed. More important, he stimulated research into all of the pathways by which ideas flow from media to society, as well as how society, in turn, affects media.

AGENDA-SETTING THEORY

Another theory relevant to communication and public opinion holds that, by and large, what mass media do is suggest to us which ideas are important; further influences or effects come from other types of communication. This view is called the **agenda-setting theory.**

In essence, the agenda-setting theory holds that the more attention the mass media give to a topic, the more importance the public will ascribe to that topic. Attention could be prompted by the size of a newspaper headline, a magazine cover, or amounts of time allotted to a topic in television or radio newscasts. Although this theory seems intuitively valid—and there are studies that support it—there are also many exceptions, most of which depend on the general conditions for agenda setting.

General Conditions of Agenda Setting

One important point to keep in mind when considering agenda setting is that the mass media convey only a tiny fraction of the news or ideas available to them. The selection process operates on several levels. A writer or filmmaker may typically use only a small part of what he or she has gained from research on a topic. Editors subsequently select only part of what is submitted to them. Finally, unless a subject is given substantial prominence in print or in a broadcast presentation, as well as frequent exposure, that topic is likely to become lost in our already oversaturated communications environment. Thus, if some topic that has the potential to capture the public's attention is consistently selected and displayed, it cannot help but shape the "idea" agenda of the reading or viewing public. Critics sometimes hold that editors have such a bias for providing readers or viewers with what they want for purposes of selling newspapers or magazines or increasing TV ratings that agenda setting is slanted toward sensational news coverage. It may have the long-range effect of emphasizing the superficial aspects of our society.

Besides agenda setting, however, the needs and biases of the public (discussed in Chapter 4) must also be considered. And it has been found that, despite the prominence given to an item in the mass media, people will pay little attention to it if it seems irrelevant to them. Accordingly, the *information needs* associated with different subdivisions of the mass audience should be a necessary part of agenda-setting theory. For example, if you are in your

20s or younger, even though you may regularly follow the news, chances are that the problems and debates about Social Security during this decade have not attracted much of your attention. Similarly, older members of our society who follow the news may not be particularly interested in the attention given to the musical superstar who can draw a half-million people to outdoor concerts. Thus, a topic must be potentially within a public's range of interests in order to allow for agenda setting by media.

Most of the research in agenda setting (such as that done by Donald Shaw and Maxwell McCombs, 1977) has first involved tabulating the amount of mass-media exposure given various topics. The audience of those media is then surveyed to see how much importance it assigns to the topics under study. Although such studies frequently show a correspondence between communications exposure and public reactions, the match is not typically a clear-cut one. Researchers like Shaw and McCombs often attribute the differences to the personal interests of newspaper readers or television viewers. The agenda-setting hypothesis seems most borne out when a topic is both potentially interesting to an audience *and* receives the attention of the mass media.

In a practical vein, it is easy to see how planners of public-information campaigns often use the mass media to alert the public's attention to a topic and then utilize telephoning, meetings, or personal letters as follow-up campaigns.

Hindrances to Agenda Setting

One bias in most studies of agenda setting is the fact that the topics involved have gained attention because of additional factors. For example, the media exposure given a particular political candidate is further influenced by media exposure given to a campaign or an election season in general. It is difficult to sort out the different exposures of the particular candidate or of certain issues for a study of agenda setting.

Furthermore, people often have many topics important to them that are not receiving media attention at all. For example, in this author's study of information sources and uses in three communities of Los Angeles, individuals in the lower socioeconomic sample mentioned personal or situational problems far more than they did issues that were prominent in the Los Angeles media. They were far more concerned about getting a better paying job or about their personal health and safety than they were, for example, about the ongoing war in Vietnam. The mass media were having little agenda-setting effect on these topics.

In fact, individuals in some subgroups of our society are often vocal in decrying the lack of prominence given in the media to issues they personally believe to be of great importance. Environmentalists, for example, feel that the nation's press overlooks serious issues of pollution and resource mismanagement. Or ask a black political activist in New York City how relevant the *New York Times* is to her cause. This lack of topical representation in the mass

Much research information on the topic of the social diffusion of ideas has come from large-scale information projects in Third World countries. For example, there have been major campaigns for family planning, as illustrated here. Despite the investment in mass media for such campaigns, word of mouth usually remains the most persuasive medium. Such campaigns, especially when sponsored by Western countries, have been criticized for representing the possible imposition of one culture's values on another. What do you think?
Henri Cartier-Bresson/ Magnum Photos, Inc.

media and the resulting frustrations felt by those concerned are cited by some as the causes for riots and demonstrations. There were no other communications alternatives.

It might also be mentioned that, especially among the less educated classes, the entertainment media may prompt more agenda setting than their news counterparts (see Chapter 14).

SOCIAL-DIFFUSION THEORY

Communication and Change

Whereas flow and agenda-setting theories examine communication and public opinion from a media standpoint, **social-diffusion theory** centers on how people use the information they get.

The communication sociologist Everett Rogers and his colleagues have contributed greatly to our thinking about how communication can spread ideas through society (see his commentary). Some of his research began in the area of agriculture, with projects designed to persuade farmers to improve their planting techniques. Other projects have involved large-scale attempts to get people in Third World countries to practice family planning methods (that is, birth control). All of these studies represent attempts by some government or agency to use communication to bring about *directed change*. Rogers's work has been of interest to business theorists because it is also a basis for studying product-marketing techniques.

Some studies in this area concern change that is relatively more self-directed—that is, change involving people who are attracted to an idea. We see this kind of change when a new hairdo spreads throughout the country

Everett M. Rogers

Two decades ago, in one of the most important studies of the diffusion of innovations, Professor James Coleman and his colleagues encountered a surprising research finding in their investigation of how doctors had decided to adopt a new antibiotic drug. Each of the physicians knew of the extensive scientific evaluations of the antibiotic drug by university medical schools and by pharmaceutical firms. But this information did not convince the physicians to begin prescribing the innovation for their patients.

The typical doctor did not adopt the new drug until a colleague who had previously adopted it had relayed his subjective evaluations of the innovation. When the colleague said, "Look, Doctor, I have used this new drug with my patients, and it works," the physician was likely to try the innovation. This peer influence was especially influential if the colleague was socially similar, such as by having graduated from the same medical school, having a similar medical practice, and being of about the same age.

We are all a great deal like the medical doctors in Professor Coleman's diffusion research study. Peer networks serve to influence us in our decisions to adopt new ideas, purchase a new consumer product, buy a home computer, wear a new clothing fashion, and so on. Usually the personal experience of someone like ourselves with an innovation is much more important than are scientific evaluations of the new idea. Peer networks convey subjective

information that we tend to trust in coping with the uncertainty that accompanies a new idea.

Why does adoption suddenly occur? Because it is at this point that interpersonal networks become activated. There are enough satisfied adopters telling their peers about the innovation to cause a sharply increased rate of adoption. Home computers are still far from this takeoff point, with only about 5 percent of U.S. households having purchased them. Home videotape recorders are at about 40 percent adoption. But cable television has reached the growth spurt, with about 50 percent adoption (of course, other factors like the availability of cable TV in a city also affect the adoption of the communications technology). Once a majority of individuals or groups has adopted something new, the rate of adoption begins to slow down and level off, as fewer and fewer individuals remain who have not already adopted the new idea.

So if we look in closer detail at why the diffusion of a new idea approaches an S-shaped curve, we see that the explanation lies in the way network influences convince us to change our behavior. And we are more likely to be persuaded by the prior experience of a social peer than by scientific evaluations of an innovation.

Everett Rogers is Associate Dean of the Annenberg School of Communications at the University of Southern California.

Suggested readings:
J. Coleman et al., *Medical Diffusion* (Indianapolis: Bobbs-Merrill, 1966).

E. M. Rogers, *Diffusion of Innovations* (New York: Free Press, 1982).

---

after a famous figure-skating star wears it in televised competition. Fashions and fads or new figures of speech are common examples of self-directed change. The media and interpersonal communication may also play a key role here.

Steps in the Diffusion of Ideas

No study has shown the diffusion of ideas to be a simple process. Individuals whose ideas or behaviors are the target for change do not simply learn about the idea from some mass-communication medium and immediately adopt it. Instead, people seem to go through a series of stages, or steps, in the process of adopting (or rejecting) new ideas. Diffusion theory emphasizes these steps and the characteristics of the people involved in them. The following is a brief description of the steps:

1. *Knowledge:* The individual gains an awareness of something new, such as a method of irrigation, birth control, pest control, or energy conservation. However, the person has not yet formed an opinion about whether that idea would be personally valuable. This is the next step.

2. *Persuasion:* In this step the individual makes attitudinal evaluations of the idea. Is the new pesticide good for me, or not? Why should I treat my water supply in a special way? What good will it do me to add these items to my diet? Do I really need computers in my business? These are not only evaluative opinions about the idea, but they are personally associated with the individual. They form the necessary basis for whether the innovation is to be adopted, the next step.

3. *Decision:* This is the point at which the individual either adopts or rejects the innovation. That is, the new idea is tried or avoided. Communication in the diffusion process typically propels a person toward decision, so that the individual has to take action even if it is rejection. Communication does not stop after this decision is made, because the individual will go on to react to his or her reactions.

4. *Confirmation:* Further communication is used to evaluate the decision that was made and the consequences of the decision. Were the benefits of water treatment actually realized? Is the crop yield improved? Did word processing actually increase clerical productivity? In this last step there may be pressure for a change of decision, particularly if the original decision was one of rejection.

These steps remind us once again that the relation between communication and our reactions is not a simple one-to-one correspondence. Dissemination of new ideas is mostly a cumulative process across a number of steps. We tend to use many forms of communication in the process of adopting or rejecting a new idea.

Early Adopters and Opinion Leaders

Social-diffusion theory has also given us a clear and relatively consistent picture of the kinds of individuals who serve as communication intermediaries in the flow of communications through social structures. Not unexpectedly, these individuals are more all-around users of communications. They typically have more contact with a greater range of information sources than does the average person. Often they know more about how or where to get information, and they tend to be in contact with more people. These individuals also exhibit typical leadership characteristics, such as in being respected by their followers. They are often knowledgeable about the new ideas. Also, they have characteristics typically found in effective communicators: empathic ability, open-mindedness, and gregarious personalities.

Another consistent finding relates characteristics of leadership to different types of societies. For example, the less developed a society is in an economic sense—that is, the more primitive, underdeveloped, or peasant-like—the more early adopters will tend to be influential sources of information on all topics, not just the idea under consideration. By contrast, in a more developed society—one that is advanced, industrialized, or technological—early adopters tend to be influential only within their specialty. In general terms, the flow of new ideas in a primitive society will include early adopters who are influential in almost everything. In an advanced society, new ideas (but not especially fads) may flow through networks of specialists.

Criticisms of Diffusion Theory

One of the most important criticisms of diffusion theory is that so much of it is based on rural or underdeveloped countries, contexts in which economic growth has been emphasized. In many cases, the growth is to be accelerated by the introduction of technology, which is meant to replace the "old ways" (for example, chemicals are to replace animal and human waste as fertilizers). The impetus for the research has come from outside the society, as when a developed country has attempted to introduce technological change into an "underdeveloped" one. Thus, there has been a one-way quality to these projects; that is, the outside agency has promoted change without much regard for the attitudes of the people who are the target of it. Bluntly speaking, it may be "forced change."

Critics of diffusion theory hold that this type of diffusion tends to be colonialist or imperialist in political orientation. They believe that the goals of these projects should themselves come under scrutiny, including consideration by the people who are asked to be the adopters. They further argue, for example, that life is more than economic or industrial growth. Moreover, critics hold that the deteriorating environmental conditions and high crime rates of advanced countries are direct arguments against rapid economic growth, especially when brought on by outsiders. (The fall of the Shah of Iran and his replacement by Muslim leaders who closed the country to American influence is another argument in support of this point.)

Critics of the theory, then, believe that direct-change attempts to promote the flow of ideas are contrary to the religious, philosophical, or political values of many societies. People should change only if they desire to. From a communication standpoint, populations involved in change should have more potential for *two-way* communication flow than the four steps of the diffusion theory indicate.

These criticisms have much in common with the discussion in Chapter 7 of the distinctions between forced compliance and conflict resolution. Just as one individual has the alternative of trying to force ideas on another person or of working out a mutually desired outcome, so, too, do political movements, governments, or social-change agencies have that alternative.

A DEPENDENCY MODEL OF COMMUNICATION EFFECTS

The Need for a Sociological Theory of Media

The problem with the theories of uses and gratifications, two-step flow, agenda setting, and social diffusion is that they are inherently constrained to certain aspects of the relation between media and opinions or social change. Each "makes a point," so to speak, but lacks the comprehensiveness needed for a broader model of communication in society. Put another way, although these theories are valuable in suggesting hypotheses within their domains, they do little to suggest a larger scheme of which they are a part. Ideally, a theory of social communication should generate the larger as well as the lesser (convergent) hypotheses. It should suggest not only how communication and society relate as a whole but also how individual behaviors, including interpersonal communication, relate to that whole.

An attempt at such a comprehensive theory is found in Sandra Ball-Rokeach's **dependency theory** (Ball-Rokeach, 1985; Ball-Rokeach and Cantor, 1986; Ball-Rokeach, Rokeach, and Grube, 1984). Among the important qualities of this theory is that it reminds us that the relations between communication and opinion are not one-way but interactive, or mutually dependent, processes. Moreover, the interactions of communication and opinion take place within and interact with a social structure. This theory also illustrates the difference in the way sociologists and psychologists analyze communication processes. Whereas in Chapter 5 we looked at theories of attitudes, which had the individual as the level of analysis, here we examine dependency theory, which analyzes the interaction of media systems, their audiences, and the structure of a society. We can then analyze individual communication within that larger framework as Ball-Rokeach (1985) has proposed.

The Concept of Dependency

One of the helpful applications of dependency theory is its reminder that we do not use media separately from the influences of the social system within which both we and the media exist. We are all integral components of one social system. The way we are likely to use and react to media will be influenced by what we have learned from our society in the past, including what we have learned through media. We will also be very much influenced by what is happening at the moment. In this respect, a given piece of mass communications, or even conversations about it, might have quite different consequences upon us, depending on our prior experiences with the topic as well as with whatever social conditions may be affecting us at the moment.

One premise of the dependency theory is that, as the society in which we live becomes more complex, we will have a more difficult time understanding its overall nature. Although interpersonal communication may help us understand our own position in our daily activities and in relations with other people, we are increasingly dependent upon other forms of communication to understand those more distant and complex aspects of our society.

This idea is compatible with most of the other functional theories that attempt to explain uses or effects of communication, as discussed in Chapter 4.

The idea that we use certain forms of communication—in particular, the public media—to understand our larger society and the world is not new. But this is only a premise of dependency theory. Audiences in complex societies are especially dependent on the information that the public media can give them. In turn, this dependency leads to complex interactions of media, audiences, and society. This is the "dependency" in the name of the theory.

The overriding strength of dependency theory is that it is comprehensive. It encourages an overall rather than a narrow or myopic view of the relation of communication with public opinion. It bypasses oversimplistic questions of whether the media have a major effect on society. It simply answers yes, and generalizes or hypothesizes certain kinds of effects. Most importantly, this theory reminds us that society affects the media. The theory reflects in a much broader sense the healthy tendency in modern social sciences to see life as a complex mixture of interacting components rather than isolated patterns of simplified cause and effect.

Impacts of Social Urbanization and Change

Two important elaborations of the dependency thesis are as follows: (1) As a society becomes more highly urban and industrialized, an audience's dependence upon media information will increase; and (2) the more a society is involved in high degrees of change or conflict, the more it will increase its dependency upon the public media.

These elaborations find considerable support in the writings of other social scientists of communication. Almost all accounts of social evolution, particularly change in developing countries, show the central role of communication in the process, for example, Daniel Lerner's work (Lerner & Schramm, 1967). So, too, after every revolution, there is usually an account of the critical role communication played in overturning the old institutions and establishing new ones.

In summary, if a society is highly industrialized, urban centered, and changing, the dependency upon communication, particularly public communications, is at its maximum. The foremost example of this may be the United States.

Dimensions of Social Effect

An important component of dependency theory is that it goes beyond the generalization that social conditions affect communication uses and effects. It does this by further holding that the cognitive, affective, and behavioral effects of using communication in these conditions can, in turn, prompt changes in society as well as in the media themselves. Again, social conditions affect how people use the media, and these uses may interact to affect both the media and social systems. These reciprocal relationships among social, media, and audience variables are the essence of this theory.

A further elaboration of this theory will be seen in the more detailed cognitive, affective, and behavioral effects that communication has on people.

Cognitive Impacts. Among the cognitive effects of media are (1) the creation or resolution of ambiguity, (2) attitude formation, (3) agenda setting, (4) expansion of belief systems, and (5) value formation or change. As we have discussed most of these concepts in the context of previous chapters, there is no reason to elaborate much further on them here. (They are all in the index if you wish to refresh your thinking.)

Ambiguity, in essence, is uncertainty about something, caused by the absence of information or by information that conflicts with what we already know. We might, for example, hear on the television news that jobs are going to be hard to get next year. Immediately we may wonder whether that situation will include the kind of job we are interested in. We may look to more media or interpersonal communication in an attempt to get additional information to compare with our present information. Media can both prompt as well as resolve ambiguity.

Attitude formation was much discussed in Chapter 5. We are constantly making generalizations about how we feel toward certain topics, events, or people. As you will recall from that previous discussion of balance theories, how we select and interpret information may be substantially influenced by a desire to maintain a type of cognitive harmony.

Among the evaluative consequences that communication has on people, we find that attitudes are often judged to be immediate and transitory, as compared with beliefs and values. Beliefs are more like generalizations about how things work, what is important, and the relation of them to our lives. That we should do all we can to stretch out the world's petroleum supplies is a belief. **Values** are often considered to be the most fundamental of our beliefs—collections of beliefs that provide us with a fundamental position on an issue. For example, believing in honesty is a value. In the context of dependency theory, these are not necessarily all of the cognitive effects of communication. However, they are the ones that may particularly interact with the nature of the audience and the social system.

Affective Impacts. The main affective consequences proposed by Ball-Rokeach are (1) that we can become desensitized to violence by excessive exposure to violent media, (2) that our fear and anxiety about parts of society can also be increased by media content, and (3) that communication can lead to changes in morale or in alienation toward society.

The first two of these affective consequences relate, in particular, to the consequences of television and film. Both can be starkly realistic and can emotionally entangle their audiences. One of the long-running accusations against dramatic television, as discussed in Chapter 14, is that it (rather than real-life social experiences) can become a basis for certain people's reality. A person may come to hold detailed stereotypical images of different ethnic, age, occupational, or sex-role characteristics based more on how they are represented on television than on how they are encountered in reality. People who are heavy users of television or film may come to see their world as excessively violent and may carry this reaction over to their everyday lives. Ball-Rokeach calls this carryover a potential for "trigger-happiness."

Morale and alienation refer to people's attitudes toward the groups or subcultures to which they belong. "Black is beautiful" was a morale-building slogan that appeared frequently in the mass media during the civil rights movement of the 1960s. (The TV commercials that show women centering their lives on the whiteness of their laundry or the lack of wax buildup on their kitchen floors have surely been a constant source of alienation.)

Behavioral Impacts. Behavioral *activations* and *deactivations* are important behavioral effects in dependency theory. Cognitive or affective effects of media use may not have an impact on society until they are translated into behavior of some type. As the term denotes, *activation* refers to ways by which media exposure spurs people to action. Direct examples are found in many types of advertising. The advertising not only encourages the formation of knowledge and attitudes about a product or service but also encourages you to act (for example, to mail in a coupon for more information). Sometimes in the psychology of motivation, the element calling for action is termed the "releaser stimulus." One contemporary example of this element is a telethon. Following an entertainment act, the host gives a pitch for the charity and you are given a toll-free phone number to call immediately in order to make your pledge. Activation, in essence, is whatever there is in media that moves you to action.

Similarly, we may be discouraged from acting for one reason or another. The absence of coverage of a topic in the media can cause inaction or deactivation. For example, politicians are forever decrying the lack of attention to their pet causes in the print and broadcast press. Furthermore, it is also possible for a message in one area of content to have a deactivating consequence upon another facet of a person's life. The constant media attention to high interest rates in 1981 and 1982 surely deactivated many people's intentions to purchase new automobiles.

The Individual in the Media System

Recently, Ball-Rokeach (1985) has proposed a sociological framework within dependency theory to hypothesize how the individual develops a media-system dependency. A particularly important premise of this elaboration of dependency theory is that an individual's relations with the media system are more determined by the interdependencies among the media and other social systems than by his or her own characteristics. Put another way, individuals are first "born into" an existing media and social system that defines the options for use; then personal characteristics (socioeconomic level, personal goals) may affect individual dependencies within those options.

Take, for example, an ordinary illiterate citizen of a medieval European village. Information options were limited to oral transactions with family, friends, or church. There was little chance of "outside" information entering that system through public media. Therefore, there would be no concomitant changes in communications or in the social structure. Yet with the eventual rise of literacy, the Reformation, and a developing economy, both the social structure and individual communication dependencies eventually changed as an interactive process. Now, compare the foregoing example with the communications options in our times, especially with regard to the new media. It is not unusual for social change to be perceptible within a few short years of our own lifetimes, in contrast to the experience of our medieval or tribal ancestors, who went many generations without change.

Dependency Theory and the New Media

As we have seen, dependency theory has been developed with a particular emphasis on the uses of public communication in society. What will be the consequences as such communication is "demassified" and individuals have a far greater range of personal information sources available to them? It seems reasonable to speculate that individuals who have the best access to needed information will be most successful in the years to come. Although this generalization has always been true, the new technologies create a far greater opportunity for us to observe its effects in a society.

What happens if you *do not* have access to the information you need or if other people control that information? For one, you will not be able to know about new opportunities or make as good decisions as the person who has information. Moreover, you may be forced into certain decisions if the other person controls the information you receive. Because the new technologies are expensive and not equally available to everyone, we may see an increasing distinction between the "information-rich" and the "information-poor" in our society. This is still another example, as in Ball-Rokeach's dependency theory, of how society and communication mutually affect each other.

Yet, we sometimes have oversimplified prescriptions to cure the gap between the information-rich and information-poor. Too often, we assume that it is simply a matter of giving everybody more access to the "facts." It may actually be more than this, as asserted in the commentary by Brenda Dervin. That we may gain "information" from many traditionally nonfactual or quasi-factual sources is an important consideration.

Brenda Dervin

Is information a thing? Virtually all the assumptions that undergird our communications systems assume so. Information is treated as a valuable commodity. Journalists collect it, librarians store it, scientists discover it. There is much talk about access to it and concern for organizing it in order to avoid overload and make maximum use of it.

Within such a context, information is treated as objective and absolute. Studies are done to determine who has got more of it and whose is more accurate. They confirm that educated, high-income, professional people are "information-rich" while others are not. These others are called the "information-poor"—victims of a knowledge or communication gap. They are seen as not having the experience, the skill, or the motivation to acquire needed information with accuracy.

But there's an alternative perspective. It says: Information is not a thing but a creation, the result of observings at specific points in time and space. The reason these observings are called "creations" is because it is assumed that it is impossible to make accurate, absolute observations. For one thing, the nature of reality is always changing. For another, all observing is constrained by past experience and the limits of current time-space. Further, since we cannot see everything and since there are lots of gaps in reality, we "make sense" by filling in the ever-persistent gaps with our own constructions. This constructing of sense is fundamental to all observing and, thus, to all information creating, whether scientific, journalistic, or otherwise.

What does this all mean to the issue of access to information? First, it means that there is a different way of looking at results that label some people "information-poor." It is possible that the relatively homogeneous group of highly educated people who control our information systems have taken their views of the world from their places in time and space and gone out of their way to see whether people who are at different times and places share them. They have found that they do not and called them *deprived*.

Second, it implies that our information systems are ignoring that which is most human about human beings, their subjectivity. They require that professional "observers" (such as scientists and journalists) omit any reference to personal motivation and report in terms of topically defined category systems (such as national versus local news or the library's card catalogue). These standard reporting procedures are examples of efficient professional structures that have little relevance to how people actually make sense of things. In effect, they remove or ignore the things that help others from different times and places understand the observings of (that is, information created by) others. This emphasis on so-called "objective information" may well be one reason for the underuse of our public information systems, even by the highly educated. In contrast, systems that leave the subjective intact (such as soap operas, advice columns, and audience participation programming) are popular among a wide range of people.

If this alternative perspective has any utility, the implications for access are clear. Access will not be improved by creating bigger communication–information systems focusing on the transmission of objective information. Rather, it will be improved by designing alternative systems that focus on the sharing of subjective observings.

Brenda Dervin is a Professor in the School of Communications at Ohio State University.

Suggested readings:

B. Dervin, "Mass Communicating: Changing Conceptions of the Audience," in *Public Communication Campaigns*, edited by W. Paisley and R. Rice, pp. 71–87 (Beverly Hills, Calif.: Sage, 1981).

B. Dervin, "Communication Gaps and Inequities," in *Progress in Communication Services*, edited by B. Dervin and M. Voight, vol. 2, pp. 73–112 (Norwood, N.J.: Ablex, 1980).

SUMMARY

Communication and change go hand in hand, no matter whether we are studying revolutions or selling toothpaste. We no longer assume, as in magic-bullet thinking, that single instances of public communication always have a direct effect. Rather, we hypothesize that most effects on public opinion are based on a mixture of communications, including interpersonal and mass. *Two-step flow theory* suggests that the media inform opinion leaders and that they, in turn, inform others.

However, there are many different theories about the effects of communications on public opinion. *Agenda-setting theory* holds that the mass media mostly alert us to topics to think about or to topics for which we will want to gather further information. There are many examples where agenda setting can be identified, but people often consider many topics important that never appear in the media.

The *social-diffusion theory* suggests that information and its acceptance flow through society in certain steps, or phases. Also, individuals who are early adopters of new ideas often have certain identifiable characteristics. Among the criticisms of diffusion theory is that it is tied to our Western, capitalistic way of life.

Ball-Rokeach's *dependency model* reminds us that there are interactions among media, their audiences, and the overall social structure. Communication not only affects society, but society, in turn, affects what media are available. In particular, individuals who live in modern, complex societies are especially dependent upon information for their existence. Communication reduces ambiguity (an example of a cognitive effect), sensitizes for certain emotional experiences (as violence is an affective impact), and sometimes influences our behavior (as with advertising). The strength of dependency theory is its comprehensiveness.

The new technologies are likely to have a most visible effect on how we gain the information necessary for our lives in modern, complex societies. At the same time, there is a danger that differences in the ability of people to gain necessary information may create a class distinction between the information-rich and the information-poor.

TOPICS FOR DISCUSSION OR BRIEF PAPERS

1. What medium do you think does the most agenda setting in modern American life? If your answer is the newspaper, is it the news columns, editorials, or advertisements that have the most influence? If your answer is television, is it the news, drama, or commercials that set the most agendas?

2. Take an example of a new product that you would like to introduce to the public to buy. Trace your promotional campaign in terms of Rogers's steps for the diffusion of ideas.

3. Analyze your own information needs. What types of information are important for your life-style? Where do you get that information? Could you improve your information sources? Explain.

4. Draw from your own experiences, and defend or criticize dependency theory. Take a stand. Give examples.

5. What implications do you think that sources of information from new media technologies have for public opinion? Give examples. Do you think that the overall effect will be good or bad? Why?

6. What is your stand on the thesis of Brenda Dervin about the importance of typically "noninformational" sources of information? Take a position and defend it.

REFERENCES AND READINGS

Agee, W. K., P. H. Ault, and E. Emery. *Introduction to Mass Communications.* 7th ed. New York: Harper and Row, 1982.

Atwan, R., B. Orton, and W. Vesterman. *American Mass Media.* New York: Random House, 1982.

Ball-Rokeach, S. J. "The Origins of Individual Media-System Dependency: A Sociological Framework. *Communication Research* 12 (1985): 485–510.

Ball-Rokeach, S. J., and M. G. Cantor, eds. *Media, Audience, and Social Structure.* Newbury Park, Calif.: Sage, 1986.

Ball-Rokeach, S. J., M. Rokeach, and J. W. Grube. *The Great American Values Test: Influencing Behavior and Belief through Television.* New York: Free Press, 1984.

Becker, S. L. *Discovering Mass Communication.* Glenview, Ill.: Scott, Foresman, 1983.

Bittner, J. R. *Mass Communication: An Introduction.* 2d ed. Englewood Cliffs, N.J.: Prentice-Hall, 1980.

Collins, R., J. Curran, N. Garnham, and P. Scannell, eds. *Media, Culture and Society.* Newbury Park, Calif.: Sage, 1986.

Davison, W. P., J. Boyla, and F. T. C. Yu. *Mass Media: System and Effects.* New York: Holt, Rinehart and Winston, 1976.

DeFleur, M., and S. L. Ball-Rokeach. *Theories of Mass Communication.* 4th ed. White Plains, N.Y.: Longman, 1982.

DeFleur, M. L., and E. E. Dennis. *Understanding Mass Communication.* Boston: Houghton Mifflin, 1981.

Dennis, E. E. *The Media Society: Evidence about Mass Communication in America.* Dubuque, Iowa: William C. Brown, 1978.

Head, S. W., and C. H. Sterling. *Broadcasting in America: A Survey of Television, Radio, and New Technologies.* 4th ed. Boston: Houghton Mifflin, 1982.

Jowett, G. S., and V. O'Donnell. *Propaganda and Persuasion.* Newbury Park, Calif.: Sage, 1986.

Lazarsfeld, P. F., B. R. Berelson, and W. N. McPhee. *The People's Choice.* New York: Columbia University Press, 1948.

Lerner, D., and W. Schramm. *Communication and Change in Developing Countries.* Honolulu: East-West Center, 1967.

McCombs, M., and L. B. Becker. *Using Mass Communication Theory*. Englewood Cliffs, N.J.: Prentice-Hall, 1979.

Paisley, W., and R. Rice, eds. *Public Communication Campaigns*. Beverly Hills, Calif.: Sage, 1981.

Rogers, E. M. *Diffusion of Innovations*. New York: Free Press, 1983.

Shaw, D. L., and M. E. McCombs. *The Emergence of American Political Issues: The Agenda-Setting Function of the Press*. St. Paul, Minn.: West, 1977.

Sterling, C. H., and J. M. Kittross. *Stay Tuned: A Concise History of American Broadcasting*. Belmont, Calif.: Wadsworth, 1978.

Turow, J. *Media Industries: The Production of News and Entertainment*. White Plains, N.Y.: Longmans, 1984.

Political Communication

THE PEOPLE'S CHOICE?

In an ideal democracy, an informed electorate would make rational decisions based on thorough examination of the evidence before casting a vote for an initiative or candidate for office. Yet the more closely we study **political communication** in democracies, the more we find voters to be uninformed, with their examination of the issues often superficial.

These generalizations might have been more expected in the early days of America, when print was the only mass medium, illiteracy rates were high, and fewer citizens had the benefit of a formal education. In this era preceding women's suffrage or minority voting rights, those who could vote often had their vote "delivered" by political organizers. One might expect that in the nineteenth century, as newspapers grew in circulation and literacy increased, the public would have had the basis to become informed. However, many have asserted that the press did as much to persuade voters as to inform them and that, by the 1920s and '30s, radio had joined in that influence. But as already mentioned in Chapter 12, that fear was countered somewhat by the famous Lazarsfeld study on the 1940 presidential elections (Lazarsfeld, Berelson, and Gaudet, 1948). As you may recall, the finding was that personal influence rather than the mass media was deemed more important by voters.

The question of sources of voter influence has grown in our times, especially with the proliferation of media types, the large investments in television advertising, and the new computer tools for conducting campaigns. According to the *New York Times* (May 24, 1987), the cost of the 1984 presidential campaign ($134 million combined for Ronald Reagan and Walter Mondale) was $36.7 million higher than 1980. The cost of U.S. Senate campaigns more than doubled ($103.0 million in 1980 and $211.1 million in 1984). Much of the increase in both cases can be attributed to communications costs, especially television advertising. Political communications is big business.

In this chapter we examine several theoretical views and research examples relating to the influences of communications in the modern U.S. political process.

THE RESEARCH PERSPECTIVE

The issue of political influence through the media has never been fully resolved in the social scientific study of communication. One reason is the lack of systematic research, but an equally important one is that the media have constantly changed (and so have the election processes). The 1950s saw the advent of television as a political medium, first in news coverage, and then by the '60s came the presidential debates. Added to these changes is the acknowledged success of the political television commercial. Although the aforementioned Lazarsfeld study stands as a classic field survey of its time, contemporary researchers recognize that in our saturated media environment, the process of studying political influence is much more complex than comparing one medium with another. We are now more inclined to study images, bases for decisions, and the decision-making process itself. There is less of a "push–pull" or even two-step flow concept of media influence and more of a dynamic, complex, interactive one. The citizen, with prior biases and motives, resides in a veritable storm of political messages, including the intrusions of direct mail and the telephone in his or her life.

The study of this modern mosaic of communication influences requires a multifaceted research approach, including attitude surveys, decision modeling, content analysis of messages, and economic data gathering. It requires combinations of research approaches, from studies of speech communication through investigations of the mass media. Moreover, the results of specialized, detailed studies of communication influence are not fully useful in an explanation of the overall process unless one can integrate them into some general model, often one requiring methods of historical and critical analysis, as in Kathleen Jamieson's book *Packaging the Presidency* (1984), which is discussed later in the chapter.

COMMUNICATION AND THE DECISION PROCESS

Political Messages as Strategic Communication

Denton and Woodward, in *Political Communication in America* (1985), stress that it is the content and purpose of communication that may make it political, not necessarily its source. It is the practical, process-oriented goal that marks communication as political, as in getting out the vote, reinforcing a campaign issue, or promoting some program of the candidate. Audiences are a particularly important consideration. Political speeches are designed for audience effects, not simply to disseminate ideas. The goals of political communication are often short-term. Most everything is done with a deadline or in reaction to current events, rather than as a part of long-range strategies. Effective political communication is usually geared to problems that the public or voters may sense at the moment.

The media are an inextricable component of the political process. Newspapers have long been recognized as a traditional part of the democratic process. Television has offered techniques for promoting candidates' images. Added to these are important media innovations, such as the use of cable television systems or video cassettes for campaign speeches.

Research Questions

The political communication researcher Dan Nimmo (1985) frequently writes on how information enters into the processes of political behavior, in general, and voting, in particular. His research relates to such issues as the contrast between the ideal of an informed electorate in a democracy and the frequent observations of low levels of information among voters. It relates, too, to the question "If voters do not use accurate information for their voting decisions, what do they use?" Possible answers are found in such concepts as the importance of political affiliation, the stereotypes voters associate with candidates, emotional issues, images of candidates, and short-term factors affecting voter decisions such as a depressed economy.

Another research issue is how the media have affected the democratic process. As already mentioned, there is the theory that before the modern media were diffused so thoroughly in society, people depended more on interpersonal affiliations (the local political ward) for voting decisions. However, as the mass media became more widely available and politicized, agenda setting affecting political attitudes could be attributed to media. Because the media were so widely diffused and often reflected varying political positions, they could be considered an agent for change. Now, however, in a period of demassification when individuals can select particular media or content of their choice, will political communication return to simply reinforcing existing opinions, rather than being an agent for promoting change or new ideas?

A Study of Proximity and Media Attention

What evidence do we have that could support generalizations about how people vote? And, in particular, what role do the mass media play? A study by Swindel and Miller (1986) provides an excellent example of how theory on the voting process can be integrated into communication research.

Swindel and Miller's study focuses upon a phenomenon called *proximity* by political communication researchers. Briefly, it refers to the premise that voters will favor candidates whose positions on issues are closest to their own. Thus, one would expect that if positions on a range of issues were defined for a given candidate, the supporters and opponents might be best differentiated in terms of proximity measures to the candidate. As an election campaign progressed, we would expect proximity measures to change as voters' preferences changed or became reinforced. Further, voter attention to political media should show some effects upon preferences as gauged by proximity measures. Swindel and Miller studied the proximity effect in data gathered during the 1980 presidential campaign and made available by the Center for Political Studies at the University of Michigan.

In one part of the study, measures were calculated for voters' proximity to the candidates (Jimmy Carter, Ronald Reagan) on the economy, national defense, governmental services, and Soviet-American relations, once before the nominating conventions and a second time just before the election. Data were also obtained that allowed the division of the voters into categories of high, moderate, and low attention to political information in the media. Table 13.1 focuses exclusively on measures of voters' preferred candidates, the average proximity score for which was 1.21. (The smaller the value, the "closer" the proximity.) The "distance" for nonpreferred candidates should be greater, which it was: 2.02.

Also as would be expected, proximity increased as the campaign progressed from time 1 to time 2. Note that there were differences according to the level of attention given to the media. The more attention given, the less the proximity change over time. Bearing in mind that these data are only for the preferred candidate, the researchers reasoned that the media may play as important a role in reinforcing existing opinions as in changing them.

Table 13.1 Voters' Proximity to Preferred Candidates as a Function of Attention to Media

		Attention to Media	
	High	Moderate	Low
Time 1	1.04*	1.21	1.23
Time 2	.94	1.04	.55

*The lower the value, the greater the proximity.

Source: S. Swindel and M. Miller, "Mass Media and Political Decision Making . . . ," in *Communication Yearbook–9*, p. 653. Reprinted by permission of Sage Publications, Inc.

Accordingly, they suggest that political researchers may be giving too much attention to studies of media and change when data such as these suggest a stabilizing effect on opinions.

A Study of Changes in Candidate Support

Another example of how researchers examine relations between communication and political decision making is found in a study by Carroll J. Glynn and Jack M. McLeod (1982), conducted at the University of Wisconsin during the 1976 presidential election between Jimmy Carter and Gerald Ford. We will examine only a portion of the study.

Individuals were interviewed in September, in October, and after the November election to gather data on candidate preference, party affiliation, estimates of how the general public supported the candidates, and various uses of the media and interpersonal communication in the campaign. This turned out to be an excellent opportunity to study change, as it was evident that opinions about candidates shifted substantially between October and November. Table 13.2 summarizes the percentages of change.

The data were analyzed to discover the degree to which party affiliation and certain communication activities or uses would mathematically predict changes in candidate support. Table 13.3 summarizes the results, which are

Table 13.2 Percentages of Support for Presidential Candidates in 1976

			Time of Interview	
		September	October	November
Candidates	Carter	38%	45%	55%
	Ford	42	42	35
	Neither	20	13	10

Source: C. Glynn and J. McLeod, "Public Opinion, Communication Process, and Voting Decisions," in *Communication Yearbook–6*. Reprinted by permission of Sage Publications, Inc., and the authors.

Table 13.3 Correlates of Changes in Candidate Support with Party-Affiliation and Communication Variables

		Non-Hard-Core Subjects		Hard-Core Subjects	
		September	October	September	October
Carter Support	Party affiliation	.018	.042	.089	.044
	Interpersonal communication	.055	.004	.112	.192*
	Newspaper use	.020	.022	.379*	.097
	Television use	.162*	.014	.107	.148
Ford Support	Party affiliation	.045	.000	.162*	.098
	Interpersonal communication	.029	.055	.379*	.255*
	Newspaper use	.095	.059	.051	.062
	Television use	.206*	.065	.013	.108

*Statistically significant (p < .05); the maximum relation would be 1; the minimum, 0.

Source: C. Glynn and J. McLeod, *Communication Yearbook–6.* Reprinted by permission of Sage Publications, Inc., and the authors.

divided between individuals who changed little throughout the campaign (the "hard-core" group) and those who showed change.

Note in this table that for the major non-hard-core group the only mathematical relation beyond a chance level was in associations between reported television use and change in candidate support. This held for both candidates. Individuals who held fairly steady in their preferences (the hard core) showed significant relations between change and interpersonal communication in several calculations and for newspaper use in the case of Carter supporters in September. It is easy to see from such analyses not only that there is a relation between communication uses and candidate support but also that the relation may vary according to the candidates or characteristics of the voters.

The Need for a New Theory

Perhaps theories that stress the importance of information in a democracy need to be revised, since evidence does not always show that information is a major factor influencing voting. Voter behavior may be more associated with fixed attitudes about issues, party affiliation, or the stereotype one holds toward a candidate. Put another way, information may be but one among many variables; and its influence may be lesser or greater depending on how strongly held are the various attitudes, affiliations, and stereotypes. It is also important to consider the role of the media in information effects on voting, because as partisanship is loosened, some voters will probably seek out information in order to reach their political decisions. Thus, the availability of information media is more important now than in a period of high partisanship and party-line voting behaviors. Theorists have also raised the issue of the amount of effort necessary to gain the information needed to make political decisions. Many of them hold that the effort may be more than it is worth to the citizen in terms of immediate gain.

Modern citizens are engaged in a much wider range of activities than their predecessors. Not only is there a burgeoning growth of media experiences, but now those media offer more personal options. So, too, do the media enlarge participation in the ritual and ceremony of political behaviors. Some of the most acknowledged persuasive strategies of television, especially commercials, are increasingly applied to political ends. If anything, the modern voter has more information on which to draw, but it is potentially more conflicting and may result in what Nimmo in his commentary calls an information crisis. Voters are likely to be affected, too, by the increasing "personalness" and interactivity of new media technologies.

"PACKAGING" THE CANDIDATE

In her award-winning book, *Packaging the Presidency*, Jamieson (1984) concludes that advertising is now the major means by which U.S. presidential candidates communicate with voters. Rejecting the contention by McGinniss (1969) in *The Selling of the President, 1968* that the 1968 presidential campaign (Richard Nixon versus Hubert Humphrey) saw the first orchestrated advertising campaign to present a "preplanned image," Jamieson traces the growth of advertising from 1952 (Dwight Eisenhower versus Adlai Stevenson) through 1980 (Reagan versus Carter). In fact, in a historical analysis, she makes the case that many early presidential elections, probably beginning with Jefferson's race against Adams, had qualities of image making in the campaigns.

Her study of campaigns beginning in 1952 reveals a transition from broadcast speeches to a major expansion of televised advertisements, including brief commercial spots. With the increased use of advertising methods has come a greater reliance on the planned image, or "packaging." Unlike many critics of contemporary politics, Jamieson sees a positive role for political advertising:

> Still, if political advertising did not exist we would have to invent it. Political advertising legitimizes our political institutions by affirming that change is possible within the political system, that the president can effect change, that votes can make a difference. As a result, advertising channels discontent into the avenues provided by the government and acts as a safety valve for pressures that might otherwise turn against the system to demand its substantial modification or overthrow. (1984, p. 452)

CAMPAIGN MANAGEMENT AND NEW TECHNOLOGIES

In the 1986 U.S. congressional elections, the *Wall Street Journal* (August 19, 1987) reported, House members spent $6.44 million and Senate members $7.65 million, respectively, on computer **hardware, software,** and services for their campaigns. Computer technology perhaps represents one of the most needed areas for research into modern political communications.

The computer has surely arrived as a tool of campaign management. It is used to manage scheduling, advance and headquarters operations, financing, volunteer activity, research, demographic targeting, and, most important, voter lists and mailings. Information technologies, especially the computer, are having a major impact on these managerial tasks, and not just in large-

Dan Nimmo

The assassination of President John F. Kennedy on November 22, 1963, ushered in the current technopolitical era. Television network news came of age through coverage of the long weekend that followed: the shock and grief in Dallas, the nation, and the world; the swearing in of a new president; the capture and then assassination of Kennedy's accused slayer, Lee Harvey Oswald; the unrelenting remorse surrounding Kennedy's casket as it sat in the rotunda of the Capitol Building; the funeral attended by world leaders of East and West; the long, slow procession to Arlington National Cemetery; the burial of the slain president; and finally, the lighting of an eternal flame that yet burns at his graveside.

It was but a prelude to the political role that television would play in the years to come. For good or ill, TV converted the conflict in Vietnam into a livingroom war. TV cameras joined President Richard Nixon in opening the doors to China on his historic trip in 1972, and then they focused on the Watergate scandal that resulted in the resignation of the same president but two years later. CBS's news anchor, Walter Cronkite, ritually counted off for television viewers each of the 444 days of the Iranian hostage crisis, much to the detriment of yet another president. And every four years, TV news reports the rise and fall of presidential aspirants trudging the nomination trails through caucuses in Iowa, the New Hampshire primary, and many Super Tuesdays.

Certainly the major political thrust of TV news was derived in part from technological breakthroughs. Satellites freed news organizations from dependence on filmed reports that could be aired only after being flown back from Saigon, Geneva, Tehran, Reykjavik, or elsewhere. Similarly, minicams freed TV correspondents from burdensome equipment, adding, for example, new dimensions to network coverage of such major political events as the presidential nominating conventions of the major political parties. But the technopolitical era is not characterized solely by the exploitation by TV network news of technological gains. Government officials and political parties make regular use of the Local Program Network and Conus, organizations that arrange satellite interviews with key politicians by local TV outlets, thus literally going over the heads of network gatekeepers. Cable TV, especially through the Cable Satellite Public Affairs Network (C-SPAN), has developed a small but nonetheless regular and vocal following of self-confessed "political junkies" adding their voices to national political discussions. And technicians, calling themselves media consultants and preferring to think of themselves as artists, saturate the airwaves with televised political advertising on behalf of clients running for office. Too often the contest is not between the candidates but between the "hired guns" mediating with voters on their behalf.

Nor is TV alone in contributing to technopolitics. With Wide Area Telephone Service (WATS), it is routine for pollsters to conduct around-the-clock soundings of popular political opinion on issues and candidates, utilizing computer-generated random-digit dialing to select representative samples. The advent of the microcomputer makes it possible for candidates for even the lowliest of offices to utilize available software packages to computerize voter contact, direct mail, fund raising, budgeting, scheduling, polling, and other tasks.

What is the impact of all of this on how we govern ourselves? There are many views, and there is much disagreement. Some observers insist, noting TV's political role, that politics has become a spectator sport. For example, they complain that Amer-

scale, highly financed campaigns. The decreasing expenses of these technologies are bringing them within reach of smaller campaigns. Although the use of computers in political campaigns began with million-dollar investments, the sophistication of microcomputers makes many of these applications available for only a few thousand dollars.

The most general application of new media technologies is to planning and scheduling. Information systems are employed to assemble a master

icans view presidential candidates in televised debates much as they do contestants on "Wheel of Fortune" or "Jeopardy," amusing entertainment to be enjoyed while munching a snack but scarcely something to be recalled beyond the game itself. Other observers disagree. By making it possible to tap citizens' opinions through polls, registering them to vote via computerized contact, informing them through instantaneous news, and educating them by public affairs programming, technopolitics *involves* people in the affairs of community and nation as never before.

Considered more broadly from the perspective of political communication as well as that of civic participation, there is another point to consider. The political scientist Benjamin Barber, for example, labels the impact of television on politics a "second American revolution." He argues that the first age of television, from its pre–World War II inception through the 1970s, could be seen as a unifying, or nationalizing, phase. TV helped us become a unified polity directly through televised coverage of political events such as presidential debates, the civil rights movement, the man-in-space program, and the Cuban missile crisis and even indirectly by creating instantly recognized entertainment celebrities such as Jack Paar or Johnny Carson—each all too willing to offer political views—as well as holding a weekly nationwide "Laugh-In" lampooning politics and politicians. Thus was bestowed a legacy of national symbols and myths cutting across diverse regions, states, sects, interest groups, and constituencies. It may not have been Marshall McLuhan's "global village," but at least there was the basis of national consensus.

But technological innovation intervened, leaving not a unifying but a fragmenting legacy. Along came UHF, cable TV, satellites, video recording, minicams, disks, interactive TV, computer networking, teleconferencing, and all the rest. A second age of television emerged that offered greater choices to audiences, more latitude for viewer activism, and a pluralizing and decentralizing of politics. Barber calls it the "New Tower of Babel." Each group, class, race, or religious sect envisions having its own mininetwork of televised, computerized communication *within* its group, rather than the communication *between* groups essential to forging a public political vision for a unified nation.

Perhaps. But American politics can scarcely be decentralized, simply because it was never centralized to begin with. A nation, not to mention a world, as diverse in interests and as conflictual in its pursuits as the United States could hardly be unified politically through technological change, nor can the cause of political division be laid at technology's door. Decentralization in politics—in spite of the rise of new technology and its political exploitation—has been and remains the norm. One suspects that, for the foreseeable future, the national political character will be shaped as much by the decentralized quality of the polity as by either the centrifugal or the centripetal forces of communications technology. Over a century and a half ago Alexis de Tocqueville observed that American politics flows from the nature of its people and their pluralized values. He would not be surprised to find that today's technopolitics is similarly derived.

Dan Nimmo is Professor of Communication at the University of Oklahoma.

Suggested readings:
B. Barber, "The Second American Revolution," *Channels* 1 (February/March 1982): 21–25, 62.

R. G. Meadow, *New Communication Technologies in Politics* (Washington, D.C.: The Washington Program, Annenberg School of Communications, 1985).

D. Nimmo and J. E. Combs, *Mediated Political Realities* (New York: Longman, 1983).

---

calendar, with time-sharing used to provide schedule inputs from a wide variety of sources; to schedule campaign evaluations to be done; and to maintain financial records.

Fund raising is a further use for computers in modern campaigns. Computers are valued not only for the data-base system mentioned earlier but also for their ability to maintain sophisticated files on donors. These files can be sorted in any order by any one or a combination of variables such as political affiliation, income level, address, amount of last donation, prior correspondence, or affiliation in certain organizations. Fund-raising software also provides the capability for a wide variety of direct-mail activities, including tailoring letters based on characteristics of the addressees in the data base. Fund raising can be evaluated relative to budget demands, and thus a manager can have better overall control over how much emphasis needs to be given to money raising of a particular type.

Most political campaigns involve the coordination of many volunteers who will be helping with mailings, organizing neighborhood coffees, walking from door to door endorsing candidates, or operating a telephone bank. An active data base of volunteers can be valuable in maintaining phone numbers, schedules, the activities volunteers are willing to do, and their commitments.

One of the activities of a modern political race is to gauge the amount and type of campaigning needed in an area based on the demographic characteristics of the voters and a knowledge of their prior voting behaviors. Computer data bases are particularly valuable for this purpose. With them, it is possible to combine census data with survey data and to use them in programs that can calculate estimated amounts of campaign activity needed for certain areas and the type of campaign that can be mounted. In general, the ability to link different data bases that represent prior research, current research, and planning models is a particularly modern use of computers in campaigns. Voter communications management also includes the telephone. Software is increasingly available to automate phone dialing and even record notes that a caller makes.

The political convention is one of the many interesting major settings of political communication. Part business meeting and part festival, conventions often simultaneously combine most forms of human communication—a full range of icons and nonverbal messages, large- and small-group meetings, organizational message exchanges, and interpersonal negotiation, all covered by the public media of communication. *Cheryl A. Traendly/Jeroboam, Inc.*

Extensive use of broadcasting no longer seems as effective for campaigning as it once did, because people have such a wide variety of broadcast alternatives to attend to, and demassification is leading audiences to expect more personalized messages. Thus we may be moving to technologies that can work with much more selective audiences than traditional mass media. The political researcher and consultant Robert Meadow summarizes many of these changes in his excellent volume *New Communication Technologies in Politics* (1985).

The computer is particularly useful because it can collate data from different sources, such as comparing past election returns with census data, new survey research, or current voter canvassing. It can also compare the costs of certain campaign alternatives with the necessity of getting out the vote for certain groups of people. The concept of **geodemographic research** is an approach that allows campaigners to identify subgroups and the issues that are particularly important to them. Campaign managers can estimate voting intentions and can integrate within these records all types of decisions, including fund raising, poll watching, media purchases, advertising strategies, voter registration, get-out-the-vote efforts, and voter identification. Geodemographics is an increasingly important concept in campaign management.

Another benefit from modern information technologies is that some of the intelligence held only by experienced political professionals can increasingly be incorporated as "artificial intelligence" in new software. Such software can assist campaign officials in deciding how to allocate funding or in predicting voting patterns.

SUMMARY

Research into *political communication* raises questions about just how campaign communications enter into the voter's decision-making process. There is reason to believe that the process may be less perfect than desired. Research into this topic takes many forms, including voter-attitude studies, media-content analyses, and historical reviews of campaign practices.

Researchers such as Denton and Woodward (1985) stress that it is the *strategic* quality of messages—the attempt to influence votes—that marks political communication. Media uses are an important part of the modern campaign process. Currently, as the public media become more personalized (demassified), there is the question of whether these media do more in reinforcing political attitude than in changing or creating them. A study of proximity by Swindel and Miller (1986) provided evidence of this reinforcement process. Glynn and McLeod (1982) added further insights into this process by noting the effects of media use on whether a person's attitudes changed over the course of a campaign. All such studies point to the need for newer, more complex models to account for interrelations among current attitudes, media uses, and voter behavior. Moreover, as new media offer increased interaction and personalization, the role of the media is likely to change.

Historical and critical research such as Jamieson's *Packaging the Presidency* is providing insights into trends in political communication. The major contribution of her research is to show the growth of political advertising in modern presidential campaigns.

New computing and communication technologies are also making important contributions to modern campaign management. The increasingly powerful microcomputer, according to Meadow (1985), is bringing to local elections capabilities that once could be provided only by large mainframe computers and large budgets.

TOPICS FOR DISCUSSION OR BRIEF PAPERS

1. Conduct a "focus group" with a few of your classmates or friends on how they would arrive at a decision about voting for a political candidate. Do the results reflect the discussion in this chapter? How much does "image" play a role?

2. Select a recent political campaign that was covered in your local newspaper. Sample articles about the candidates at specific points in the campaign period. How much of the coverage was devoted to campaign issues, how much to "image," and how much to "human interest" items? Do you think press coverage encourages a superficial view of an election?

3. Write down notes of your perceptions of television advertising in the most recent presidential election, and have a friend do the same. What types of messages were in the ads you remembered most? What images were promoted? Did you and your friend agree or disagree on coverage, and why? What generalizations might you draw about presidential campaign advertising on television?

4. Obtain a copy of Jamieson's *Packaging the Presidency* and review it. Do you agree with her on the positive uses of television advertising? Why?

5. Go to a microcomputer software store or catalog and try to locate computer programs that would be useful for local political campaigns. (Or locate a local firm or consultant who might use them.) What programs are available? What will they accomplish for the campaign? What effects do you think the growth of computer use might have on local campaigns?

REFERENCES AND READINGS

Arteton, F. C. *Teledemocracy: Can Technology Protect Democracy?* Newbury Park: Sage, 1987.

Campbell, A., et al. *The American Voter.* New York: Wiley, 1960.

Denton, R. E., Jr., and G. C. Woodward. *Political Communication in America.* New York: Praeger, 1985.

Glynn, C. J., and J. M. McLeod. "Public Opinion, Communication Processes, and Voting Decisions." In *Communication Yearbook 6*, edited by M. Burgoon. Beverly Hills, Calif.: Sage, 1982.

Jamieson, K. H. *Packaging the Presidency*. New York: Oxford University Press, 1984.

Lang, G. E., and K. Lang. *Politics and Television Revisited*. Newbury Park, Calif.: Sage, 1984.

Lazarsfeld, P. F., B. Berelson, and H. Gaudet. *The People's Choice*. New York: Columbia University Press, 1948.

McGinniss, J. *The Selling of the President, 1968*. New York: Simon and Schuster, 1969.

McQuail, D., and K. Siune, eds. *New Media Politics*. Newbury Park, Calif.: Sage, 1986.

Meadow, R. *New Communication Technologies in Politics*. Washington, D.C.: The Washington Program, Annenberg School of Communications, 1985.

Nimmo, D. *Political Communication and Public Opinion in America*. Santa Monica, Calif.: Goodyear, 1978.

Nimmo, D. "Information and Political Behavior." In *Information and Behavior*, edited by B. D. Ruben. New Brunswick, N.J.: Transaction Books, 1985.

Nimmo, D., and K. R. Sanders, eds. *Handbook of Political Communication*. Beverly Hills, Calif.: Sage, 1981.

Swindel, S. H., and M. Miller. "Mass Media and Political Decision Making: Application of the Accumulated Information Model to the 1980 Presidential Election." In *Communication Yearbook 9*, edited by M. L. McLaughlin. Beverly Hills, Calif.: Sage, 1986.

Entertainment

COMMUNICATION FOR FUN AND PROFIT

Despite the primary attention that social scientists devote to the informational or persuasive aspects of communication, much of human communication, from interpersonal to public, reflects *entertainment* purposes. This is communication for enjoyment, for relaxation, for companionship, for escape from the pressures of everyday life, or for excitement. Entertainment as an entire message or a part of a complex message is usually immediately pleasurable or otherwise rewarding.

Entertainment pervades most levels and forms of communication. For example, theories of interpersonal communication often point out the key role of enjoyment and immediate satisfaction in everyday conversations. As for the mass media, you need only add up the content of television to sense our appetite for mass entertainment. Newspapers carry more entertainment than most editors would like to admit. The motion picture industry is a multibillion-dollar-a-year business. In fact, combining all of its forms, entertainment is usually among the top five businesses in the United States. In time as well as in money, our number-one communications business is mainly for fun and profit.

In this chapter we examine some examples of research into entertainment, including studies of entertainment's effects, of television viewing, of cultural impacts, of violent entertainment, and of child socialization.

THE RESEARCH PERSPECTIVE

Research into entertainment reflects a rich mix of methods. For example, there are the relatively straightforward surveys of television viewing or newspaper and magazine reading, all of which are a basis for setting advertising rates. There are the more theoretically oriented survey studies to determine and attempt to explain audience tastes. Scholars conduct experiments to assess the effects of media content under carefully controlled conditions. Further, there is considerable growth of qualitative research into media, as in critical analyses of media content—for example, assessing the image of women in prime-time television. Also, U.S. television programming is of considerable interest in international communication research, as it is often asserted that TV conveys a distorted image of American life.

As we will see in this chapter, a major line of social scientific research into the effects of entertainment focuses upon social learning. Researchers find that many of the images of society; stereotypes of sex roles, age levels, and ethnic groups; and strategies for behavior may be learned more from entertainment media than from informational media. Perhaps the prime-time situation comedies have had more of an effect on our lives than we realize. But, after all, Shakespeare did say that "all the world's a stage."

THE MAJOR EFFECTS OF ENTERTAINMENT

Pleasure as a Primary Effect

What about the uses of entertainment? Unlike research into two-step flow, agenda setting, or the social diffusion of information, research into entertainment has gotten much less attention from communication theorists. It is reasonable to assume that we get our rewards (or thrills!) from a multitude of entertainment options that constantly compete for our attention. For purposes of discussion, we can refer to the immediate satisfactions of entertainment (such as pleasure or escape) as a primary effect. Psychologically speaking, we can equate many of the effects of entertainment with its use as **leisure** in our lives.

Leisure remains a scantily studied aspect of social behavior. Perhaps this is so because many of the cultures that make up the industrialized Western world put a premium on work rather than on relaxation and enjoyment. Theoretically, leisure is much more than just nonwork. It is a time during which we hope to derive satisfaction from rest, relaxation, deliverance from boredom, as well as feelings of personal enlightenment and growth. In essence, we divide the twenty-four hours in our day among sleeping; work; obligatory activities such as housework, shopping, and child care; and leisure. The mark of modern industrialized civilizations seems to be that we are increasingly using the entertainment media as a primary leisure activity. This is particularly true in the United States, and television is by far the dominant leisure activity for many citizens.

Social Learning as a Secondary Effect

The secondary effects of mass-media entertainment have received the bulk of social scientists' attention. Researchers' concern is with the way in which entertainment leads to **social learning.**

Most research into social learning has involved the possible negative effects of television entertainment—in particular, the consequence of media-portrayed violence. Another topic involves the effects of television on our attitudes toward people of different ethnic, gender, or age groups—that is, how the media promote certain social attitudes. The paradox is that while we pursue the media for entertainment ends, we may also be engaging in mass social learning, taking on the values of the images we are using mainly for escape or sheer pleasure. The effects may be especially pronounced on our children, as you can see from the commentary by Aimee Dorr, a noted authority on children and television.

From a positive viewpoint, social learning has led to the use of the media to promote constructive social-learning experiences, as, for example, in the production of antidrug or antismoking campaigns or in the development of the well-known children's television series "Sesame Street." Projects in this area are often referred to as "prosocial" uses of media.

TELEVISION AS A LEISURE ACTIVITY

Patterns of Leisure Activities

It is common knowledge that many groups in the U.S. population spend substantial amounts of time with television. For example, Nielsen surveys reported that average household TV usage per day passed the 6-hour mark during the 1970–1971 television season. By the 1979–1980 season, it had passed the 6½-hour mark; and in 1985–1986, it was 7 hours and 10 minutes.

If people spend so much time watching television, how has this affected the time spent on other activities? John Robinson (1981) attempted to answer

Aimee Dorr

Television. The word once called forth wondrous visions and terrible fears of what the medium would mean for American children. Optimists saw it as a master teacher, a window on the world, an activity uniting the family. Pessimists saw it as a time waster, a purveyor of distasteful content, an activity isolating each child with an electronic baby-sitter. Optimists sought to hasten television's arrival into the home; pessimists sought first to delay it and then to minimize its impact. It did not take long for the pessimists to fail, as during the 1960s television became a part of virtually every American household.

Now that a generation of television-reared children have become men and women rearing their own children with television, should the optimists of the past be glad? Did they accurately foresee the future? Some people today answer yes, and again yes. They point to television's contributions to children's development and education. Television brings physical processes and events, great people, faraway places and peoples, and important stories to life and makes them available to all children, even those who cannot read. It is as close to a real-life experience as children can get without being there. Sometimes it is actually better, because it can slow life down, repeat it, zoom in close to it, and move back from it. Television can even lead children to experience fear, anger, and disgust without ever having to suffer through the real-life experiences that would normally provoke such feelings. Finally, those who look on the bright side applaud the fact that most television viewing goes on in children's own homes, often with others in the room or close by, and that its content is a frequent topic of children's conversations with family and friends.

Hearing all these claims for the good that television does, the pessimists of yesterday and today clamor for an opportunity to present their side. They agree that televised presentations are lifelike, that even very young children can understand at least some of what is presented. At a minimum they can imitate the actions of characters on television. But "what characters and what actions!" the pessi-

mists exclaim. They find much of what television presents and most of what children choose to view to be trivia and sometimes even trash. It is sex, violence, consumerism, ridicule, racism, sexism, and ageism—not the good things in life—that entertain children for several hours each day. Those who look on the dark side note that such entertainment is chosen in place of playing with other children, amusing oneself, studying, and doing chores.

Amid these conflicting claims about television, one easily asks where reality is. Clear-thinking men and women have argued this very point for decades now. You should too. Television programming is undeniably attractive to children, with information, stories, and advertisements that are easier to understand than are those in any other medium except film. Because television is a superb medium for presenting some aspects of the world to children, we should all be especially concerned about the programming menu it offers and the diet children choose. How can we make television content the best possible? How can we lead children to prefer the best? How can we teach them to interpret television's messages properly and use them wisely? And how can we be sure they spend enough time actively experiencing the world, mucking in it, and trying things out, not just sitting home watching the world go by on a large-size, full-color television screen?

Aimee Dorr is a Professor in the Graduate School of Education at the University of California at Los Angeles.

Suggested readings:

G. Comstock, S. Chaffee, N. Katzman, M. McCombs, and D. Roberts, *Television and Human Behavior* (New York: Columbia University Press, 1978).

R. Liebert, J. Neale, and E. Davidson, *The Early Window: Effects of Television on Children and Youth* (Elmsford, N.Y.: Pergamon Press, 1973).

E. L. Palmer and A. Dorr, eds., *Children and the Faces of Television: Teaching, Violence, Selling* (New York: Academic Press, 1980).

D. Pearl, L. Bouthilet, and J. Lazar, *Television and Behavior: Ten Years of Scientific Progress and Implications for the Eighties* (Washington, D.C.: U.S. Government Printing Office, 1982).

this question by comparing two studies done a decade apart. During those ten years, time spent by Americans in viewing television had substantially increased. The results of his comparison are summarized in Table 14.1.

There are several interesting points to note in the table. You can see, for example, that even in 1965 the predominant form of leisure activity was playing records and watching television (mostly watching television). In fact, television was the fourth most time-consuming activity during the waking hours of men and women. Time spent with "the tube" was exceeded only by work, housework, and eating.

Table 14.1 also illustrates that television was the activity that gained the most in allocated time during the decade between 1965 and 1975. By 1975, it not only dominated free-time activities but now accounted for more time than that spent in eating or doing housework. Television was the second most engaged-in activity during a person's waking hours. In round figures, about 40 percent of people's free time, on the average, was spent in watching television.

Table 14.1 Differences in Use of Time for Obligatory and Free-Time Activities, 1965–1975

		1965 minutes/day	Differences 1975 minutes/day	Difference minutes/day
Obligatory Activities	Work	253	228	−25
	Trip to work	26	24	−2
	Housework	126	103	−23
	House repair	21	18	−3
	Child care	37	34	−3
	Shopping	54	46	−8
	Eating	119	116	−3
	Sleeping	457	472	+15
	Personal care, other	51	70	+19
	Total	1144	1110	−34
Free-Time Activities	Study	15	23	+8
	Organization	6	4	−2
	Religion	10	12	+2
	Entertainment	21	17	−4
	Visiting (and meals out)	64	54	−10
	Sports	8	11	+3
	Hobbies, other active leisure	10	11	+1
	Radio	4	2	−2
	Records, TV	89	132	+43
	Magazines, etc.	14	17	+3
	Newspapers	21	14	−7
	Resting, other	20	22	+2
	Travel	21	24	+3
	Total	296	330	+34
	Total minutes/day	1440	1440	

Source: John P. Robinson, "Television and Leisure Time: A New Scenario," *Journal of Communication* 31, no. 1 (Winter 1981): 125. Used by permission.

Obviously, since there are only twenty-four hours in a day, the increase in time spent viewing television must be taken from some other activities. The sometimes heard claim that we are sleeping less and watching TV more does not hold up, according to the figures in Table 14.1. You can see that the average time spent sleeping actually increased over the decade, as did time spent with personal care. Perhaps the most conservative generalization that can be made about the differences is that, as the overall figures indicate, people reported half an hour more free time in 1975 than they did in 1965. Probably, then, a substantial share of this increased free time was spent in watching television. Of course, this does not definitely mean that there was a segment of newly available free time and that people decided to watch television. Quite the opposite could also be the case: that people simply spent more time watching television and took that time away from a variety of other activities.

Robinson also compared activities that compete or go along with television viewing, as based on the figures in Table 14.1. These are summarized in Table 14.2. Among the generalizations shown in this table are that as people tended to have additional leisure time in 1975, they tended to spend it more with at-home activities than with activities outside the home. The increased time spent in viewing television reflected not only a decrease in time spent at work and on other such obligatory activities but also a reduction in time spent with away-from-home recreation. Such patterns have been used by business forecasters to predict an expanding market for home entertainment devices and services.

Table 14.2 Away-from-Home and At-Home Activities That Compete with and Complement Television Viewing

	Away-from-Home Activities	At-Home Activities
Competitive with television	Work Religion Visiting Bars, parties Shopping, travel	Personal care
In between	Sports, outings Entertainment Studying Organizational participation	Book, magazine reading Child care Housework Hobbies Eating
Complementary with television		Radio, records Resting Newspaper reading Sleeping

Source: John P. Robinson, "Television and Leisure Time: A New Scenario," *Journal of Communication* 31, no. 1 (Winter 1981): 128. Used by permission.

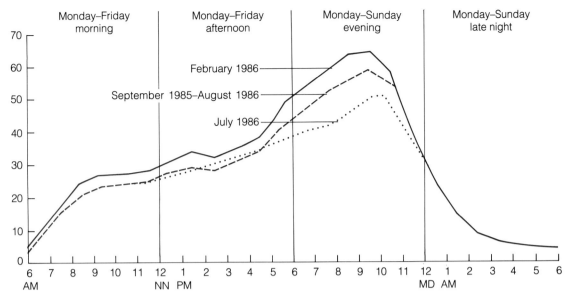

Source: A. C. Nielsen Co., *1987 Nielsen Report on Television*, p. 5. Copyright © 1987 by A. C. Nielsen Co.

Figure 14.1
Percentage of House-
holds Using Television,
by Hour of Day and
Season

What People Watch

Although viewing patterns vary from weekday to weekend and by seasons of
the year, two highly reliable patterns have been found across most audience
surveys over the last several decades. One of these, as shown in Figure 14.1,
is that viewing tends to build from almost zero during the early morning
hours (3 to 5 A.M.) to a peak at roughly 8 P.M. to 10 P.M. daily, but with
seasonal variations. Note in this figure the seasonal differences where Feb-
ruary and July are separated from the curve for the annual average. More
people watch prime-time television in winter than summer, but the overall
daily curves are very similar in terms of the hourly pattern.

Another reliable pattern is the preference American audiences show for
various types of evening television programs, as shown in Figure 14.2. Note
how informational programs (the right side of the figure) draw a consistently
smaller audience than any of the specific types of entertainment programs.
Note, too, that this comparison even includes the nightly news programs in
the informational category. (American television is truly entertainment!) Situation comedies are usually the most favored type of entertainment program,
with general dramas, suspense or mystery dramas, and feature films vying
for second place.

You can also see in Figure 14.2 that tastes differ according to segments
of the viewing population. For example, children are most attracted to situation comedies during the evening hours, and they are about the only audience for cartoons presented during the day (not shown here). Women over

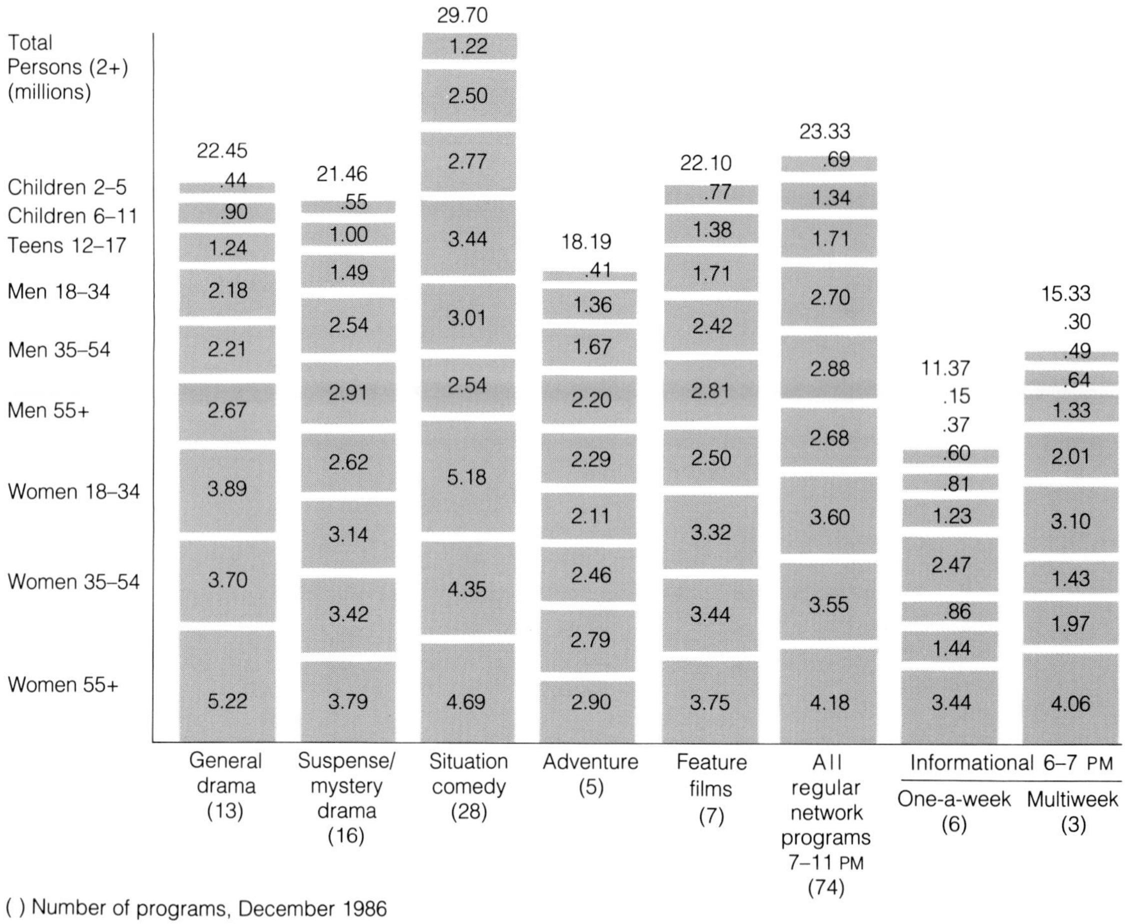

	General drama (13)	Suspense/ mystery drama (16)	Situation comedy (28)	Adventure (5)	Feature films (7)	All regular network programs 7–11 PM (74)	Informational 6–7 PM One-a-week (6)	Informational 6–7 PM Multiweek (3)
Total Persons (2+) (millions)	22.45	21.46	29.70	18.19	22.10	23.33	11.37	15.33
Children 2–5	.44	.55	1.22	.41	.77	.69	.15	.30
Children 6–11	.90	1.00	2.50	1.36	1.38	1.34	.37	.49
Teens 12–17	1.24	1.49	2.77	1.67	1.71	1.71	.60	.64
Men 18–34	2.18	2.54	3.44	2.20	2.42	2.70	.81	1.33
Men 35–54	2.21	2.91	3.01	2.29	2.81	2.88	1.23	2.01
Men 55+	2.67	2.62	2.54	2.11	2.50	2.68	2.47	3.10
Women 18–34	3.89	3.14	5.18	2.46	3.32	3.60	.86	1.43
Women 35–54	3.70	3.42	4.35	2.79	3.44	3.55	1.44	1.97
Women 55+	5.22	3.79	4.69	2.90	3.75	4.18	3.44	4.06

( ) Number of programs, December 1986

Source: A. C. Nielsen Co., *1987 Nielsen Report on Television*, p. 11. Copyright © 1987 by A. C. Nielsen Co.

Figure 14.2
Audience Size and Composition by Selected Program Type for Regularly Scheduled Network Programs, 7–11 P.M.

55 years of age constitute the largest viewer group and are most attracted to general drama. Teenagers and men in the 18–34 age group watch the least television. Men in the 35–54 age group watch the most informational programs.

Although we cannot be sure of how well these patterns will persist in the years to come, several trends became noticeable in the mid–1980s. One is that overall time spent watching television is still increasing slightly. But this increase includes growth due to audiences adding cable and pay-television services. Viewing of over-the-air television seems to be decreasing slightly. Overall time spent with television would be greater, however, if video cassettes and disks were included in the figures. Figures would also increase slightly if the use of the television set with computers, especially for game playing, were included. Bear in mind that these uses are all mainly *entertainment*. If direct broadcast satellite or electronic text services ever become popular, we have every reason to believe that time spent with television will increase still more. The question is where we will get the extra hours.

THE CULTIVATION THESIS

We have stressed many times in this book that communication is how the rules of our society "get into" us. In Chapter 12, on public opinion, we discussed theories of how information affects society. The **cultivation thesis** acknowledges the effects of information but stresses a more comprehensive point: that the sum of our communication experiences "cultivates" our image of reality.

Media Images as "Reality"

We pause for a moment to explore more thoroughly what *image* and *reality* mean in terms of this thesis. Our daily perceptions are filled with items, events, people, actions, and so on that we observe directly. This is a kind of *reality as directly experienced*. These are firsthand observations, ones we can see, touch, or even check on. But we also gain many impressions of our world indirectly from the reports of others, including the texts, sounds, and images conveyed to us by communications media. You may never have been to China, for example, but you have many impressions, or images, of what China is like because of media representations.

Some of our media use is prompted by a need for information about a great variety of things that we cannot experience directly. If we want to learn more about China, it is easier to go to the library than to travel to the opposite side of the world. As we spend more and more of our time with media, our view of the world around us—that portion not directly experienced—will be very much a product of what we experience in media representations. Experiences restricted to media can easily distort what may exist in reality. It is this distortion that causes visitors to China to be so surprised by the hustle and bustle of city life when they have mainly experienced media images of rural life. It is the same with European visitors who assume that it is easy to see "real" cowboys and Indians when they visit the United States or with tourists who assume that Hawaii is all war canoes and hula girls. Many a young person has been attracted to Hollywood by its glamorous movie image only to find that the reality is quite the opposite.

Also, as discussed in Chapter 12, part of media distortion is due to the lack of objectivity or "truth" of the information that flows through society. The cultivation thesis extends this bias to the even greater amounts of media experiences we have that are not necessarily based on fact but on drama or fantasy. Individuals who spend much of their time with entertainment media may come to expect a world that is more based on the imaginations of writers, set designers, directors, and performers than on fact.

Television is getting more exciting all the time. Studies show that many children now devote more sustained attention to television than to any other communications source, including their parents. Despite numerous studies of the effects of televised violence on children, there is still disagreement as to the social consequences. We do know, however, that by their teenage years, many young people turn away from television viewing in favor of other recreational activities, including spending time with one another. *Jane Scherr/ Jeroboam, Inc.*

Cultivation by Television

We can consider the cultivation effect in everyday experiences with prime-time television. For example, if the majority of a person's experience with crime is based on TV police shows, where violence abounds, we might expect that person to believe that the everyday life of a police officer is full of action when, in fact, it is not. Or that person might assume that U.S. society is riddled with everyday violence. (We may have our problems, but crime in society is not nearly as frequent as that displayed on television.) This, in essence, has been the thesis of George Gerbner and his research associates in studying the consequences of television violence on the viewing audience.

Gerbner has pursued the cultivation thesis with two types of studies. One has been an annual analysis of the content of prime-time television programs. The other has been a study of the differences in images of society held by heavy viewers of television as compared with light viewers.

Content Analysis of Violence. In the content-analysis research, measures are taken of the following aspects of a sample of television programs:

> percentage of programs with violence
> rates of violent acts per program
> rates of violent acts per hour
> percentage of characters involved in violence

These components are combined in a mathematical formula to yield an overall violence index: the higher the value, the greater the measure of violence. Figure 14.3 summarizes findings for the violence index from the 1967 through 1978 television seasons.

The analyses in Figure 14.3 are subdivided by weekend, children's programming, and different prime-time hours. As you can readily see, despite the condemnation of television violence found so often in the popular press and even in the report of a government commission, violence continues at a relatively high rate in network programming. Roughly 80 percent of the programs sampled portray one kind of violence or another. When these data are analyzed on a per-program basis, the results show an average of about five violent incidents per program, or an average rate of about 7.5 an hour. If this rate is accurate and you watch about three hours of television daily, then you would expect to witness well over 8000 violent incidents in the course of a year! No doubt about it: American television portrays a substantial amount of violence.

Effects of Violence on Social Images.   Most of the complaints about violence on television are coupled with the assumption that violence will become part of viewers' attitudes and images of everyday life. Yet, with only a few exceptions, there have been no attempts to study these consequences directly. One exception is the second type of research engaged in by Gerbner and his associates. These studies have compared light and heavy viewers of television in terms of how they answer certain questions about society.

Some of the studies are based on the results of questionnaires administered to a national sample of the U.S. population (see Gerbner et al., 1979). Other studies by Gerbner and his colleagues have involved selected groups

Figure 14.3
Television Violence
Analyses from 1967
to 1978

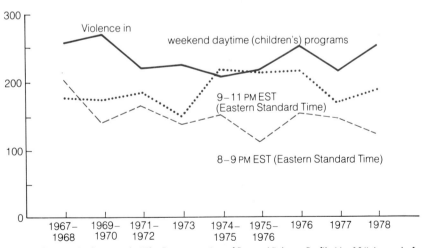

Source: George Gerbner et al., "The Demonstration of Power: Violence Profile No. 10," *Journal of Communication* 29 (1979):185. Used by permission.

of viewers. One example of the latter involved the students in a New Jersey middle school (seventh and eighth grades), whose average age was roughly 13 years. Among the questions asked of these students was:

> Think about the number of people who are involved in violence each week. Do you think that 1 person out of every 100 is involved in some kind of violence in any given week, or is it closer to 10 people out of every 100?

Gerbner and his fellow researchers hypothesized that the students who heavily watched television would tend to select the answer indicating a greater amount of violence in the populace—an amount that, indeed, was an overestimate of real figures. They called this the "television answer" because television exaggerates the number of people involved in violence. "Light" viewers were those watching up to four hours of television a day; "heavy" viewers were those watching more than four hours. Heavy viewers in almost all of the subgroups overestimated the amount of violence when answering the question. Moreover, certain subgroups estimated more violence than others. For example, heavy viewers who were female, who read the newspaper every day, who watched TV news every day, or whose father had no college degree, tended to overestimate even more than other heavy viewers. According to the researchers, being a potential victim of violence (that is, a female potential victim), being exposed to news of violence (newspapers, TV), and perhaps having a less educated family to influence opinion might all be deeper reasons for being affected by media. This is the type of evidence used in the cultivation research project, and it is extended to other types of images or symbols that predominate on television (for example, images of women).

Problems with Cultivation Research

Like all of the other theories concerning the broad effects of communication on society, cultivation research and theory are not without critics. One general criticism of the type of evidence just presented is that, although it shows a relationship between heavy viewing and estimates of violence, the theory does not demonstrate at all that the former is the cause of the latter. That is, there may be other reasons that cause this relationship. It might be conceivable that people who overestimate the amount of violence in society have a greater appetite for watching television. There is also the problem that what is identified and counted in a television program does not necessarily predict what is perceived and interpreted by a viewer. As Horace Newcomb (1980) has pointed out, how individuals perceive and interpret the so-called "symbols" of their culture may not be adequately reflected in "counts" of TV acts of violence or in answers to general questions about the world.

A more comprehensive criticism of cultivation research has been offered by Paul Hirsch (1980, 1981), who, in reanalyzing data drawn from the same national surveys used by Gerbner and his colleagues, finds little evidence in favor of the cultivation thesis. The arguments for and against the cultivation thesis are illustrative of the pros and cons of social scientific research assumptions and methods in modern communication.

BEHAVIORAL EFFECTS OF VIOLENCE

Even if cultivation theory were largely correct—and we do not have sufficient evidence to know this—there is still the question of the effects of media violence on a viewer's subsequent behavior. As you may recall from Chapter 5, the link between attitudes and behavior is not entirely predictable. We may say that one of the consequences of entertainment is an effect on social attitudes, but does the effect go any further than this? Herein lies one of the primary theoretical questions not only about the effects of entertainment in general but also about violence in particular. Let us next examine some of the theoretical pros and cons.

An Aggressive Stimulation Theory

The psychologist Leonard Berkowitz (1962), long an authority on aggression, focused a major part of his studies on the question of how media (often motion picture clips) might affect aggressive tendencies in individuals. Somewhat in contrast to cultivation theory, Berkowitz's **aggressive stimulation theory** places much more emphasis on likely interactions between the content of the depicted aggression and the circumstances and attitudes of the individual.

One basic hypothesis borne out in most of his studies is that media-depicted violence definitely can increase an individual's state of physical and emotional arousal. Generally, an individual's intention to engage in aggression was found to increase (1) as a function of the degree of violence depicted in the medium, (2) if the violence seemed justifiable ("the other person deserves to get it!"), and (3) if the individual saw a similarity between the depicted violence and a situation that she or he had faced or experienced. Berkowitz's experiments typically involved college students who viewed different versions of a boxing match, so edited as to present the aggression as justified or unjustified. In one experiment, the participants were intentionally insulted so as to stir up their likely feelings of aggression prior to seeing the film clip.

Similarly, Berkowitz showed that aggressive tendencies could be reduced by conditions opposite to those just described, plus the additional factor that if the consequences of violence (pain, suffering) were shown, an individual's aggressive tendencies were inhibited.

Although the Berkowitz research has given us more detailed ideas on the possible relations between violence in media and subsequent behaviors—especially in tying effects to the psychological state of the individual—there are still many arguments that indicate that the effects of media violence are not so predictable. For one, there is the problem of relating the behavior of college students watching experimental films and filling out questionnaires to people in real situations. Indeed, there is another theory that is almost the complete opposite of Berkowitz's. We will turn to it for purposes of contrast.

The Symbolic Catharsis Hypothesis

The essence of the **symbolic catharsis hypothesis** is that viewing violence allows a person to "let off steam," so to speak, thereby decreasing the probability of that person's engaging in actual violence.

Most of the attention given to this hypothesis has been focused on the research of the psychologist Seymour Feshbach (1971). Obviously, this is a controversial theory, because it is used against the many critics of violence on television. This theory says that although, as in Berkowitz's theory, media-depicted violence may arouse an individual, the vicarious experience of the aggression reduces the probability of that individual's engaging in aggressive acts.

There are individual differences, too, in this theory. For example, if a person has been reared in a family context in which aggressive tendencies have been the way of life, he or she is thought more likely to feel a cathartic effect from media aggression than an individual who has developed strong internal controls. Put another way, some people have a greater need to release their aggression, and certain media give them that opportunity. Perhaps this is why televised violence as "entertainment" often draws a large audience, not to mention the size of the audiences for books and films in this category.

Which theory is correct? There are arguments and evidence favoring both, although in balance Berkowitz's approach might be slightly favored. What seems more likely, however, is that how a person responds to media violence is more a result of the characteristics and circumstances of that individual and less of the content of the medium than most theories stress. For this reason, we will turn again to social-learning theory for a few more specifics.

THE CONCEPT OF MODELING

Causes of Imitation

We have already stressed that if a person's experiences are based on media as opposed to real-life situations, we can expect media to have consequential effects on that person's attitude, images, and perhaps behaviors. Certainly, too, the greater the frequency of media exposure, the greater the probability of these effects. Yet, common experience as well as research evidence consistently reminds us that there is *more* to the effects formula. At least one component of this "more" is the *modeling potential* of a media portrayal. That is, what characteristics of content would encourage an individual to pattern his or her behavior after a media presentation? What persuades us to imitate what we experience in media? The answer to this question has been found to incorporate several factors: the "attractiveness" of media characters, their potential relation or relevance to the individual, and the relevance of further "significant other" characters in the media content.

As in the psychology of interpersonal attraction (Chapter 7), some media characters, no doubt coupled with the attractiveness of the performer playing them, can be more influential than others. In one series of studies, the television researchers Byron Reeves and Bradley Greenberg (1977) found that the following factors influence whether a youngster expresses an interest in "behaving like" certain TV characters:

good looks
strength
similarity to most boys or girls
likability
same or greater age

Presumably, then, these children would be more likely to model the behavior of certain characters than of others, and this tendency might be relatively independent of the frequency of exposure to the portrayal.

Next, there is the degree to which an individual can "identify" with a media character. How much can a TV viewer, a moviegoer, or the reader of a book see himself or herself in the role of a principal character in the portrayal? And this question does not necessarily restrict the viewer or reader to characters of the same sex, age, or ethnic group. What seems important is an identification with personality similarities, with how one reacts to situations, or with similar family or group contexts.

Although the formal research literature is mixed on this point, we certainly see everyday examples of the influence of media figures on hair styles, fashion, and even styles of speech (remember the Fonz?). Moreover, film and sports stars are paid millions to endorse products, a practice that would certainly cease were it not so effective.

Finally, the psychologist Albert Bandura (see, especially, 1977) has written extensively on how media portrayals can convey vicarious approval for depicted behaviors. We are much more likely to imitate a behavior if we have seen it portrayed in a positive and reinforcing context. Not only do we look for the apparent satisfaction gained by the "model" engaged in the behavior, but we also look for the fact that other characters convey a "social approval" of the behavior.

Modeling and Expectancy-Value Theory

We can bring most of the foregoing components of modeling full circle by relating them in terms of Martin Fishbein's expectancy-value theory, introduced in Chapter 5. This combination is summarized in Figure 14.4, which was used to theorize about the probability of children's modeling their behavior after television portrayals.

Figure 14.4
Probability of Modeling as Predicted by Expectancy-Value Theory

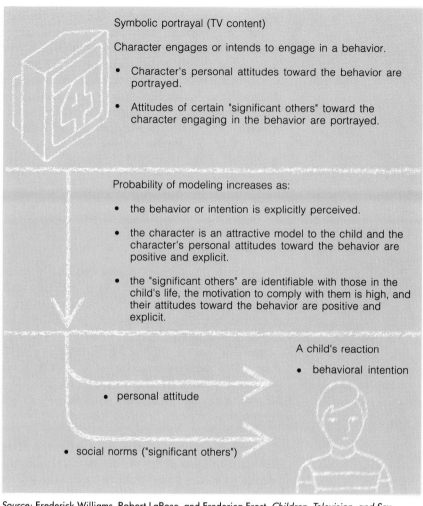

Symbolic portrayal (TV content)

Character engages or intends to engage in a behavior.

- Character's personal attitudes toward the behavior are portrayed.

- Attitudes of certain "significant others" toward the character engaging in the behavior are portrayed.

Probability of modeling increases as:

- the behavior or intention is explicitly perceived.

- the character is an attractive model to the child and the character's personal attitudes toward the behavior are positive and explicit.

- the "significant others" are identifiable with those in the child's life, the motivation to comply with them is high, and their attitudes toward the behavior are positive and explicit.

A child's reaction

- behavioral intention

- personal attitude

- social norms ("significant others")

Source: Frederick Williams, Robert LaRose, and Frederica Frost, *Children, Television, and Sex-Role Stereotyping* (New York: Praeger, 1981), p. 145. © Praeger Publishers, 1981. Reprinted by permission.

In essence, expectancy-value theory holds that if you can identify yourself and your "significant others" in a media portrayal and if there is a promise of personal and social reward related to a specific behavior, your intentions to engage in that behavior will increase in probability.

This theory places much more of the responsibility for the social effects of entertainment media on the decisions of the individual than do most others. You may, for example, view all types of televised violence, and with considerable frequency, but whether you will imitate it depends on how much you can identify yourself and your significant others in the portrayal as well as on how much you sense you will gain both personal and social reward if you do engage in the action.

Ellen Wartella

The influence of the new technologies on children is the subject of much current speculation. Computers are expected to help children "learn more and faster" as they revolutionize the nature of education. Such are the expected benefits of the electronic media.

At the same time, critics call video-game parlors "dark hangouts" where time and money are squandered. Video games themselves are accused of causing arthritis in users, among other physical and moral maladies. More than a few communities have passed ordinances barring minors from video-game parlors or restricting the location and use of the parlors in other ways.

The voices of the Pollyannas and Cassandras are not new to twentieth-century media. With the introduction of film in the second decade of the century, radio in the 1920s, and television in the 1950s, there have been proclamations of the great social benefits and predictions of great evils to be derived from each new medium. Both sides have spoken some truth. What lessons are there to be learned when speculating on the likely influences on children of today's new media?

First, it is likely that the greatest impact of the new media will be on how children spend their time. Sitting in front of a video terminal will replace watching TV. By the same token, today's college students were children of television. Many of their parents worried about the amount of time they spent in front of the tube. But in the generation before that, their grandparents worried about how much time their children spent next to the radio. That children spend "too much time" with new media is a recurring concern.

Secondly, the new media will influence both what children think about their world and how they think about it. The striking characteristic of today's new media is that they demand an active role of the user—for example, to choose among the 40 or 50 cable channel offerings, to engage in the play of a video football game, or to interact with a computer. They allow child users to actively manipulate a medium and make it more responsive to their wishes and needs. A popular view in child development today holds that children's intellectual development is a function of their active organization and manipulation of their environment. To the extent that the environment provides rich and demanding challenges, children's intellectual functioning should be enhanced. The new media are likely to provide just such challenges.

Before I begin to sound too much like the Pollyanna I spoke of earlier, however, let me point out that all of the potentially "good effects" of new media are dependent on their providing "good" sorts of content for children. We need child advocates who will ensure that child viewers receive the best sort of programming possible, or else the Cassandras may be right.

Fortunately, a third lesson to be learned from past media innovations is that new media have always lived up neither to their great potential as proponents have suggested nor to their great evil consequences as opponents have argued. Rather, new media tend to blend into the context of children's lives and provide an influence among others, such as family, school, and peer group, in socializing children to American culture.

Ellen Wartella is Associate Professor in the Institute of Communication Research at the University of Illinois at Urbana-Champaign.

Suggested reading: E. Wartella, A. Alexander, and D. Lemish, "The Mass Media Environment of Children," *American Behavioral Scientist* 23 (1979): 33–52.

SOME FINAL NOTES

The potential for modeling from communications media may increase substantially in our time. As we increase the variety of broadcast and print content through new technologies, we broaden the opportunity to locate content especially relevant to our individual needs and tastes. We may be markedly increasing the probability of finding content with which we can readily "identify" and which we can possibly "model." This is one implication of the uses of several of the new communications technologies by children, as discussed in the commentary by the media effects researcher Ellen Wartella.

In particular, the demassification of the media may also herald an era of more directly influential media. After all, the more a medium and its content are specifically relevant to our personal needs, the less likely it is that there are intervening steps between the original communicator and ourselves. Perhaps this is the final demise of two-step flow theory.

SUMMARY

If we added up all of our uses of mass media, entertainment would stand out on top. We invest more time and money in entertainment than in any other medium. An important theoretical question is whether entertainment, like news and information, has consequences for society. Research indicates not only that it has effects on our opinions and attitudes but also that such effects may be greater than those from the other uses of mass media. This is the *social-learning* thesis: that we acquire attitudes and even ways of behaving from what we perceive in supposedly entertaining media.

Americans spend the greatest amount of their *leisure* time in viewing television. Moreover, as the amount of leisure time has increased for Americans, we have devoted a portion of that newfound time to television viewing. Again, entertainment is the favorite program type.

The *cultivation thesis* holds that people who are heavy viewers of television will tend to confuse reality with images presented by the media. In the work of Gerbner and his colleagues, for example, heavy viewers of television assume that there is more violence in society than either statistics indicate or light viewers assume. Content analyses consistently show that substantial amounts of violence are portrayed daily on television, and despite public criticism, the level of violence continues. However, the cultivation thesis is not without its critics, some of whom maintain that the counts of violence are overdone and that what is portrayed on television is not necessarily what people interpret.

Opinions about the consequences of violence portrayed by media also differ. One position is that we are stimulated to think or act aggressively by violence in the media *(aggressive stimulation theory)*. A counterposition is that viewing violence can have a cathartic effect: we can blow off steam, so to speak *(symbolic catharsis hypothesis)*.

Further theory suggests that certain qualities of television characters will encourage behavioral modeling by viewers, especially young ones.

TOPICS FOR DISCUSSION OR BRIEF PAPERS

1. How much of your waking day do you spend in leisure activities? Is the amount anywhere near the estimates described in this chapter? What is your favorite leisure activity, and why?

2. Why do you watch television? Or if you watch very little, explain why. What are your opinions about television as a leisure activity? Is it wasted time?

3. What are your interpretations of the cultivation thesis? Do you think that the estimates of violence on television are accurate, too low, or too high? Personally, what are your opinions about violence on television?

4. Examine the arguments pro and con about the aggressive stimulation theory of Berkowitz and about Feshbach's symbolic catharsis hypothesis. Which do you favor, if either? Why?

5. Have you ever modeled your own behavior after a media figure? What made that figure attractive to you?

REFERENCES AND READINGS

Bandura, A. "Social Learning Theory of Identificatory Processes." In *Handbook of Socialization Theory and Research*, edited by D. A. Goslin. Chicago: Rand McNally, 1969.

Bandura, A. *Social Learning Theory*. Englewood Cliffs, N.J.: Prentice-Hall, 1977.

Bandura, A., D. Ross, and S. A. Ross. "Vicarious Reinforcement and Imitative Learning." *Journal of Abnormal and Social Psychology* 67 (1963): 601–607.

Berkowitz, L. *Aggression: A Social Psychological Analysis*. New York: McGraw-Hill, 1962.

Davis, D. K., and S. J. Baran. *Mass Communication and Everyday Life: A Perspective on Theory and Effects*. Belmont, Calif.: Wadsworth, 1981.

Feshbach, S., and R. Singer. *Television and Aggression*. San Francisco: Jossey-Bass, 1971.

Fishbein, M., and I. Ajzen. *Belief, Attitude, Intention, and Behavior*. Reading, Mass.: Addison-Wesley, 1975.

Gerbner, G., and L. Gross. "Living with Television: The Violence Profile." *Journal of Communication* 26 (1976): 173–196.

Gerbner, G., L. Gross, N. Signorielli, M. Morgan, and M. Jackson-Beeck. "The Demonstration of Power: Violence Profile No. 10." *Journal of Communication* 29 (1979): 177–196.

Hirsch, P. M. "The Scary World of the Nonviewer and Other Anomalies: A Reanalysis of Gerbner et al.'s Findings on Cultivation Analysis, Part I." *Communication Research* 7 (1980): 403–456.

Hirsch, P. M. "On Not Learning from One's Own Mistakes: A Reanalysis of Gerbner's et al.'s Findings on Cultivation Analysis, Part II." *Communication Research* 8 (1981): 3–37.

Newcomb, H. "Assessing the Violence Profile Studies of Gerbner and Gross: A Humanistic Critique and Suggestion." *Communication Research* 5 (1980): 264–282.

Palmer, E. L., and A. Dorr, eds. *Children and the Faces of Television: Teaching, Violence, Selling*. New York: Academic Press, 1980.

Reeves, B., and B. S. Greenberg. "Children's Perceptions of Television Characters." *Human Communication Research* 3 (1977): 113–127.

Robinson, J. "Television and Leisure Time: A New Scenario." *Journal of Communication* 31 (1981): 120–130.

Turow, J. *Media Industries: The Production of News and Entertainment*. White Plains, N.Y.: Longmans, 1984.

Wartella, E., A. Alexander, and D. Lemish. "The Mass Media Environment of Children." *American Behavioral Scientist* 23 (1979): 33–52.

Williams, F., R. LaRose, and F. Frost. *Children, Television and Sex-Role Stereotyping*. New York: Praeger, 1981.

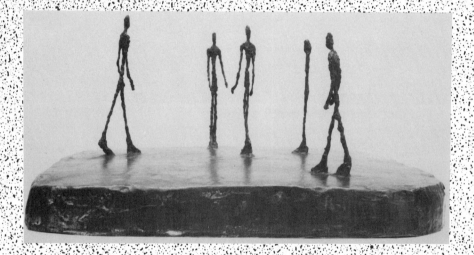

Challenges
from the Future

Reflecting the author's premise that communication is changing

greatly in our times, especially as a result of the introduction of

many new communication technologies, the final chapter of this

volume introduces the concept of the information society.   A

major purpose is to challenge you to contemplate the personal

and professional challenges raised by these changes.

Alberto Giacometti's *City Square,* 1948 (page 288).
Bronze, 8½″ x 25⅜″ x 17¼″. Collection, The Museum of
Modern Art, New York, Purchase.

The Information Society

TECHNOLOGY AND SOCIAL CHANGE

Many have come to call ours the **information society** because of the vast expansion of information technologies in our lives. This expansion includes the application of these technologies in the home, office, and public environments, including computers, satellites, videotape, compact disks, fiber optics, integrated circuits, **artificial intelligence,** and **robotics.**

As we have seen in previous chapters, these technologies are changing our means for interpersonal, group, organizational, and public communication. As we are challenged and aided by these advances in information technology, it is critical that we understand the larger consequences for our immediate and longer-term futures. Our attempts to study modern communications must go far beyond such specialties as speech communication, journalism, broadcasting, or organizational communication. We must see how these different contexts of communication may be coalescing into one all-pervasive context within which we will be carrying out our personal and professional lives. It is not so much that we can expect to see the replacement of traditional communication contexts but that these contexts will increasingly overlap.

For example, how can we best use the newer technologies to increase the range and effectiveness of personally satisfying communications in individual, group, organizational, or even public contexts? Our ability to join with other individuals in point-to-point, highly personal configurations is greater now than ever before in history. Will we take best advantage of it? It is one thing to have new opportunities for interpersonal communication, but it is another to have the *skills* necessary to move communication to that powerful transactional level.

The new technologies also allow us to form groups or communities whenever we can be connected on a telecommunications network. What groups will we want to join? Will we be able to join them? By the same token, will we be able to avoid certain groups? When we communicate in groups that are assembled electronically, how can we be most effective?

Never before in history have so many people had so much information at their fingertips. We need only to make a withdrawal from the "information bank" to get what we need. But how do we know what we need? If we get too much information, how do we make the best decision with it? What if we wish to keep certain information to ourselves? Will the new information environment allow privacy?

In this chapter we review the broad social and economic consequences of the new means of communication. The growth of large-scale communications systems is an important component of such concepts as Daniel Bell's "Post-Industrial Society" (1976), Peter Drucker's "Age of Discontinuity" (1969), Simon Ramo's "Century of Mismatch" (1970), Marc Porat's economic analysis of the "Information Economy" (1977), or my own thesis in *The Communications Revolution* (1983) that this change is revolutionary. The exponential growth and new opportunities afforded by communications are a component in theories of the future envisioned by Marshall McLuhan (1964),

Buckminster Fuller (1969), and Alvin Toffler (1980). Although these views of our future are not completely consistent with one another and are certainly not without critics, they do offer a generalization important to those of us studying modern communications: The final revolution in communication is not so much in the technologies themselves but in their social consequences.

EIGHT AREAS OF CHANGE

One of the problems with visions of the future is that they bias us to look for the future "out there." Parts of this future are already happening, however, particularly in the social impacts of the new communications technologies. Many social impacts of the new technologies have already permeated the traditional institutions and services of our society, and they continue to do so. An examination of some of these areas may lead us to conclude that the so-called communications revolution is not going to come crashing down on us but is already evolving in our everyday environment.

Following are brief comments about changes in the eight areas of information businesses, transportation, politics, health care, work, leisure, education, and national development. They are the changes that will affect your personal and professional future.

1. The Information Business

One distinct characteristic of change in the economic sector is the projected growth of what some call the information business. This business has to do with all the products and services we associate with communications, from delivering the mail to designing, building, and selling computers. It involves many products and services that most people have never thought of as being related. Figure 15.1 is a summary of the wide-ranging components of this business, as envisaged by a Harvard research group.

Notice in the figure how communications *products* (looking toward the bottom of the chart) used for printing, storage of information, or books are distinguished from communications *services* (top of chart) such as the mail, telephone services, broadcasting, and financial services. In other words, the information business involves items that we manufacture and market as well as services that we provide. The modern versions of **desktop publishing** fit into this contrast. There is the sale of the equipment as contrasted with offering publishing services.

Another distinction in Figure 15.1 is between communications products and services that are like information "conduits" (left of chart). Conduit types of business are services like the mail or businesses that retail products such as copiers, dictation equipment, or simply paper. The delivery of financial

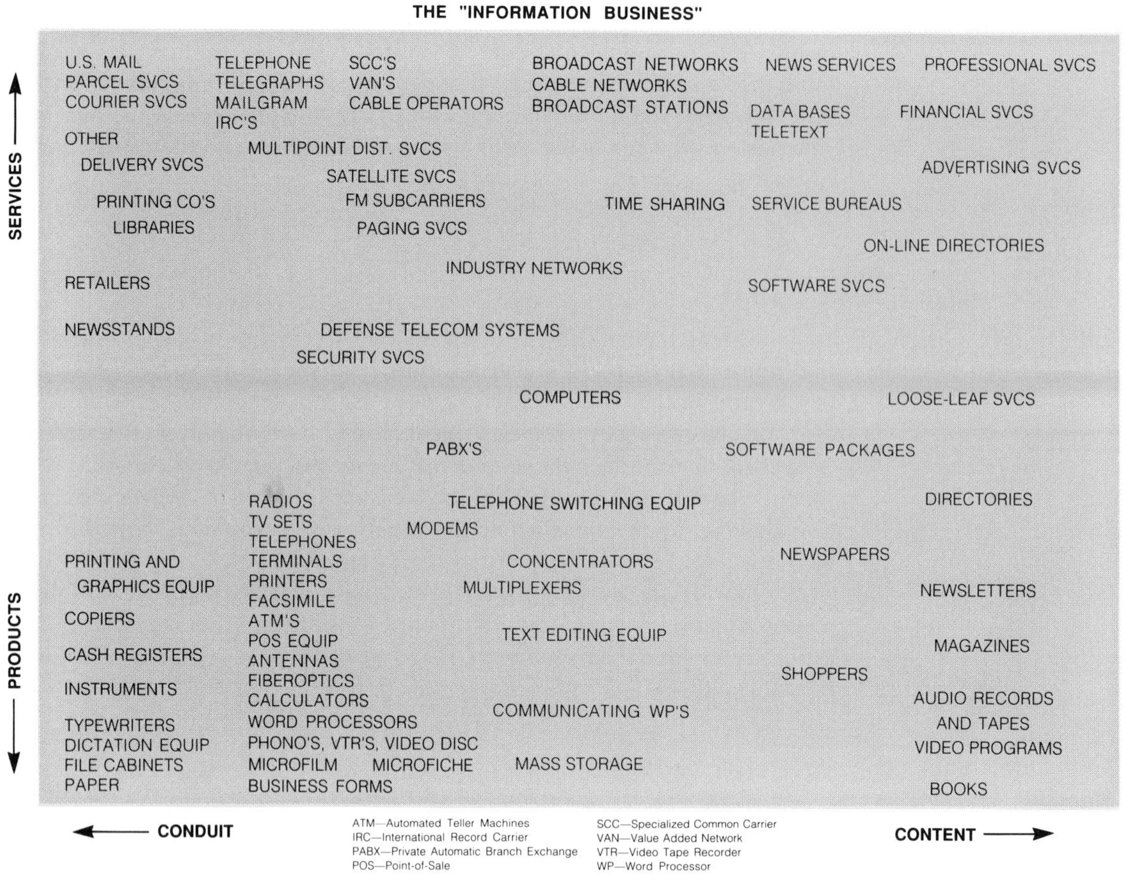

Figure 15.1 — The Information Business

U.S. MAIL	TELEPHONE	SCC'S	BROADCAST NETWORKS	NEWS SERVICES	PROFESSIONAL SVCS
PARCEL SVCS	TELEGRAPHS	VAN'S	CABLE NETWORKS		
COURIER SVCS	MAILGRAM	CABLE OPERATORS	BROADCAST STATIONS	DATA BASES	FINANCIAL SVCS
	IRC'S			TELETEXT	
OTHER	MULTIPOINT DIST. SVCS				
DELIVERY SVCS					ADVERTISING SVCS
	SATELLITE SVCS				
PRINTING CO'S	FM SUBCARRIERS		TIME SHARING	SERVICE BUREAUS	
LIBRARIES	PAGING SVCS				
					ON-LINE DIRECTORIES
	INDUSTRY NETWORKS				
RETAILERS				SOFTWARE SVCS	
NEWSSTANDS	DEFENSE TELECOM SYSTEMS				
	SECURITY SVCS				

Vertical axis (left): SERVICES (top) → PRODUCTS (bottom)
Horizontal axis: CONDUIT ← → CONTENT

		COMPUTERS		LOOSE-LEAF SVCS
	PABX'S		SOFTWARE PACKAGES	
	RADIOS	TELEPHONE SWITCHING EQUIP		DIRECTORIES
	TV SETS	MODEMS		
	TELEPHONES			
PRINTING AND	TERMINALS	CONCENTRATORS	NEWSPAPERS	
GRAPHICS EQUIP	PRINTERS	MULTIPLEXERS		NEWSLETTERS
	FACSIMILE			
COPIERS	ATM'S			
	POS EQUIP	TEXT EDITING EQUIP		MAGAZINES
CASH REGISTERS	ANTENNAS			
INSTRUMENTS	FIBEROPTICS		SHOPPERS	
	CALCULATORS			AUDIO RECORDS
TYPEWRITERS	WORD PROCESSORS	COMMUNICATING WP'S		AND TAPES
DICTATION EQUIP	PHONO'S, VTR'S, VIDEO DISC			VIDEO PROGRAMS
FILE CABINETS	MICROFILM MICROFICHE	MASS STORAGE		
PAPER	BUSINESS FORMS			BOOKS

← CONDUIT   CONTENT →

ATM—Automated Teller Machines
IRC—International Record Carrier
PABX—Private Automatic Branch Exchange
POS—Point-of-Sale
SCC—Specialized Common Carrier
VAN—Value Added Network
VTR—Video Tape Recorder
WP—Word Processor

Figure 15.1
The Information Business

Source: Copyright © 1980 by the President and Fellows of Harvard College.

services (such as accounting), advertising, and products such as magazines or books represent "content" types of business (right of chart).

One contribution of the analysis shown in Figure 15.1 is that many of the new communications technologies affect whole clusters of services or products or the operations involving conduit or content. For example, the computer is now used extensively in retailing services, and it is also used to aid in the editing of television programs. The communications satellite can be used to deliver the mail electronically, and it is also used by a publisher such as Dow-Jones to "deliver" content for each morning's *Wall Street Journal* to different printing plants in separate parts of the United States. It is likely that as we witness the further growth of communications technologies in our society, we will see their direct effects upon most of the constituents of the information business.

2. Trading Communication for Transportation

There are now many instances in which we substitute communication for transportation. In research circles, these are called communication–transportation trade-offs. One with us for many years has been our use of the "Yellow Pages" to let our "fingers do the walking." In recent years, "tele-shopping" has become big business. We can think of these examples as a substitution of electronic movement for people movement. Most types of home entertainment that have evolved in the present century are, in a sense, transportation–communication trade-offs because the entertainment is brought to our homes rather than making us transport ourselves across town.

In some respects, we can look at the growth of communication–transportation trade-offs in terms of services that are deliverable to the home by communications networks. For example, a study by Herbert Dordick and his associates (1981) predicted that banking and entertainment services will be used in roughly 50 percent of all households in the United States by 1995. Other projections of adoption of nontraditional means for receiving traditional services, with percentage of households expected, are:

> information such as addresses, telephone numbers, calendar of events: 45 percent
>
> home security such as fire and police alarms: 40 percent
>
> shopping by catalog: 30 percent
>
> directories of goods and services: 30 percent
>
> personal message systems: 30 percent
>
> games: 30 percent
>
> public information such as laws, regulations, elections: 25 percent
>
> library services: 20 percent

(See the commentary by Herbert Dordick.)

Teleconferencing in all its forms is another example of a communica-tion–transportation trade-off. When we think of teleconferencing, business applications usually come to mind. This type of conferencing can save travel time and costs by bringing people together via television, telephone, and computer links.

There is already a question of whether teleconferencing may not alter the power structure in meetings, giving the advantage to people who are better "on camera" or to groups that have superior equipment or control over the conference. Regardless, teleconferencing is rapidly becoming a fact of life in the business world and in government. As communications networks become more accessible and less expensive or as fuel costs rise, we can certainly expect teleconferencing to increase.

Herbert S. Dordick

In the Information Era, the home is emerging as the information center, and the consumer is the major promoting force. This is unusual; in the past it was the government, either as NASA or the Defense Department, that provided the nation's technological push.

Look into your homes and your daily life. There is hardly a home in the country that does not have at least a half-dozen microprocessors timing ovens and operating washing machines, waking you up in the morning, tuning your radios and television sets, selecting the multiple channels on your cable TV, regulating air temperature, and correcting your typewritten mistakes. Your home may be one of the several million with personal computers, putting you squarely into the Information Era.

The home is being "networked." The communications revolution has wired the home, linking it with many communications services. The telephone, which reaches into over 96 percent of all of the nation's households, is changing beneath our fingertips. "POTS" (Plain Old Telephone Services) are rapidly becoming sophisticated information services, and we will see some tied into our television sets. With intelligence being provided inexpensively for each household by the massive stored program electronic switches at the telephone central office, it becomes quite clear that new telephone networks might very well become the computer networks for the future information household.

Cable television will soon be purchased by more than 50 percent of all households in the nation, and by the end of the century, 90 percent of all households are expected to be on the cable. Cable television is becoming the prime deliverer of entertainment into the home; tomorrow's theater seats will be in homes on cable-satellite networks.

Few if any households in the nation are not within reach of a television and radio broadcast signal, and those not directly "connected" are reached in other ways. For years, engineers knew that the broadcast signal was full of empty "space" or unused bandwidth. Teletext and other forms of electronic publishing are now being transmitted on these empty spaces to test homes. The electronic newspaper is not that far off for those who want to pay the relatively high cost of financial information. The "dark" hours of the broadcast signal—usually just after midnight until the early morning hours—can be used to transmit or "download" information to households and businesses so that electronic newspapers can be available to you at your breakfast table.

Then there are the new low-powered broadcast stations that can provide more local information ser-

The business environment is not the only application of teleconferencing. Some are already using it to "go to school." Perhaps you have heard of Instructional Television Fixed Service facilities, where students are seated in a classroom that is normal except for the existence of two or three remotely operated television cameras. These cameras capture the image of the instructor or images of any notes or charts that are to be presented. The images and sounds are then transmitted into remote classrooms, often in companies where the students work and where they are seated before small television receivers. In the remote classrooms it is possible to "raise one's hand" electronically by pressing a buzzer that will sound in the master classroom. The student's question can then be transmitted to the master classroom as well as over the whole classroom network.

Still another fascinating application of communication–transportation trade-offs is in the concept of the "new rural society," as envisioned by the late Peter C. Goldmark (1972). The idea was to create a highly pleasant living

vices to the home. And where neither broadcast nor low-powered broadcasting reaches homes, the Direct Broadcast Satellite will fill in the gaps. While the consumer or business cannot send information easily by means of broadcast modes, terrestrial or satellite, the telephone remains a most convenient return device. You send your information "upstream" by telephone or cable and the broadcast system or cable system "downloads" your information to the appropriate parties. Consider the possibility of keeping your bank informed weekly (or even daily) by telephone of your money transactions, then having the bank send you daily balance statements over its "dark"-hour broadcast signals, suitably coded, of course, to preserve your privacy.

With the computer chip rapidly entering into our lives, we shall find ourselves doing more for ourselves from our homes or offices and from our cars or while we jog or walk about.

We have become a self-service society, doing more for ourselves instead of having others do things for us. We entertain ourselves in the home with pay TV rather than going to movies or the theater. We want to shop, bank, and work in the privacy of our homes. We are privatizing our lives.

Is this a new phenomenon? Not really. It seems that people have shifted from public or community activities to more privatized activities over the centuries. Gustave Flaubert described how Parisians moved in their very private salons until they became bored and sought more public activities. Tolstoy vividly described the St. Petersburg aristocracy excitedly awaiting Napoleon to lift them out of their boredom, hoping that he would somehow enliven their lives through some glorious community event. And he did!

During the 1960s, we Americans joined forces and communes and paraded down Pennsylvania Avenue and lived in Mississippi towns in order to express dissatisfaction with international policies and racial inequality. Today, we have found these communal activities less rewarding and effective for making change, so we have shifted to a more privatized way of life and of dealing with what we now perceive to be more personal issues.

The new communications and computing technologies that are giving us the Information Era seem to be very suitable for our life choice today. Tomorrow we may find them equally suitable as a means of altering our life-style as we once again become more public.

Herbert S. Dordick is Professor of Communications at Temple University.

Suggested reading: H. S. Dordick, H. G. Bradley, and B. Nanus, *The Emerging Network Marketplace* (Norwood, N.J.: Ablex, 1981).

---

environment while at the same time preserving the advantages of the city. In describing his strategies for developing this new society, Goldmark found that the greatest single problem in urban decentralization was likely to be reduction in operating efficiency because of the stretching of communication links. The key to decentralization, then, would be to devise new types of communications networks that would let a community spread out.

The plan was to interconnect as fully as possible everybody in the community. This linking was just as critical to the community as streets, electricity, and other utilities are to a modern city. Stretching was to be done by having all homes connected just as if they were in physical proximity, perhaps even more so. There were to be further layers to this network, including radio and television broadcasting, two-way cable communications systems, videotext services, and networks linking the operating components of community government, as well as emergency service, travel services, schools, libraries, and health services. The objective was to maintain most of the communication advantages of the urban environment but to do so in such a way that the community would be free of the type of physical congestion and environmental pollution typically found in the great cities.

By the same token, the traditional concept *community* takes on different physical forms when we think of communities as they are formed on communications networks. Too often we think of a community in geographic terms, but it can just as well refer to a community of interest. The freedom from geographic and transportation factors that communications provides is a basis for new types of communities, ones assembled via communications networks.

3. Changing Systems of Governance and Politics

As discussed in Chapter 13, perhaps no type of change is more visible in modern election campaigning than the uses of media as well as polling systems to get candidates elected to office. Our election campaigns are increasingly taking on the characteristics of a "media blitz." Candidates are packaged and promoted with all the same techniques used to sell patent medicines and breakfast foods. In presidential debates, as described by Elihu Katz and his colleagues (1962), candidates are seen more in terms of their television image than in terms of their ability as officeholders.

We already have the capability for instant polling, or "dial-in" voting, via the telephone or two-way interactive cable-TV systems. All major election campaigns take advantage of polling, and we can expect campaigns to increase their use of new information-gathering techniques. Moreover, we are seeing the use of such techniques by elected officials to test the acceptance of their upcoming decisions.

The new communications networks have already changed the relationship between geographic factors and the span of government control. As you can see on most historical maps, the borders of empires and states were shaped by geographic factors such as mountains, seas, and the transportation pathways of rivers and overland passages. Until the nineteenth century, most government communications networks were limited by the extent of the transportation system. But with the invention of the telegraph, the communications networks of nations were able to transcend transportation problems. Later advances of telephone and radio made possible changes in political orders heretofore restricted by geographic and transportation limits. Highly dispersed nations such as the United States and the Soviet Union would have been impossible before the improvements in transportation and communication systems.

Given that the U.S. Congress was originally established as a link between the population and the ruling government, we might even ask ourselves if the new communications networks have made this system obsolete. During the years since the American Revolution, we have transformed the speed of communications from the speed of a horse or sailing ship to the speed of light. Through computers we are automating the storage, manipulation, and retrieval of potentially infinite amounts of political information. With modern news coverage, crises are played out directly on our television screens. No longer are political perceptions delayed by the times necessary for transportation systems to deliver the news. No longer does government perception of public reaction depend on a flow from citizens through elected representatives to the central government. Our political discourse is rapidly being transformed from the written document and spoken word to an electronic communications network enveloping all.

We are faced with a challenge of adjusting our democracy away from the constraints of the eighteenth century and toward the advantages of the twenty-first. Representative government is not dead, but some of our ways of practicing it are becoming obsolete.

4. New Dimensions in Health Care

One of the greatest areas of growth in the service industries in modern society has been in health care. It is noteworthy that this field is also marked by a high rate of adopting technology. Although many of these technologies are used in direct diagnosis and laboratory testing, some are communications devices.

There is "telemedicine," for example, the delivery of health-care information over communications links. The idea of using communications to deliver a physician's advice over long distances goes back to the early use of radio for ship-to-shore medical emergencies. Now, especially with the growth of telecommunications networks aided by satellites, we can expect telemedicine to grow. There have already been successful experiments in the use of satellite communications to link remote areas with centralized medical facilities (for example, the ATS-6 satellite projects in India and North America). These included regular telemedical diagnoses and treatments of individuals separated by thousands of miles. Although telemedical costs are high, it is possible that other paid services provided simultaneously by the telecommunications network (TV broadcasting, education, navigation, business data links) could contribute to covering expenses.

On another front, there is even speculation that computers might someday replace the bedside physician. As outlined in a book entitled *The Post-Physician Era*, Jerrold S. Maxmen (1976) predicts that in fifty years the computer will replace the physician as the primary agent of health care. Highly specialized physician researchers working with paramedical personnel and computers could monitor and constantly improve automated medical decision systems. The necessary human link between the computer and the patient would be a health-care professional selected for talents in interpersonal communication and sensitivity toward the ill. Simple medical advice would be dispensed directly by the computer to the patient, probably right in the home.

Whether or not Maxmen's prediction is eventually realized, the development of regional and national, if not international, information files that hold the collective experiences of a great variety of physicians is growing. These assemblages, by including rare or exceptional cases, increase the diagnostic power of the entire health-care field. Not only do such systems provide a center for pooling the collective experiences of experts, but they can continually accumulate new diagnostic experiences as well.

Even if Maxmen has predicted too great a role for the computer in medicine, it is nevertheless still gaining an important place. We are already experiencing the growth of computer applications in medicine—for example, in research files, medical record keeping, and general administration. Just as the computer aids the designer or manager in other fields, it may aid rather than replace the physician. We should expect a computer-assisted medicine to evolve in ways not dissimilar to computer-aided design or computer-assisted management.

Although we have emphasized computers and telecommunications networks in this discussion, there is another relevant dimension. This is the distorted public image of medicine and health care that has been created by the mass media, particularly by entertainment television. A decade or so ago, for example, we had "Dr. Kildare" and "Ben Casey," later "Marcus Welby," and then "Medical Center," "Emergency," "General Hospital," "St. Elsewhere," and the ever-popular reruns of "M*A*S*H." Much of the public attitude regarding medical issues is influenced by these show-business treatments. Attitudes are also distorted by sensationalist news coverage of such weighty issues as birth control, abortion, mental health, patients' right to use certain unapproved medicines (new compounds for AIDS treatment), test-tube babies, surrogate mothers, and the recent popular exploitations of genetic manipulation.

Somehow, we must use the new opportunities for public communication to alert society enough to important medical issues to keep people informed and provide a forum for full and balanced deliberation. In the next century, if not sooner, we may have to debate the use of biomedical techniques that have the power to alter life itself.

There is an even more basic use of our communications technologies in medicine: *to promote a positive public attitude about personal health*. Too often we consider "health" only as the opposite of "disease" rather than as a positive goal to be sought in everyday living. If we were to invest as much in our national media for a campaign to build highly positive attitudes toward physical and psychological health as we do to buy patent medicines, sugar cereals, and deodorants, we might accomplish as much for disease prevention as all the other technologies have accomplished in the curing of those diseases.

5. New Types and Contexts of Work

Even the nature of work is changing. More people are engaged in the gathering, storing, reformulating, and transforming of information than ever before in history. *Knowledge* is a basic resource in our high-technology society. Closely associated with these changes is the burgeoning growth of telecommunications and the computer-related industries and services discussed earlier as the information business. One need only look to the classified ads in any of

In the communications society many jobs and careers involve the use of computers and telecommunications, either directly or indirectly. Computers have largely replaced typewriters for word processing and are now being transformed into multipurpose workstations for electronic mail, calculations, transactions processing, and for storage and retrieval of information. Many large corporations say that computers allow them to operate with fewer workers as well as managers. Social critics respond with the crucial question of where the displaced workers will find new careers. *Photo Edit*

our major papers to see evidence of rapidly expanding employment opportunities in such areas as computer-assisted management, operations analysis, programming, and electronic funds management, as well as in the design and manufacture of all the technologies necessary to perform these services.

Although executives are not yet, nor will they probably ever be, working in absolutely paperless offices, there is hardly a manager who has not been affected by the necessity to adopt office communications technologies. These include the automation of accounting systems, word processing, electronic mail, filing, and other technologies that generally fall under the term *computer-assisted management*. The traditional tasks of an office in record keeping, information gathering and dissemination, product or services monitoring, and general coordination are all being influenced by the revolution in information technology.

There are many good reasons to expect that the qualitative impact of information technologies will be as significant as their quantitative impact. From this perspective, one focus is on characteristics of the so-called "knowledge worker," the individual involved in the interpretation of information. Engineers, physicians, teachers, managers of data systems, financial analysts, and individuals in research and development are a few of the workers in this occupational area. What is important is not the detailed definition of this occupation but the rapid increase in the number of knowledge-based careers in our society. The qualitative change is that many more people are now more dependent on the manipulation of information and knowledge in their work. For example, many of today's executives must rapidly become experts in new systems for office automation, which are mainly methods for handling information.

The environment for work is also changing. You may be working flexible hours rather than a fixed schedule. You may be working at home for part or all of your time. Even career patterns seem to be changing. Individuals may work for a number of years and then change careers as technological breakthroughs offer new opportunities. Occupational changes may also involve a return to universities for new career training. All these alternatives are made possible, in part, by changes in the communications environment.

6. The Growth of Electronic Leisure Activities

We discussed leisure at some length in Chapter 14 and emphasized that it is the basis for a major business in the United States. It is paradoxical that we know so little about activities at which we all like to spend some time each day and that business sees as a large growth area in our postindustrial economy. Our modern challenge is to broaden the concept of leisure, to see it as a necessary and fulfilling part of life, and, most of all, to learn how to use it. Leisure is not just nonwork. It is a time for personal growth, recovery from fatigue, and deliverance from boredom. We already know that viewing television is the nation's number-one leisure activity. Our sets are on an average of just over seven hours a day.

Despite the emergence of arts and cultural channels and sports alternatives now offered via cable television, there is still no firm basis for believing that we will have an improved type of television in our future leisure time. (Some of the new arts channels have already been discontinued.) New technologies are exceedingly expensive. In order that investors can get a return on their money, mass-marketing techniques and advertising are spilling over into cable and satellite television services and into rental videotapes. The new television is becoming disturbingly similar to the old.

As long ago as 1959, Wilbur Schramm and his associates warned us that it is not what television does to us that counts, but what we do with television. The revolution in communications technology is transforming the television marketplace. Perhaps before mass marketing takes its toll in moving our current program mediocrity from one set of technologies to another, we should try to take advantage of this transformation to use television for more varied and constructive areas of leisure.

What about new forms of electronic leisure activities? From 1977 through 1982, the video-game industry (game machines and game programs) grew from virtually nothing to an estimated $3-billion business, only to collapse a year or so later. The video disk was thought to be the home entertainment playback machine of the future, but it faded as the price of tape machines broke beneath the $500 mark. The compact disk with recorded music arrived with little fanfare but has now established a firm market. Digital tape and high-definition television are next on the horizon. What's next? And will it be temporary or permanent?

7. The Nonrevolution in Education

Education stands out from the other social-impact areas of our present discussion in a most unfortunate way. Although education abounds with opportunities for the use of communications technologies, it remains the institutional sector of our society that is taking the least advantage of the technology revolution. As compared with, say, medical practices or transportation, education has changed little in the last century.

Suppose, for example, the year was 1930. If you had a serious infection, there were no antibiotics. The miracle drugs did not become available until the 1940s. You certainly could not have gotten a comfortable airplane flight fifty years ago. Yet if you were able to go back in time and visit a school in 1930, most of the basic educational practices would be comparable with today's (and some would argue that they were better!). Although most of us can recall the use of motion pictures or filmstrips as an occasional technological aid to education, their current use in schools is practically nonexistent. Educational television has never achieved particularly widespread adoption. The most innovative projects in the uses of television for learning—"Sesame Street," for example—have come from outside the regular educational institutions.

Although television is often thought of only as an entertainment medium, it can have effective instructional uses. For example:

> Television is a great attention-getter.
> The most talented teachers can be available for all.
> It is a powerful medium for illustrating social concepts.
> Children identify personally with television characters.
> Television is excellent as a discussion-starter.
> Production techniques can make complex topics understandable.
> Television instruction is cost-efficient.

But, alas, we make little constructive use of television in education. As the social critic Mayra Mannes once said, "We are a generation who wasted a miracle."

Equally unfortunate is that it now appears that the microcomputer is falling behind the exciting expectations for it in public education. The microcomputer is a natural for managing drills in such basics as reading, writing, or mathematics. Nor do computers necessarily replace teachers; they mainly make them more effective, leaving more time for them to concentrate on complex tasks. Why should a human be forced to correct spelling errors over and over again when a machine can do it so well? Small computers are excellent for:

> *Perceptual drills:* Computers can provide exercises in letter and number recognition, left-to-right orientation for reading, or visualization of geometric concepts.

Simulations: Abstract problems are made concrete by using shapes, sounds, and movements on the computer screen. (For example, the concept of multiplication can be simulated as the successive adding of numbers.)

Language recognition: Vocabulary can be built by pairing pictures with word texts or sound-synthesized "spoken" words. Other uses are displays of different grammatical configurations; exercises in the analysis of pre-fixes, suffixes, and words; and exercises in the construction of compound words.

Written composition: As students prepare a written composition of their own, the computer can check on punctuation, spelling, and other grammatical characteristics, even giving an estimate of readability.

Friendly expert: The computer has a collection of facts from which the student can draw evidence to answer given questions. (For example, the file could include gas-mileage information for a variety of contemporary automobiles, and the student would be asked to identify the best, worst, and average categories.)

A further and most obvious benefit is to use telecommunications to bring the home directly into the educational system. It is possible to imagine homework assignments completed and transferred to a school file via personal computers in the electronic network. It may be, in fact, that as the communications technologies of telephone, computer, and television grow together in the home, we may well spend as much time bringing school to us as we do in transporting ourselves there.

8. National Development and World Order

One of the most far-reaching consequences of the new communications technologies is that they are shrinking our world environment. The affairs of nations on opposite sides of the globe are increasingly impinging on one another. We can see this closeness, for example, in debates over the "new world information order." The advanced industrial nations control most of the world's communications services and manufacturing capabilities. Many nations argue that most international information flow is one-way, from the powerful nations to the weaker ones. As developing nations (such as India and Indonesia) are potentially threatened by this form of "electronic colonialism," they are arguing for a greater access to, and control over, the world's communications networks. For example, they argue that the richest 10 percent of the world's nations use 90 percent of the broadcasting spectrum. Developing countries are demanding their share of the benefits of the technology revolution. Rightly, their leaders see modern communications as a critical resource (see the commentary by Yash Pal).

Another increasingly frequent criticism from other nations is that many of our internationally distributed media products have a one-way cultural quality to them. That is, they tend to present life only as we in the United

Yash Pal

The electronic revolution, computers, and space technology have brought forth an era where lines of communication can be established, in principle between all people on this earth. One can build visions where every human being would be an active agent in an interacting network of humanity. Education would be universal, ignorance would be wiped out, and the only remaining gaps—between the rich and the poor, privileged and not-so-privileged, powerful and weak—would be those that arise even in a normal transactional relationship between equals.

However, this is but a vision. Powerful technologies are more likely to be used for concentration of power than otherwise, unless there is a conscious effort to augment these with other subsidiary technological elements, social goals, and regulatory practices. The slogan "free flow of information" is often invoked to oppose social, ethical, or organizational constraints. But we know that all free flows are down the potential gradients, from highlands to lowlands, and can indeed flood the mass of people living down in the valleys, in spite of the best benevolent intentions of some of the people residing on the hilltops.

Potential gradients exist both across countries and within countries. A poor developing country with very inadequate communications and educational infrastructure might be well advised to invest in a broadcast satellite. The simplest and easiest option would be to generate all the messages in one central place with the help of a few clever communicators and let the rest of the millions soak up their showered wisdom. It would also be very economical to fill up most of the broadcast time with sports events and reruns of "I Love Lucy" and Hollywood extravaganzas. All this may pacify the populace, may also lead to some information transfer, but will it lead to development? A system develops if its elements interact with one another to occasionally create a new configuration. True communication implies exchange, the involvement of two or more people each giving to and taking from the others. Unless the input to the satellite is provided through many sources representing the real, live, experience of such interactions, the system will be a homogenizing venture at best and a centralizing (and indoctrinating) scheme at worst.

So far, we have been rather conventional in selecting from among the infinity of roadways for communication made possible by new communications technologies. There is too much emphasis on widening the already traveled highways, too few gateways, and too many gatekeepers. Unless we work for an autonomous access to the bulk of humanity in the wilderness of long-distance communications, the dream of creating a thin universe of intimacy on this earth will remain but a dream.

The pity is that now we have the means to realize it.

Yash Pal has served as Secretary-General of the United Nations Conference on the Exploration and Peaceful Uses of Outer Space. In his native India, he is Professor at the Tata Institute of Fundamental Research, Distinguished Scientist, Indian Space Research Organization, and Honorary Professor at the Physical Research Laboratory.

States or the Western world see it, without due regard or consideration to the cultures or ways of other peoples. Put another way, media, like individuals' language behavior, can have critical characteristics when examined as *intercultural communication*.

Even now the methods for international relations are changing. We have seen the rise of electronic diplomacy in our time, as meetings between heads of state were prompted by the questions and challenges of television news commentators. As leaders of government appear directly on television, or, for that matter, as revolutionaries appear directly on television news shows, the normal channels of international diplomacy are bypassed altogether.

Since the Vietnam War, we have seen a tightening loop around the occurrence of world events, their instantaneous transmission to us, our reaction to them, and our reactions to our reactions. Most citizens of the United States followed the details of World War II in morning newspaper headlines (with adjacent maps of battlefronts). This lag often made it possible for presidential commentary to accompany the news of the event, thus shaping public interpretation of it. International negotiations were reported mostly in terms of what diplomats wanted the public to think, coupled with whatever scraps of additional news reporters could uncover. In today's world media environment, it is common for a president to witness the breaking news at the same time as a nation of viewers.

Certainly, for the United States, television in the Vietnam War marked a turning point in coverage of international crises. On-the-spot television reporting was delivered directly to the nation's living rooms each evening, often contradicting President Lyndon Johnson's policy announcements. The direct message of the devastation of war had already been digested by the public. We could also see this reporting a decade later when President Jimmy Carter was reduced to a TV bystander like ourselves during the hostage crisis in Iran. Iranian revolutionaries cleverly bypassed diplomatic channels altogether, giving interviews on prime-time TV news programs. A still more vivid and tragic example of the instantaneous presence of media-conveyed news was the explosion of the space shuttle *Challenger*. News traveled so fast that many individuals witnessed the immediate aftermath of the disaster as they found their way to the nearest television set.

The communications revolution has put the world in our living rooms!

YOUR PERSONAL AND PROFESSIONAL CHALLENGES IN THE INFORMATION AGE

What will the information society mean to you? Practically speaking, as you plan for an optimal personal and professional life, what decisions do you face for yourself as well as your country?

Here are just a few of the challenges:

1. How can we better understand the transformations that the new technologies bring to our traditional institutions and services? Are there common characteristics among these applications? For example, can an understanding of computer-assisted management in business contribute to computer-assisted medicine? Can adoption of innovations in medicine aid us in accelerating adoption of new technologies in education?

2. If we do gain a deeper understanding of the impacts of communications technologies on institutions and services, can we use this understanding to maximize desired effects? What are these desired effects? How do we accommodate a balance between goals of efficiency and social benefits? How can applications be directed toward solving such global problems as the threat of nuclear holocaust, the population explosion, food shortages, drought, pollution, and resource conservation?

3. How does the political context affect the growth and applications of the new technologies? For example, will the current deregulation of communications technologies in the United States further stratify the information-rich and the information-poor? In a climate of deregulation, how can programs with social goals be implemented? On the other hand, how much and what kinds of control will stifle efforts for growth toward commercial (that is, profit) goals? What are the interactions between the growth of communications technology in communist countries as opposed to that in free-enterprise countries?

4. What about the management of information technologies? If we understand their impacts and can define goals, how can we ensure that we are promoting optimum applications? Are contemporary theories of management enough to aid us in this direction? How can the technologies themselves assist in their management? What new types of managers and new training programs are implied?

5. What are the prospects of going beyond the traditional goals in applications of communications technologies? What are the highest levels of accomplishment, reward, or gratification in the applications of these technologies for information, education, management, entertainment, or persuasion? If we have the capabilities for reaching high goals, do we know what goals we are seeking?

These questions present you with a fundamental and concrete option. *You can be the shaper of the social consequences of tomorrow's new technologies or the one who is shaped.* This is the final personal and professional challenge of being alive in what may be the greatest period of change in the history of human communication.

SUMMARY

Although the purposes of human communication remain much the same, we are in the midst of a veritable revolution in the development of new types of communications to serve these purposes. But the ultimate revolution is not so much in these new technologies as in their social uses and consequences.

Eight areas of impact are:

1. *The information business:* There is a relation among the manufacture of communications products, the delivery of services, and the ways in which these center either on the "conduits" or the "content" of communication.

2. *Transportation:* We are already substituting communication for transportation in such areas as home entertainment, decentralized communities, and teleconferencing.

3. *Politics and governance:* Television, in particular, is used to "sell" political candidates, especially their images. Furthermore, new types of polling make it possible to gather public opinion nearly instantaneously. Com-

munications systems greatly expand the influence of government as compared with governance based on transportation systems.

4. *Health care:* Telemedicine vastly expands the range of health-care delivery. There is even speculation that computers might replace the bedside physician. The use of modern communications systems to promote positive attitudes about health might offer the greatest payoff of all.

5. *Work:* The nature and contexts of work are changing. More people are working in the information and knowledge fields than ever before. Also, the new technologies make it more feasible to work flexible time schedules or to work at home.

6. *Leisure:* The business of leisure activities is big and growing. Television remains the number-one leisure pastime in the United States. Will it grow? Will it be replaced by new forms?

7. *Education:* Unfortunately, education has been slow to adopt the new technologies of communications, although many of them could greatly expand the services of our educational system. We already know the capability of television as an excellent instructional medium. But perhaps the greatest boon to education will come with the small computer.

8. *Development and world order:* Many nations realize the importance of communication and are calling for a greater share of the world's communications pathways. International television has put wars in our living rooms and changed the nature of diplomacy.

The ultimate challenge of the information society is the degree to which we can apply the new technologies for direct human benefits, *shaping them rather than being shaped by them.*

TOPICS FOR DISCUSSION OR BRIEF PAPERS

1. What are your thoughts on the concept of a "postindustrial" society? Do you agree with Daniel Bell and others on this social and economic transition? Take a position, and defend it.

2. Select one of the eight areas of social impact discussed in this chapter and do some research on it. What are current trends in that particular area? What are examples beyond the ones discussed? What consequences does the impact hold for your personal future?

3. What do you think the federal government's role should be in social change? As discussed in Chapter 13 regarding regulation, should the government give free rein to change (as with deregulation), or should it control it?

4. If we can have almost unlimited access to new forms of communication, what do we want? What is *good* communication? What values should we associate with desired benefits of new types of communication?

5. What are your personal and professional career goals in the information society. Sketch out a plan, and share it with others.

REFERENCES AND READINGS

Bell, D. *The Coming of Post-Industrial Society.* New York: Basic Books, 1976.

Dordick, H. S., H. G. Bradley, and B. Nanus. *The Emerging Network Marketplace.* Norwood, N.J.: Ablex, 1981.

Drucker, P. *The Age of Discontinuity.* New York: Harper and Row, 1969.

Ferguson, M., ed. *New Communication Technologies and the Public Interest.* Newbury Park, Calif.: Sage, 1986.

Fuller, R. B. *The Prospects for Humanity.* New York: Bantam, 1969.

Goldmark, P. "Tomorrow We Will Communicate to Our Jobs." *The Futurist* 6 (1972): 35–42.

Katz, E., and G. Wedell. "The Debates in the Light of Research: A Survey of Surveys." In *The Great Debates*, edited by S. Kraus. Bloomington: Indiana University Press, 1962.

Maxmen, J. *The Post-Physician Era.* New York: Wiley, 1976.

McLuhan, M. *Understanding Media: The Extensions of Man.* New York: McGraw-Hill, 1964.

McPhail, T. L. *Electronic Colonialism.* 2d ed. Newbury Park, Calif.: Sage, 1986.

Nillis, J., F. R. Carlson, P. Gray, and G. J. Hanneman. *The Telecommunications–Transportation Tradeoff.* New York: Wiley, 1976.

Pelton, J. *Global Talk.* Brighton, England: Harvester Press, 1981.

Porat, M. U. *The Information Economy.* Washington, D.C.: U.S. Department of Commerce, 1977.

Ramo, S. *Century of Mismatch.* New York: David McKay, 1970.

Rice, R. E., and Associates. *The New Media.* Beverly Hills, Calif.: Sage, 1984.

Rogers, E. M. *Communication Technology.* New York: Free Press, 1986.

Schramm, W., J. Lyle, and E. Parker. *Television in the Lives of Our Children.* Stanford, Calif.: Stanford University Press, 1960.

Sheppard, C. S., and D. Carol. *Working in the Twenty-First Century.* New York: Wiley, 1980.

Taber, M. *The Myth of the Information Revolution.* Newbury Park, Calif.: Sage, 1986.

Toffler, A. *The Third Wave.* New York: Morrow, 1980.

Williams, F. "Doing the Traditional Nontraditionally." In *Communications and the Future*, edited by H. F. Didsbury, Jr. Bethesda, Md.: World Future Society, 1982.

Williams, F. *The Communications Revolution.* New York: New American Library, 1983.

Williams, F. *Technology and Communication Behavior.* Belmont, Calif.: Wadsworth, 1987.

Williams, F., ed. *Measuring the Information Society*. Newbury Park, Calif.: Sage, 1988.

Williams, F., and R. E. Rice. "Communication Research and the New Media Technologies." *Communication Yearbook 7*, edited by R. Bostrom, pp. 200–224. Beverly Hills, Calif.: Sage, 1983.

Williams, F., R. E. Rice, and E. M. Rogers. *Research Methods and New Media*. New York: Free Press, 1988.

Glossary

A

Advertising A commercial communications practice in which a sponsor purchases space or air time for a given message; rates typically depend on the size and type of audience reached.

AEJMC Association for Education in Journalism and Mass Communications.

Agenda-setting theory The view that public concern for certain issues depends on the prominence that media writers and editors give them; it holds that the media are less effective in promoting particular attitudes than in determining which issues will receive attention.

Aggression An act of forceful behavior, an attack; often implied to be negative.

Aggressive stimulation theory The view that violence in media can lead people to employ violence in their personal lives.

Alphanumeric The digital and alphabetic characters used in computer text or code.

AM Amplitude modulation (see Modulation).

Amplifier Any device that takes a signal and increases its power by drawing power from a source other than the signal itself.

Analog Relating to representations or transformations that bear some physical relationship to the original; usually refers to voltage, frequency, resistance, or mechanical translation.

Argument An attempt to influence through facts, inferences, logic, or reasoning.

Artificial intelligence Computer programs that perform functions, often by imitation, usually associated with human reasoning and learning.

Attitude A feeling, belief, or idea that affects how we may respond to stimulation; for example, George tends to favor Republican candidates for office: he has a positive attitude toward Republicans.

B

Balance (psychological) A mental or emotional state that is free from conflict; during this state our attitudes toward ideas, people, or events are in harmony with one another.

Bandwidth The width of an electronic transmission path or circuit in terms of the range of frequencies it can pass; a measure of the volume of communications traffic that the channel can carry. A voice channel typically has a bandwidth of 4000 cycles per second; a TV channel requires about 6.5 million cycles per second.

Binary A numbering system having only two digits, typically 0 and 1.

Bit *Bi*nary digi*t*: a unit of information with two values or states such as 0 and 1 or yes and no. In an electrical communication system, a bit can be represented by the presence or absence of a pulse.

Broadband communication A communications system with a bandwidth greater than voiceband. Cable television is a broadband communications system with a bandwidth usually from 5 MHz to 450 MHz.

Byte A group of bits processed or operating together. Bytes are often a 32-bit group.

C

Cable television The use of a broadband cable (coaxial cable or optical fiber) to deliver video signals directly to television sets; contrasted with over-the-air transmissions. Current systems may have the capability of receiving data inputs from the viewer and of transmitting video signals in two directions, allowing pay services and video conferencing from selected locations.

Catharsis A relieving of ideas or emotions by bringing them to the surface; a purging of the emotions.

Some of these definitions are adapted from other works by the author, namely, *Technology and Communication Behavior* (Belmont, Calif.: Wadsworth, 1987) and *The Executive's Guide to Information Technology* (with H. S. Dordick; New York: Wiley, 1983).

Cathode ray tube A device often used as the display unit or screen for a computer; called CRT for short.

CATV Community antenna television; the term used to refer to the forerunner of cable television systems.

Cellular radio (telephone) A radio or telephone system that operates within a grid of low-powered radio sender–receivers. As a user travels to different locations on the grid, different receiver–transmitters automatically support the message traffic.

Channel Technically, a segment of bandwidth that can be used to establish a communications link. A television channel has a bandwidth of 6 MHz; a voice channel, about 4000 Hz.

Chip An electronic device made up of interconnected transistors, diodes, and other components.

Chronemics In nonverbal communication, the use of time as a communication device—for example, arriving late at party in order to make a special impression.

Coaxial cable A cable consisting of a conductor surrounded by another conductor in the form of a tube that can carry broadband signals by guiding high-frequency electromagnetic radiation.

Cognitive dissonance theory A theory based on the premise that humans tend to behave in ways that will reduce or avoid psychological discomfort (see Dissonance).

Communication The processes of creating, transmitting, receiving, and interpreting messages between a source and receiver.

Communication hierarchy The patterns of management communications across the levels of an organization; these are often downward, with feedback coming upward.

Communication rules (in organizations) Formal and informal guidelines for communication activities, including which communications are expected of individuals in different communication roles.

Communicative competence What we have to know about the social uses of language in order to communicate most appropriately in any given situation.

Computer A system, usually of electronic circuitry, that can receive, store, process, and present information according to a program given to it.

COMSAT Communications Satellite Corporation. A private corporation authorized by the Communications Satellite Act of 1962 to represent the United States in international satellite communications and to operate domestic and international satellites.

Congruity theories A body of theories based on the premise that our attitudes toward concepts will tend to average out if those concepts are shown to be related. For example, your attitude toward capital punishment and your attitude toward a particular political candidate may affect each other.

Content analysis The systematic identification, classification, and, sometimes, quantification of the parts of messages, for example, counting the number of acts of violence in a television program.

Correlation The relationship between two sets of measures, as in the relation between IQ and reading ability; more generally, a relationship between events.

CPU The central processing unit of a computer.

CRT See Cathode ray tube.

Cultivation thesis The theory that attendance to mass media content will create expectations as to behavior; for example, if television typically portrays criminals as dark and shifty-eyed, then viewers will expect that stereotype in reality.

Curiosity A desire to know, to find out about something; sometimes considered a basic psychological drive.

D

Data base Information or files stored in a computer for subsequent retrieval and use.

Decoding The process by which message signals are received and reconstituted into a form interpretable by a communication receiver (usually a person).

Demassification The trend toward smaller and more precisely identified groups (audiences) rather than the large, anonymous ones for the traditional mass media (for example, radio, television, newspapers) and especially toward the new technologies (cable TV, pay TV, video cassette, special text information services).

Dependency theory The view that public communications do not affect society as a one-way process but that the media, their audiences, and social structures mutually interact with one another.

Deregulation The easing or dropping of regulatory laws or agreements; in communications, this especially refers to easing of regulations governing broadcasting and telephone services.

Desktop publishing Use of computer technology to set type, design pages, and otherwise create camera-ready copy for printing.

Digital transmission A type of transmission in which messages are numerically coded into binary (0 or 1) units; a sound or picture pattern can be "sampled" for critical features and converted into digital form.

Direct broadcast satellite (DBS) A satellite system designed with sufficient power so that inexpensive earth stations can be used for direct residential or community reception, thus reducing the need for local networks.

Dish An informal term referring to a ground antenna (earth station) in satellite communications.

Disk A magnetized surface capable of storing binary information.

Dissonance An uncomfortable mental or emotional state in which thoughts, feelings, or actions are in conflict with one another; for example, you are eating chocolate cake, yet you know you want to lose weight.

Drive reduction A lessening of our unsatisfied needs (or drives) brought about by some kind of behavior; for example, we can reduce our hunger drive by eating.

Drop The link that connects a subscriber's television set in the home to the outside cable TV system.

E

Electromagnetic spectrum In communications, that portion of the frequency range of energy that includes light and radio waves.

Electronic mail The delivery of correspondence, including graphics, by electronic means, usually the interconnection of computers, word processors, or facsimile equipment.

Electronic publishing Distribution of print or graphics to the consumer electronically rather than by paper.

Empathy An individual's ability to sense personally and accurately the feelings and emotions of others.

Encoding The process of translating a message into transmittal form via a communications medium.

Entertainment Pleasure, escape, attention arousal; in communication, a function served by media or personal behaviors.

Expectancy-value theory The view that our intentions to behave in certain ways are predictable from our attitudes about personal rewards and from how we think others who are important to us will feel about our actions.

Experimental research A study in which the researcher intentionally manipulates some part of a situation so as to test the effects on another part; for example, showing children violence in a television program can be part of an experiment to see whether it affects their play behavior.

F

Facsimile A system for the transmission of text or images; a black and white reproduction of a document or a picture transmitted over a telephone or other transmission system.

Fax See Facsimile.

Federal Communications Commission (FCC) A board of five members (commissioners) appointed by the president and confirmed by the Senate under the provision of the Communications Act of 1934. The FCC has the power to regulate interstate communications.

Feedback Technically, the reception by the source of its transmitted signals or of signals returned by the receiver. More generally, any response by an individual or audience that is interpreted by a communication source; for example, applause heard by a public speaker or a letter written to the newspaper editor.

Feeder The neighborhood transmission lines of a cable television network, which stand between the major distribution trunk lines and the drops into houses or apartments.

Fiber optics Glass strands that allow for the transmission of modulated light waves for communication.

FM Frequency modulation (see Modulation).

Frequency The number of recurrences of a phenomenon during a specified period of time; electrical frequency is expressed in hertz, equivalent to cycles per second.

Frequency spectrum Usually the range of frequencies of electromagnetic waves useful for radio communication.

Function In communication, the purpose for which a message is created or the purpose that motivates an individual to seek out or attend to that message; studying functions is a type of communication research.

Functional theory A view of why humans use different types of communication to meet their needs.

G

Gatekeeper General term used to describe an individual, office, or business that controls communications access or flow. An editor is a gatekeeper.

Geodemographic research In political communication, the use of community and personal statistics to plan election campaigns or explain outcomes.

Gigahertz (GHz) 1 billion cycles per second.

Group communication Communication among individuals who are usually in one another's presence and who all have an opportunity to contribute; a field of communication study.

H

Haptics In nonverbal communication, the use of touch to communicate.

Hardware The electrical and mechanical equipment used in telecommunications and computer systems (see Software).

Head end The electronic control center of a cable television system; usually located at or near the antenna site.

Hertz (Hz) The frequency of an electric or electromagnetic wave in cycles per second, named after

Heinrich Hertz, who detected such waves (see also Kilohertz, Megahertz, Gigahertz).

High-resolution TV Television picture scanning systems that are above the present European or American standards, usually over 1000 lines.

Holograph A method of image reproduction on a flat surface that gives the appearance of three dimensions.

Humanistic theories Views that stress the distinctive capabilities of the human being, including choice, and maintain that humans are not just the product of their environmental experiences.

I

ICA International Communication Association

Icon Any image or object that might portray a meaning concretely or resemble one from prior learned associations.

Iconicity The degree to which an image or object concretely portrays a meaning.

Information Facts, reports, or data; the reduction of uncertainty; one of the main functions of communication.

Information society Generally refers to our modern society in which knowledge, education, research, and uses of computers and telecommunications are a basis for economic growth.

Information technology A general term referring to computers, telecommunications, and their combinations and any other technology that incorporates them.

Inoculation (in persuasion) Presentation of only parts of a forthcoming argument, allowing an individual to build up defenses against the full argument.

Instruction A basic communication function; messages that teach skills, understanding, insights.

Interactive Relating to communication situations in which messages are readily exchanged between the communication source and the receiver.

Intercultural communication Communication exchanged across international borders, particularly where the values and backgrounds of the countries are different; a field of communication study.

Interpersonal communication Communication between two individuals that is a part of a developing social relationship (as contrasted with impersonal communication); a field of communication study; also called relational communication.

Intrapersonal communication Communication within or to oneself.

J

Journalism The profession of news gathering, interpretation, writing, and publishing; a field of communications study.

K

Kilohertz (Khz) 1000 cycles per second.

Kinesics The study of nonverbal symbols communicated by facial, hand, or bodily gestures.

L

Language Linguistic definition: the relationship between spoken sounds (or written counterparts) and their intended meanings. Social definition: the system of spoken symbol and meaning relationships shared by a group of people.

Large-group communication A communication level in which there are too many individuals present for each to have a chance to participate, as in a small group; usually more than 25 people.

Laser "Light amplification by simulated emission of radiation"; an intense beam that can be modulated for communications.

Laser disk A recording and playback technology in which a highly focused light beam scans a recording surface.

Learned Acquired from experience or instruction, as in knowledge or skills.

Leisure Time away from the normal obligations of work that may be occupied by recreation, creative activities, diversions, pursuit of pleasurable gratifications, or doing nothing.

Linguistic rule A fundamental association between sounds and meanings that allows us to generate a spoken form of our language or to generate a meaning when we respond to the form.

Linguistic theory The description of the rules for a language.

Low-power television A special form of television licensing for stations whose signals will not exceed a 15-mile radius.

M

Management The controlling and directing of the activities of individuals in an organization; the application of resources (money, personnel, materials) to make a profit or perform a nonprofit objective.

Mass communication A process by which media that are originated by organizations or businesses are widely distributed in an anonymous society and, in turn, are used by the society and affect it; a field of communication study. In this book, mass communication is seen as a part of the larger concept of Public communication (see also Demassification).

Meaning Our mental recognition of something that is represented, referred to, intended, or described; our response to a symbol.

Media extension Generally refers to the uses of technologies for the expansion of human capabilities for communication; for example, writing allows for the recording and preservation of spoken language; printing allows for wide dissemination of written language.

Medium (plural, **media**) Anything capable of storing or transmitting symbols—for example, the air (as in speech), paper, a telegraph wire, or the broadcast wave; often used generally to denote a type of communication, for example, print.

Megahertz (Mhz) 1 million cycles per second.

Message A symbol or collection of symbols initiated by a source and capable of interpretation by a receiver or receivers.

Microchip A complex electronic circuit with multiple solid-state devices engraved on a surface.

Microsecond One-millionth of a second.

Microwave The short wavelengths from 1 GHz to 30 GHz used for radio, television, and satellite systems.

Millisecond One-thousandth of a second.

MIS Management information system, a configuration of computers and telecommunications used to support organizational and business communication.

Model A representation of something, that is, of its physical characteristics, its actions, its main features.

Modem A device that provides for digital computer communication over voice-grade (or better) telephone lines.

Modulation A process of modifying the characteristics of a propagating signal, such as a carrier, so that it represents the instantaneous changes of another signal. The carrier wave can change its amplitude (AM), its frequency (FM), its phase, or its duration (pulse code modulation) or combinations of these.

Motivation The expectation of reward or satisfaction of needs that impels us to act or think in certain ways.

MSO Multiple system operator, a company that operates several television cable systems.

Multiplexing A process of combining two or more signals from separate sources into a single transmission system from which the original signals can be recovered.

N

Nanosecond One-billionth of a second.

Narrowband communication A communication system capable of carrying only voice or relatively slow speed computer signals.

Narrowcasting Radio or television meant for a specialized audience.

Natural medium A means of communication adapted to the unaided human senses or effectors, for example, speech or sight.

Network Technically, the organization of a communication system, such as the linking of the computers in an organization; in group communication, individuals who regularly share information; in broadcasting, a group or system of stations.

Nonverbal communication Meaningful sounds or patterns of voice, gestures, facial expressions, bodily postures, and even objects or designs that go beyond the formal language system.

O

On-line In referring to a computer or terminal, actively connected to a telecommunications or another computing system.

Opinion The expression of ideas or attitudes about a concept; distinguished from values, a deeper, more general attitude.

Organizational communication Communication that takes place in a business, office, or some other type of functional group, supporting the functions of the organization; a field of communication study.

Organizational role A set of duties, responsibilities, or behaviors expected of a person occupying a particular position in an organization; a job description.

P

Pagination In newspaper production, the use of computer-assisted design to plan the layout of a full page.

Paralanguage All of the meaningful features of speech beyond the basic language symbols.

Personal attraction Qualities that motivate one person to get to know another person.

Personal communication Communication initiated or interpreted relative to the motives or needs of an individual; for example, telling another person how important his or her ideas are; the focus of interpersonal, or relational, communication.

Personal rewards Satisfaction of particularly individual needs, such as the need for feeling good about ourselves, for security, for understanding, and for physical or monetary benefits.

Persuasion The attempt to influence another person's beliefs, attitudes, or actions through communication.

Physical needs Requirements for maintaining human bodily existence (sometimes called biological or physiological "drives").

Political communication The communication involved in election campaigns; campaign management; a field of communication study.

Pornography Content that is meant to arouse a person sexually.

Primary group An individual's immediate family; relatives, a kinship group.

Process A series of events, a sequence; often used to emphasize that communication is ongoing and dynamic.

Proxemics In nonverbal communication, the use of space as a communication device; for example, standing close to a person in order to intimidate him or her.

Proximity In communication, the state of individuals being in potentially close contact with each other, either physically or in their beliefs.

Psycholinguistics The study and theory of how language behavior reflects linguistic rules; for example, how we know which words in a sentence are verbs; how we learn this.

Psychological needs Our requirements to feel satisfied about ourselves and our existence; to assume that others feel positive about us.

Psychology The science of human mental and physical behaviors.

Public access channel A cable television channel set aside for programming originated by private individuals or groups.

Public communication A modern context of large-scale communication in which the audience can be either anonymous or segmented and identified; includes uses of new media technologies; includes mass communication, in which the audience is generally anonymous (see Mass communication).

Public opinion The attitudes, ideas, or information held by large numbers of people; can be studied by survey research.

Public switched telephone network The more formal name given to the commercial telephone business in the United States; includes all of the operating companies.

Purposive Serving some goal; acting with an intent to accomplish something; fulfilling a function.

R

Receiver Anything capable of interpreting messages, for example, you reading this page.

Relational communication Message exchanges that are part of the process for forming social relationships; essentially the same as interpersonal communication.

Reward A personal pleasure, gain, or satisfaction of a need resulting from behaving in a certain way; a reward may be either subtle (as in a feeling of accomplishment or recognition) or concrete (as in being paid well).

Rhetoric The study of human discourse, of sources of effectiveness in discourse; the study of discourse in antiquity; *rhetoric* meaning senseless communication is a slang term.

Robotics The use of electronic control techniques, as programmed on microprocessors, to operate mechanical sensing and guidance mechanisms in manufacturing and assembly processes.

S

Satellite In communications, a radio or television receiver and transmitting device orbiting the earth and capable of broadcasting signals over a wide area.

SCA Speech Communication Association of America

Secondary group An ad hoc collection of individuals communicating together for some purpose, for example, children playing a game, the staff of an office, a football team.

Selective perception Attention only to what seems in agreement with your existing attitudes, opinions, beliefs, or what will not cause displeasure; for example, smokers tend to avoid news stories about lung cancer.

Semantics The study of meaning in messages and language.

Slow-scan television A technique of placing video signals on a narrowband circuit, such as a telephone line, that results in a picture changing every few seconds.

Small-group communication More than 3 or fewer than 25 individuals in a communication situation; few enough people so that most everyone can contribute to the discussion.

SMATV Satellite master antenna television; the use of satellite dishes on multiple dwellings to capture signals that are then transmitted over wires to residents.

Social approval Satisfaction based on the fact that those persons ("significant others") who are important to us feel positive about our behavior.

Social-diffusion theory A view that attempts to explain the relationship between the flow of new ideas in society and changes in attitudes and behaviors, as when farmers use new agricultural methods or consumers buy new products.

Socialization The process of learning the ways, or rules, of a society.

Social learning Observations of situations, individuals, or behaviors that affect our personal attitudes and behaviors; in public-communication theory, learning acquired from media images or characterizations.

Social science The study of human behavior, relations, institutions, and cultures.

Social stereotype A set of qualities associated with a particular group or class of people; for example, the belief that all lumberjacks are big and tough-talking is a stereotype.

Sociolinguistics The study and theory of the relations of social aspects of communication situations to the way we use language.

Software In computing, the program instructions that direct a computer's operations. More generally in communication, any program or content material for a communications system (for example, materials in an instructional technology center).

Solid state Referring to devices that allow transformations or manipulations of small electrical currents because of the conductive properties of their materials.

Source Anything capable of initiating communications, for example, a person speaking.

Spectrum Technically, the range of wavelengths of electromagnetic energy; more generally, the range of broadcast frequencies.

Stereotype The expectation that an individual or group will look and behave in certain ways, whether or not the assumption is valid.

Strategic In communication, the use of messages or technologies according to a plan and with a particular effect in mind—for example, an advertising campaign specifically aimed at turning out votes for a candidate or investment in new telecommunications devices for the main purpose of reducing costs.

STV Subscription television.

Surveillance A close watch kept over what is happening in your environment; one of the needs satisfied by communication.

Survey research A method of study that involves sending questionnaires or using the telephone to contact individuals for research purposes.

Symbol Something that represents an idea, object, event, or feeling but that itself has no physical relation to what it represents (for example, the word *chair*).

Symbolic catharsis hypothesis A theory holding that seeing violence in the media (for example, television) reduces one's hostilities and tendency to do violence.

T

Tariff The published rate for a service, equipment, or facility established by the communication common carrier.

Technology In communication, the devices or methods that we develop to extend communication capabilities, for example, computers or telecommunications devices.

Telecommunications The sending of messages over a wired, optical, or broadcast system.

Telecommuting The use of computers and telecommunications to enable people to work at home. More broadly, the substitution of telecommunications for transportation.

Teleconference The visual, sound, or text interconnection that allows individuals in two or more locations to see and talk to one another in a long-distance arrangement.

Telemarketing A method of marketing that emphasizes the creative use of the telephone and other telecommunications systems.

Teletext The generic name for a set of systems that transmit alphanumerical and simple graphic information over the broadcast (or cable) signal, using spare line capacity in the signal for display on a suitably modified TV receiver.

Time-sharing The simultaneous use of a computer by two or more users. The large computers used by the information utilities can accommodate many simultaneous users.

Transactional Relating to communication situations in which each exchange of messages influences the next, as in negotiating an agreement.

Transmitter The equipment that creates broadcast carrier waves and imposes information upon them by modulation.

Transponder The electronic circuits of a satellite, which receive a signal from the transmitting earth station, amplify it, and transmit it to earth at a different frequency.

Trust Confidence that another person will act positively toward you, that his or her actions will be favorable and predictable.

Two-step flow theory The view that the mass media do not influence the public directly but are the source of information that opinion leaders use, in turn, to influence the average citizen.

U

UHF Ultrahigh frequency (see VHF).

Uplink The communications link from a transmitting earth station to a satellite.

Uses and gratifications theory A body of research that attempts to describe and explain how people use different media to satisfy their personal and social needs.

V

Values Deep seated attitudes that can be generalized across a variety of concepts; attitudes reflective of one's culture.

Variable Any phenomenon that affects another phenomenon; for example, group pressure, as a variable, may cause a person to conform his or her attitudes (another variable) to the attitudes of the group.

VDT Video display terminal of a computer.

VHF Very high frequency; a frequency range above traditional broadcast frequencies but lower than ultra high frequency (UHF).

Video disk   An audiovisual medium that uses a reflecting surface and laser technology for master recording and consumer playback.

Videotext   The generic name for a computer system that transmits alphanumerical and simple graphic information over a telephone line or TV cable for display on a video monitor.

W

WATS   Wide Area Telephone Service; a service offered by telephone companies in the United States that allows customers to make dial calls to telephones in a specific area for a flat monthly charge or to receive calls "collect" at a flat monthly charge.

Appendix

Communication Analysis and Skill Building

Note: This appendix contains several questionnaires and forms to be used in carrying out certain exercises. Instructors of classes using *The New Communications* as a required text or students in classes using this text as a required text may reproduce the number of questionnaires or forms needed to complete a given exercise. Otherwise, permission to reproduce this material must be obtained in writing from the publisher. (For information, see the copyright page at the beginning of this book.)

Many of the theoretical concepts of human communication become much more understandable to us if we attempt to experience them firsthand. This is the primary motive for including the following exercises. A secondary one is that all of us can improve our communication skills by guided practice.

The exercises in this section reflect skill building in both *analysis* and *performance* as related to a variety of types of communication.

EXERCISE 1 — USES AND GRATIFICATIONS

General Description

In this exercise, you analyze people's motives (Chapter 4) for using communications of different types. First, you are to gather data for the questionnaire that is part of this exercise. Second, you are to analyze the results.

Objectives

to witness how people will respond when asked how they fulfill their communication needs

to experience one of the ways in which social scientists have gathered information about gratifications

to gain experience in analyzing and reporting one's social science research findings

Directions for Gathering Data

1. Make two copies (by retyping or photocopying) of the questionnaire given for this assignment. Fill in the first one yourself. Then get a person *at least 20 years your senior* (a parent if you wish) to fill in the other.

2. Follow these instructions for the questionnaire. Be sure to explain them personally to the individual who gives you data:

Below are ten personal needs that we often gratify by using communications of some type.

First, on a scale of 1 to 6, rate how important each of these needs is to you personally. 1 = critically important, 2 = quite important, 3 = somewhat important, 4 = neutral to me, 5 = generally not important, 6 = not important at all.

Second, for each need, assign an "X" to the one medium that is most important in fulfilling that need. Put an "O" by those media that are irrelevant. Leave the others blank.

Directions for Reporting Your Study

Interpret your results, and report them in a paper divided into the following sections:

1. Results
   a. Interpret your findings for the younger person sampled.
   b. Interpret your findings for the older person sampled.
   c. Compare the findings.

2. Implications: Answer these questions:
   a. In general, do we use a different communications medium for each different personal purpose? If not, which media seem to serve similar purposes?
   b. Beyond face-to-face communication, which medium do you think is ultimately of the most overall value to people? Why?
   c. If you were going to try to influence the older person to vote in a certain way, which media would you use, and why?

(Attach the completed questionnaires to your paper.)

QUESTIONNAIRE

(Two copies needed)

Respondent's age _____ *sex* _____ *Do not give name.*

1. To escape the pressures of everyday life: Importance = _____ .
   newspapers ( )   magazines ( )   television ( )   radio ( )
   movies ( )   records, tapes ( )   books ( )   telephone ( )
   face-to-face conversations ( )

2. To find out what is going on in the world: Importance = _____ .
   newspapers ( )   magazines ( )   television ( )   radio ( )
   movies ( )   records, tapes ( )   books ( )   telephone ( )
   face-to-face conversations ( )

3. To be in a festive mood: Importance = _____ .
   newspapers ( )   magazines ( )   television ( )   radio ( )
   movies ( )   records, tapes ( )   books ( )   telephone ( )
   face-to-face conversations ( )

4. To find out what is going on in my city: Importance = _____ .
   newspapers ( )   magazines ( )   television ( )   radio ( )
   movies ( )   records, tapes ( )   books ( )   telephone ( )
   face-to-face conversations ( )

5. To learn about things, to study: Importance = _____ .
   newspapers ( )   magazines ( )   television ( )   radio ( )
   movies ( )   records, tapes ( )   books ( )   telephone ( )
   face-to-face conversations ( )

6. To experience beauty: Importance = _____ .
   newspapers ( )   magazines ( )   television ( )   radio ( )
   movies ( )   records, tapes ( )   books ( )   telephone ( )
   face-to-face conversations ( )

7. To develop good taste: Importance = _____ .
   newspapers ( )   magazines ( )   television ( )   radio ( )
   movies ( )   records, tapes ( )   books ( )   telephone ( )
   face-to-face conversations ( )

8. To kill time: Importance = _____ .
   newspapers ( )   magazines ( )   television ( )   radio ( )
   movies ( )   records, tapes ( )   books ( )   telephone ( )
   face-to-face conversations ( )

Adapted from research reported by E. Katz, M. Gurevitch, and H. Hass, "On the Use of Mass Media for Important Things," *American Sociological Review*, 38 (1973):164–181.

9. To understand more about myself: Importance = _____ .
   newspapers ( )   magazines ( )   television ( )   radio ( )
   movies ( )   records, tapes ( )   books ( )   telephone ( )
   face-to-face conversations ( )

10. To thoroughly enjoy myself: Importance = _____ .
   newspapers ( )   magazines ( )   television ( )   radio ( )
   movies ( )   records, tapes ( )   books ( )   telephone ( )
   face-to-face conversations ( )

NONVERBAL COMMUNICATION*

General Description

This exercise involves experimenting with certain aspects of nonverbal communication (Chapter 3). It is composed of two parts. In the first part you are to use nonverbal cues to communicate with other people and observe what they do in response. In the second part you are to prepare a report that describes what you did, what you observed, and what you thought about it all.

Objectives

to become aware of some of the nonverbal means by which messages can be communicated

to become aware of some of the ways in which people will respond when unusual nonverbal messages are communicated

to experience one of the ways in which social scientists have gathered information about nonverbal communication

to gain experience in reporting social science research activities and findings

Directions for Communicating and Observing

1. Read over the list of nonverbal communication situations (following). Choose three you would like to do.

2. Do each once, each time with a different person. The people should be either friends or acquaintances, never strangers, but they should not be familiar with the assignment before you give your performance.

3. When you give your performance, pay close attention to everything the other person does. Stop the performance when you feel the person has recognized and responded to your nonverbal communication. Right then be sure to give the person an explanation of what you have been doing and why.

Nonverbal Communication Situations (Choose 3)

1. While you are having a conversation with someone you know, look directly at him or her the whole time you talk, but stare at the floor or the wall the whole time the other person talks. Keep up this pattern during the whole conversation.

*An original version of this exercise was developed by Professor Aimee Dorr, now of the University of California at Los Angeles.

2. When entering an uncrowded area (nearly empty elevator, library room, dining area, and so on), sit or stand very close to an acquaintance. That is, sit or stand closer than you usually would with that person in that situation.

3. After conversing with an acquaintance for a while normally, change the topic and. talk with a lot of hesitations, *ums, hums, wells,* and the like in your sentences.

4. While talking with someone you know, sit or stand with your back straight and your arms folded across your chest. Don't vary your physical position during the entire conversation.

5. During a conversation with an acquaintance, maintain a smile. Try to keep smiling for the entire conversation.

Remember: It is important to explain what you have done to the other person(s) involved after you have completed your performance. When you write down what happened, be sure to record your observations of what the other person(s) did, not their explanations of what they did or why they did it.

Directions for Written Assignment

As soon as possible after giving your performance and your explanation, you should make notes for yourself about:

1. what you did, in as complete detail as possible

2. the conditions under which you did it (for example, place, time of day, characteristics of the person you did it to, who else was around)

3. how the person responded (for example, moved away, stopped talking, changed topics, talked faster, asked what was the matter, asked where you were going, frowned, turned and looked at wall or floor, sat up straighter)

4. what other people did, if anything

5. how you felt

Assemble your notes into a report in the following form.

FORM FOR REPORT ON NONVERBAL EXPERIMENTS

Name: _____ Exercise: _____ Date: _____

First Performance
What I did:

To whom, where, etc.:

How person responded:

_____

Second Performance
What I did:

To whom, where, etc.:

How person responded:

_____

Third Performance
What I did:

To whom, where, etc.:

How person responded:

_____

On a second sheet of paper write a brief summary of what you learned about nonverbal communication. Describe how you communicated, how successfully you could do it, and how you felt doing it. Discuss what your communications seemed to mean to the other people and how they showed that they had received your messages. If people responded differently, speculate about why that might be.

INTERPERSONAL VARIATIONS

General Description

Interpersonal, or relational, communication (Chapters 7, 11) varies considerably according to how well we know the other person. There are four parts to this exercise. The first part requires you to have conversations with three persons with whom you have varying relationships. Second, observe the interpersonal communication process with these three persons. Third, summarize and record each conversation on an Observation Sheet (see the sample in this exercise). Fourth, prepare a brief report on the differences in your conversations.

Objectives

to become aware of how communication between persons varies according to their knowledge of each other

to gain experience in gathering information through interviews and observations

to learn how to record, report, and interpret information (data) gathered through interpersonal communication and observation

Directions

1. Select one topic that will be used in all three conversations. Possible topics include sports, politics, religion, culture, or music.
2. Develop a list of seven to ten questions to be discussed in each conversation. Plan that each conversation will last no longer than fifteen minutes and no less than ten.
3. Conduct conversations with three different types of people:
    a. a person with whom you are very friendly (a best friend, family member, roommate)
    b. someone with whom you have a distant relationship (a classmate you have just met, your boss, a person you usually say little more than "hello" to)
    c. a total stranger
4. When preparing for your conversations be sure to have your Observation Sheet (follow the sample form) ready to fill in *after* each discussion (not in the presence of the other person).
    a. In the first part of the Observation Sheet you are to describe briefly the information that you acquired in the conversation.

b. The second part of the sheet asks you to pay particular attention to (1) the language used (was it descriptive and detailed or nondescriptive and very general?), (2) feelings and thoughts disclosed by both you and the other person, and (3) your estimates of feelings about the conversations themselves.

Directions for the Written Assignment

1. Be sure you have an Observation Sheet filled in for each of the three conversations. These are to be handed in.

2. Prepare a one- to two-page written report contrasting the results of the three conversations. Stress differences in what you have learned about theory and practice in interpersonal communication.

OBSERVATION SHEET

INTERPERSONAL COMMUNICATION

Name: _____ *Date:* _____ *Topic:* _____

Interview Type (from assignment): _____

1. Please give a very brief summary of the topic and questions discussed.

2. Please answer these questions:

   a. What is the relationship between you and the other person? Did it change during the conversation?

   b. How much did either of you stray from the topic? Who caused this?

   c. How much that was new did you learn about the other person?

   d. How much did the other person learn about you?

   e. How "personal" versus "impersonal" was the conversation? And how do you know about this?

COMPLIANCE VERSUS CONFLICT RESOLUTION

General Description

This exercise involves contrasting interpersonal exchanges that are purposely set up to promote compliance or conflict resolution. Do two of each. After each exchange, ask the other person to fill in a brief questionnaire concerning the interaction. Your report of this exercise involves an analysis and interpretation of these questionnaires.

Objectives

to experience the differences you prompt in people when you appear "to want to get your way" (compliance) versus "to want to reach a mutually satisfactory outcome" (conflict resolution)

to gain experience in administering a questionnaire and interpreting the results

to gain experience in reporting your observations and analyses of interpersonal communication

Directions

1. Look over the following suggested topics, and select one you wish to discuss for about ten minutes with each of four individuals. These persons should be individuals you know but not close friends. (Perhaps you can select them from a university class.) Ask them to help you with a class assignment on people's attitudes about the topic that you select. The topics are:
    a. Marijuana should be legalized (or not).
    b. Abortion should be legalized (or not).
    c. The military draft should be reinstated (or not).
2. Conduct an approximately ten-minute conversation with each person on that same topic, but in so doing, make this important distinction:
    a. *With two of the persons, try to convince them right off of your opinion on the topic; get them to comply with your ideas.*
    b. *With the two others, try to ferret out their opinions and respect them while offering your own.*

    At the conclusion of each conversation, ask the other person to fill in the questionnaire, which you can duplicate from page 333.
3. Examine the information that you have obtained, and prepare a brief written report that includes:
    a. a description of the topics, the persons interviewed, and the length of the interview

b. the differences in the other person's reactions as contrasted between the compliance and conflict-resolution situations

c. any other observations you made

d. copies of the questionnaire

Student's name _____

Note: The above individual is gathering the following information for a university class assignment and would be appreciative if you could answer the following questions. It is not necessary to put your name on this questionnaire, and the results will remain anonymous. Please fill in:

Topic discussed:

What was your opinion on the topic?

Did the above person agree with you?

How tolerant was the above person of your opinions?

How would you rate your conversation on the spectrum below (check one)?

not pleasant __ : __ : __ : __ : __ really pleasant

Would you like to discuss the topic further?

very much __ : __ : __ : __ : __ not at all

Did you change your own mind on the topic as a result of the discussion?

not at all __ : __ : __ : __ : __ yes, I did

Comments:

GROUP-COMMUNICATION ANALYSIS

General Description

An analytic attitude about group processes can improve your effectiveness in them. This exercise has four parts. First, organize and conduct a small-group discussion on a topic of your choice. Second, during the discussion make notes in terms of Bale's Interaction Process Analysis (Chapter 9). Third, ask participants to complete brief questionnaires regarding their participation. Fourth, analyze your results, and prepare a brief summary report of your findings.

Objectives

to gain experience in organizing and conducting a group discussion

to gain experience in gathering information on group-process analysis

to learn how to record, report, and interpret information (data) gathered from group-process analysis

in all, to develop an analytic attitude about group-communication processes

Directions

1. Select one topic that will be interesting for two or three of your friends or classmates to discuss with you. It should be a topic on which there will be differing views, opinions, or even facts. For example, you might discuss the chances for a football team to win a national championship, who is the best current popular music group, or how long some current hair or dress fashion is likely to last.

2. Make up an Interaction Process Analysis Form that generally follows the format of the one in this exercise (or photocopy that one). Put in the names of your discussants.

3. Conduct a discussion that lasts at least fifteen minutes on the selected topic. Try to get the others to participate without your constantly having to prompt them. As the discussion progresses, try to make appropriate tab marks on your Interaction Process Analysis Form. But be careful that it does not interfere with the discussion process.

4. At the conclusion of the discussion, ask the participants to each fill in their Participant Evaluation Forms (see the example in this exercise). Then, after they have given you the forms, ask them how they felt about the discussion (interesting, boring, and so on).

5. With your results, prepare a brief written report that includes the following items:

    a. What was generally talked about? Was anything agreed upon? What was the greatest aspect of disagreement?

    b. How was the "spread" of participation? Did everybody participate, or did one person dominate the discussion? Why did participation work the way that it did?

    c. What relationships can you draw between your Interaction Process Analysis results and the participants' Evaluation Forms?

    d. What overall generalizations would you draw about setting up future discussions?

INTERACTION PROCESS ANALYSIS FORM

Categories	Participants						
Seems friendly							
Dramatizes							
Agrees							
Disagrees							
Shows tension							
Seems unfriendly							
Gives suggestions							
Gives opinions							
Gives information							
Asks for information							
Asks for opinions							
Asks for suggestions							

PARTICIPANT EVALUATION FORM

What topic did you discuss?

What was your main personal position on that topic?

Who said the most in this discussion, you or somebody else? Describe.

Please rate your feelings about the discussion by placing one check mark on each of the scales below.

I thought the discussion was:

　　interesting __ : __ : __ : __ : __ boring

I felt that all participants:

　　had their say __ : __ : __ : __ : __ did not get enough chance to talk

My general degree of satisfaction with the discussion was:

　　not satisfied __ : __ : __ : __ : __ very satisfied

Discussions like these are:

　　very useful or fun __ : __ : __ : __ : __ a waste of time

Generally I thought that everybody:

　　agreed with one another __ : __ : __ : __ : __ did not agree at all

Comments:

FACT-FINDING INTERVIEW

General Description

In this exercise, you try to obtain information (Chapters 4, 12) through a personal interview, as you might if you were a news reporter. Write up a summary of the interview. Then have the person you interviewed check this summary and also give you his or her evaluation of your interview style.

Objectives

to gain experience in conducting interviews and sorting out facts

to practice writing up summaries of facts

to gain feedback on your interviewing behavior

to gain experience in evaluating interpersonal communication behavior as involved in interviewing

Directions

1. Select a topic and an individual who is knowledgeable about certain facts on that topic and who is willing to be interviewed by you. This might be a professor in your university, a friend, or a person in a business of some type. (For example, you might interview the manager of a supermarket about how shelf location of goods affects buying.) Work with a topic that is of particular interest to you and about which you might prepare a paper for another class or write an article for the school paper.

2. Conduct an interview with the person you have selected. You will need a minimum of twenty to thirty minutes for this. Feel free to take notes as you get the facts.

3. Write up your summary of the facts. Then send a copy along with your Interview Evaluation Form to the individual whom you interviewed. You might deliver these materials in person. In either case, enclose a stamped, self-addressed envelope for the person's reply.

4. Prepare a brief written report that includes the following:

   a. What are your overall observations of the accuracy and general degree of success in conducting the interview. Base these on the feedback you obtained from your interviewee plus your own feelings.

   b. What suggestions can you make for improving your own interview style?

   c. Enclose your fact summary and the Interview Evaluation Form.

INTERVIEW EVALUATION FORM

Dear _____

    For a class assignment, as well as to improve my interview skills, I would like to ask you to check over the main facts drawn from my recent interview with you. Also, could you take a moment to give your evaluation of how well the interview was conducted?

    A stamped, self-addressed envelope is enclosed for your convenience.

       Sincerely,

_____

    Please respond by placing one check mark on each scale.

How clear and to the point was I in asking questions?

    very clear __ : __ : __ : __ : __ not clear at all

Did I seem to understand the facts when you gave them?

    did not seem to __ : __ : __ : __ : __ yes, very much so

How would you rate my overall manner or bearing?

    very effective __ : __ : __ : __ : __ quite ineffective

Suggestions for improvement (please write in):

ORAL PRESENTATION

General Description

This exercise involves preparing and presenting an oral presentation where the goal is persuasion (Chapters 4, 5, 8). The exercise involves three steps. First, select a topic, and analyze how you might try to get your audience (a college class) to believe or act in a certain way. Second, prepare and deliver the presentation, and ask your audience to fill in your Presentation Evaluation Form (in this exercise). Finally, prepare a brief written report on your analysis of the evaluations obtained from your audience, with suggestions for the future improvement of your presentation style and strategies.

Objectives

to give you experience in audience analysis for persuasion

to give you practice in planning and delivering an oral presentation

to provide you with audience feedback on your oral effectiveness

to provide you with experience in interpreting audience reaction and improving your oral presentation capabilities

Directions for Preparing the Presentation

1. Review the materials in Chapters 4 and 5 on the nature of persuasion and persuasive strategies. Select a topic that would be interesting and realistic to your audience (a college class). This topic should get your listeners to believe or act in a specific way. Be able to state your topic in a form such as these:

    a. "to get my audience to agree that women should register for military service"

    b. "to get audience members to promise that they will vote for candidate X"

    c. "to get my listeners to give me $1 in return for giving them my 'Handy Guide for Getting A's on Exams'"

    d. "to get my audience to sign up for four hours of volunteer work at the Children's Hospital"

2. Analyze your audience's likely motives for agreeing with your persuasive purpose. Develop a ten-minute oral presentation wherein you will attempt to persuade your audience to accept your proposition. Consider dividing your presentation into these parts:

    a. *Introduction:* Get the audience to feel friendly and receptive toward you.

b. *Main body:* Tell your audience what you want. Then concentrate on all of the main reasons that might be likely to persuade the listeners to agree with you.

c. *Conclusion:* Remind members of your audience of what you want them to do. Then summarize the main reasons why they should accept your proposition.

3. At the conclusion of your presentation, distribute the Presentation Evaluation Form; collect it when completed.

4. Analyze the audience's evaluations, and then prepare a short written report that includes the following points:

a. What was your main purpose?

b. What audience motives did you try to appeal to?

c. On the Presentation Evaluation Form, what percentage of the audience agreed with your proposition?

d. How did listeners rate your general effectiveness?

e. What do you feel needed improvement the most?

PRESENTATION EVALUATION FORM

Speaker's name _____ *Date* _____

What exactly do you think the speaker wanted you to believe or to do?

I thought that the speaker was (check one position on each scale):

unclear ___ : ___ : ___ : ___ : ___ clear

sincere ___ : ___ : ___ : ___ : ___ insincere

alert and energetic ___ : ___ : ___ : ___ : ___ dull and lazy sounding

not believable ___ : ___ : ___ : ___ : ___ believable

well organized ___ : ___ : ___ : ___ : ___ disorganized

Relative to what the speaker wanted me to believe or to do, I:

accept fully ___ : ___ : ___ : ___ : ___ do not accept at all

For what reasons did you accept or reject the speaker's proposition? Please explain.

What did you like best about the speaker?

What did you like least about the speaker?

WRITTEN NEWS REPORT

General Description
We often take news writing for granted (Chapter 12). Why not see how well you do it yourself? This exercise has three steps. First, prepare a brief news report of your choice. Second, have your report evaluated by another person (and there is the possibility that you will evaluate the report of another person). Finally, respond to that evaluation.

Objectives

to give you experience in separating facts from opinions, objectivity from subjectivity, in your own writing

to give you experience in evaluating the quality of news writing

to provide you with experience and criticism of your written expression in general

Directions for Preparing Your News Report

1. Select any topic that would lend itself to a brief news article. (For example, it could be the report of a meeting, a campus event, or the announcement of something.) You will want a topic that can be adequately covered in about 500 words (two typewritten pages).

2. Research the topic carefully; check your facts. Then prepare your report, observing the following suggestions:

   a. Write your report with the most important idea first and the least important last.

   b. Include facts and figures, even direct quotations if you wish.

   c. Do not use any personal references to yourself (no "I," "me," and so on); keep yourself and your opinions out of the article.

   d. Remember the journalist's "five Ws + H." That is, be sure to include the *what? where? who? why? when?* and *how?* of your topic.

Directions for Evaluations

1. Have another person (preferably a classmate selected at random or by your instructor) evaluate your written report in terms of the Written News Report Evaluation (in this exercise). If your instructor assigns it, you may also evaluate the work of another person.

2. Write a one-page follow-up to the evaluation of your report, stressing how you can improve upon your written expression.

WRITTEN NEWS REPORT EVALUATION

The writer's name: _____ *Evaluator's name:* _____

The news topic: _____ *Date:* _____

Please place one check mark on each of the following scales:

I found the report:

easy to read __ : __ : __ : __ : __ hard to read

disorganized __ : __ : __ : __ : __ organized

very informative __ : __ : __ : __ : __ not informative at all

very objective __ : __ : __ : __ : __ full of personal opinion

Were the five Ws and the H complete (if relevant)? Please describe:

I felt that the factual quality of the report was:

very complete __ : __ : __ : __ : __ quite incomplete

not believable __ : __ : __ : __ : __ believable

The greatest strength of this report was (describe):

The greatest shortcoming of this report was:

My advice to the writer is:

COMPARATIVE ANALYSIS OF MASS-MEDIA NEWS

General Description

It is easy to see how the news varies between newspapers and television (Chapters 12, 13). This exercise is composed of two parts. In the first, you are to keep track of how two news items (one local, one national or international) are covered in the newspaper and television news over a four-day period. In the second part, you are to write a summary describing what would happen if an individual used only one of the two media as his or her sole news source.

Objectives

to become more aware of differences in how news is represented in newspapers as compared with television

to gain experience in gathering information through content analysis

to gain experience in interpreting your observations and reporting them

Directions

1. Choose two topics that are current news items. Make sure that both are ongoing items and not simply one-time events. They should be items that are being carried both in the newspapers and on television. One topic should be a local item, the other national or international.

2. Keep track of how these items are covered in a local newspaper and by a local television station. Use the Content Analysis Log (see the sample) as a guide for recording your observations. Notice that the log covers four days.

3. When your logs are completed, analyze them and prepare a report that includes the following points:

    a. A summary of the facts (amount of coverage, emphasis, and so on) that contrasts the newspaper and TV coverage of the two topics

    b. Your interpretations of these facts; impressions of differences in the two media

    c. Speculations on the consequences, in general, to a person who gets his or her news only from television or only from the newspaper (differences for local or national and international?)

CONTENT ANALYSIS LOG OF COMPARATIVE NEWS COVERAGE

Make a separate log for each of the two topics.

Name: _____ Date: _____

Topic: _____

For each entry give a short description of coverage, including length, major points, and focus.

Day	Newspaper	Television
First		
Second		
Third		
Fourth		

EXERCISE 10

COMMUNICATION AND LIFE PLANNING

General Description

This exercise involves getting you to think about your longer range future and the role of modern communications in it (Chapter 15). The exercise involves preparing a report in response to a series of written questions. It is suggested that this paper serve as a topic for further group discussion.

Objectives

to give you the opportunity to think formally about your future; to see how communications capabilities and choices fit into it

to encourage you to see the importance of personal communication ability and the ability to use modern technologies to your personal and professional advantage

to give you experience in expressing your ideas in writing

Directions for Preparing Your Report

Part 1 The Present

Prepare a brief description (about 500 words) of yourself and your life at the present time. Who are you? How does communication fit into who or what you are? How are you in communicating with other people? What are your strengths, weaknesses?

Part 2 Personal Goals

In about 500 words, describe your long-range personal (not professional) goals. What life-style appeals most to you (fast city pace, country-style, settle down, or . . .)? How does communication fit into this desired personal life-style? What kinds of communication will be especially important for this life-style? If somebody had to sum up the kind of person you are, what would you like to have him or her say?

Part 3 Professional Goals

In another 500 or so words, explain where you want to be professionally in the next thirty years. What professional accomplishments will you want to be known for? Can you keep your personal and professional goals in harmony? How will different types of communication abilities fit into your plans? (Will you have to be especially person-oriented in your communication?)

Part 4 Priorities for Right Now

Given your above goals, what priorities would you like to exercise in your present choice of activities? What do you want to get to work on? What uses of communication are especially involved? What are your specific priorities for the next twelve months?

Index

Fishbein, Martin, 96, 281
Fitzpatrick, Mary Anne, 223, 225
FM (frequency modulation), 119
Freedom of speech and the press, 205
Fuller, Buckminster, 292
Functional theories of communication motivation, 69–72
Functions of communication, 62–63
  entertainment, 74, 76–77
  information, 73–75
  instruction, 74–75, 77–78
  persuasion, 75, 78–81

G
Geodemographic research, 263
Gerbner, George, 76–77
Goldmark, Peter C., 296–97
Gottman, J. M., 222
Gray, Elisha, 115
Group communication, 158. *See also* Groups
  analysis of, 168–71
  differences in, 164–65
  Interaction Process Analysis of, 168–69
  in large groups, 29, 31, 34
  large versus small, 158, 159
  network analysis of, 169–71
  in small groups, 29, 31, 33–34
Groups. *See also* Group communication
  brainstorming in, 165
  communication in, 160–61, 164–65
  conformity in, 164–65
  leadership types in, 165–67
  life cycle of, 162–63
  media of communication in, 160–61
  motivation of, 164
  primary, 158
  risky shifts in, 165
  secondary, 158
  types of, 158–60
Gutenberg, Johann, 109, 110

H
Haptics, 53
Health care, new communication technologies in, 299–300
Heider, Fritz, 89
Hirsch, Paul, 278–79
Humanistic theory of communication motivation, 65–69

I
Iconics, 55
Impersonal communication, 142, 143
  in organizations, 177
Influence, psychology of, 86–87
  and argument, 97–100
  and attitude-behavior problem, 93–95
  balance theory of, 87–90
  dissonance theory of, 91–93
  expectation-value theory of, 95–97
  in everyday lives, 86–87
  inoculation theory of, 92–93
Information, 73–75. *See also* Political communication; Public communication; Public-opinion formation
  access to, 247–48
  binary, 56–57
  demassification of, 234–35
  distortion of, 248, 275, 276
  Marxist criticism of presentation of, 74–75
  and public opinion, 235–49
  sharing, 149
  and social change, 293–94
  as social need, 73–75
  use of, by voters, 254, 255, 258–59
Informational businesses, new communication technologies in, 293–94. *See also* Communications industry; Teleconferences
Information society, 292
Inoculation theory, 92–93
Instruction, 74–75
  through entertainment, 76
  and new technologies, 78, 303–4
  through persuasion, 78
  "Sesame Street" as, 78, 303
  as social need, 74–75, 77–78
  through television, 303

Interaction Process Analysis (IPA), 168–169
Intercultural communication, 48
Interpersonal communication, 15–16, 29, 30, 33. *See also* Communication; Relational communication
  and advertising, 79–81
  and attitude-behavior problem, 93–95
  and avoidance of dissonance, 91–93
  balance and harmony in, 87–90
  components of process of, 146–55
  content analysis of, 38
  effective characteristics of, 153–55
  impersonal, 142, 143
  in marriages, 221–24
  via media, 145
  personal, 142, 143
  and persuasion, 78–81
  and psychological needs, 64–65
  and psychology of influence, 86–87
  sociolinguistic study of, 51–52
  transactional, 142–44
Interpersonal communication, characteristics of effective
  assertiveness, 153
  empathy, 154
  open-mindedness, 153–54
  persuasiveness, 154–55
  self-concept, 153
Interpersonal communication process, components of
  attraction, 147–48
  avoidance of stereotyping, 148–49
  conflict resolution, 152
  development of trust, 149–52
  information sharing, 149
  motivation, 148
  proximity, 146–47
Interpersonal relationships. *See* Relational communication
Intrapersonal communication, 29, 30, 33

J
Jamieson, Kathleen, 255, 259

Public communication
(*continued*)
deregulation of, 202, 207–8
dissonance avoidance in,
91–92
expectancy-value theory of,
281–82
government role in, 198
influence of, 79
market research in, 204
media institutions in, 200–201
media of, 194–95
modeling as effect of, 280–81
multiplicative capabilities of,
36, 195–96
needs satisfied by, 69–72,
200
and new technologies, 197
organizational aspects of,
196–97
as public process, 194–95,
199–201
regulation of, 202, 205–7
social context of, 195, 199
Public-opinion formation
by agenda setting, 237–39
dependency model of,
243–48
direct, 235–37
and flow of ideas from mass
media, 235–37
and new technologies, 236,
247
and political communication,
254, 255, 258–59
research perspective into,
234–35
by social diffusion, 239–42
by two-step flow, 236–37
Putnam, Linda L., 180

R
Radio
content selection in, 202
demassification of, 208–9
effects of, on public opinion,
235
"narrowcasting" in, 209
and new technologies, 128–29
regulation of, 202, 204
as traditional medium,
118–19, 120
Receiver, in communication
process, 11
Recording. *See* Sound-recording
devices

Regulation, of public
communication, 202, 205
and deregulation, 207–8
principles of, 205–7
Relational communication, 217.
See also Interpersonal
communication
between acquaintances, 226,
227
competitive exchanges in,
223–24
differences in, 222
disengagement process in,
226–30
effects of gender differences
on, 224–26, 227
in marriages, 221–24
and new media, 230–31
persuasion in, 78–79
research perspective into,
217–18
steps in evolution of, 218
types of, 219–21
Rewards, in communication, 62
Rice, Ronald E., 160–61
Risky shift phenomenon, 165
Robinson, John, 269–72
Robotics, 292
Rogers, Everett M., 239, 240

S
Satellite communications,
125–28, 294
Schramm, Wilbur, 19, 21, 302
Secondary groups, 158
Selective attention, 80
Selective exposure, 80
Selective perception, 90
Self-concept, in interpersonal
communication, 153
Self-disclosure, in marriage,
224–26
Sender, in communication
process. *See* Source, in
communication process
"Sesame Street," 76, 78, 269,
303
Shannon, Claude, 26
Short, John, 145
Small-group communication, 29,
31, 33–34. *See also* Group
communication; Groups
content analyses of, 38
versus large-group
communication, 158, 159

Social change, through
communication technology,
292–93. *See also*
Computers; New
technology
Social-diffusion theory, 232–42
Social learning, 268, 269
Social rewards, 96
Social scientific research, in
communication, 24
Sociolinguistic theory, 51–52
Sound-recording devices
and digital technology,
129–30
traditional, 119, 122
Source, in communication
process, 11, 13, 24–29
in different contexts, 30–32
and functional categories of
communication, 74–75
Survey research, 234
Symbolic catharsis hypothesis,
280
Symbols, 8, 46–47
as basis of communication, 8,
9, 11
examples of, 6–7
lanugage as, 9–10, 47–48
and meaning, 9
and media extensions, 48–49
nonverbal, 52–57
our history as users of, 8

T
Tannenbaum, Percy, 93, 94–95
Technology, new. *See* New
technology
Technopolitics, 260–61
Teleconferences, 34
as communication–
transportation trade-off, 295
Interaction Process Analysis
of, 169
and new technologies, 133,
184
and "personalness," 231
two-way video, 161
Telegraph, 108, 109, 112–13,
115, 298
Telephone
and digital communication,
128
and group communication,
160–61
and interpersonal
communication, 145

TO THE STUDENT

Now that you have read all about communication as a *process* and the importance of *feedback*, may I invite you to give me your personal and frank opinions on THE NEW COMMUNICATIONS? Please fill in this questionnaire and mail it to me c/o the publisher. Thank you.

School Name: _____

Instructor's Name: _____

Title of the Course: _____

Was this a quarter or semester course? _____

Year in school? _____

What is your major? _____

Relative to other college textbooks that you have used, how would you rate THE NEW COMMUNICATIONS? Please place one check mark on each of the scales below.

easy to read __ : __ : __ : __ : __ hard to read

interesting __ : __ : __ : __ : __ dull

up to date __ : __ : __ : __ : __ out of date

learned much from it __ : __ : __ : __ : __ learned little from it

In the next edition of THE NEW COMMUNICATIONS, what would you like to see added? Would you like to see anything deleted or changed? (Describe)

_____

_____

_____

_____

_____

Sincerely,

Frederick Williams

FOLD HERE

FOLD HERE

Dr. Frederick Williams
Wadsworth Publishing Company
10 Davis Drive
Belmont, CA 94002

CUT PAGE OUT